07/08
31.18

POPULATION
CONTROL

Also by Steven W. Mosher

Hegemon: China's Plan to Dominate Asia and the World

China Attacks (with Chuck DeVore)

A Mother's Ordeal: One Woman's Fight Against China's One-Child Policy

Korea in the 1990s: Prospects for Reunification (ed.)

The United States and the Republic of China: Democratic Friends, Strategic Allies, and Economic partners (ed.)

China Misperceived: American Illusions and Chinese Reality

Journey to the Forbidden China

Broken Earth: The Rural Chinese

POPULATION CONTROL

Real Costs, Illusory Benefits

Steven W. Mosher

Transaction Publishers
New Brunswick (U.S.A.) and London (U.K.)

To my wife, Vera, without whom nothing would be possible

Library of Congress Catalog Number: 2007045617
ISBN: 978-1-4128-0712-8 (case) ; 978-1-4128-0713-5 (paper)
Printed in the United States of America

Library of Congress Cataloging-in-Publication Data

Mosher, Steven W.
  Population control : real costs, illusory benefits / Steven W. Mosher.
      p. cm.
  Includes bibliographical references and index.
  ISBN 978-1-4128-0712-8
      1. Birth control. 2. Population policy. I. Title.
HQ766.M59 2008
304.6'66—dc22   2007045617

Contents

List of Tables

List of Figures

Acknowledgments

This book would never have been written without the support and encouragement of one remarkable man, Father Paul Marx, O.S.B., Ph.D. My debts to him are many. He founded, in 1989, the Population Research Institute, my institutional home for the past 12 years. He invited me to join him at PRI in 1995, beginning a collaboration that has lasted to the present day. Although he formally retired in 1999, he continues, at the age of 87, to offer daily aid and encouragement for our work, including the writing of this book. It is my fondest hope that he is pleased by its publication.

When I joined PRI, I found myself in the company of several energetic colleagues, chief among whom were researcher James A. Miller and investigative reporter David Morrison. Jim, as we called him, was a statistician by training, and was superb at tracking down often obscure data sources to make his compelling, numbers-based arguments. David, for his part, had a strong sense of justice, and traveled to the far corners of the globe in pursuit of those who violated the rights of women and families. Jim is no longer with us, and David has continued his journalism career elsewhere, but references to their earlier work abound in these pages.

I should also like to warmly thank my long-time executive assistant, later editor of the *PRI Review*, Sarah Kramer (*nee* Dateno), and my editorial assistant, Cheryl Metzger. Sarah and Cheryl share well-deserved reputations for meticulousness, which have saved the manuscript from many errors. Those that remain are my own.

I am indebted to many others besides who have given me information, encouragement, and the benefit of their expertise, including (but not limited to) Allen Carlson, Greg Clovis, Ginny Hitchcock, Angela Franks, Patrick Cunningham, Gail Instance, Randy Engel, Nancy Creger, Francis Kelly, Gerard Joseph, Rita Joseph, Vernon Kirby, Joel Bockrath, Carlos Polo, Brian Clowes, Dr. Stephen Karanja, Kateryna Cuddeback, David Tennessen, Michael Bird, Pat Reihle, Nicholas Eberstadt, Austin Ruse, Linus Clovis, Jean Guilfoyle, Donald Bishop, Dr. Joe McIlhaney, Jr., Dr. Stanley K. Monteith, Larry Carosino, Robert George.

Early drafts of sections of Chapters 2, 3, and 6 appeared in past issues of the *PRI Review,* and appear here with permission. The author gratefully acknowledges the following publisher for permission to use previously published material:

Princeton University Press, Julian Lincoln Simon, *The Ultimate Resource*, 1981, Figure 20-1, page 278.

Introduction

For over half a century, the population controllers have perpetrated a gigantic, costly and inhumane fraud upon the human race, defrauding the people of the developing countries of their progeny and the people of the developed world of their pocketbooks. Determined to stop population growth at all costs, the controllers have abused women and targeted racial and religious minorities (Chapter 5), undermined primary health care programs (Chapter 6), and encouraged dictatorial actions if not dictatorship (Chapter 3). They have skewed the foreign aid programs of the United States and other developed countries in an anti-natal direction (Chapter 7), corrupted dozens of well-intentioned nongovernmental organizations, and impoverished authentic development programs (Chapter 8). Blinded by zealotry worthy of Al-Qaeda, they have even embraced the most brutal birth control campaign in history: China's infamous one-child policy, with all its attendant horrors (Chapter 3).

They cannot even define what they are against: There is no workable demographic definition of "overpopulation." Instead the controllers conjure up images of poverty—low incomes, poor health, unemployment, malnutrition, overcrowded housing—to justify their anti-natal programs. The irony is that their war on people has in many ways caused what it predicted—a world that is poorer materially, less diverse culturally, less advanced economically, and plagued by incurable diseases, not to mention the many curable but ignored ones.

But the controllers have not only studiously ignored the mounting evidence of their multiple failures, they tiptoe around the biggest story of them all: Fertility rates are in free fall around the globe. The world's population of six plus billion will never double again, but will peak in a few decades at somewhere around 8 billion, and then it will *begin to decline*. Eighteen countries already fill more coffins than cradles each year, and the number of dying countries is growing steadily (Chapter 1).

The silence of the controllers concerning the coming birth dearth is hardly surprising. Their movement was born in the dark fear of the "unchecked growth in human numbers" of the poor, the illiterate, and the other. As that phantasm evaporates in the face of falling fertility, so should the population control movement. The trouble is that movements with billions of dollars at their disposal, not to mention thousands of paid advocates, do not go quietly to their graves. Moreover, many in the movement are not content to merely achieve *zero* population growth, they want to go negative. In their view, our current numbers should be reduced down to one or two billion or so—an end that would keep them fully employed for a couple more centuries while they implement a global one-child policy.

Enough already. If couples around the world are self-regulating their own fertility downward, surely everyone can agree that we don't need the controllers any more. We never did.

Part I

The Population Problem

1

The White Pestilence

One remarks nowadays all over Greece such a diminution in natality and in general manner such depopulation that the towns are deserted and the fields lie fallow. Although this country has not been ravaged by wars or epidemics, the cause of the harm is evident: by avarice or cowardice the people, if they marry, will not bring up the children they ought to have. At most they bring up one or two. It is in this way that the scourge before it is noticed is rapidly developed. The remedy is in ourselves; we have but to change our morals.
—Polybius (204-122 B.C.)[1]
N.b. Rome annexed the Greek states in 146 B.C.

Demography is destiny.
—Auguste Comte[2]

Most of us grew up on a poisonous diet of overpopulation propaganda. Remember the lifeboat scenarios in high school biology, where we had to decide who we were going to push overboard, lest we all die. Recall the college class in which we were assigned to read Paul Ehrlich's *The Population Bomb*, which begins with the author mournfully intoning "The battle to feed all of humanity is over," and ends by advocating the abandonment of entire continents to famine and death in order to "cut ... out the cancer [of population growth].[3] Look up the speeches of former Vice President Al Gore, who warned of an "environmental holocaust without precedent"—a "black hole" in his words—that will engulf us if we do not stop having babies.[4] In this and a myriad of ways we have been force-fed—and most of us swallowed whole—the nasty theory that there were *too many people*, along with its even more terrible corollary that it is necessary to practice *inhumanity* in order to save humanity—or some worthy fraction thereof.

What if overpopulation is, as economist Jacqueline Kasun has re-marked, a *false* dogma? What if the assorted population controllers, radical environmentalists, self-serving politicians, and others are wrong about our breeding ourselves off the face of the planet? From Ehrlich on, they have been peddling a worst-case scenario—times *ten*. Everyone has read passages similar to the following, taken from James Coleman and Donald Cressey's *Social Problems*, one of the standard social science textbooks from the 1990s:

> The world's population is exploding. The number of men, women and children is now over 5 billion. ... If the current rate of growth continues, the world's population will double again in the next 40 years...the dangers of runaway population growth can be seen in historical perspective... It took all of human history until 1800 for the world's population to reach 1 billon people. But the next ... 1 billion was added in only 130 years (1800-1930), [the next billion] after that in 30 years (1930-1960), and the next in 15 years (1960-1975). The last billion people were added in only 12 years (1975-1987). *If this trend (of runaway population growth) continues the world will be soon be adding a billion people a year, and eventually every month*[5] (italics added).

Since even the most frantic of population alarmists now agree that the world's population in the early 1990s was only increasing by some 90 million per year (an increment which has since fallen to 76 million) there was zero chance that the world would "soon be adding a billion people a year," much less " every month." But literally millions of col-lege students learned otherwise and, like me, began to obsess about the numbers.

Over six billion of anything is a mind-boggling number, and not just for the numerically challenged. Few people have the independence of mind to grasp what this number truly represents: A great victory over early death won by advances in health, nutrition and longevity. Even fewer are aware that the world's population will never double again. In fact, as we will see, it is already close to its apogee.

Like other Baby Boomers, I lived through the unprecedented dou-bling of the global population in the second half of the 20th century. Never before in human history had our numbers increased so far, so fast: from 3 billion in 1960 to 6 billion in 2000. But Ehrlich and Company, I came to see, glossed over the underlying reason: Our numbers didn't double because we suddenly started breeding like rabbits. They doubled because *we stopped dying like flies*. Fertility was falling throughout this period, from an average of 6 children per woman in 1960 to only 2.6 by 2002.[6]

Life expectancy at birth, on the other hand, was steadily rising, climbing from 46 years in 1950-1955 to over 65 years from 2000-2005. The less developed countries saw the most dramatic increases: life spans there lengthened from 41 to 63 1/2 years.[7] You don't have to be a rocket scientist to understand that, with everyone living half again as long, there will be more of us around at any given time. Longer life spans in fact account for about half of all population growth over the last half century. The happy fact that billions of us were cheating death for decades at a time would seem cause to celebrate, not to mourn.

Population control enthusiasts refused to celebrate. They were too fixated upon the numbers. Those riding the population train to fame, fortune and government funding scarcely deigned to notice improved life-spans. Moreover, they seemed completely oblivious to what demographer Joel Cohen calls "the most important demographic event in history." This occurred around 1965—our census numbers aren't accurate enough to be more precise—when the population growth *rate* peaked and then began to fall. From adding 2.1 percent to the world's population each year world population growth dropped to increments of only 1.2 percent by 2002. To put the matter plainly, the population train began to brake in 1965. It has been losing momentum ever since.[8]

On the fantasy island of overpopulation human numbers are always exploding, but a close look at the real world reveals a different reality. The unprecedented fall in fertility rates that began in post-war Europe has, in the decades since, spread to every corner of the globe, affecting China, India, the Middle East, Africa, and Latin America. The latest forecasts by the United Nations show the number of people in the world shrinking by mid-century, that is, before today's young adults reach retirement age. Many nations, especially in Europe, are already in a death spiral, losing a significant number of people each year. Listen closely, and you will hear the muffled sound of populations crashing.

The old "demographic transition" charts showed birthrates leveling off precisely at the replacement rate. But many of today's young adults in Europe and elsewhere are too enamored of sex, the city, and the single life to think about marriage, much less about replacing themselves. A single Swedish woman may eventually bear one child as her biological clock approaches midnight, of course, but she is unlikely to bear a second. What was supposed to be the perfect family—a boy for you and a girl for me and heaven help us if we have three—has been scorned by moderns on their way to extinction. The declining number of traditional families has been unable to fill the fertility gap thus created.

This is the *real* population crisis. This population implosion, by reducing the amount of human capital available, will have a dramatic impact on every aspect of life. Peter Drucker, the late management guru, wrote back in 1997 that "The dominant factor for business in the next two decades—absent war, pestilence, or collision with a comet—is not going to be economics or technology. It will be demographics."[9] Drucker was particularly concerned with the "increasing *under*population of the developed countries," but a decade later this reproductive malaise has spread even to the less developed world, and is a truly global phenomenon.[10]

By 2004, the United Nations Population Division (UNPD) found that 65 countries, including 22 in the less developed world, had fertility rates that were below the level needed to ensure the long-term survival of the population.[11] Most of the rest, the agency warned, were likely to enter this danger zone over the next few decades. According to the agency's "low-variant" projection, historically the most accurate, by 2050 three out of every four countries in the less developed regions will be experiencing the same kind of below-replacement fertility that is hollowing out the populations of developed countries today.[12] Such stark drops in fertility, cautioned the UNPD, will result in a rapid aging of the populations of developed and developing countries alike. With the number of people over 65 slated to explode from 475 million in 2000 to 1.46 billion in 2050, existing social security systems will be threatened with collapse.[13] It will prove difficult, if not impossible, to establish new ones.

These sobering projections show that the population of the world will continue to creep up until about the year 2040, peaking at around 7.6 billion people.[14] This is only a fraction more—one-sixth or so—than the 6.5 billion that the planet supports at present. Then the global population *implosion*, slow at first, but accelerating over time, begins. We fall back to current levels by 2082, and then shrink to under 5 billion by the turn of the next century. That population will be much older than we are today.

If this impending population implosion catches you by surprise, you have the UN Population Division (UNPD) to thank. The agency buries its "low-variant" projection deep within its biennial reports, where only demographic bores like me bother to look. Reporters looking for quick stories skim the UNPD's press releases and the "executive summary," which highlight the "medium variant" projection of 9 billion plus by mid-century. But the "medium variant," despite its moderate-sounding name, is anything but middle of the road. All of its numbers hang on a single, unexplained, and incredibly unrealistic assumption—also deeply interred in the UNPD reports—that *all countries will approach a "fertility floor" of 1.85 children per woman over the next half century.*

How was this "fertility floor" determined? The UNPD report does not say. Why would fertility in countries like Mexico fall to 1.85 and no further? The UNDP report offers no explanation, despite the fact that many countries have already fallen through this supposedly solid "floor." And what about those countries? How will Italy or Spain, for example, manage to climb back up to the "fertility floor" after spending the last two decades in the "fertility basement?" The UNPD report is silent.

The "low variant" projection, which has global fertility falling gradually to 1.35, seems preferable for a host of reasons. First and foremost, it has been historically the most accurate. For two decades and more, the low variant has been a better predictor of population growth. Second, the low variant accurately reflects the fertility rates in dozens of developed countries around the globe. Fertility rates between 1.1 and 1.6 are typical of post-modern societies, even those with strong pro-natal policies. In fact, the UN Population Division admits as much, writing that "in recent years fertility has fallen well below replacement to reach historically unprecedented low levels (1.3 children per woman and below) in most developed countries as well as in several less developed ones." The "low variant" makes the intuitively reasonable assumption that, as additional nations modernize, they will behave demographically like modern nations. Finally, the only effective counter to falling fertility, as we will see in later chapters, is strong religious faith, combined with a tax structure that completely shelters young couples from taxes. But religious faith, in Europe and some other developed countries at least, has long been on the wane. And taxes are on the rise—in part to pay for an increasing number of elderly.

What happens to the world's population *after* 2050 depends on the fertility decisions of those not yet born. It is impossible to predict accurately. But all of the current trends point downward. Women around the world were averaging 5.0 children in 1970. This had fallen to 2.6 by 2002—not far above replacement rate fertility of 2.3—and it is projected to drop to 1.54 children per woman by the year 2050.[15] But who's to say that it will stop there? Shaped by powerful, if partially hidden, economic, political and cultural forces, the one-child family appears well on the way to becoming a universal norm in many countries. Pockets of higher fertility, driven by religious motivations and traditional values, will still exist. But, as in present-day Japan or Germany, most families will have no more than one child. The number of the aged will skyrocket, and the world's population will be in free fall.[16]

This is the *real* population problem.

More Coffins than Cradles

This barren world of tomorrow can already be glimpsed in the Europe of today. For all of Europe, from Ireland in the west to Russia in the east, is aging and dying. French historian Pierre Chaunu has coined an apt phrase for the strange infecundity of present-day Europeans and their overseas descendants, who are failing to produce enough children to replace themselves. He calls it the White Pestilence.

The phrase contains a ghostly echo of the Black Death of the Middle Ages, which emptied out the cities and towns of the continent in successive pandemics of bubonic plague from 1347 to 1352. But unlike the Black Death, Chaunu's White Pestilence does not fill up the graveyards; it empties out the maternity wards. And it is not the result of bacteria that infect our bodies' so much as dark, anti-natal thoughts that invade our minds. These are reinforced by an economic system that puts a premium on expanding the work force at the expense of maternity, and a political system that weakens families, putting those with children at a financial disadvantage that is both unjust and shortsighted.[17] Europe, along with its offspring in North America, Australia, and New Zealand, for some time now has been refusing to pay its debts to those who provide for the future in the most fundamental way—by providing the next generation—and are thus mindlessly committing a form of collective suicide.

Just how bad is the White Pestilence likely to be? Obscured by debates over epiphenomena like exploding immigration and bankrupt pension funds is the brute fact that Europe is already suffering from a devastating, crippling shortage of people. The populations of no fewer than thirteen European countries, including Russia, Poland, and Hungary, have already begun to crash.[18] The total fertility rate for Europe, including the former Soviet Republics, currently averages an anemic 1.4 children per woman, and no increase is in sight.[19] As a result, the current population of 728 million will plunge to only 557 million by the year 2050, a drop similar in magnitude to that occurring during the Black Death.[20] At that point, Europe will be losing 3 to 4 million people a year. If the crash continues—and there is no reason to expect it not to—the White Pestilence will over time prove far more lethal than its medieval predecessor. Three out of four Europeans will have disappeared by the end of the 21st century, and the population will number only 207 million. By then the population decline will be irreversible, with the surviving Europeans averaging more than 60 years of age.

Well before this time, the aging of the population will have created unbearable strains on social security and health care systems. By mid-century, seven nations—Austria, Bulgaria, the Czech Republic, Greece, Italy, Romania and Spain—will have populations with an *average age* above 55. At the current time, 1.6 workers support one young or retired dependent. By the middle of the century, each worker will have to support one dependent, placing a huge tax burden on the rapidly-declining work force—and further driving down fertility.

Europe is already suffering tremendous economic and social dislocation caused by a rapidly-aging population and, in Western Europe, massive in-migration. Baby bonuses and child allowances, such as Poland's 1,000 zloty bonus (about $320) to the mothers of newborns, have done little to alleviate the problem. If Europe's problems are bad now, as its population is just beginning to dip, it is frightening to think about how much worse they will become during the coming demographic free-fall.

The plunge has already begun in Russia, Ukraine, and Belarus. The disintegration of the Soviet Union in 1991 triggered a sharp drop in Russian births, which have stayed low in the years following because of the sudden loss of a social system that formerly provided employment and housing for nearly every Russian, the ongoing economic stagnation, and a general lack of confidence in the future. Current Russian birthrates are the lowest in the nation's history, substantially lower than those achieved during the upheavals of World War I and the Russian Revolution, and equaled only by the worst year of World War II when German armies overran the western third of the country. Russia's population is already decreasing by three-quarters of a million people each year; Ukraine's, by a quarter million.

By 2003 the birthrate had been so low for so long that Russian leaders became concerned. Russian President Vladimir Putin warned the Russian parliament that the lack of babies was "a serious crisis threatening Russia's survival."[21] Three years later, Putin put in place a one-time payment of $9,000 upon the birth of a second child, along with additional cash and child-care subsidies for additional children.[22] But the crisis, apparently, continues. Russia's population is slated to decrease from 143 million in 2005 to 112 million in 2050. This is the UNDP's medium variant projection, which unrealistically assumes that most Russian couples will start having two children again.[23] It is hard to see how a country can lose a quarter of its population and build a modern economy at the same time. Yet the converse is also true: Until the Great

Russian Depression ends the birthrate is likely to say low. The largest country in the world seems locked into a fatal spiral; a dance of death between demography and depression.

Birthrates are higher—although still running below replacement levels—in Western Europe. What might appear cause for celebration, however, is in fact cause for concern as well. For birthrates in many Western European countries are being "propped up" by more fertile immigrants. France's estimated Total Fertility Rate, for instance, is running at 1.86 children per woman.[24] This is high by European standards, but much of this fertility is attributable to mostly Muslim immigrants. The French government forbids the collection of statistics by race or religion ("We are one people," it maintains), but demographers believe that the immigrant population is about 10% of the whole, and that it is out-reproducing the native-born French population by two or three to one. The department of Seine-Saint-Denis has both the highest percentage of immigrants in the country—about one-quarter of the population of the department is foreign, mostly Muslim—and also the highest birthrate. Subtracting the 3 or 4 children of the average immigrant leaves the native population averaging only 1.3 children or so, about the European average.[25]

In 1987 Antonella Pinnelli, a Rome-based sociologist and demographer, called the continent's flight from fertility "very worrisome, because when a society loses the will to reproduce, it loses its vitality."[26] Two decades of rock-bottom birthrates later, Italy and other European countries are in danger of losing more than their vitality. Their history, traditions and, indeed, their very existence are at risk. The cross of St. George, the English national flag, has now been banned in British prisons, only the first of what will undoubtedly be many efforts to culturally appease a growing Muslim population. In the end, however, only the numbers matter. Demographers now estimate that France, for example, will be as much as 40% Muslim by 2050.

"In demographic terms, Europe is vanishing," remarked then-Premier Jacques Chirac in 1984. "[Soon] our countries will be empty."[27] Empty of Gauls, Teutons, Britons, and Slavs perhaps. But other tribes, more fruitful than the modern-day European ones, will certainly come to occupy the pleasant lands north of the Mediterranean. And the surviving Europeans will retreat to their retirement homes, as the Neanderthals once retreated across the same terrain before the advance of Cro-Magnon Man. In France, as in most of Western Europe, the successor population is already in place.

Going Down, Down Under ...

The epidemics that swept through the New World, as well as Australia and New Zealand, in advance of European colonization find their modern-day parallel in the White Pestilence, which is once again emptying out these lands. Not that they were ever "overpopulated" by any stretch of the imagination. Take Australia, for example. With only 20.6 million people scattered across nearly 3 million square miles of land, the dominant carnivore in many parts of the country is not man, but the dingo.

My introduction to Australia's emptiness came in 1992 when I was invited to testify before the Australian Senate. After landing in Sydney, which at 4 million people is Australia's largest city, I picked up my rental car at the airport and headed south on the main superhighway bound for Canberra, the capital. Within a half hour this bustling freeway had shrunk to a lightly trafficked two-lane country road. For the next three hours I drove through open grassland broken only by scattered stands of eucalyptus trees and an occasional farmhouse. I recall passing through only one town of any size. *And this is one of the more populated parts of rural Australia*, I had to keep telling myself. The land "beyond the black stump," as the Aussies call the virtually uninhabited Outback, lay two hundred miles to the west.

Despite Australia's pressing population problem—too few people—Aussies are presently averaging only about 1.7 children. Cardinal George Pell, Archbishop of Sydney, has warned that "We need to start rethinking this [anti-natal] attitude if we want enough people around when we are old to care for us, pay taxes to support us, and if necessary, go to war to defend us."[28] Gail Instance, the dynamic head of Australia's Family Life International, is even blunter. "Common sense tells us that we are committing national suicide. We had better make up our minds about who we want to give this country to—since we don't seem to want it ourselves."[29]

Canadians are even more reckless with their country's future—the fertility rate is an anemic 1.5—and for just as little reason. Canada is the world's second largest country, second only to Russia, but has a population that is, at only 32.4 million, many times smaller. And it is likely to become smaller still. Tom Wonnacott, who teaches statistics and demography at the University of Western Ontario, puts it this way: "For every 100 Canadians in this generation, there are fewer than 80 children in the next." His prediction: "Another generation of baby bust will give us a Canada where there are more people aged 65 than any other age—and a lot fewer workers to support retirees."[30]

Latins Still Loving—But Not Procreating

The image of the loving Mexican mamacita surrounded by a passel of barefoot children remains scratched on the minds of Americans, even when it has largely vanished in the dusty pueblos of Mexico itself. Government-enforced sterilization campaigns, along with simple modernity, have dramatically shrunk family size south of the border in recent years. When I speak to American audiences, they are invariably surprised to learn that the average young Mexican family now numbers no more children than its American counterpart.

Then where do all the Hispanic young men come from that they see cutting grass in front of apartment complexes, working in construction zones, or shopping in Wal-Mart, people frequently ask. Many are children of the 1970s and 1980s, I answer. A one-time drop in infant mortality rates produced the largest cohort in Mexican history. But, once again, it wasn't that Mexicans suddenly started breeding like rabbits. It was rather that their children stopped dying like flies.

Today their numbers are dropping rapidly. "The Mexicans are getting uppity," one California farmer, himself of Hispanic descent, complained to me laconically. He was increasingly dependent on immigrants from Central America, he told me, to prune and tend his orchard. The desperate bands of young men we see swimming the Rio Grande or scaling border fences are no longer exclusively Mexican, but come from countries not just south of our border, but *south* of Mexico, such as Guatemala, Honduras, El Salvador, and Columbia.

When President Bush in 2006 ordered National Guard troops to assist the beleaguered Border Patrol, Mexican government officials were indignant that the United States was "militarizing" its hitherto peaceful southern border. What they failed to mention was that Mexico's *own* southern border, in this case with Guatemala, has been heavily guarded for some time and for the same reason. Responding to the flood of illegals from more fecund countries further south, units of the Mexican Army are on constant patrol there.

But Central and South American countries, too, are seeing their birthrates fall. Most Latin American countries are now rapidly approaching replacement rate fertility, if they are not already there, according to the UNPD. Women in Brazil, the largest South American country, currently average only 2.3 children. The inhabitants of Argentina, Columbia, Uruguay, and Chile are even less fertile.

Islam Contracepted

The millions of Muslims flooding into Europe are not being driven out of their homelands by population pressure so much as they are being drawn into a demographic vacuum as Europe empties itself of offspring. There are still pockets of high fertility in the Islamic world—impoverished Afghanistan has one of the highest birthrates in the world—but the trend is towards three- and even two-child families.[31] Indonesia, at 223 million the largest majority Muslim country, had a 2.4 fertility rate in 2005, according to the UNPD.

In recent years a number of Muslim countries have seen fertility declines that are among the largest ever recorded. The only two majority Muslim countries in Europe, Albania and Bosnia-Herzegovina, dropped their birthrates farther and faster than most of their neighbors. In the less-developed world, Kuwait, Algeria, Iran, and Tunisia all saw their fertility rate drop by two-thirds during the last three decades of the twentieth century. All were at or below replacement by 2000. The "least developed countries," UN parlance for the poorest of the poor, generally saw smaller declines. But here, too, the Muslim states of Bangladesh, Sudan, and the Maldives all cut fertility by a third or more, and are currently averaging three or four children.[32]

The Koran, like the Torah and the Bible, comes down firmly on the side of natality. But Islam lacks a central religious authority, and any imam can issue a *fatwa*—an Islamic religious opinion. Knowing this, the population control movement has sought out and cultivated liberal Muslim clerics, encouraging them to rethink Islam's traditional encouragement of childbearing.

One of the earliest Muslim countries to be targeted for re-education in this way was Egypt. As the Middle Eastern country with the largest population, it was listed as a "country of concern" in a key National Security Council study in the early 1970s.[33] The UN Population Fund immediately moved in, among other things helping to set up an International Center for Population Studies and Research at Al-Azhar University in Cairo. In the years following, it carried out a series of projects on "Population in the Context of Islam" which were consciously designed to shift religious opinion.

Nevertheless, it was 1988 before the Grand Imam of Al-Azhar University could be induced to issue a major *fatwa* affirming the acceptability of family planning "for personal and national justification." He decreed that contraceptive use was permissible "in the case of a three-child family who can afford more children physically and financially, but who want no more children because their country has a population problem."[34] Consequently, the Egyptian birthrate has fallen sharply in recent years, and by 2006 women were averaging only 2.74 children.[35]

In Iran the Western-engineered shift in religious opinion was even more dramatic. The Islamic Revolution of 1979 ushered in a government of ayatollahs committed to the Koranic injunction that children are blessings and opposed to all forms of birth control. Yet, by the early 1990s, the depression induced by the flight of Western investors, along with the continuing, unrelenting efforts of the population controllers, induced the Iranian government to change its policy. Departing from the traditional Islamic understanding of the blessing of children, the government began a foreign-inspired and supported campaign against the large family.

The principal architect of Iran's population control program was Hossein Malek-Afzali, a physician who was, like most population controllers, trained in the United States, in his case at the University of California at Los Angeles. Television programs openly promoted family planning, as did the ayatollahs at religious services. Many a village mullah began devoting part of his Friday sermon to encouraging his followers to visit the local birth control center. A network of volunteers was set up to go house-to-house, while the government began offering free contraceptive services—including pills, condoms, IUDs and the contraceptive patch—and free sterilizations.[36]

The program, in conjunction with Iran's continuing economic turmoil, soon began to make inroads into the fertility of the population. *The Washington Post* reported in 1992 that the government had already paid for 200,000 tubal ligations and 7,500 vasectomies.[37] The brief flourishing of fertility following the Islamic Revolution quickly subsided and family size in 2006 stood at 1.79 children and falling.

Birthrates are also falling in relatively prosperous, westernized Turkey, despite the exhortations of government leaders to have more children. "Our population which is nearing 65 million is not enough," warned Turkish Prime Minister Necmettin Erbakan of the Islamist Refah Party in 1995. "Population is the power by which we shall establish right in the world," he told a cheering crowd. "These would-be westerners [i.e., population control advocates] are trying to reduce our population. We must have at least four children."[38] As the fertility rate fell past 2.5 children per women in 2002, Recep Tayyip Erdogan, soon to become Turkey's prime minister, attacked contraception as "straight out treason to the state." "Have babies," he urged Turks. "Allah wants it."[39]

The most geopolitically charged exception to the small family norm is the Palestinians. The late Yassir Arafat once said that "the womb of the Arab woman is my best weapon." Those wombs, it turns out, are still churning out nearly five children each, almost twice as many as the average Jewish woman.[40] Not only that, the reverse Diaspora of Jews back to Israel is over. Immigration has slowed to a trickle. One consequence of losing the baby wars is that in 2005 Jews became a minority in Greater Israel. Perhaps it is no coincidence that Israel pulled out of Gaza that same year. Uprooting a few thousand Israeli settlers may have seemed a small price to pay for ridding itself of 1.3 million unassimilated Palestinians. Israel's historical claim to what the United Nations calls "occupied Palestinian territories" may be recorded in the Torah, but there are limits to how many Palestinians that Israel can absorb. Unilateral disengagement now may be preferable to being overwhelmed from within by an ever-expanding Palestinian Muslim block. As always, demography is proving to be destiny.

Japan: Land of the Setting Sun

A decade and a half ago, the Japanese economic boom appeared well nigh unstoppable. Industry was flourishing under the guidance of *Long Range Vision* plans issued by elite bureaucrats at the Ministry of International Trade and Industry (MITI). The *salarimen*, as the Japanese middle class are called, were grinding away at their customary 70-hour work week. Economic growth was consistently running at 4 to 5 percent a year, and Japan's trade surplus with the United States was surging toward the $100 billion mark.

Conceding defeat, Harvard academic Ezra Vogel wrote a book called *Japan as Number One,* admonishing Americans that we were falling behind because of our lack of Japanese-style "central direction" and "government and business cooperation." We should, he advised us, "adopt policies more suited to the postindustrial age."[41] Others feared that if we didn't join them, they might beat us. *The Coming War with Japan* had the yellow peril once again leading a "Greater East Asia Co-Prosperity Sphere," and once again threatening Pearl Harbor.[42] Both became bestsellers.

It wasn't long thereafter that the Japanese economy ran into a brick wall. Economic growth stalled, averaging an anemic one percent growth for most of the 1990s. During the Asian economic downturn of 1998, Japan's GNP actually *shrank* by 2.8 percent. Never number one, the

Rising Sun soon slipped to fourth, behind the European Union and China.[43]

The experts told us that crony capitalism, corruption, and protectionism were to blame. But when has this not been true in post-World War II Japan? The Liberal Democratic Party has been in power since it was formed by a coalition of three conservative parties in 1956. It is bound together less by a political philosophy than by loose alliances between factional leaders who trade favors, give and accept bribes, and are periodically disgraced and forced out of office by scandal. The subterfuges used by Japanese bureaucrats to keep out foreign-made goods in key industrial sectors are legion. Don't bother looking for American-made cars on Japanese highways; you won't see any.

What really happened in the 1990s is that the yellow peril turned quietly grey. For over four decades now, the Japanese people have been having too few little Mikis and Yosukus to replace themselves. The Japanese fertility rate first fell below replacement around 1960. After fluctuating around 2.0 for the next 15 years, it began to sink again in 1975. By 1990 it had reached 1.57, leading Japanese journalists to invent the term "1.57 shock." Further shocks followed at regular intervals: "1.53 shock" in 1992, "1.47 shock" in 1993, and the "1.38 shock" in 1998. Since then the fertility rate has hovered around 1.4 children per woman. The voluntary childlessness of the Japanese exceeds even the forced-pace population reduction of China's one-child policy.

This prolonged Japanese birth dearth has resulted in what Yamada Masahiro of Gakugei University calls the world's first "low-birthrate recession." With ever smaller cohorts of new workers, the *salarimen* have been getting wrinklier and their ranks thinner, year by year. The depopulation crisis has already forced Japan to slash pensions and raise the retirement age from 60 to 65 to keep pension funds afloat. By 2040, says the Organization for Economic Co-operation and Development (OECD), the rise in the ratio of dependent old to working young may be reducing Japan's growth in living standards by three-quarters of a percentage point per year, cutting Japan's GNP by 23 percent by mid-century as a result.

Japan is on the brink of a major demographic meltdown. Japan's population of 127 million has stopped growing and—if the birthrate continues at this low level—will soon begin to shrink at an alarming pace. According to UN estimates, by the year 2050 Japan will have 35 million fewer people than it does now. The 92 million Japanese who remain will have a median age of 54, with those aged 75-80 constituting the largest five-year population cohort. The ratio of workers aged 20-65 to retirees will have fallen to just over one-to-one. By then, barring a striking upturn in fertility, Japan's complete demographic collapse is virtually assured: Projections show so few women of childbearing age that the population decline will inevitably accelerate. A population bust, like an explosion, proceeds in geometric progression.

Yet there are foreign observers, like Victor Mallet of the *Financial Times*, who are celebrating the decline of the Japanese population as good for the world and for Japan itself. Mallet bases his optimism on the fact that the "the labor force has been rising this year as older people rejoin the workforce and more women take jobs. Robots and immigrants ... will also help to keep the economy growing."[44] Each of his proposed measures, however, is either a temporary stopgap measure, or is self-defeating. The newly rehabilitated elderly will soon be forced to retire again, this time for good. As for women joining the work force in greater numbers, this will surely drive the birthrate down even more, exacerbating the labor shortage over time. Nor is immigration likely to solve Japan's problems. It would take an estimated 600,000 immigrants *a year* to offset the impending decline in the labor force, an influx of such magnitude that would shake Japan's homogenous and insular monoculture to the core.

Staking Japan's future on the promise of robot manufacture seems an equally dubious proposition. While it is true that more than half of the world's industrial robots—57 percent to be exact—are located in Japan, few jobs off the assembly line are suited for robots, at least at their present level of sophistication.[45]

Mallet's *laissez faire* attitude towards Japan's demographic crisis is emphatically not shared by the Japanese leadership. Reacting to reports that the 2006 total fertility rate had dropped to 1.25, the then-prime minister, Shinzo Abe, announced on January 26, 2007, that he would "set out a full-scale strategy to reverse the declining birthrate." A "Strategic Council to Study Measures to Support Children and Families" has been established, with instructions to report back by mid-year on ways to encourage more births that go beyond the current—and largely ineffectual—child allowances. Still, it remains to be seen whether any post-modern society, including Japan's, can revive a sagging birthrate.[46]

The old age tsunami that is about to hit Japan will not spare other Asian countries. The Four Tigers—Taiwan, Hong Kong, South Korea, and Singapore—are already getting long in the tooth. China and India, the world's two demographic giants, are tottering along not far behind.

China and India: Grey and Male

When China's geriatric leaders, then led by the diminutive septuage-narian Deng Xiaoping, embarked upon the one-child-per-couple policy in 1979, they did not imagine that they were remaking the country in their own demographic image. But—with China's population rapidly aging and its sex ratio ever more skewed in favor of men—this is exactly what is happening. The face of China is slowly coming to resemble the Politburo of the Chinese Communist Party, that is to say, it will be grey and overwhelmingly male.

For some years, Chinese women have been averaging 1.7 children, a birthrate so low that by 2020 China's median age will be older than that of the United States. Between now and 2025, the number of people over 60 is set to double in size, from roughly 140 million today to more than 300 million. As these massive numbers of elderly begin heading for the exits, by mid-century China could be losing a quarter of its population each generation.

China's increasingly elderly population will also be increasingly male. The one-child policy has made little girls an endangered species, as many couples, desperate for a son, sacrifice any daughters they may happen to conceive to keep their quota open. Within a few years of the introduction of the one-child policy, hundreds of thousands of baby girls were being drowned, smothered, or abandoned at birth each year. Even some villagers in relatively wealthy areas like the Pearl River Delta, where female infanticide was unknown in earlier times, quietly began to do away with daughters.[47]

The arrival of ultrasound machines in China has added a new dimension to this tragedy. Pregnant women, commonly brought in by husbands or in-laws anxious for male offspring, undergo ultrasounds to determine the sex of the child they are carrying. If the image on the screen reveals male genitalia, the family celebrates its good fortune. If the unfortunate fetus lacks that apparatus, however, her life is quickly extinguished. Such sex-selective abortions, as they are called, along with female infanticide, have resulted in a ratio of male to female births of 117 to 100. This means that over 10 percent of all girls conceived in China are killed in *utero*. Only women can have babies, of course, and the selective elimination of so many of their number hastens the day of China's depopulation.

The country where Paul Ehrlich experienced his "overpopulation" epiphany—India—is similarly transforming itself into a country of old men, although at a slower pace, and with great regional variations. "Old India," as Nicholas Eberstadt has called it, consists of large urban centers and much of the rural South. Cities like New Delhi, Mumbai (Bombay), and Kolkata (Calcutta) have sub-replacement fertility, as do southern states like Kerala and Tamil Nadu. Birthrates in the rural North, however, are still high.[48]

India's *de facto* two-child policy is neither as well known nor as brutal as China's. But this policy, in conjunction with modernity, has effectively brought the average fertility rate down to about 2.9 or so. Add to this the ubiquitous ultrasound machines found in every rural clinic throughout the country, and the longstanding preference for sons, and you find many families with more than one son, but few with more than one daughter. A startling number of unborn babies have died after an ultrasound revealed their sex to parents determined to avoid raising, educating, and paying a dowry for a girl.

The real demographic horror show is not India's projected debut as the world's most populous country (taking over this distinction from China), but the elimination of an entire generation of baby girls.

American Exceptionalism

The United States seems set to avoid the geriatric trap that has begun swallowing up populations elsewhere in the developed world. Birthrates, which fell below 2.1 following the legalization of abortion in 1973, have actually inched back up to replacement in recent years. Part of the reason for our relative prolificacy has to do with the generous tax breaks that American couples with young children have enjoyed beginning in the mid-1990s. Each child born in 2007 qualifies its parents for an additional $4650 deduction against their income and an additional $1,000 credit against their tax liability. The happy result is that an American couple of modest income with two or more children pays virtually no income tax. The situation is far different in Europe where a similar couple may turn over 50 percent of its income to the state and receives back only a paltry monthly subsidy.

The continuing strength of religious sentiment in the United States is another factor. Fertility is strongly influenced by whether you focus on the here-and-now, as post-Christian Europeans do, or live with the hereafter in mind, as many Americans do. Immigrants, most of whom regard babies as a blessing rather than a burden, have also contributed to the baby bump. The population ticker at the U.S. Census Bureau hit

300,000,000 on October 17, 2006, and seems set to increase for some decades to come.

The Crisis of the Empty Cradle

Unlike the endlessly propagandized "crisis caused by our burgeoning numbers," the crisis of the empty cradle has crept upon us quietly. Classic "demographic transition" theory assumed that parents in pre-modern societies were motivated to have many children to ensure that at least two survived to adulthood. Cradles were kept full because so many newborns departed via coffins so soon after their arrival. Reduce the infant and child mortality rate, the theory went, and parents would adjust their childbearing downward to compensate. A new and stable equilibrium of low mortality *and* low fertility would result in zero population growth.

No such equilibrium was ever reached. In the developed countries, trends like more education, especially for women, high taxes, the widespread availability of birth control devices, legalized abortion, the move from farm to city, the decline of religious belief, anti-natal propaganda and the dominance of a radically individualistic, materialistic worldview have caused the birthrate to continue to plummet ever lower. Materialism, in its various forms and guises, is probably the chief culprit, given that it creates an overarching worldview in which children are cast as the enemies of wealth and happiness. I once received a letter from a friend who lives in Florida. A neighbor of his, a young woman who commutes 50 miles one way to work, was bemoaning how little time she had to spend with her four-year-old son. My friend suggested that she sell her $40,000 SUV and get a job closer to home. Not only would she have more time to spend with her son, he told her, she would probably also be money ahead. She shook her head. "You don't understand," she said. "My husband and I *love* this SUV." Who was it that said that no man can serve two masters? The young woman in Florida apparently believes that she is driving an SUV. But in fact it is driving her.

Of all the factors affecting fertility, all but one works to keep the cradle empty. The sole exception is the raft of advances in human reproductive technology. But helping tens or even hundreds of thousands of infertile couples to conceive a child hardly counterbalances the millions who consciously limit themselves to one or no children.

Those who actually work in the field of reproductive endocrinology have long admitted what the population controllers are loath to admit, that fertility delayed is fertility denied. At a gathering of the American Fertility Society held in San Antonio in the mid-1990s, the speaker, Dorothy Mitchell-Leef, a prominent reproductive endocrinologist, asserted that "modern American women have been sold a bill of goods." American women have been encouraged by both "doctors and authoritative voices in the culture" to believe that they could start a family just as easily at 38 as at 22—perhaps even more easily, because in their late thirties they would be financially better off. Medical advances—injected hormones, in vitro fertilization, and screening of genetically damaged fetuses—made the usual biological limits seem old-fashioned. Not only is this picture false, she went on, but the fallacy of this view has been known for decades. A French study, conducted way back in the 1970s, followed women with infertile husbands who were trying to get pregnant through artificial insemination. The results showed that the chances of conception diminished sharply with age, with fertility showing a significant drop after age 30 and a sharp decline after 35. It was time, Mitchell-Leef asserted, for doctors to "begin telling women that if having children was a high priority, they should think of having them earlier in life rather than later." Her audience of professional American women, many of whom had experienced firsthand the "grief felt by women whose infertility treatments had failed, burst into applause."[49]

The overall pattern in the developed world seems too evident to ignore. Once people are educated, urbanized, and begin to enjoy a certain level of wealth, birthrates plummet. More and more couples live in urban conditions where children provide no economic benefits, but rather are, as the Chinese say, "goods on which one loses." Education delays marriage and provides other options for women besides marriage and family. For materially minded couples in countries where the state provides old age benefits, and charges high tax rates in consequence, the way to get ahead is to remain perpetually childless. Why give up a second income to bring a child into the world who will never, at least in material terms, repay your investment? Why provide for your future in the most fundamental way, by providing the next generation, if the government has pledged to keep you out of the poorhouse in your dotage anyway.

As Phillip Longman has remarked, the modern nanny state has created a strange new world in which the most "successful" individuals in material terms are the most "unfit" in biological terms. In all previous ages of human history wealth and children went hand-in-hand. Wealth made it possible to marry earlier, to bring more children into the world, and ensured that more of these children survived. Numerous progeny in turn virtually guaranteed continued family prosperity. But no longer. The cradle-to-grave social welfare programs found in developed countries, along with the heavy tax burden these demand, have not merely made the care and feeding of children superfluous to wealth; they have made children themselves wealth's enemy.[50]

True enough, some may answer. But what is behind the radical declines in fertility that we are now seeing among still poor peoples in Asia, Africa, and Latin America? Peoples who do not yet dream of SUVs, of education beyond the village primary school, or even employment outside the family field? Why are people in countries where the state does not even provide a bare minimum of support for the elderly also radically downsizing their families? Why, in countries where infant mortality rates are still relatively high, are couples failing to fill empty cradles?

The answer is that the demographic implosion that has occurred "naturally" in the developed world has been in large part imposed by force on the less fortunate, less powerful peoples of the world. The United States and other developed countries consciously set out in the 1960s to engineer a radical decline in Third World fertility. Weak nations, dependent on the United States and Europe for financial aid, military security, or access to markets, were bullied or suborned into mandating anti-natal measures. Paid for by the West, these measures ranged from the free provision of contraceptives to enforced sterilization programs. Hapless villagers worldwide have been subjected to clever marketing schemes, bait-and-switch health ploys, anti-family TV soap operas, and even blunt coercion in an effort to deprive them of the free exercise of their fertility.[51]

Their governments, despite having adopted population control programs under duress, are slow to abandon them even after birthrates begin to plummet. South Korea, for example, in 1961 embarked on a family planning program at the insistence of the U.S. government. The program quickly evolved into a *de facto* two-child-per-family policy, complete with strong punitive measures against those who dared violate this limit. Civil and military officials with more than two children, for example, were denied promotions or even demoted. Third and higher order children were declared ineligible for medical insurance coverage, educational opportunities, and other government benefits. Couples who agreed to sterilization were given priority access to scarce public housing. This did matters stand for three long decades.

By the time the government began to rethink this policy in the mid-1990s, the fertility rate had dropped to an anemic 1.7 children, the population was aging rapidly, and the South Korean economy had developed a full-blown labor shortage. Moreover, the country was experiencing an epidemic of sex-selective abortions, in which Confucian-minded parents anxious for sons were ending the lives of girl fetuses because of their gender. With young women in increasingly short supply, the population was poised to drop precipitously.

It was 1996 before the South Korean government finally got out of the population control business, announcing on June 4th of that year that all restrictions on childbearing would be lifted. No new pro-natal measures were enacted, however, unless one counts the government's promises that public health clinics would soon begin offering infertility treatment (in addition to birth control) and that it would crack down on sex-selective abortions.[52]

But if the government thought that, left to make their own decisions about family size, the Koreans would begin reproducing themselves, it badly miscalculated. Thirty-five years of anti-natal education and policies, combined with South Korea's rapid modernization, had done its work. With nary a pause, the birthrate continued to drop. It reached an all-time low of 1.2 in 2004, with the South Korean population now poised to shrink in absolute numbers.[53]

Thailand was another country that, strongly encouraged by the U.S. government, undertook a full-blooded population control program in 1962. Forty-five years later, its demographic profile resembles that of the dying West. Its villages are bereft of children, its schools are closing down for lack of students, and its population is rapidly aging. The average Thai mother today has 1.6 children, well below the replacement rate level of 2.2.

Many in Thailand are now having second thoughts. Tiang Phadthai-song, a researcher from Chiang Mao University in Northern Thailand, is among those who believe that "the family planning program has been too successful." In 1997, when the TFR was passing 1.9, Tiang published a paper called "The collapse of Thai society: the impact of family planning," in which she detailed the demographic disaster awaiting the Thai people. End family planning policies, she urged the government, so that the birthrate can once again rise to replacement levels.[54] Her pleas have fallen on deaf ears, even as the birthrate continues to fall.[55]

Many countries still have foreign-funded programs in place that they find uncongenial and which compromise their future. Take sparsely populated Bolivia, for example, a country whose nine million inhabitants are spread out over an area the size of Texas. The democratically elected government regards both its fertility rate (4.0) and its rate of population growth (2 percent per annum) as "satisfactory"—both have been falling in recent years—and has specifically adopted a hands-off policy of "no intervention" in these matters.[56] Yet the population control establishment is not content to leave well enough alone. The U.S. Agency for International Development (USAID) and others pour tens of millions of dollars into reproductive health programs in that country, which have the effect, not unintentional, of further reducing the birthrate.

The profound changes in the human condition caused by long-term, below-replacement birthrates can rightly be termed a "Demographic Revolution." But unlike the Industrial Revolution of the nineteenth century, or the Information Revolution of the late twentieth, or the Democratic Revolution that succeeded the fall of the Soviet Union in Eastern Europe (if not in Russia itself), all of which vastly improved the lives of billions, most of the consequences of the ongoing Demographic Revolution will be negative.

Population growth has been an important escalator of consumer demand. Try selling cars, houses, refrigerators, or anything else, for that matter, in a depopulating country. Or try to seek profitable investments in the stock market when millions of elders start liquidating their IRAs and 401Ks to survive. This is not to say that some few sectors of the economy, such as pharmaceuticals and health care, will not expand. But as Peter Drucker clearly saw, shrinking demand elsewhere will more than offset these gains in a few sectors.

Falling birthrates are also drastically shrinking family circles. Consider China's forced pace fertility reduction program known as the one-child-per-family policy. The first generation of children born under this policy has no brothers or sisters. These only children are now producing a second generation who are missing not only siblings, but uncles, aunts, and cousins as well. Demographer Nicholas Eberstadt of the American Enterprise Institute looks ahead to a world in which "for many people, 'family' would be understood as a unit that does not include any biological contemporaries or peers" and that we may live in "a world in which the only biological relatives for many people—perhaps most people—will be their ancestors."[57] Lacking close family ties, many seniors will be socially isolated and painfully lonely. As Ben Wattenberg has remarked, "Young DINKs (double income, no kids) may be cute. Old LINKs (low income, no kids) may be tragic. Clergymen say that the saddest funerals are those in which the deceased has no offspring."[58]

Modernity alone would have been sufficient to effect a demographic transition in South Korea and elsewhere, but the population engineers were not content to wait. They artificially induced a precipitous fall in birthrates by strict, nationwide anti-natal policies and, with the assistance of US family planning funds, have produced a full-blown Demographic Revolution.

The hundreds of millions of dollars that foreign agencies like USAID poured into Korea's two-child policy is but a tiny fraction of the $100 billion or so that has been spent on fertility reduction programs in the world at large. Imagine putting billions of dollars into programs to undo the Industrial and Information Revolutions, and you will understand the insanity of our current approach. We are making the old age tsunami predicted by Peter Drucker, Nicholas Eberstadt, Ben Wattenberg, and others even worse. And, even as we do so, we are causing a vast flood of human misery, as we will see in the chapters to come.

Notes

1. Polybius, *The Histories*, Volume 6. Quoted in Robert de Marcellus, "A Foundering Civilization," *Human Life Review* 28(1-2) (Winter/Spring 2002):7-18.
2. The phrase "Demography is destiny" is generally attributed to Auguste Comte (1798-1857), a 19th-century French mathematician and sociologist.
3. Paul Ehrlich, *The Population Bomb* (Ballantine Books, 1968; a Sierra Club edition followed in 1969, to which the following page citations refer.) The "battle … is over" phrase is from the Prologue. For the denial of food aid, see pages 143, 148.
4. Al Gore's *Earth in the Balance: Ecology and the Human Spirit* (Boston: Houghton Mifflin, 1992) is filled with such bombast. See, for instance, pages 177, 40 and 78.
5. The quote is from Chapter 17, entitled "Population." *Social Problems*, 4th ed. (Boston: Addison Wesley Educational Publishers, 1990) 487.
6. U.S. Census Bureau, *Global Population Profile 2002*, 22.
7. Table IV.1. "Life Expectancy at Birth by Development Group and Major Area, Estimate and Medium Variant, 1950-1955, 2000-2005, and 2045-2050", United Nations Secretariat, Department of Economic and Social Affairs, Population Division. *World Population Prospects: The 2004 Revision*, Volume III, Analytical Report, p. 55. The increase in life expectancy in the less developed world would have been even more dramatic without the onset of the HIV/AIDS epidemic, and the resurgence of malaria, in Africa. In Chapter 6 we will explore the extent to which population control programs are responsible for rising mortality in Africa.
8. Joel Cohen, "Human Population: The Next Half Century," *Science* (2003) 302:1172-1175. The U.S. Census Bureau puts the percentage at 2.2 percent and the years at 1963-1964. See the U.S. Census Bureau's *Global Population Profile 2002*. (Washington, D.C.: U.S. Government Printing Office, 2004) 3.
9. Peter Drucker, "The Future that Has Already Happened," *Harvard Business Review*, September/October 1997, pp. 20, 22, 24.
10. Some researchers have attempted to make the case, counterintuitive at best, that an aging and shrinking population will not create serious economic and social

problems. I have not been generally impressed by these efforts. Economist Phil Mullan, for example, has written *The Imaginary Time Bomb* (I. B. Tauris, New York: 2002), a self-described effort to debunk unfounded anxiety about the consequences of societal aging. Mullan's conclusion, that "The economic importance of population changes is often grossly exaggerated," (p. 212) seems remarkably modest in view of his thesis. It is also one that, given the incessant scaremongering over the population bomb, I have no trouble assenting to.

11. Very low fertility is not limited to the more developed regions. Of the 148 countries and territories defined by the UN Population Division as "less developed regions," 22 have below replacement fertility. The United Nations has issued two recent reports on this surprising development (2000, 2003), and a number of articles have been dedicated to this topic (Morgan, 2003; Goldstein, Lutz and Testa, 2003; Billari and Kohler, 2004).

12. The UN Population Division labels its three principal population projections the "high variant," the "medium variant," and the "low variant." Each is calculated using different assumptions about future fertility. The medium variant unrealistically assumes that all countries will approach a "fertility floor" of 1.85 over the next half century. It does not explain how this "fertility floor" was determined, nor does it explain how countries such as Italy will regain the "fertility floor" after spending the last two decades in the "fertility basement." The high variant is even more unrealistic. It assumes that the fertility rates of all countries will converge on 2.35, a fertility rate that has been achieved by *no* developed country, even those with strong pro-natal policies. I favor the low variant, which has fertility falling to 1.35. *World Population Prospects: The 2004 Revision, Volume III, Analytical Report*, 33.

13. United Nations Secretariat, Department of Economic and Social Affairs, Population Division. World Population Prospects: The 2004 Revision [working paper]. Volume I, "Comprehensive Tables."

14. The UN Population Division's medium variant projection, which assumes that the TFR in low fertility countries will rise to 1.85, is 9.1 billion. Only the Intergovernmental Panel on Climate Change (IPCC), in its *Special Report on Emissions Scenarios*, is still discussing a total population of 15.1 billion by 2100, a number that is supported by no demographic projections that I know of.

15. Replacement rate fertility is the level of fertility at which each successive generation of women produces exactly enough offspring so that the same number of women survive to have children themselves. Replacement rate fertility is often said to be 2.1 children per woman over her reproductive lifetime, but this is in fact the replacement rate fertility of a relatively developed country. For the globe as a whole, the replacement rate fertility estimated by the U.S. Census Bureau in 2002 was 2.3. See *Global Population Profile, 2002* available at http://www.census.gov/prod/2004pubs/wp-02.pdf, especially p. 21.

16. A June 29, 1999 report from the UN Population Division projected that by 2050 1 person out of every 5 will be 60 years or older. By 2150, this figure will be 1 in every 3.

17. For a good discussion of how the liberal welfare state relentlessly suppresses fertility, see Phillip Longman, *The Empty Cradle: How Falling Birthrates Threaten World Prosperity [And What To Do About It]*, esp. Chapters 10 and 12.

18. The nations whose populations are currently declining are Russia, Ukraine, Romania, Belarus, Bulgaria, Georgia, Kazakhstan, Hungary, Poland, Moldova, Lithuania, Latvia, Armenia, Czech Republic, Serbia and Montenegro, and Estonia. Were it not for massive immigration from Eastern Europe, the populations of Spain, Italy and Germany would be declining as well.

19. Table 3. "Total Fertility for the World, Major Development Groups and Major Areas, 1970-1975, 2000-2005, 2045-2050, by Projection Variants." In *WPP 2004, Analytical Report*, xxi.
20. Table 1. "Population of the World, Major Development Groups and Major Areas, 1950, 1975, 2005, 2050, by Projection Variants." *WPP 2004, Analytical Report*, xviii.
21. *Wall Street Journal*, January 24, 2003.
22. C. J. Chivers, "Putin urges plan to reverse slide in the birth rate," *The New York Times*, May 11, 2006.
23. United Nations Population Division, "World Population Prospects: The 2004 Revision Population Database," http://esa.un.org/unpp/p2k0data.asp. Another UNDP publication, *World Population to 2300*, has Russia's population declining to 101.5 million by 2050, and to 80 million by the end of the century. See *World Population to 2300* (UNDP, 2004, Tables 5, 8, and Figure 39). The Russian decline is alarming because it is fed not only by a declining and well-below replacement level birthrate, but also by an unprecedented rise in the numbers of early deaths of working-age men. The dramatic increase in deaths of Russian men aged 30 to 50 has pulled down male life expectancy from a 1991 average of 63.5 years—which was already well behind most other nations—to an astonishing 57.7 years in 2004. "Russian population declining as births, life expectancy drop," *The Washington Times*, 26 September 2006, p. A12. The World Bank's 2005 report, *Dying Too Young: Addressing Premature Mortality and Ill Health Due to Non Communicable Diseases and Injuries in the Russian Federation*, also pegs male life expectancy at 57.7.
24. This is the estimate given in the CIA's *The World FactBook*. https://www.cia.gov/cia/publications/factbook/geos/fr.html. Other estimates are comparable.
25. See "France's End," by Joseph D'Agostino, for an extended discussion of Muslim immigration and Europe's new demographic realities. *PRI Review* 15(5) (November/December 2005):1, 6-7.
26. "Falling Population Alarms Europe," *The Washington Times*, 2 December 1987, pp. 1, 8, at 8.
27. Ibid.
28. Tess Livingstone, *George Pell: Defender of the Faith Down Under*. (San Francisco: Ignatius Press, 2002) 314.
29. Personal communication, November 2005.
30. Tom Wonnacott, "Census shows youth will be missing from next generation," *PRI Review* (May/June 2003) 13(3): 5-6.
31. Muslim majority countries near or below replacement birthrates include Algeria at 2.5, Azerbaijan at 1.85, Bosnia-Herzegovina at 1.32, Tunisia at 2.0, Iran at 2.12, Kuwait at 2.4, Lebanon at 2.3, and Turkey at 2.5., Indonesia at 2.4., and the United Arab Emirates at 2.5. Egypt and Libya, at 3.3 and 3.0 respectively, are higher, with Saudi Arabia and Iraq, at 4.0 and 4.8 respectively, are higher still. Afghanistan, on the other hand, has a reported TFR of 7.5, one the highest in the world. From the 2004 WPP.
32. The figures come from Table III.5. "Ten Countries and Areas with Largest Per Cent Declines in Total Fertility, by Development Group, 1970-1975 to 2000-2005," UNDP, WPP, 43.
33. Egypt was listed as a country of special concern in "National Security Study Memorandum 200," Chapter 5.
34. "Al-Azhar Fatwa Committee's point of view on birth planning," PMID: 12343622 [PubMed - indexed for MEDLINE], Population Sciences (Cairo, Egypt), 1988; (8):15-7, http://www.ncbi.nlm.nih.gov/entrez/query.fcgi?db=pubmed&cmd=Search&itool=pubmed_AbstractPlus&term=%22Al%2DAzhar+Islamic+Research+

Academy%2E+Fatwa+Committee%22%5BCorporate+Author%5D.

35. As I have explained, I have here used the low variant projection of the UN Population Division, which shows a TFR for 2005-2010 of 2.74. The earlier numbers for the 2000-2005 period were, of course, higher at 3.3. The 2006 CIA's *The World FactBook* gives a figure of 2.83.

36. "Fewer Means Better," *The Economist*, 5 August 1995, 41.

37. "Iran Promoting Birth Control in Policy Switch," *The Washington Post*, 8 May 1992.

38. Yeni Yuezul, quoted by Youssef Courbage, "Nouveaux horizons démographiques in Méditerrané," (Paris: National Institute of Demographic Studies, 27 February 1995), http://www.ined.fr/englishversion/publications/collections/courbage/chapter3.pdf (accessed 7 November 2006).

39. "Contraception is Treason, Turkish Islamist Leader Says," *Agence France Presse*, 16 February 2002.

40. The WPP gives the TFR for "Occupied Palestinian Territory" as 5.00 (medium variant) or 4.75 (low variant) for 2005-2010. For Israel it reports 2.66 (medium variant) and 2.41 (low variant).

41. Ezra Vogel, *Japan as Number One*. Selangor, Malaysia: Pelanduk Publications, 2001.

42. George Friedman and Meredith Lebard, *The Coming War with Japan*. Boston: St. Martin's Press, 1991.

43. On a Purchasing Price Parity basis.

44. Victor Mallet, "Procreation does not result in wealth creation," *Financial Times*, 4 January 2007.

45. For a discussion of robots and the Japanese future, see Eamonn Fingleton's, *In Praise of hard Industries* (Boston: Houghton Mifflin, 1999).

46. "Prime Minister Abe to set up a strategic council to counter the falling birthrate," *Asahi Shimbun* (28 January 2007), 1. Abe's Minister of Health, Hakuo Yanagisawa, tried to directly encourage women to have more children by saying: "The number of childbearing machines is fixed. Each [women] should do her best." Needless to say, this clumsy word choice provoked calls for his resignation. See "Prime Minister reprimands health minister for his inappropriate remarks referring to women as "child-bearing machines," *Tokyo Shimbun* (29 January 2007), 2.

47. I witnessed the arrival of female infanticide to the Pearl River Delta during my fieldwork there in the early 1980s.

48. Nicholas Eberstadt, "Growing Old the Hard Way: China, Russia, India," *Policy Review*, Hoover Institution, April/May 2006, http://www.hoover.org/publications/policyreview/2912391.html. See also, "Old Age Tsunami," "Opinion" section, *WSJ*, 15 November 2005.

49. Scott McConnell, "Delayed Motherhood: Is it Good for Society?" *New York Post*, 24 May 1995.

50. See Phillip Longman's *The Empty Cradle*, for an extended discussion of this problem, especially Chapter 7, "The Cost of Children." *The Empty Cradle: How Falling Birthrates Threaten World Prosperity and What to Do About It* (New York: Basic Books, 2004), 240 pp.

51. In the absence of a general theory of fertility change, it is impossible to offer any reliable, quantitative estimates of the precise impact of these diverse programs. But, as we will see in succeeding chapters, these programs have often been coercive in character and their impact on fertility necessarily dramatic. To put it another way, one doesn't require a general theory of fertility change to interpret or explain the low fertility rate of a woman who has been forcibly sterilized.

52. "Government to Do Away With Birth Control Policy," *Korea Times*, 5 June 1996.
53. In 2006, the number of babies born in the city of Seoul increased slightly, but it seems unlikely that this is the beginning of a resurgence in Korean births. "New Babies Rise Again in Seoul," Kang Shin-woh, *Korea Times*, 19 January 2007.
54. "Thailand's Grim Harvest," *PRI Review* 7(1) (January/February 1997):14.
55. According to the U.S. Census Bureau's International Data Base, the Total Fertility Rate in 2005 was 1.6. See http://www.census.gov/cgi-bin/ipc/idbsum.pl?cty=TH (accessed on March 5, 2007).
56. U.N. Population Division, *World Population Policies, 2005*, http://www.un.org/esa/population/publications/WPP2005/Publication_index.htm.
57. Nicholas Eberstadt, "World Population Implosion," *The Public Interest*, 1996.
58. "The Bomb that Fizzled," Ben Wattenberg, *New York Times Magazine*, 23 April 1997.

2

The Malthusian Delusion and
the Origins of Population Control

It is astonishing, what a propensity Mr. Malthus
has to try experiments, if there is any mischief to be
done by them. He has a perfect horror of experi-
ments that are to be tried on the higher qualities
of our nature, from which any great, unmixed, and
general good is to be expected. But in proportion
as the end is low, and the means base, he acquires
confidence, his tremours forsake him and he ap-
proaches boldly to the task with nerves of iron.
     –William Hazlitt, *A Reply to the "Essay on Population"*
                    by the Rev. T. R. Malthus[1]

The first population bomber of the modern age was, by profession at least, ill-suited to the task. The Rev. Thomas Malthus, Anglican clergyman, predicted in 1798 that there would be standing room only on this earth by the Year of Our Lord, 1890.

A London talk by Benjamin Franklin had inflamed Malthus' imagination. The American polymath had proudly proclaimed to his English audience that the population of their former colonies was growing at a rate of 3 percent a year. The good parson, who fancied himself something of a mathematician, knew that this meant that America's population was doubling every 23 years or so. He pondered this remorseless geometric progression during the long walks he was accustomed to take in the English countryside, becoming increasingly concerned about the staggering numbers—2, 4, 8, 16, 32, 64—that would soon result. He imagined the boroughs filling up with people, until every available nook and cranny was choked with human misery. How could this coming hoard of humanity possibly be fed, he wondered? How could sufficient grain be grown in the green fields he was passing, even if every moor,

31

hedgerow, and woodland was brought under cultivation? An arithmetic increase in the food supply—2, 4, 6, 8—was the best that could be hoped for. But with men multiplying geometrically and food only arithmetically, the number of people would inevitably outstrip the food supply. It was perhaps the very simplicity of the parson's notion that gave it such a strong grip on his mind. Better minds than his would soon fall prey to the same delusion.

Malthus published his speculations in 1798 in a tract called *An Essay on the Principle of Population.* Despite its scholarly sounding title, this was the original "population bomb." It contained no images of exploding ordinance (these would be reserved for our less genteel age), but like its latter-day imitators it aroused great public concern by painting a picture of imminent catastrophe brought on by the unchecked growth in human numbers. Such a fate, Malthus argued, could only be avoided by stern, even pitiless, measures. The problem, as he saw it, was that the death rate in England was in marked decline. Before the advent of modern means of sanitation and medicine roughly 40 out of every thousand people had died each year. But as the Industrial Revolution spread, it brought better housing and nutrition for the poor, and provided the means for public authorities to underwrite public health and sanitation measures. The death rate had dropped to 30 per thousand and was still falling. Malthus proposed to undo all this:

> All children born, beyond what would be required to keep up the population to a desired level, must necessarily perish, unless room be made for them by the deaths of grown persons.... Therefore ... we should facilitate, instead of foolishly and vainly endeavoring to impede, the operations of nature in producing this mortality; and if we dread the too frequent visitation of the horrid form of famine, we should sedulously encourage the other forms of destruction, which we compel nature to use. Instead of recommending cleanliness to the poor, we should encourage contrary habits. In our towns we should make the streets narrower, crowd more people into the houses, and court the return of the plague. In the country, we should build our villages near stagnant pools, and particularly encourage settlements in all marshy and unwholesome situations. But above all, we should reprobate [I.e., reject] specific remedies for ravaging diseases; and restrain those benevolent, but much mistaken men, who have thought they were doing a service to mankind by projecting schemes for the total extirpation of particular disorders.[2]

These were strange, almost diabolical, views for a member of the Christian clergy to hold. Were his emotions in synch with his intellect? Did Malthus really mourn over baptisms, while celebrating funeral rites with a particular zest? His population control measures were denounced by many of his fellow Christians, who rejected them as an offense against charity, not to say common sense. Karl Marx and Frederick Engels weighed in as well, damning his theories as an "open declaration of war of the bourgeoisie upon the proletariat," and Malthus himself as a "shameless sycophant of the ruling classes, terrified by Europe's burgeoning working class and the French Revolution.[3] His theories were embraced, however, by members of the British upper class. An increasingly barren lot themselves, they feared that the poor were becoming too prolific, not to mention too powerful at the polls and in the marketplace. These Malthusians, as they came to be called, helped to ensure that their founder's "Essay on Population" was a commercial success, appearing in no fewer than six editions from 1798 to 1826. Population horror stories have sold well ever since.

Life spans lengthened and general health improved throughout the nineteenth century, but Charles Darwin gave the Malthusians something new to brood over. Not only were the poor too prolific, but by having all those children—most of whom, to make matters worse, now survived childhood—they were rapidly dumbing down the population. For the prosperous and privileged, who found themselves increasingly outnumbered by the great unwashed, this was the "survival of the fittest" in reverse. This dyspeptic view was given intellectual respectability by Francis Galton, a cousin of Darwin himself. In his *Inquiries into Human Faculty and Its Development,* Galton gave a pseudo-scientific gloss to what he saw as the declining genetic stock of the nation. To counter this "dysgenic" trend, he proposed an active policy of "eugenics," a word he coined meaning "good births." Eugenics would encourage more children from the fit, and fewer—or no—children from the unfit, with the ultimate goal of engineering the evolutionary ascent of man.

Such views were eagerly embraced by the secular humanists of the early twentieth century, who—as in our day—were busily thinking of ways to improve the natural man at the same time that they reduced his numbers. Malthus, in particular, proved a fit precursor to Planned Parenthood founder Margaret Sanger, who also opposed helping the poor. Philanthropy, she wrote, following the good reverend, merely bred and perpetuated "constantly increasing numbers of defectives, delinquents and dependents."[4] Such aid supported, at a "terrific cost to the community," a "dead weight of human waste."[5]

While Malthus was content to wait for plague, pestilence, and putrification to check human numbers (he opposed contraception and abortion), Sanger, not one for half-measures, wanted to stop the "unfit" from conceiving children in the first place. She stated forthrightly, "We cannot improve the race until we first cut down production of its least desirable members."[6] She hoped to accomplish this aim through the promotion of birth control, but sterilization was a good option for those who couldn't or wouldn't contracept. The government should get involved, she believed, in providing a monetary incentive to coerce "the ever increasing and numerous dependent, delinquent and unbalanced masses" into being sterilized.[7] "[A]sk the government to first take off the burdens of the insane and feeble-minded from your backs," she urged. "Sterilization for these is the remedy."[8]

Setting up the American Birth Control League (as Planned Parenthood was first called), Sanger sought to put her beliefs into action.[9] To ensure "the elimination of the unfit," she opened birth-control clinics in America targeting the poor and the disabled.[10] Since the "unfit" lived abroad too, she spread her eugenic beliefs throughout the world through population control, which would ensure eugenic "quality" over mere population quantity.[11] Sanger often compared humanity to a garden, which required the proper soil, fertilizer, and sunlight. "Do not forget this," she further advised, "you have got to fight weeds."[12]

Her project attracted the notice of those who considered themselves "fit"—and who does not? In particular, however, the wealthy eugenicists of Sanger's day threw themselves into the eugenic project with gusto. Sanger's goal, in her own words, was "to create a race of thoroughbreds."[13] Although she failed in this venture, as Hitler would fail even more spectacularly after her, she did manage to round up quite a stable of wealthy supporters. These with names like Rockefeller, Duke, Scaife, Lasker, Sulzberger and Dupont, were easy marks for Sanger's arguments because they prided themselves on being the product of superior bloodlines.[14] In reality, most of Sanger's "thoroughbreds" had no great natural gifts; but for the accident of inherited wealth, would have had merely middle-class prospects.

The Nazis took active measures to purify the blood lines and improve the stock of the "superior" Aryan race that went well beyond anything that most eugenicists, even in their darkest moments, had envisioned. The entire eugenics project went into eclipse, its advocates heatedly denying that they had ever meant any such thing as Dachau, Auschwitz, Bergen-Belsen, etc. For all that, population "quality" remained a concern of the population control community and, carefully disguised, would gradually over time creep back into its discourse. When John D. Rockefeller III drew up the draft charter of the Population Council in 1954, for example, he included a paragraph calling for the promotion of research so that "within every social and economic grouping, parents who are above the average in intelligence, quality of personality and affection, will tend to have larger than average families." Thomas Parran, a former surgeon general and one of the few Catholics in Rockefeller's circle, objected that "Frankly, the implications of this, while I know are intended to have a eugenic implication, could readily be misunderstood as a Nazi master race philosophy."[15] The paragraph was quietly dropped.

While Rockefeller and others could easily be shamed into silence on the need to *remodel* humanity, the horror of the Holocaust did not prevent them from talking publicly about the continuing need to *reduce* human numbers. After World War Two the United States and other developed countries had sent many medical and aid workers overseas, and these "benevolent, but much mistaken men," as Malthus had scornfully called them, were successfully eliminating many of the infectious diseases which had long plagued the developing world. While birthrates remained high, mortality rates were falling. The populations of Latin America, Africa, and Asia were beginning a period of rapid growth, as Europe and America had a few decades before. With the help of Rockefeller and other men of great wealth, controlling this growth was soon to be placed on the national agenda.

The Dilettante and the Huckster

Population growth seems to arouse a primal fear in the wealthy, who somehow feel threatened by the poor in their numbers. How else to explain the epiphany experienced by John D. Rockefeller III, grandson of oil tycoon John D. Rockefeller, Sr. and one of the wealthiest men in the world, when he encountered the impoverished masses of the developing world. A dilettante who had never held a steady job,[16] he made extended journeys to Asia and Africa after the war. He came away convinced that Western efforts to check what he saw as runaway population growth must take precedence over economic development.[17] He had found the cause that would consume his life. The peasant societies of Asia, Africa and Latin America would never be the same.

Rockefeller's efforts to win over his fellow Rockefeller Foundation trustees to his new passion failed, however. The majority believed (correctly, as history would show) that Western technology, particularly American agricultural know-how, would enable the peoples of the world to continue to feed themselves. They rejected his controversial proposal to develop new birth control methods and export these to the developing world. Denied access to the family fortune, Rockefeller used his own money—a sure sign of the true believer—to set up the Population Council in 1952. The council posed, and still poses, as a neutral, scientific organization, but its purpose in Rockefeller's mind was clear—to control global population growth. Although his brother Nelson worried about the negative impact that these fringe activities might have on his own political career, the family as a whole supported the Rockefeller scion's efforts, although whether this was from shared conviction or simply to help him find himself is not clear. The family attorney opined that "My own feeling is that he [Rockefeller III] has the time to do it and that one of the things that he most needs is some activity which will occupy his full time five days a week. It seems to me that if he works at this conscientiously for a year or two he might make a consequential dent in the problem...."[18] In fact, he was to work as the president, later as the chairman, of the Population Council for the next quarter century. As for the "dent" in humanity that this produced, it was considerable.

As unlikely as it sounds, the dilettante threw himself into his new role as the world's first population control technocrat with almost evangelical fervor. He gathered the best minds on the subject together, and trained more, building a global network of population experts who shared his anti-natal views. He funded research to find easier, more reliable and, above all, more *permanent* ways of contracepting and sterilizing the poor. He established regional centers for demographic training and research in Bombay (1957), Santiago (1958), and Cairo (1963), and national centers in many countries, understanding these as stepping stones to instituting full-scale population control programs. Such centers and the experts they produced, explained Frederick Osborn, his right-hand man at the Council, "stimulated recognition of the dangers of the too-rapid growth of local population."[19] No doubt they did, since this was precisely why they were set up in the first place.

As time went on, Rockefeller became increasingly involved in "action programs" as well, providing grants for the purchase of contraceptives, as well as technical personnel to actually oversee their distribution in developing countries. He helped to set up national family planning programs in South Korea, Malaysia, Hong Kong, Sri Lanka, and elsewhere. But the most important thing that he did, using his own funds and those of like-minded super-rich, was to work quietly behind the scenes to help convince the U.S. federal government, with its deep pockets, to sign on to his agenda.

Rockefeller would not have succeeded without the help of a man, Hugh Moore, whom he came to detest. The irrepressible Moore had money, too, but unlike the "old money" of the Rockefellers he had made it himself, peddling the idea of a paper cup into a multimillion dollar manufacturing concern—the Dixie Cup Company—whose product was familiar to every American. Moore's epiphany on population did not come while on a grand tour of Asia, but in a distinctly pedestrian way—while reading a book.

The book was *The Road to Survival,* a hell-bent-for-leather account of the dangers of overpopulation written by William Vogt, the national director of the Planned Parenthood Federation of America.[20] As Moore read how population growth was "the basic cause of future wars" and "the spread of tyranny and communism," alarm bells went off in his head. Moore credited Vogt "for really waking me up," and then and there decided to make population his sole concern.[21] He formed the Population Action Committee and called for immediate mobilization against the impending crisis. "Who among us," he used to shout at meetings, "will come up with a plan for starting a CONFLAGRATION?"[22] According to his biographer, Lawrence Lader, Moore's "methods were often designed purposefully to stimulate controversy and thereby focus public attention. With time running out, people have to face raw facts.… A warning should be shouted from the rooftops."[23] Moore believed that people needed to be scared, really scared, in order to become aware of the disaster that loomed before them. And what better way to scare them than with an image of a bomb, and talk of an explosion.

The bomb had leveled Hiroshima and Nagasaki. By the early 1950s the Soviets had it too, and the Cold War was in full swing. America anguished over the thought of bombs—their explosive power no longer expressed in tons, but megatons—ready to lay waste to the world. Moore deliberately played on these fears with a pamphlet called *The Population Bomb,"* which he mailed to 1,000 leaders in business and the professions.[24] It declared that "Today the population bomb threatens to create an explosion as disruptive and dangerous as the explosion of the atom, and with as much influence on prospects for progress or disaster, war or peace." The coming "population explosion" would be the mother of all calamities, leading to widespread famine and crushing tax rates, the spread of communism and the scourge of war, plus every other imaginable environmental and social ill in between. All this was written in what Lader calls a "whiplash phraseology [that] stung a dormant public." Eager to convince others of the correctness of his cause, Moore inflated future human numbers to justify his radical plan to restrict human fertility. The hype was nowhere more evident than on the booklet's cover. It featured a drawing of a world teeming with humanity, with standing room only on all continents. (Africa, already the prime target of the population controllers, was front and center.) Coming out of the North Pole was a lit fuse. A pair of scissors with long, sharp blades was poised to give it the snip. The scissors were labeled "population control."

The controversy sparked by the publication of the pamphlet delighted the huckster in Moore. Over the next decade and a half, he mailed, free of charge, hundreds of thousands of copies of the booklet to every group of politicians, educators, officials, journalists and people of influence he could think of. One and a half *million* copies later, this relentless promoter had made the "population bomb" the doomsday metaphor of choice. He had engraved the image of mushroom clouds of people, boiling up from the surface of the planet in an unconstrained frenzy of procreation, on the consciousness of most Americans. He had convinced many that "population control" would stop the spread of communism. And he had captured the imagination of a young butterfly expert by the name of Paul Ehrlich, who later asked to borrow the title for his own book on the dangers of overpopulation.

Rockefeller was one of the first to receive a copy of *The Population Bomb*, along with a letter of explanation from Hugh Moore. "We are not primarily interested in the sociological or humanitarian aspects of birth control," Moore wrote. "We are interested in the use which Communists make of hungry people in their drive to conquer the earth."[25] Rockefeller and his circle were predictably offended by both Moore's crude style and his alarmist rhetoric. Frederick Osborn worried that Moore's "Madison Avenue techniques" might "set the [population control] movement back ten years," and urged that distribution of the pamphlet be halted.[26] Low-key and scientific-minded, Rockefeller fretted that phrases like "population explosion" and "population bomb" might create an atmosphere of panic. One can almost hear Moore chuckle, since panic was precisely what he was trying to provoke, seeing it as the surest way to massive government intervention.

Rockefeller, too, was convinced that the federal government needed to get involved in population control, but it was the outspoken Moore who paved the way. When his old friend, William H. Draper, was appointed by President Eisenhower to chair a committee to study foreign aid, Moore seized his chance.[27] He saturated the Wall Street financier and other committee members with material on the dangers of overpopulation, arguing that economic aid was being nullified by population growth.[28]

When the Draper Report appeared in 1959, it was the first official government report to endorse population control.[29]

In 1961, as the U.S. Congress was considering a major foreign aid bill, Moore launched an advertising campaign in the *New York Times*, the *Wall Street Journal*, the *Washington Post*, and *Time* magazine. Among the earliest ads were two designed to put the nation's first Catholic president, who had earlier rejected the Draper Report, "on the spot," in Moore's phrase. The full-page ads were headlined an "Appeal to President Kennedy," and called for the federal government to address the "population explosion."[30] Draper, at Moore's urging, returned to Washington and undertook a one-man lobbying campaign for the cause. With Rockefeller and his colleagues also working behind the scenes to encourage federal intervention, these wealthy men were about to impose their will on the U.S. Congress. It would, in turn, impose its will on the world.

Applying the Economic Lash

The U.S. Foreign Assistance Act of 1961 represented a radical departure from previous notions of foreign aid, such as feeding the hungry or arming our allies, because it took population control as a fundamental aim:

> The Congress declares that the individual liberties, economic prosperity, and security of the people of the United States are best sustained and enhanced in a community of nations which ... work together to use wisely the world's limited resources in an open and equitable international economic system.... *Development assistance ... shall be concentrated in countries which will make the most effective use of such assistance ... the President shall assess the commitment and progress of countries ... by utilizing criteria, including ... control of population growth...*"[31] (italics added).

The effect of this language was to enshrine in U.S. law two core beliefs of the population control movement, namely, that population growth is a national security issue, and that foreign aid should be given chiefly to countries which control it. A subsequent provision of the bill is even more radical, for it enlists all U.S. aid programs, from education and health to rural development and disease control, into the war on people:

> [A]ll appropriate activities proposed for financing under this chapter shall be designed to build motivation for smaller families through modification of economic and social conditions supportive of the desire for large families, in programs such as education in and out of school, nutrition, disease control, maternal and child health services, improvements in the status and employment of women, agricultural production, rural development, and assistance to the urban poor, and through community-based development programs which give recognition to people motivated to limited the size of their families.[32]

Those who think that U.S. foreign aid is principally intended to feed the hungry, reduce the incidence of disease, or promote economic development are mistaken. The proper end of *all* foreign aid, according to this and subsequent laws, is nothing other than fertility reduction. Governments that want access to U.S. foreign assistance must not only agree to "control their population growth," they must accept programs that are consciously designed to shrink family size and reduce fertility rates. The 1961 bill was Maoist-style social engineering at its worst, but moderate and conservative American politicians mostly voted for it, convinced as they were by Moore, Draper, and others that in stopping the birth of babies they were stopping the spread of communism.[33] George H. W. Bush, who headed the special Republican Task Force on Population and Earth Resources while serving in Congress in the late 1960s, was among those who supported the change. Bush writes that he was "impressed by the arguments of … Draper that economic development overseas would be a miserable failure unless the developing countries … control[led] fertility.[34]

The Dark Legacy of Doctor Reimert Thorolf Ravenholt, Population Czar

Malthusianism, that "monstrous doctrine of unreason," as Paul Johnson has called it,[35] was now official U.S. policy. The United States had made it its business to stop women in the developing world from having "too many" children. (We, not they, would define how many was "too many.") To carry out this sweeping mandate, the Office of Population was set up within the United States Agency for International Development (USAID) in 1966, and a physician by the name of Reimert Thorolf Ravenholt was appointed as its first director.

Dr. Ravenholt had massive amounts of aid money at his disposal, the State Department at his beck and call and, of course, a mandate from Congress itself. No ordinary bureaucrat, he was to become a law unto himself—a "Population Czar," if you will. By the end of his tenure in 1979, Ravenholt had put firmly in place the powerful interlocking directorate of U.S.-funded population control organizations that continues to assault women around the world today.

Who was Dr. Ravenholt? An epidemiologist by training, he apparently looked upon pregnancy as a disease, to be eradicated in the same way one eliminates smallpox or yellow fever. He was also, as it happened, a bellicose misanthrope.[36]

He took to his work of contracepting, sterilizing, and aborting the women of the world with an aggressiveness that caused his younger colleagues to shrink back in disgust. His business cards were printed on condoms, and he delighted in handing them out to all comers. He talked incessantly about how to distribute greater quantities of birth control pills, and ensure that they were used. He advocated mass sterilization campaigns, once telling the *St. Louis Post-Dispatch* that one-quarter of all the fertile women in the world must be sterilized in order to meet U.S. goals of population control and to maintain "the normal operation of U.S. commercial interests around the world." Such rigorous measures were required, Ravenholt explained, to contain the "population explosion" which would, if left unchecked, so reduce living standards abroad that revolutions would break out "against the strong U.S. commercial presence."[37]

Ravenholt denounced those at USAID and elsewhere who argued that the proper end of U.S. assistance was economic development or social reform, saying dismissively that "the one thing these people don't seem to want to do is family planning."[38] He declared that "the biggest threat to mass population programs stems from 'revisionist tendencies' promulgated by those unduly concerned with 'irrelevant' issues of social policy or even general health care."[39]

His enemies responded that he had a "myopic" focus on population control and a "bellicose" personal style.[40] Charming he was not. To commemorate the bicentennial of the United States in 1976, he came up with the idea of producing "stars and stripes" condoms in red, white, and blue colors for distribution around the world. When Randy Engel of the U.S. Coalition for Life, in congressional testimony, criticized what she called this "harebrained scheme," Ravenholt sent her packets of condoms in Tahitian blue colors.[41] Another time, at a dinner for population researchers, Ravenholt strolled around the room making pumping motions with his fist as if he were operating a manual vacuum aspirator—a hand-held vacuum pump for performing abortions—to the horror of the other guests.[42]

Like nearly all population controllers, he saw abortion as an essential element of his anti-people strategy, human rights as secondary, and people of religious sentiment as opponents. He condemned "religious opposition to birth control" for "greatly aggravat[ing] Africa's population problems.... Most harmful to Africa has been the Helms Amendment, authored by Catholic zealots, blocking provision of much-needed abortion services.[43] Also, religious fanatics in the Congress have further vitiated U.S. population program assistance. Access to abortion is important in every land to enable individual women to avoid bearing unwanted children;

but Africa must now urgently choose between making abortion services generally available or accepting catastrophic increase in the killing fields."[44] In other words, if you don't kill children in utero, they will kill each other after birth because of the purported stresses of "overpopulation."

Ravenholt was an unapologetic Malthusian, who not only believed that birth control was the "key to public safety, freedom from hunger, and development," but argued against "interventionist" medical programs to save the lives of infants and children. The birthrate must be driven down first, or at least simultaneously. He offers the following summary of his point of view:

> [T]he main admonition to be made to those persons and organizations in advanced nations wishing to help the Africans is … Beware! Do not harm the communities and nations you seek to help with public health programs! Unfortunately, that admonition has often been neglected by those seeking to help the Africans. A main case in point is the powerful interventionist prevention of infant and child mortality by the many means our society now readily offers: grants of food, potable water, antibiotics, immunization, etc. How could these be harmful? Quite simply, *they are enormously harmful to African societies when the deaths prevented thereby are not balanced by prevention of a roughly equal number of births.* It is the population excesses resulting from well-intentioned but population-unbalancing interventionist activities which are largely driving today's killing fields in Africa. Many infants and children rescued from preventable disease deaths by interventionist programs during the 1970s and 1980s have become machete-wielding killers.… [P]ublic health interventionists for Africa must learn that the benefit or harm of very proposed health interventionist program is inescapably dependent upon whether it aggravates or improves the population [situation].… [T]hey must not blithely assume that if their interventionist program "only increases the child population by 10 percent" it does no harm.[45]

As the U.S. population czar, Ravenholt did not set out to organize a huge in-house population control bureaucracy to achieve his goal of eliminating excess people. Rather, after the American fashion, he collaborated with existing organizations, like the International Planned Parenthood Federation (IPPF), the Population Council, and the Association for Voluntary Sterilization (AVS, more recently, Engender Health) to carry out family planning programs in countries overseas. He selected smaller organizations to play specific, highly specialized, roles, providing them with grants that were often 10 times or more their previous annual budgets.[46] The structure set up by Ravenholt thus resembles a conglomerate, with headquarters, USAID, directing its various subsidiaries in different steps in the manufacture, testing, marketing, and delivery of its wide array of anti-natal products.

Once the pipeline was in place, the radical Dr. Ravenholt set out to flood the developing world with condoms, birth controls pills, and other contraceptives. Ravenholt's "inundation" method was called by one observer "the most massive medical experiment in the history of the world," albeit one completely lacking in safety controls.[47] Ravenholt, reports Angela Franks, "would choose pills of varying types and brands each year, basing his choice solely on which pharmaceutical company offered the lowest bid, without taking into account possible side effects."[48] One of these "bargains" was a huge supply of high-estrogen birth-control pills, which Ravenholt obtained at a deep discount from the pharmaceutical company Syntex *after* this pill was declared unsafe by the Food and Drug Administration (FDA). Another was a defective intra-uterine device (IUD), the Dalkon Shield, which he got at half price from a manufacturer besieged with lawsuits. He was sending container loads of Depo-Provera (a hormonal contraceptive) overseas over a decade before it was approved by the FDA for use in America. (We will examine the health consequences of such irresponsible actions in detail in Chapter 6.)

The sheer number of devices he and his successors have shipped over time is staggering. From 1968 to 1995, the Office of Population shipped more than 10.5 billion condoms, over 2 billion cycles of abortifacient birth control pills, more than 73 million abortifacient IUDs, and over 116 million vaginal foaming tablets to the "undeveloped countries of the Third World." In the 1990s, the abortifacients Norplant and Depo-Provera were added to the arsenal, and by 1995 nearly a quarter of a million units of Norplant, and almost 4 million doses of Depo-Provera had been shipped.[49] The tables in Appendix A detail the year-to-year USAID shipments of the various contraceptives up to 2005.[50] With the exception of Norplant, all of these devices are sourced in the United States, which USAID has not hesitated to point out to congressmen skeptical of the merit of the program.

From 1968 to 1995, the Office of Population spent more than $1 1/2 billion to buy, test, store, ship and deliver contraceptive and abortifacient devices. Less than a third of this actually went to purchase condoms, pills, and injectables. The rest of the money went for shipping, testing and, above all, marketing them. USAID currently uses Panalpina, an international shipping firm, to provide for "the warehousing of contraceptives worldwide," as well as for shipping. (Container-loads of condoms and other contraceptives deteriorate quickly in the tropical heat and humidity, so USAID has been paying closer attention to storage in recent years.) For its services, Panalpina received almost $24 million from 1992-97.[51] Contraceptives are tested by a North Carolina firm, Family Health International (FHI), which is under contract to "verify that the quality of contraceptive products, such as condoms and pills, shipped by USAID to other countries meets strict standards."[52]

The real challenge for Ravenholt was in "marketing" these devices to wary Third World couples. Contrary to population control propaganda about a huge "unmet need" for contraception among the world's people, the actual demand for these drugs and devices is quite low.[53] The poor, of course, do have real "unmet needs"—for practically everything else *besides* contraceptives. Lest the devices languish in run-down warehouses until their expiration date and have to be thrown away (a not uncommon fate), the population czar developed highly sophisticated distribution, promotional, and advertising campaigns—still in use today—to push them onto the local population.

Physician-dominated health programs were the favored approach, but these often failed to increase "contraceptive prevalence"—the percentage of couples contracepting—in countries where doctor visits were a rarity, or where most physicians refused to collaborate. If this happened, Ravenholt would turn to community-based programs, where hired "facilitators" would be paid a bounty for finding "acceptors." The term "accepter" itself, as Donald Warwick has noted, "suggests passive receipt of goods delivered by others."[54] At the same time, social marketing programs would be brought in, in which street vendors and shop keepers of all kinds were trained to hand out contraceptives with other purchases. Massive programs of "contraceptive social marketing" are still used today to motivate people in places like Kenya and Nigeria to accept and use the great quantities of contraceptives that Ravenholt's successors at USAID think that they "need."

Other programs relied upon advertising and entertainment. USAID's chief condom pusher, for example, an organization called Population Services International (PSI), uses aggressive and ubiquitous advertising campaigns to flood the media with a pro-condom message. These campaigns involve, to use PSI's own martial language, a constant "barrage of radio spots and films shown on television, in cinema halls, and on [PSI's] fleet of mobile film vans", all extolling the virtues and benefits of condom usage.[55] Like the loudspeakers that bleated the Thought of Chairman Mao all day long in Chinese communes, there would seem to be no escape from these forced feedings of anti-natal propaganda. Radio soap operas and traveling puppet shows are also utilized to spread the word. In Bangladesh, according to PSI, the "audience turnout among the entertainment-starved rural population is enormous, averaging between

3,500 and 4,000 viewers per show. On some occasions, as many as 10,000 [people] have been known to turn out."[56] To further drive home the message, during the intermission break, the contraceptive promoter passes out party favors, "sample products such as oral contraceptive pills ... or condoms."

Throughout his long tenure in office, Ravenholt maintained his single-minded focus on controlling population growth by contracepting, sterilizing, and aborting as many women as possible. He was impressed by China's "startling success" in population control, saw it as an expression of "the collective will of the people," and claimed that it had been brought about by "peer pressure."[57] He considered himself to be above the law, and would not take no for an answer. If democratically elected governments refused family planning assistance, Ravenholt did an end-run around them, funding nongovernmental organizations (NGOs) in their countries to carry out population control activities, or quietly funding organizations to come in from abroad, a practice which still continues today.[58] If staff members went to a country that forbid contraceptives, sterilizations, or abortions, they were expected to smuggle in as much contraband as they could in their suitcases, explaining to bemused customs inspectors that these were for personal use only.[59] He advocated air-dropping contraceptives into countries where they were in short supply.

Although he left office in 1979, over two decades later his dark legacy lives on, as the Population Reference Bureau recently confirmed: "Ravenholt began a program that has devoted $8 billion to population and reproductive health.... While today's program differs from his, especially in its emphasis on reproductive health [which itself is largely a fig leaf for family planning], its programmatic underpinnings remain Ravenholt's."[60]

Ravenholt himself recently concurred with this assessment: "During the last two decades dedicated believers in the USAID mission of providing assistance for curbing excess fertility and population growth in the less developed world have worked to keep alive as much as possible of the powerful population program we created at USAID during the 1970s."[61]

McNamara's Folly: Bankrolling Family Planning

At the same time that Ravenholt was setting up his "powerful population program," the nations of Western Europe, along with Japan, were being encouraged by the administration of President Lyndon B. Johnson to make family planning a priority of their own aid programs. International organizations, primarily the United Nations and its affiliated agencies, were also being leveraged on board. Together, they helped to create and maintain the illusion that the international community was solidly behind population control programs. (It wasn't, and isn't, as we shall see.) But it was the World Bank and its billions that was the real prize for the anti-natalists. They captured it when one of their own, Robert McNamara, was appointed its president in 1968.[62]

McNamara came to the World Bank from the post of secretary of defense, where he had unsuccessfully prosecuted the Vietnam War by focusing on "kill ratios" and the "pacification of the natives" instead of victory. A former automobile executive, he was prone to cost-cutting measures, which sometimes proved to be false economies. He decreed that a new class of ship—the fleet frigate—should have only one propeller instead of the customary two. This saved the expense of a second turbine and drive train, but the frigate—known in the Navy as McNamara's Folly—lacked speed, was hard to berth, and had to be retired early.[63] The population policies he was to advocate suffered from similar defects.

When the boards of the World Bank and the International Monetary Fund convened on October 1 of that year, President Lyndon Johnson made a surprise appearance.[64] Technology in the underdeveloped nations, he said, had "bought time for family planning policies to become effective. But the fate of development hinges on how vigorously that time is used."

The stage was now set for McNamara to get up and attack the "population explosion," saying that it was "one of the greatest barriers to the economic growth and social well-being of our member states." The World Bank would no longer stand idly by in the face of this threat, McNamara said, but would:

- Let the developing nations know the extent to which rapid population growth slows down their potential development, and that, in consequence, the optimum employment of the world's scarce development funds requires attention to this problem.
- Seek opportunities to finance facilities required by our member countries to carry out family planning programs.
- Join with others in programs of research to determine the most effective methods of family planning and of national administration of population control programs.[65]

It quickly became evident that "the optimum employment of the world's scarce development funds" meant in practice that the World

Bank, the International Monetary Fund (IMF), and its network of regional development banks would act as loan sharks for the anti-natalists, pressuring sovereign nations into accepting family planning programs on pain of forfeiting vital short-term, long-term, and soft loans.[66] This practice is well known in the developing world, as when a Dhaka, Bangladesh daily, *The New Nation*, headlines: "WB [World Bank] Conditions Aid to Population Control."[67]

McNamara also began providing loans for population and family planning projects, including those that involved abortion (both surgical and through abortifacient chemicals). By 1976 the National Security Council (NSC) was able to praise the World Bank for being "the principal international financial institution providing population programs."[68] Details are hard to come by, however. The World Bank is one of the most secretive organizations in the world, besides being effectively accountable to no one. What is known is that there is a carefully segregated Population Division, which reportedly employs some approximately 500 people. But those who work on conventional development projects are not privy to what goes on in this division, which is off-limits to all but those who work there.[69]

A rare, inside look at the organization's activities in this area is provided by a recent World Bank report, entitled *Improving Reproductive Health: The Role of the World Bank*. Written in a distinctly self-congratulatory tone, the document reveals that the Bank has spent over $2.5 billion over the last twenty-five years to support 130 reproductive health projects in over 70 countries. Indonesia and Lesotho, for example, have been the site of "'information, education and communication' campaigns about sex and reproductive health." India has been the beneficiary of several different programs, which the report claims have "helped bring India two-thirds of the way towards her goal of replacement level fertility." No mention is made of the fact that the Indian campaigns have been notorious for their coercive tactics, or that McNamara visited India in 1976, at the height of the compulsory sterilization campaign, to congratulate the government for its "political will and determination" in the campaign and, one would suspect, to offer new loans for its continuance.[70]

The World Bank also promotes abortion. *Improving Reproductive Health* openly admits that, since the 1994 Cairo Conference on Population and Development, the first of the World Bank's goals in the area of reproductive health has been "providing access and *choice* in family planning" (italics added). Except for its candor, this promotion of abortion should come as no surprise. In Burkina Faso, for example, we are told that World Bank projects have included "mobilizing public awareness and political support" (that is, lobbying) for abortion and other reproductive health services.

The Bank has long been accused of pressuring nations, such as Nigeria, into legalizing abortion. As recently as 1990 abortion was virtually unthinkable as an official family planning practice in Nigeria. The Planned Parenthood Federation of Nigeria was even forced to defend itself that year against allegations that it promoted the sale and use of "contraceptives" that were abortifacient in character. A year later—and two months after approval of a $78 million World Bank population loan—the government announced proposals for allowing abortion under certain circumstances.[71] (I will discuss the case of Nigeria in more detail in the following chapter.)

Population control loans skyrocketed after the Cairo conference. The Bank reported that, in the two years that followed, it had "lent almost $1 billion in support of population and reproductive health objectives."[72] The numbers have been climbing since then. But even this is just the tip of the iceberg. As economist Jacqueline Kasun notes, "Given the conditions which the bank imposes on its lending, the entire $20 billion of its annual disbursements is properly regarded as part of the world population control effort."[73]

Despite his predilection for population control, McNamara never abandoned more conventional aid modalities, roads, dams, power plants, and the like. Not so James Wolfensohn, who headed the Bank from 1995 to 2005. Asked at the 1996 World Food Summit in Rome how the World Bank understood its mission towards the developing world, Wolfensohn replied that there was a "new paradigm" at the Bank. "From now on," Wolfensohn said, "the business of the World Bank will not be primarily economic reform, or governmental reform. The business of the World Bank will primarily be social reform." The Bank has learned, he added, that attempt to reform a nation's economics or government without first reforming the society "usually means failure."

The benefits to nations who are willing to fall into line in the "civil society" will be immediate and intensely attractive. "The World Bank will be willing to look favorably on any reasonable plan for debt reduction—and even debt forgiveness," Wolfensohn told the assembled reporters, "provided that the nation in question is willing to follow a sensible social policy." Wolfensohn went on to tell reporters that population control activities are a *sine qua non* for any social policy to be considered "sensible."[74]

The World Bank is also, according to Wolfensohn, prepared to begin "directly funding—not through loans" certain NGOs in the countries involved, to further ensure that governments adopt "sensible social policies." Thus fueled with money from the World Bank, the heat these favored NGOs will be able to generate on their governments to adopt, say, population control programs, including legalized abortion, will be considerable.[75] Of course, other international organizations, not to mention USAID and European aid agencies, have been using this tactic for many years with great effect. Recalcitrant governments (that may innocently believe that they do not have a population "problem") are thus sandwiched between the demands of international lenders and aid givers on the one hand, and the demands of "local" NGOs—loud, persistent and extremely well-funded by those same aid givers—on the other.

Rapid Spread of Programs

With the United States, international organizations, and an increasing number of developed countries now working in tandem to strong-arm developing countries into compliance, anti-natalist programs spread with startling rapidity. By the late 1960s, American family planning field workers bearing boxes of contraceptives were a common sight in many countries. The villages they approached, residents of a calmer, more congenial world, rarely rejected these gifts outright. "[The workers] were so nice," one Indian man later remarked, "And they came from distant lands to be with us. All they wanted was that we accept the [foam] tablets. I lost nothing and probably received their prayers. And they, they must have gotten some promotion."[76]

This villager's shrewd guess could not have been closer to the mark. From the beginning, the success of population control programs has been measured not by declines in fertility, but by the numbers of "acceptors" it generates. Those workers who meet their quotas of acceptors are promoted; those country programs that meet their targets are expanded. Since those that fail on either count are terminated, there is little incentive to make sure that all this contraceptive largess is used for its intended purpose. One villager used his free boxes of vaginal foaming tablets, their contents undisturbed, to build a little temple in his living room to the local Hindu fertility god.

The hundreds of millions of dollars being poured into such programs ensured that they would, like a cancerous growth spreading throughout the human body, metastasize throughout the world. Bernard Berelson, the head of the Population Council, happily reported in 1970 that:

In 1960 only three countries had anti-natalist population policies (all on paper), only one government was offering assistance [that is, funding population control programs overseas], no international organization was working on family planning. In 1970 nearly 25 countries on all three developing continents, with 67 percent of the total population, have policies and programs; and another 15 or so, with 12 percent of the population, provide support in the absence of an explicitly formulated policy ... five to ten governments now offer external support (though only two in any magnitude); and the international assistance system is formally on board (the UN Population Division, the UNDP, WHO, UNESCO, FAO, ILO, OECD, the World Bank).[77]

The recklessness with which Ravenholt, McNamara and others forced crude anti-natal programs upon the developing world dismayed many even within the movement. Ronald Freedman, a leading sociologist/demographer, complained in 1975 that, "If reducing the birthrate is that important and urgent, then the results of the expanded research during the 1960s are still *pathetically inadequate. There are serious proposals for social programs on a vast scale to change reproductive institutions and values that have been central to human society for millennia*"[78] (italics added). This was social engineering with a vengeance, Freedman was saying, and we don't know what we are doing!

With even committed controllers saying "Slow down!" one might think that the anti-natalists would hesitate. But their army had already been assembled and its generals had sounded the advance; it could not be halted now. Even Freedman, rhetorically throwing up his hands, conceded that "many people ... are eager for knowledge that can be used in action programs aimed at accelerating fertility decline," and that the programs would have to proceed by "a process of trial and error." These *trials*, it goes without saying, would be funded by unwitting taxpayers in the developed world; while the *errors,* murderous and costly, would be borne by poor women and families in the developed world.

What justification was offered for this massive investment of U.S. prestige and capital in these programs? Stripped of its later accretions—protecting the environment, promoting economic development, advancing the rights of women—at the outset it was mostly blatant self-interest. McNamara, who headed an organization ostensibly devoted to the welfare of the developing countries, had told the World Bank's Board of Governors in 1968 that "population growth slows down their potential development." But he told the *Christian Science Monitor* some years later that continued population growth would lead to "poverty, hunger, stress, crowding, and frustration," which would threaten social, economic and military stability. This would not be "a world that anyone wants," he declared.[79] It was certainly not the world that many in the security establishment wanted, as secret National Security Council deliberations would soon make starkly clear.

The Cold War Against Population

As the populations of developing world countries began to grow after World War II, the U.S. national security establishment—the Pentagon, the Central Intelligence Agency, the National Security Agency, and the National Security Council—became concerned. Population was and is an important element of national power, and countries with growing populations would almost inevitably increase in geopolitical weight. This was obviously a concern in the case of countries opposed to U.S. interests, such as the Soviet Union and China. But even allies might prove less pliable as their populations and economies grew. Most worrisome of all was the possibility that the rapidly multiplying peoples of Asia, Africa, and Latin America would turn to communism in their search for independence and economic advancement *unless their birthrate was reduced.* Thus did population control become a weapon in the Cold War.

Perhaps the first "successful" population control program was carried out in post-war Japan. Prostrated by the war, Japanese leaders humbly acceded to MacArthur's suggestion that abortion be legalized. While it was publicly maintained that the devastated Japanese economy could not support more people, the general's interest was apparently in fighting the next war—in utero, as it were. He must have been pleased as the birthrate fell by half over the next few years.[80]

MacArthur anticipated, in both style and substance, a secret directive issued by the National Security Council. "Our officials must know about the facts of population growth and be fully persuaded of the importance of this issue," the NSC wrote in May 1976. "They must then find suitable occasion and discreet means to bring the message most persuasively to the attention of LDC [less-developed country] leaders whose influence is decisive in shaping national policies and programs."[81]

What the NSC then went on to describe what sounded a lot like a covert operation. Washington should not be forward or assertive about its anti-natal agenda, it said, but "selective and low-key," relying instead upon outside agencies and the LDCs themselves to promote its agenda. "It is important that the LDC's take more of a lead on population issues at international conferences and at home…. We must help ensure that international organizations like IBRD [the World Bank group], WHO, UNDP, UNICEF, and UNFPA, as well as private voluntary organizations, play an active, positive role in support of population programs." An appearance of international unity and consensus was to be carefully created. The war on people was not the United States versus everyone else; at least, *they* were not to think so.

The NSC singled out for special praise "encouraging" trends in three countries now well known for abuses—China, India, and Indonesia. Indeed, the agency seems to have had China in mind when it noted approvingly that "population programs have been particularly successful where leaders have made their positions clear, unequivocal and public, while maintaining discipline down the line from national to village levels, marshalling governmental workers (including police and military), doctors and motivators to see that population policies are well administered and executed. Such direction is the *sine-qua-non* of an effective program."

While privately commending coercion—how else can the reference to "maintaining discipline" and "marshalling ... police and military" be understood?—US officials were cautioned against publicly praising such programs: "We recommend that US officials refrain from public comment on forced-pace measures such as those under active consideration in India ... [because that] might have an unfavorable impact on existing voluntary programs."

Most importantly, the true—that is, anti-natal—purpose of the programs was not to be mentioned at all costs: "[W]e should avoid the language of 'birth control' in favor of 'family planning' or 'responsible parenthood,' with the emphasis being placed on child spacing in the interests of the health of child and mother and the well-being of the family and community."

In other words, our Cold War against people was to be carefully disguised as an innocent program to improve infant and maternal health. "We have only the best interests of your mothers and children at heart," foreign aid recipients are told in sugared tones. "We're not sterilizing your women to prevent them from having children, only to protect them from the danger of dying in childbirth." It was a clever ruse that would take in many, both in targeted countries and here at home. And, as we will see in Chapter 10, it is still in use today. Those who are out to reduce the numbers of mothers and children like to pose as their protectors.

Earth First (People Last): The Environmental Movement Signs On

Every sorcerer deserves an apprentice. Hugh Moore, grand wizard of the population explosion, got his in the person of a young Stanford

University entomologist by the name of Paul Ehrlich. In the very first sentence of his very first book, Ehrlich proved beyond all doubt that he had already mastered Moore's panic-driven style. "The battle to feed all of humanity is over," he wrote. "In the 1970s the world will undergo famines—hundreds of million of people will starve to death in spite of any crash programs embarked upon now."[82]

In fact, he had gone Moore one better, as overzealous acolytes are prone to do. His book should have been named *The Population Explosion*, instead of *The Population Bomb*, for according to Ehrlich the "bomb" had already gone off and there was nothing to do now but wait for the inevitable human die-back. "Too many people" were, in his words, chasing "too little food."[83] The most optimistic of Ehrlich's "scenarios" involved the immediate imposition of a harsh regimen of population control and resource conservation around the world, with the goal of reducing the number of people to 1.5 billion (about a fourth of its current level) over the next century or two. Even so, about a fifth of the world's population would still starve to death in the immediate future.

Such a prediction took pluck, for when the book appeared in 1968 there was no hint of massive famine on the horizon. The days of Indian food shortages were past. (We wouldn't learn about China's man-made calamity of the early 1960s until decades later.) The Green Revolution, about which more will be said in Chapter 5, was starting to pay off in increased crop yields. And experts like Dr. Karl Brandt, the Director of the Stanford Food Research Institute, rebuked Ehrlich, saying that "Many nations need more people, not less, to cultivate food products and build a sound agricultural economy ... every country that makes the effort can produce all the food it needs."[84]

But it wasn't his forecast of a massive human die-off that catapulted Ehrlich into the front rank of environmental prophets. (In a leitmotif that has since become familiar, the book left readers with the impression that this might not be such a bad thing.) Rather it was his startling claim that our reckless breeding had jeopardized earth's ability to support life. All life, not just human life. Our planet was literally dying. Not only were we Children of Earth killing ourselves, we were going to take "Mother" to the grave with us as well.

Heavily promoted by the Sierra Club, *The Population Bomb* sold over three million copies. Ehrlich became an instant celebrity, becoming as much of a fixture on the *Tonight Show* as Johnny Carson's sidekick, Ed McMahan. He commanded hefty lecture fees wherever he went (and he went everywhere), and always drew a crowd. People found it titillating to hear about the end of the world. Likening the earth to an overloaded spaceship or sinking lifeboat, issuing apocalyptic warnings about the imminent "standing room only" problem, he captured the popular imagination. His prescriptions were always the same: "Join the environmental movement, stop having children, and save the planet."[85]

While Ehrlich fiddled his apocalyptic tunes, Moore burned to commit the growing environmental movement firmly to a policy of population control. His ad campaign, still ongoing, began suggesting that the best kind of environmental protection was population control. "Whatever Your Cause, It's a Lost Cause Unless We Control Population," one ad read. "Warning: The Water You are Drinking May be Polluted," read another, whose text went on to equate more people with more pollution. A third, addressed to "Dear President Nixon," claimed that "We can't lick the environment problem without considering this little fellow." It featured a picture of a newborn baby.

Moore went all out for the first Earth Day in 1970, printing a third of a million leaflets, folders, and pamphlets for campus distribution. College newspapers received free cartoons highlighting the population crisis and college radio stations a free taped show (featuring Paul Ehrlich). With his genius for marketing, Moore even announced a contest with cash awards for the best slogans relating environmental problems to what he called "popullution" [population pollution]. Students on over 200 campuses participated. The winner, not surprisingly, was "People Pollute."[86]

By 1971 most of the leading environmental groups had signed on to the anti-natal agenda, having been convinced that reducing the human birthrate would greatly benefit the environment. Perhaps it was their interest in "managing" populations of other species—salmon, condors, whales, etc.—that predisposed them to impose technical solutions on their own species. In any event, many of them were population hawks, who believed that simply making abortion, sterilization, and contraception widely available was not enough. "Voluntarism is a farce," wrote Richard Bowers of Zero Population Growth as early as 1969. "The private sector effort has failed ... [even the expenditure] of billions of dollars will not limit growth." Coercive measures were required. He proposed enacting "criminal laws to limit population, if the earth is to survive."[87]

Those who held such views were not content to merely stop people from multiplying; they demanded radical reductions in human numbers. The group Negative Population Growth wanted to cut the-then US population of 200 million by more than half, to 90 million.[88] Celebrated oceanographer Jacques Cousteau told the *UNESCO Courier* in 1991, "In order to stabilize world populations, we must eliminate 350,000 people per day." Garrett Hardin of "The Tragedy of the Commons" fame opined that the "carrying capacity" of the planet was 100 million and that our numbers should be reduced accordingly.

To carry out these decimations, Malthusian solutions are proposed, as when novelist William T. Vollman opined that "there are too many people in the world and maybe something like AIDS or something like war may be a good thing on that level."[89] And lest we have compunctions about resorting to such measures, we should bear in mind, as Earth First! Founder Dave Foreman wrote, "We humans have become a disease, the Humanpox."

The Feminist Dilemma

The most radical of the feminists had a different definition of disease. Why should women be "subject to the species gnawing at their vitals," as Simone de Beauvoir wrote in her feminist classic, *The Second Sex?* Why endure pregnancy at all, if contraception, sterilization and, especially, abortion, could be made widely available? With the legalization of abortion in the United States in 1972, feminists increasingly looked overseas, eager to extend their newfound rights to "women of color" elsewhere in the world. They had read their Ehrlich as well as their Beauvoir, and knew that the world had too many people, or soon would. But family planning, especially abortion, provided a way out. "Let us bestow upon all the women of the world the blessing that we women in the privileged West have received," elite feminists said to themselves. "The freedom to indulge our sexual appetites—like men—without fear of pregnancy. We will, at the same time and by the same means, solve the problem of too many babies. For surely impoverished Third World women do not actually want all those children they are bearing. Patriarchy has made them into breeding machines, but we will set them free."

At the time, the population control movement remained ambivalent over the question of abortion. Hugh Moore had long wanted it as a population control measure, but Frank Notestein was still arguing in the early 1970s that the Population Council should "consistently and firmly take the anti-abortion stance and use every occasion to point out that the need for abortions is the proof of program failure in the field of family planning and public health education."[90]

The women's movement would not be put off with the promise of a perfect contraceptive. They knew, better than anyone (and often from painful personal experience) that contraception, because of the inevitable failures, *always* led to abortion. This is why, as Sharon Camp, then of the Population Crisis Committee, wrote "both abortion and contraception are presently on the rise in most developing countries."[91]

Abortion was, in the end, accepted by most controllers because it came to be seen as a necessary part of the anti-natal arsenal. The Rockefeller Commission, established by President Nixon, wrote that "We are impressed that induced abortion has a demographic effect wherever legalized" and on these grounds went on to call for "abortion on demand."[92] The Population Council followed the Commission in endorsing abortion as a means of population control by 1975.

In the end, feminist advocacy of abortion had proven decisive. The feminists had given the population control movement an additional weapon, abortion, to use in its drive to reduce human fecundity, and were encouraging its aggressive use.

At the same time, it was soon apparent to many feminists that birth control was not an unmixed blessing for Third World women, who continued to be targets of ever-more aggressive programs in places like Indonesia, India, and Bangladesh. They began to demand further changes in the way programs were carried out, starting with male contraceptives and more vasectomies. Frank Notestein wrote of the feminists' shifting demands that, "As second-generation suffragists they were not at all disposed to allow the brutish male to be in charge of contraception. Women must have their own methods!" But now they "complain violently that the men are trying to saddle the women with all the contraceptive work. You can't please them if you do, and can't please them if you don't."[93]

Although expressed somewhat crudely, Notestein's comment pointed up the dilemma faced by feminists. On the one hand, they sought to impose a radically pro-abortion agenda on population control programs, whose general purpose—fertility reduction—they applauded. On the other they tried to protect women from the abuses that invariably accompanied such programs. But with the exception of the condom, other methods of contraception all put the burden on women. Vasectomies could easily be performed on men, but it was usually the woman who went under the knife to have her tubes tied. And only women could undergo abortions. So, as a practical matter, the burden of fertility reduction was placed disproportionately on women. And when programs took a turn towards the coercive, as they were invariably prone to do in the Third World, it was women, overwhelmingly, who paid the price.

Feminist complaints did lead to some changes, but these were mostly matters of presentation. Population controllers did learn, over time, how to better disguise the true, anti-natal purpose of their efforts. They mastered a different language or, rather, several different languages, switching from one to the other as circumstances demanded. When Western feminists need to be convinced of the importance of supporting the programs, reproductive rights rhetoric is the order of the day. Thus we hear Nafis Sadik telling Western reporters on the eve of the 1994 UN Conference on Population and Development that the heart of the discussion "is the recognition that the low status of women is a root cause of inadequate reproductive health care."

Such language would ring strange in the ears of Third World women, who are instead given soothing lectures about "child-spacing" and "maternal health." Population control programs were originally unpopular in many Middle Eastern countries and sub-Saharan countries until they were given a face lift, with feminist input, and presented as programs to "help" women. As Peter Donaldson, the head of the Population Reference Bureau, writes, "The idea of limiting the number of births was so culturally unacceptable [in the Middle East and sub-Saharan Africa] that family planning programs were introduced as a means for promoting better maternal and child health by helping women space their births."[94] William Vogt, past president of the Planned Parenthood Federation of America, was even blunter: "It seems to me that perhaps we could ... spread birth control under the guise of maternal health."[95]

The feminists did not imagine, when they signed onto the population control movement, that they would merely be marketing consultants. It is telling that many Third World feminists have refused to endorse population control programs at all, arguing instead that these programs violate the rights of women while ignoring their real needs. It must be painful for Western feminists to contemplate, but their own movement has "co-opted," to use Betsy Hartmann's term, by another movement for whom humanity as a whole, and women in particular, remain a faceless mass of numbers to be controlled, that is to say, contracepted, sterilized, and aborted. For despite the feminist rhetoric, the basic character of the programs hasn't changed. They are a numbers driven, technical solution to the "problem of overpopulation"—which is, in truth, a problem of poverty—and they overwhelmingly target women.

This is, in many respects, an inevitable outcome. To accept the premise that the world is overpopulated and then seek to make the resulting birth control programs "women-friendly," as many feminists have, is a fateful compromise. For it means that concern for the real needs of women is neither the starting point of these programs, nor their ultimate goal, but merely a consideration along the way. Typical of the views of feminists actively involved in the population movement are those of Sharon Camp, who writes "There is still time to avoid another population doubling, but only if the world community acts very quickly to make family planning universally available and to invest in other social programs, like education for girls, which can help accelerate fertility declines."[96] Here we see the population crisis mentality in uneasy alliance with programs for women which, however, are justified chiefly because they "help accelerate fertility declines."

The alliance between the feminists and population controllers has been an awkward affair. But, as the third of the three most anti-natalist movements in history, the radical feminists gave the population controllers new resources, new constituencies, new political allies, a new rhetoric, and remain staunch supporters even today.

The Population Firm and Its Funding

Over the past decade, the Population Firm has become more powerful than ever. Like a highly organized cartel, working through an alphabet soup of United Nations agencies and "nongovernmental organizations," its tentacles reach into nearly every developing country. It receives sustenance from feeding tubes attached to the legislatures of most developed countries, and further support through the government-financed population research industry, with its hundreds of professors and thousand of students. But unlike any other firm in human history, its purpose is not to produce anything, but rather to destroy—to destroy fertility and to prevent babies from being conceived and born. It diminishes, one might say, the "oversupply" of people. It does this for the highest of motives—to protect all of us from "popullution." Those in poor countries who do not subscribe to its ideology it bribes and browbeats, bringing the combined weight of the world's industrial powers to bear on such pockets of resistance.

In 1991, the United Nations estimated that a yearly sum of $4.5 to $5 billion was being directed to population programs in developing countries. This figure, which has grown tremendously in the last 15 years, includes contributions from bilateral donors such as the United States, the European nations and Japan, from international agencies like those associated with the United Nations, and from multilateral lending institutions, including the World Bank and the various regional development banks. It includes grants from foundations, like Ted Turner's UN Foundation, and wealthy individuals, like Warren Buffet, all of whom work together to advance their cause. Yet still more is demanded. The World Watch Institute insisted, in January 1999, that "the amount of money needed each year (in addition to current expenditures) to provide reproductive health care for all women in developing countries is $12 billion." [97]

The best illustration of how these various organizations interact to generate such huge sums comes from the pages of a lawsuit filed by one its minor players, the Washington, D.C.-based Population Institute, against the Reagan administration. The Institute's complaint centered on the 1985 decision of USAID to deny funding to the UN Fund for Population Activities (UNFPA) because of its involvement with China's program of forced abortion and sterilization. In an effort to prove that the Institute had "standing" to sue, the Institute's president, Werner Fornos, was amazingly candid about the substantial sums of money his Institute had received over the years to lobby the U.S. government on behalf of worldwide population control.

Wrote Fornos: "In fiscal year 1985 the Population Institute received $150,000 from UNFPA and ... expected to receive an additional $100,000 when AID released ... [funds] that it had earlier withheld from UNFPA." Because of the funding cut-off, Fornos had to inform "seven employees of the Population Institute—about one-third of my staff—that we no longer have funds to pay their salaries. Additional lay-offs may become necessary if UNFPA is not funded by AID, and thus cannot fund the Population Institute."[98]

By Fornos' own admission, he has an extremely cozy relationship with UNFPA. Indeed, he propagandizes for US population control funding that winds up in his own pockets. Demanded James Miller: "Let Fornos raise his funds the old-fashioned way—by his own efforts—and stop sticking the American taxpayer with his personal bills."[99]

Aside from the money budgeted for anti-natal programs, a vast amount of money not explicitly designated as "population" financing is used to further the family planning effort. As Elizabeth Liagin notes, "During the 1980s, the diversion of funds from government non-population budgets to fertility-reduction measures soared, especially in the U.S., where literally hundreds of millions from the Economic Support Funds program, regional development accounts, and other non-population budgets were redirected to "strengthen" population planning abroad."[100]

An almost unlimited variety of other "development" efforts—health, education, energy, commodity imports, infrastructure, and debt relief, for example—are also used by governments and other international agencies, such as the World Bank, to promote population control policies, either through requiring recipient nations to incorporate family planning into another program or by holding funds or loans hostage to the development of a national commitment to tackle the "over-population" problem.

In its insatiable effort to locate additional funds for its insatiable population control programs, USAID has even attempted to redirect "blocked assets"—profits generated by international corporations operating in developing nations that prohibit the transfer of money outside the country—into population control efforts. In September 1992, USAID signed a $36.4 million contract and "statement of work" with the accounting firm Deloitte and Touche to act as a mediator with global corporations and to negotiate deals that would help turn the estimated $200 *billion* in blocked assets into "private" contributions for family planning in host countries. The corporations would in return get to claim a deduction on their US tax return for this "charitable contribution." The Profit initiative, as it is fittingly called, is not limited to applying its funds directly to family planning "services," but is also encouraged to "work for the removal" of "trade barriers for contraceptive commodities" and "assist in the development of a regulatory framework that permits the expansion of private sector family planning services." This reads like a bureaucratic mandate to lobby for the elimination of local laws which in any way interfere with efforts to drive down the birthrate, such as laws restricting abortion or sterilization.[101]

The central idea of the population controllers—that people in their numbers were somehow the enemy of all that is good—continues to reign supreme in Washington. J. Brian Atwood, who administered the U.S. Agency for International Development in the early days of the Clinton administration, put it this way: "If we aren't able to find and promote ways of curbing population growth, we are going to fail in *all* of our foreign policy initiatives" (italics added). Atwood also went on to announce that the United States "also plans to resume funding in January [1994] to the UN Fund for Population Activities (UNFPA)," funding that the previous two presidents had held in abeyance because of concerns about the UNFPA's participation in forced abortion in China.[102]

Secretary of State Warren Christopher offered a similar but even more detailed defense of population programs the following year. "Population and sustainable development are back where they belong in the mainstream of American foreign policy and diplomacy." He went on to say, in a line that comes right out of US National Security Study Memo 200, that population pressure "ultimately jeopardizes America's security interests." But that's just the beginning. Repeating a now familiar litany, he claimed of population growth that: "It strains resources. It stunts economic growth. It generates disease. It spawns huge refugee flows, and ultimately it threatens our stability.... We want to continue working with the other donors to meet the rather ambitious funding goals that were set up in Cairo."[103] Such rhetoric is not forthcoming from the senior members of the Bush administration, but Ravenholt's "powerful population program," mandated by legislation and fueled by continued congressional appropriations, remains in place.

The movement was never more powerful than in 2007 in terms of money, other resources, and political clout.

*　　*　　*

Like a wave that crests only seconds before it crashes upon the shore, this appearance of strength may be deceiving. There are signs that the anti-natal movement has peaked, and may before long collapse of its own overreaching. US spending on coercive population control and abortion overseas has long been banned. In 1998 the U.S. Congress, in response to a flood of reports about human rights abuses, for the first time set limits on what can be done to people in the name of "voluntary family planning."[104] Developing countries are regularly denouncing what they see as foreign interference into their domestic affairs, as the Peruvian Congress did in 2002. Despite strenuous efforts to co-opt them, the opposition of feminists to population control programs (which target women) seems to be growing.[105] Many other groups—libertarians, Catholics, Christians of other denominations, the majority of economists, and those who define themselves as pro-life—have long been opposed.

As population control falls into increasing disrepute worldwide, the controllers are attempting to reinvent themselves, much the same way that the Communists in the old Soviet Union reemerged as "social democrats" following its collapse. Thus organizations working in this area have found it wise to disguise their agenda by adopting less revealing names. Thus Zero Population Growth in June 2002 became Population

Connection. The Association for Voluntary Surgical Contraception the year before changed its name to Engender Health.

Documents prepared for public consumption by the UNFPA and other population control agencies now routinely cloak their plans in language about the "empowerment of women," "sustainable development," "safe motherhood," and "reproductive health." Yet the old anti-natal zeal continues to come through in internal documents. When Thoraya Obaid assumed control of the UNFPA in 2002 she pledged to "slow and eventually stabilize population growth" in a presentation to her new bosses on the UN Commission on Population and Development. "Today I want to make one thing very clear," she told them in no uncertain terms. "The slowdown in population growth does not mean we can slow down efforts for population and reproductive health—quite the contrary. If we want real progress and if we want the projections to come true, we must step up efforts.… While population growth is slowing, it is still growing by 77 million people every year."[106]

The various deceptions adopted by the anti-natalists will, in the end, avail them nothing. For, as we will see, their central idea—the Malthusian notion that you can eliminate poverty, hunger, disease, and pollution by eliminating the poor—is bootless. Reducing the numbers of babies born does not in itself solve political, military, economic, or environmental problems, as millions of well-meaning Westerners have been propagandized into believing. On the contrary, it often creates them. Yet where population control programs are concerned, these costs have been largely ignored (as the cost of doing business) while the benefits to people, the environment, and to the economy, have been greatly exaggerated.

Population control programs cause real harm to real people in the area of human rights, health care, and the development of democratic institutions. These shortcomings are most vividly on display in China, whose longstanding one-child policy is much admired by the population controllers. It is to that country that we shall next turn.

Notes

1.   Quoted in Midge Decter, "The Nine Lives of Population Control," Michael Cromartie, Ed., *The Nine Lives of Population Control.* (Washington, D.C.: Ethics and Public Policy Center, 1995), 15.
2.   Quoted in Allan Chase, *The Legacy of Malthus: The Social Costs of the New Scientific Racism.* (New York: Knopf, 1977), 7.
3.   Quotes are from Ronald L. Meek, ed., *Marx and Engels on the Population Bomb,* 2nd edition. (Berkeley, California: Ramparts Press, 1971), 16, 70. Engels also wrote, "Too little is produced, that is the cause of the whole thing [the population problem]. But *why* is too little produced? Not because the limits of produc-

tion—even today and with present-day means—are exhausted. No, but because the limits of production are determined not by the number of hungry bellies but by the number of *purses* able to buy and to pay. Bourgeois society does not and cannot wish to produce any more." From Frederick Engels letter to F.A. Lange of 29 March 1865, Chapter 6, "The Pressure of Population Upon the Means of Employment," 87.

4. Margaret Sanger, *Pivot of Civilization.* (New York: Brentano's, 1922), 108.

5. Ibid., 112.

6. Letter of Margaret Sanger to Frederick Osborn, December 29, 1939, from the Planned Parenthood Federation of America Records, Sophia Smith Collection, Smith College, Northampton, Massachusetts. Cited in Angela Franks, *Margaret Sanger's Eugenic Legacy: The Control of Female Fertility.* (Jefferson, N.C.: McFarland, 2005), 12.

7. Margaret Sanger, "Lasker Foundation Award Speech," October 25, 1950, Margaret Sanger papers, Library of Congress, Washington, D.C. Cited in Franks, 188.

8. Margaret Sanger, "The Function of Sterilization," *Birth Control Review*, October 1926, 299. Cited in Franks, 179. Many rejected the views of the Eugenicists, including G. K. Chesterton, who accused them of suffering from "a hardening of the heart with a sympathetic softening of the head," and for presuming to turn "common decency" and commendable deeds" into "social crimes." G. K. Chesterton, *Illustrated London News*, 14 February 1925.

9. Sanger founded the American Birth Control League in 1921. In 1939 the organization changed its name to the Birth Control Federation of America, before settling on the Planned Parenthood Federation of America in 1942. See Alan E. Guttmacher, "The Planned Parenthood Federation of America, Inc., General Program," in Mary Steichen Calderone, ed., *Manual of Family Planning and Contraceptive Practice*, 2nd edition. (Baltimore: Williams and Wilkins, 1970), 91-96. Cited in Kasun, 216. See also the timeline in Franks, 256-58.

10. Margaret Sanger, "Birth Control and Racial Betterment," *Birth Control Review*, February 1919, 11-12. Cited in Franks, 49.

11. See the history in Franks, 127-49.

12. Sanger, ed., *The Sixth International Neo-Malthusian and Birth Control Conference*, vol. IV, Religious and Ethical Aspects of Birth Control, "The Children's Era," (New York: ABCL, inc., 1926), 53. Cited in Clement Mulloy, *Margaret Sanger vs. The Catholic Church.* (Ph.D. Dissertation, University of Arkansas, 2000), 110.

13. The banner of the November 1921 issue of the *Birth Control Review*, cited in Franks, 49. See also her unpublished piece, "We Must Breed a Race of Thoroughbreds," 1929, Margaret Sanger papers, Library of Congress, cited in Franks, 49.

14. See Franks, 37-40, 150-78.

15. Quoted in Donald T. Critchlow, *Intended Consequences: Birth Control, Abortion, and the Federal Government in Modern America.* (Oxford University Press: Oxford, 1999), 23.

16. He occupied his time serving as a trustee of the Rockefeller Foundation, the Rockefeller Institute, and 35 other boards or committees. He joined the navy a year after Pearl Harbor, at a time when almost all young men of his age were already in service, only to be assigned as a special assistant to the undersecretary of the navy. See Critchlow, 20.

17. Visiting Dhaka, Bangladesh, in 1963, Rockefeller and his party passed through narrow, dusty streets cluttered with people and animals of all descriptions," smelling of "bad meat, urine, and sweat." The party came to "the west bank of the river at dusk. . . . the sand swarmed with people. Rockefeller said nothing for at least

twenty minutes. He stood beside an over-turned oil drum, confronted by the chaos so remote from the orderly presentations on the 56th floor of the R.C.A. building. Here at last was what he had come to see, the plain reality of the so-called "population explosion." … "The numbers," he said, "the sheer numbers of it … the quality, you see, goes down." From John Enson Harr and Peter J. Johnson, *The Rockefeller Conscience* (New York: Scribner, 1991).

18. Quoted in Donald Critchlow, *Intended Consequences*, 22.
19. Quoted in Critchlow, 28.
20. William Vogt, *The Road to Survival*, with an introduction by Barnard Baruch (New York: William Sloane Associates, 1948), 463-464. Vogt also wrote *People! Challenge to Survival* (New York: William Sloane Associates, 1960), the flavor of which may be suggested by his endorsement of the idea of "an anti-fertility agent to be added to the rice, grain or salt, that would cut our birth rate…" (229).
21. Hugh Moore to Malcolm W. Davis, Carnegie Endowment for International Peace, 10 November 1949, Moore Papers, Box 2, Princeton University. Cited in Critchlow, 31. Moore was warned that Vogt was not an expert in population matters—"there is just enough truth in [Vogt's] book to make it dangerous," Frank G. Boudreau of the Milbank Memorial Fund told him—but Moore found Vogt's warning of imminent catastrophe credible anyway. Ibid. 31.
22. Lawrence Lader, *Breeding Ourselves to Death*, with a Foreword by Dr. Paul R. Ehrlich (New York: Ballantine Books, 1971), 3.
23. Ibid., 3.
24. Hugh Moore, *The Population Bomb* (New York: Hugh Moore Fund, 1954).
25. Hugh Moore, Will L. Clayton, and Ellsworth Bunker to John D. Rockefeller 3rd, 26 November 1954, RG 2, Box 45, RA. Quoted in Critchlow, 32.
26. Quoted in Critchlow, 32. See also, Lader, 3.
27. The full name of the committee, which was established in 1958, was the Committee to Study the United States Military Assistance Program. It was intended to study the effectiveness of US foreign aid in countries where we had mutual-assistance pacts.
28. "The climax was a seven-page telegram from Moore," Draper later recalled, "making it clear that if the committee didn't deal with the population issue we'd be derelict in our duty." Quoted in Lader, *Breeding Ourselves to Death* (New York: Ballantine Books, 1971).
29. Eisenhower would later publicly distance himself from the Draper Report, saying at a press conference about American family planning assistance that "I cannot imagine anything more emphatically a subject that is not a proper political or governmental activity or function or responsibility." The U.S. government, he stated, should not "interfere with the internal affairs of any government." Quoted in Critchlow, 44.
30. The ads appeared in the *New York Times* (27 August 1961), and the *Wall Street Journal* (28 August 1961). The Moore quote is from Moore's letters to Draper as quoted in Critchlow, 47, also footnote 104, p. 245.
31. Committee on Foreign Affairs, Committee on Foreign Relations, *Legislation on Foreign Relations Through 2005*, "Current Legislation and Related Executive Orders," Vol. 1 (Government Printing Office, Wash., D.C., January 2006), 19, 22, emphasis added. Accessed on 8 March 2007 at http://www.dsca.osd.mil/programs/LPA/2006/faa_aeca.pdf. Also quoted in *PRI Review* 1(3) (May/June 1991): 4. Donald P. Warwick's *Bitter Pills: Population Policies and Their Implementation in Eight Developing Countries* (Cambridge: Cambridge University Press, 1982) contains a useful summary of the interaction between the population control lobby and the Congress that led to the establishment of a strong population unit inside of USAID. See esp. 44-47.

32. Ibid., 45.
33. This language was repeated in the International Development and Food Assistance Act of 1978, section 104(d) of which provides that American foreign aid "shall be administered so as to give particular attention to … the impact of all programs, projects, and activities on population growth. All … activities proposed for financing … shall be designed to build motivation for smaller families … in programs such as education … nutrition, disease control, maternal and child health services, improvements in the status and employment of women, agricultural production, rural development, and assistance to the urban poor." In its Section 102 on "Development Assistance Policy" the act says US aid would be "concentrated" in countries that demonstrate their "commitment and progress" by their control of population growth." An explanatory footnote in the Report on Population and Development Assistance by the House Select Committee on Population states that "the whole of AID's development assistance effort" was intended to be included within the population-control provisions of Section 104. 22 U.S. Code, sec. 2151-1; 22 U.S. Code, sec. 2151(b). House Select Committee on Population, Report, Population and Development Assistance", 95th Congress, 2nd Session (Washington, D.C.: U.S. Government Printing Office, 1978), 111. Also quoted in Kasun, 103-104.
34. George H.W. Bush, "Foreword," Phyllis Tilson Piotrow, ed., *World Population Crisis: The United States Response.* (New York, Praeger Publishers: 1973). This was reprinted in the *Population and Development Review* 14(4) (December 1988), as "George Bush on Population: An Early Statement," 751-2. Bush praised R. T. Ravenholt and then-Assistant Secretary of State Philander P. Claxton, Jr., by name as "determined individuals … who were willing to urge their superiors ahead" [on population matters].
35. Paul Johnson, *A History of the English People* (New York: Harper and Row, 1985), 276.
36. Ravenholt's views include the following: "Although American blacks still heap incessant blame upon contemporary white populations because earlier white populations owned black slaves, this is an inappropriate onus; rather, American blacks should thank their lucky stars that the institution of slavery did exist in earlier centuries; if not, these American blacks would not exist: their ancestors would have been killed by their black enemies, instead of being sold as slaves. The only way Africans were then able to get to America was in slave ships; and because their ancestors were transported here as slaves, many millions of blacks are living far better in America than are their cousins in Africa—where starvation and the killing fields prevail." R. T. Ravenholt, "Africa's Population-Driven Catastrophe Worsens," unpublished paper dated June 2000 available at www.ravenholt.com. There are so many problems with this paragraph it is difficult to know where to begin. Suffice to say that it is better to die a free man than to live in chains.
37. *St. Louis Post-Dispatch*, 22 April 1977.
38. Berelson to files, 31 October 1973, Berelson Files, Population Council Papers (unprocessed), RA. Quoted in Critchlow, 178.
39. Ravenholt is quoted in David Heaps, "Report on the Population Council Prepared for the Ford Foundation," December 1973, Population Council Files (unprocessed), RA. Quoted in Critchlow, 186.
40. Ibid.
41. Randy Engel, personal communication, 4 March 2007. Mrs. Engel recounts that "I put the package safely away for the next USAID Congressional hearing at which time I asked the Chairman of the hearings to return the condom packet to Ravenholt. That was the last time Ravenholt pulled that stunt."

42. Quoted in Kasun, 105.
43. The Helms Amendment, authored by Senator Jesse Helms of North Carolina, forbids US funds from being spent directly on abortions. It has not prevented USAID, under the direction of Ravenholt's successor, from giving funds to organizations that then turn around and promote or perform abortions themselves. This is why the Mexico City policy, which forbids such a sleight-of-hand, was necessary.
44. R. T. Ravenholt, "Africa's Population-Driven Catastrophe Worsens," unpublished paper dated June 2000 available at www.ravenholt.com. Accessed May 2006.
45. Ibid.
46. Similarly, family planning programs in the United States were set up using existing organizations like Planned Parenthood Federation of America. While people like Bernard Berelson of the Population Council wanted to set up a "Federal Department of Population and Environment ... with the power to take whatever stops are necessary to establish a reasonable population size" for the United States, reorganizing the various agencies that were hitherto involved, this approach was rejected. See Donald Critchlow, *Intended Consequences* (Oxford University Press; Oxford, 1999). Berelson's proposal appeared in "Beyond Family Planning," *Studies in Family Planning* 38 (February 1968):1-16. While these organizations call themselves "non-governmental," many of them receive upwards of 90 percent of their funding from the federal trough, and it would be more accurate to call them quasi-nongovernmental organizations, or QNGOs (pronounced kwang-goes). Without the regular and generous subsidies they receive from the government, most QNGOs would shortly cease to exist in any recognizable form.
47. Cited in Angela Franks, *Margaret Sanger's Eugenic Legacy: the Control of Female Fertility* (MacFarland: North Carolina, 2005), 169.
48. Franks, 169.
49. In the fall of 1989, USAID's quarterly newsletter, *USAID Highlights* 6:4, boasted that, "Since 1968, USAID has purchased $567.7 million worth of contraceptives for distribution to 75 [undeveloped] countries—6.9 billion condoms, 1.6 billion cycles of oral contraceptives, 49.7 million intrauterine devices (IUDs), and 16.5 million vaginal foaming tablets. To this must be added shipments from 1990-95 of 3.6 billion condoms, over 400 million cycles of birth control pills, more than 23 million IUDs, over 100 million vaginal foaming tablets, nearly a quarter of a million units of Norplant, and almost 4 million doses of Depo-Provera. See *Contracts and Grants and Cooperative Agreements with Universities, Firms and Non-Profit Institutions Active During the Period October 1, 1994–September 30, 1995*, popularly known as *The Yellow Book, 1995*, USAID, Washington, D.C. Appendix A gives complete figures for all condoms and contraceptives shipped from 1990 onwards.
50. It should be noted that the operative word is shipments—the quantities actually sent abroad—which may be considerably lower than the amounts that were procured in the first place.
51. Panalpina provided USAID with warehousing and shipping services. Under one contract (CCP-3057-C-00-2019-00), covering the period 22 June 1992 to 1 January 1997, USAID's requirements for "freight forwarding and warehousing of contraceptives worldwide" were being handled by Panalpina at a cost of $23,909,166.
52. FHI promotional brochure, undated. This connection with USAID is particularly ironic since Stephen Mumford, one of FHI's leading lights, has been associated with the unregulated sterilization of thousands of women with quinacrine hydrochloride pellets, a strong acid. See David Morrison, "Burn, Baby, Burn," *PRI Review* 6(5) (September-October 1996):1.
53. US population controllers had met with a disappointing "absence of widespread public demand" and an "underutilization of ... outreach," they reported in 1978

to the U.S. Congress. House Select committee on Population, Report, *Population and Development Assistance*", 95th Congress, 2nd session (Washington, D.C.: U.S. Government Printing Office, 1978), 55-59 *passim.*

54. Donald Warwick, Bitter Pills (Cambridge: Cambridge University Press, 1982), 43.
55. PSI Special Reports, Report No. 2/1993, 11.
56. PSI Profile: Social Marketing and Communications for Health, 2-sided flier on "Bringing Mass Media to Rural Populations through Mobile Video Vans," November 1994.
57. Reimert Thorolf Ravenholt, "China's Birthrate: A Function of Collective Will," Paper presented to the Annual Meeting of the Population Association of America, 27 April 1979. How the Chinese people could express their "collective will" without free elections or opinion polls Ravenholt doesn't say.
58. Duff G. Gillespie, "Reimert T. Ravenholt, USAID's Population Program Stalwart", *Population Today* 28 (October 2000):7.
59. Ibid. Gillespie reports that "If you went to a country that forbade contraceptives, you were to carry two suitcases—one for clothes, the other for contraceptives."
60. Duff G. Gillespie, "Reimert T. Ravenholt, USAID's Population Program Stalwart", *Population Today* 28 (October 2000):7.
61. R. T. Ravenholt, "Africa's Population-Driven Catastrophe Worsens," unpublished paper dated June 2000 available at www.ravenholt.com. Accessed July 2003.
62. It should be noted that the World Bank, despite its title, is predominately an American institution. The head of the World Bank is an American, and its headquarters are in Washington, D.C. At the time of its founding at the 1944 Breton Woods conference, a special division was created at the Treasury Department to oversee its activities. That bureau, called the National Advisory Council on International Monetary and Financial Policies (the "NAC" to insiders), monitors US investments in global lending institutions—the World Bank, the International Monetary Fund, and the regional development banks—to ensure they are sufficient to maintain a dominant position. At the same time, the NAC works with an inter-agency task force to make certain that the policies of the World Bank reflect those of the U.S. government. The 1988 annual report of the NAC states that "the council [NAC] seeks to ensure that … the … operations [of the World Bank and other international financial institutions] are conducted in a manner consistent with U.S. policies and objectives…" International Finance: National Advisory Council on International Monetary and Financial Policies, Annual Report to the President and to the Congress for the Fiscal year 1988, (Wash., D.C., Department of the Treasury), Appendix A, p. 31. Quoted in Jean Guilfoyle, "World Bank Population Policy: Remote Control," *PRI Review* 1(4) (July/August 1991):8.
63. I served on board a ship of this class, the *USS Lockwood*, from 1974-76. As the Main Propulsion Assistant—the officer in charge of the engine room—I can personally attest that this fleet frigate, as this class of ship was designated, was anything but fleet. On picket duty, it could not keep up with the aircraft carriers that it was tasked with protecting from submarine attacks.
64. The 1968 meeting was the 23rd joint annual meeting of the boards of governors of the World Bank and the International Monetary Fund. The two organizations always hold their annual meetings in tandem, underscoring their collaboration on all matters of importance.
65. McNamara moderated his anti-natal rhetoric on this formal occasion. More often, he sounded like Hugh Moore, as when he wrote: "the greatest single obstacle to the economic and social advancement of the majority of the peoples in the underdevel-

oped world is rampant population growth.... The threat of unmanageable population pressures is very much like the threat of nuclear war.... Both threats can and will have catastrophic consequences unless they are dealt with rapidly." *One Hundred Countries, Two Billion People.* (London: Pall Mall Press, 1973), 45-46. Quoted in *The 9 Lives of Population Control*, p. 62. McNamara never expressed any public doubts about the importance of population control, although he did once confide in Bernard Berelson that "many of our friends see family planning as being 'too simple, too narrow, and too coercive.'" As indeed it was—and is. The quote is from Critchlow, 178.

66. See Fred T. Sai and Lauren A. Chester, "The Role of the World Bank in Shaping Third World Population Policy," in Godfrey Roberts, ed., *Population Policy: Contemporary Issues* (New York: Praeger, 1990). Cited in Kasun, 104.

67. "WB [World Bank] Conditions Aid to Population Control," *The New Nation,* 7 September 1994, 1. Cited in Kasun, 104.

68. U.S. International Population Policy: First Annual report, prepared by the Interagency Task Force on Population Policy, (Washington, D.C., U.S. National Archives, May 1976). Quoted in Jean Guilfoyle, "World Bank Population Policy: Remote Control," *PRI Review* 1(4) (July/August 1991):8.

69. Personal communication with the author from a retired World Bank executive who worries that, if his identity is revealed, his pension may be in jeopardy.

70. Peter T. Bauer and Basil S. Yamey, "The Third World and the West: An Economic Perspective," in W. Scott Thompson, ed., *The Third World: Premises of U.S. Policy.* (San Francisco: Institute for Contemporary Studies, 1978), 302. Quoted in Kasun, 105.

71. The Nigerian case will be discussed in more detail in the Chapter 4. See Barbara Akapo, "When family planning meets population control," *Gender Review*, June 1994, 8-9.

72. Word Bank, 1995 Annual Report, p. 18. Quoted in *PRI Review* 5(6) (November/December 1995):7.

73. Kasun, 277.

74. David Morrison, "Weaving a Wider Net: U.N. Moves to Consolidate its Anti-Natalist Gains," *PRI Review* 7(1) (January/February 1997):7.

75. Ibid.

76. Cited in *Innocents Betrayed* (Front Royal, VA.: Population Research Institute, 1997), 4.

77. Bernard Berelson, "Where Do We Stand," paper prepared for Conference on Technological change and Population Growth, California Institute of Technology, May 1970, 1. Quoted in Ronald Freedman, *The Sociology of Human Fertility: An Annotated Bibliography.* (New York: Irvington Publishers, 1975), 3. It's worth noting that Freedman's book was a subsidized product of the institution Berelson then headed. As Freedman notes in his "Preface," the "staff at the Population Council were very helpful in reading proof, editorial review, and making detailed arrangements for publication. Financial support was provided by the Population Council" (p. 2).

78. Freedman, 4.

79. *Christian Science Monitor*, July 5 1977. McNamara went on to say that, if present methods of population control "fail, and population pressures become too great, nations will be driven to more coercive methods."

80. Among other things, MacArthur published a report, drafted by the Natural Resource Section of his Supreme Commander Allied Powers (SCAP) office, which argued that the "discrepancies" between Japan's burgeoning population and its limited resources could not be met in any "humane" way except by a reduction of the birthrate. The Japanese Diet followed in 1948 by passing the Eugenic Protection

Law, which made abortion, sterilization and contraception widely available. The imagined "discrepancies," combined with a high forced savings rate and a drive for exports at all costs, gave way to a post-war economic boom that vaulted Japan into the first rank of nations. See David Cushman Coyle, "Japan's Population," *Population Bulletin* 15(7):119-136.

81. *U.S. International Population Policy: First Annual Report*, prepared by the Inter-agency Task Force on Population Policy, (Washington, D.C., U.S. National Archives, May 1976). Quoted in Elizabeth Liagin, "America vs. Everyone Else," *PRI Review* 6(6) (November/December 1996):5

82. Paul R. Ehrlich, *The Population Bomb* (New York: Ballantine books, 1968).

83. The first three sections of Ehrlich's book were called, "Too many people," "Too little food," "A dying planet."

84. Daniel Lyons, *Is There a Population Explosion?* (New York: Catholic Polls, 1970), 5.

85. Ehrlich has continued his scaremongering to the present day, writing one book after another, each one chock full of predictions of imminent disasters that fail to material-ize. People wonder why Ehrlich doesn't learn from his experiences. The answer, I think, is that he has learned very well. He has learned that writing about "overpopu-lation and environmental disaster" sells millions of books. He has learned that there is no price to pay for being wrong, as long as he doesn't admit his mistakes *in print* and glibly moves on to the next imagined disaster. In one sense, he has far outdone Hugh Moore in this regard. For unlike Moore, who had to spend his own money to publish the original *The Population Bomb*, Ehrlich was able to hype the population scare *and* make money by doing so. He is thus the archetype of a figure familiar to those who follow the anti-natal movement: The population hustler.

86. Lawrence Lader, *Breeding Ourselves to Death,* 79-81.

87. Richard M. Bowers to ZPG members, September 30, 1969, Population Council (unprocessed), RZ. Quoted in Critchlow, p. 156.

88. In later years, as U.S. population continued to grow, NPG has gradually increased its estimate of a "sustainable" U.S. population to 150 million. See Donald Mann, "A No-Growth Steady-State Economy Must Be Our Goal," NPG Position Paper, June 2002.

89. Quoted in David Boaz, "Pro-Life," *Cato Policy Report* (July/August 2002), 2.

90. Frank Notestein to Barnard Berelson, February 8, 1971, Rockefeller Brother Fund Papers, Box 210, RA. Quoted in Critchlow, 177. These concerns, while real enough to Notestein, apparently did not cause him to reflect on the fact that he was a major player in a movement that "detracted from the value of human life" by suggesting that there was simply too much of that life, and working for its selective elimination.

91. Population Action International, "Expanding Access to Safe Abortion: Key Policy Issues," Population Policy Information Kit 8 (September 1993). Quoted in Sharon Camp, "The Politics of U.S. Population Assistance," in Mazur, *Beyond the Numbers*, 126.

92. Critchlow, 165.

93. Frank Notestein to Bernard Berelson, April 27, 1971, Notestein Papers, Box 8, Princeton University.

94. Peter Donaldson and Amy Ong Tsui, "The International Family Planning Move-ment," in Laurie Ann Mazur, ed., *Beyond the Numbers* (Washington, D.C.: Island Press, 1994), p. 118. Donaldson was, at the time, president of the Population Refer-ence Bureau, and Tsui was deputy director of the Carolina Population Center.

95. Quoted in Angela Franks, *Margaret Sanger's Eugenic Legacy: The Control of Female Fertility,* 245.

96. Sharon Camp, "Politics of U.S. Population Assistance," in *Beyond the Numbers*, 130-1. Camp for many years worked at the Population Crisis Committee, founded by Hugh Moore in the early 1960s. It has recently, perhaps in recognition of falling fertility rates worldwide, renamed itself Population Action International.
97. "Matter of Scales Spending Priorities," *World Watch Magazine*," January-February 1999, World Watch Institute, http://www.worldwatch.org/node/764.
98. Lawsuit, *The Population Institute et al. vs. M Peter McPherson et al.*, Civil Acton No. 85-3131, U.S. District Court for the District of Columbia, affidavit of Werner H. Fornos, 3.
99. James Miller, "Fornos whines for population grants," *PRI Review* 5(5) (September/October 1995):16.
100. Quoted from Elizabeth Liagin, "Profit or Loss: Cooking the Books at USAID," *PRI Review* 6(3) (November/December 1996):1.
101. Ibid.
102. John M. Goshko, "Planned Parenthood gets AID grant...." *Washington Post*, November 23, 1993, A12-13.
103. Reuters, "Christopher defends U.S. population programs," Washington, D.C, December 19, 1994.
104. The Tiahrt Amendment, about which more in Chapter 5.
105. See Betsy Hartmann, *Reproductive Rights and Wrongs.* (Boston: South End Press, 1995).
106. Thoraya Ahmed Obaid, "Reproductive Health and Reproductive Rights With Special Reference to HIV/AIDS," Statement to the U.N. Commission on Population and Development, April 1, 2002.

3

The Chinese Model

"We have had sufficient experience now with population programs to realize that they can easily become a vehicle for elite pressure on the poor. I fear that the elevation to legitimacy of "beyond voluntary family planning" measures lends itself to precisely such pressure. ... Of course one might claim that such measures are in the 'ultimate' interest of the poor, but this view leaves one in the uncomfortable position of having to define the person, group, or institution that is better able to judge the interests of the poor than the poor themselves."

—Richard Easterlin, *World Development Report 1984 Review Symposium*[1]

Li Aihai, happily married and the mother of a 2 1/2-year-old girl, had a problem. She was four months pregnant with her second child. Sihui County family planning officials had come to her home and told her what she already knew: She had gotten pregnant too soon. She hadn't waited until her daughter was four years old, as Chinese law required of rural couples. The officials assured her that, because her first child had been a girl, she would eventually be allowed a second child. But they were equally insistent that she would have to abort this one. It was January, 2000.[2]

She pleaded that she had not intended to get pregnant. She was still wearing the IUD that they had implanted in her after the birth of her first child, as the law required. They were unsympathetic. Report to the family planning clinic tomorrow morning, they told her as they were leaving. We'll be expecting you.

Aihai had other plans. Leaving her little daughter in the care of her husband, she quietly packed her things and went to stay with relatives in a neighboring county. She would hide until she brought her baby safely into the world. Childbirth-on-the-run, it was called.

71

When the county family planning officials discovered that Aihai had disappeared, they began arresting her relatives. While her father-in-law managed to escape with her daughter, her mother-in-law and brother-in-law were arrested. Her own mother and father, brother and sister, and three other relatives were also imprisoned over the next few weeks. In all nine members of her extended family were arrested, hostages to the abortion that was being demanded of her.

But Aihai, knowing that her family supported her pregnancy, stayed in hiding. And her relatives, each refusing to tell the officials where she had gone to ground, stayed in jail.

Three months later the family planning officials struck again. The date they chose, April 5, was an important one on the Chinese traditional calendar. It was the festival of Qingming, or "bright and clear," a day on which rural Chinese men, by ancient custom, "sweep the graves" of their ancestors. Starting with the grave of their own deceased parents, they visit in turn the graves of grandparents, great-grandparents, and ancestors even further removed. At each stop they first clean off the headstones and weed the plot, and then set out a feast for the deceased, complete with bowls of rice, cups of rice liquor, and sticks of incense.

Why did the family planning officials pick this day of all days? Was it a further insult to the Li family, several of whom were languishing in their jail? Or was the day chosen for a very practical reason: With most of the men and boys away in the hills feting their ancestors, the village would be half-deserted, and they could carry out their plan without opposition.

The family planning officials came to the village in the company of a wrecking crew armed with crowbars and jackhammers. These fell upon Aihai's home like a horde of angry locusts. They shattered her living room and bedroom furniture into pieces. They ripped window frames out of walls and doors off of hinges. Then the jackhammers began to pound, shattering the brick walls, and to knocking great holes in the cement roof and floors. By the time they completed their work of destruction, you could stand on the first floor of Aihai's home and look up through two stories and the roof to the blue sky above. The wrecking crew then moved on to her parents' house, and then to her in-laws'. At day's end, three homes lay in ruins. The family planning officials confiscated the family's livestock and poultry, and then disappeared.

Aihai remained in hiding, out of reach of the family planning officials, for two more months. It wasn't until her child was actually born, she knew, that he would be safe. Abortions in China are performed up to the very point of parturition, and it is not uncommon for babies to be killed by lethal injection even as they descend in the birth canal. Only after she had given birth—to a beautiful baby boy—did she make plans to return home.

Aihai came back to find her family in prison, her home destroyed, and family planning officials furious that she had thwarted their will. Underlying their anger was hard calculation: Every "illegal" child born in their county was a black mark on their performance, depressing annual bonuses and threatening future promotions. But family planning officials, like most Chinese officials, have access to other sources of income. If you want your relatives released, they now told Aihai, you must pay a fine of 17,000 renminbi (RMB) (about US$2,000). Now this is a huge sum by Chinese standards, the equivalent of two or three years' income. It was many days before she was able to beg and borrow enough from family and friends to satisfy the officials' demands, and win her family's release.

No sooner had she paid one fine than she was told she owed another, if she wanted to regularize her son's status. He was currently a "black child," family planning officials explained to her. Because he was conceived outside of the family planning law, he did not exist in the eyes of the state. As a nonperson, he would be turned away from the government clinic if he fell ill, barred from attending a government school of any kind, and not considered for any kind of government employment later in life. He would not even be allowed to marry or start a family of his own. The government had decreed that "black children" would not be allowed to reproduce; one generation of illegals was enough. There was an out, however. If she were able to pay another fine of 17,000 RMB, however, her son would be issued a national identity number, and would be treated like everyone else—almost. She would still be required to pay double fees for his school supplies.

She was not surprised when she was ordered to report for sterilization. The population control regulations, she knew, were unyielding in this regard. Two children and your tubes are tied. This time she made no effort to resist the authorities. Having a second child had bankrupted her family. Having a third was out of the question. Her newborn son would have no younger siblings.

Even so, Aihai considers herself far more fortunate than Ah Fang, the wife of a neighboring villager. Married at 19 to an older man in a time-honored village ceremony in front of dozens of relatives and friends, Ah Fang is considered by everyone she knows to be his wife. Everyone, that is, but the local Communist authorities, whose unbending family planning regulations prohibit women from marrying until they reach the age of 23.

When Ah Fang became pregnant there was no chance that she would be allowed to carry her child to term, even though it would have been her first. The one-child policy does not apply to couples who are, in the view of the Chinese state, merely cohabiting. For them—and for single mothers of all ages—there is a *zero*-child policy. Ah Fang was ordered to present herself at the local clinic for an abortion. She went in as instructed on September 27, 2001. She has been careful not to criticize the authorities, but her friends have been less reticent. "She wanted to keep her baby," they complain openly, "but the law forbade it."[3]

*   *   *

Such personal tragedies, far from being rare, could easily be multiplied almost beyond belief. I met many "Li Aihai"s and "Tang Ah Fang"s (the names are, of course, pseudonyms) while living in a village in Guangdong province from 1979 to 1980, and have met many in the years since. But it would be impossible to know them all. For the history of China's 25-year experiment in "controlling reproduction under a state plan" is littered with literally millions—no, *tens* of millions—of such victims of forced abortion and forced sterilization.[4]

At the beginning of 1980, the Guangdong provincial government secretly ordered a 1 percent cap on population growth for the year. Local officials complied the only way they could—by launching a family planning "high tide" soon thereafter to terminate as many pregnancies as possible. The rules governing this high tide were simple: No woman was to be allowed to bear a second child within four years of her first, and third children were strictly forbidden. Furthermore, all women who had borne three or more children by November 1, 1979, were to be sterilized.

Over the next few weeks I became an eyewitness to every aspect of this draconian campaign. I went with young mothers to family planning "study sessions" where they were browbeaten by senior Party officials for getting pregnant. I followed them as they were unwillingly taken under escort to the commune clinic. I watched—with the permission of local officials who were eager to demonstrate their prowess in birth control to a visiting foreigner—as they were aborted and sterilized against their will. I will never forget the pain and suffering etched on the faces of these women as their unborn children, some only days from birth, were brutally killed with chemical weapons—poison shots—and then dismembered with surgical knives.

The demands of China's family planners escalated as the 1980s unfolded.[5] The one-child policy, first suggested by Deng Xiaoping in a hard-line 1979 speech, was in place nationwide by 1981. The "technical policy on family planning" followed two years later. Still in force today, the "technical policy" requires IUDs for women of childbearing age with one child, sterilization for couples with two children (usually performed on the woman), and abortions for women pregnant without authorization. By the mid-1980s, according to Chinese government statistics, birth control surgeries—abortions, sterilizations, and IUD insertions—were averaging more than thirty *million* a year. Many, if not most, of these procedures were performed on women who submitted only under duress.

The principal modification of the one-child policy occurred in the mid- to late-1980s when, in response to rising rates of female infanticide, the government relaxed the policy in the countryside for couples whose first child was a girl. In some parts of China this has devolved into a de facto two-child policy. Some rural officials found the selective enforcement of a mixed policy—one child for couples whose first child was a boy, two children for couples who first child was a girl—impossible to manage. Others, including the officials who run Sihui County in Guangdong province, where Li Aihai lives, are doing quite well at giving everyone two chances at a son, but no chance for two sons.

A quarter century after the Chinese got deadly serious about family planning, the program continues to be carried out against the popular will by means of a variety of coercive measures. In presenting the program to foreigners, who can be squeamish about such things, Chinese family planning officials are careful to emphasize "voluntarism." In speaking to their own cadres, however, the only form of coercion ever condemned is the actual use of physical force—tying down pregnant women for abortions, for instance. But while force is frowned upon, it is rarely, if ever, punished. Home-wrecking, unlawful detentions, heavily punitive fines, and like measures continue to be, as they have been from the late 1970s, the whip hand of the program. Women are psychologically and physically pressured to abort unauthorized children to the point of being dragged to the abortion mill. Networks of paid informants are used to report on unauthorized pregnancies of neighbors, family, and friends. Entire villages are punished for out-of-plan births. Officials conduct nighttime raids on couples suspected of having unauthorized children, and they keep detailed records on the sexual activity of every woman in their jurisdiction—so much for privacy. And to make the coercive regime complete, the "family planning centers" have prison cells—complete with bars—to detain those who resist forced abortion or sterilization. Forced sterilization is used not only as a means of population birth control, but sometimes as *punishment* for men and women who disobey the rules.[6]

The result of this systematic and relentless coercion is that millions of IUD insertions, sterilizations, and abortions continue to be performed each year. The national family planning journal continues to issue thinly disguised injunctions to get the job done at all costs. Officials are exhorted to take "real action" and "effective measures" to achieve "practical results." In short, Deng Xiaoping's no-holds-barred approach still dominates the program. "Use whatever means you must [to reduce China's population]," China's paramount leader ordered Party officials back in 1979, "Just do it."[7] They have been "just doing it" ever since.

The Chinese government maintains that abuses are the exception, not the rule, and constitute deviations—local aberrations—from national policy. But when the Guangdong provincial government orders 25,000 abortions to be carried out in Huaiji County, as it did in 2001 in response to reports of laxity in the local family planning program, this can hardly be described as a "local aberration." Nor can the forced abortion campaign undertaken by the Guangxi provincial government in the spring of 2007, complete with huge remedial fines for those who had successfully birthed babies outside of the state plan, be regarded as anything other than the expression of national policy. The Chinese program remains highly coercive not because of local deviations from central policies but as a direct, inevitable, and intentional consequence of those policies.

This is no secret. Articles in the Chinese media openly speak of the need for coercion in family planning, and senior officials continue to endorse the policy as currently practiced. Chinese Prime Minister Zhu Rongji, for instance, said on October 13, 1999 that "China will continue to *enforce* its *effective* family planning policy in the new century in order to create a favorable environment for further development" (italics added). In its *White Paper on Population*, released on December 19, 2000, the People's Republic of China (PRC) avows that it will continue the one-child policy for another fifty years. The *White Paper* actually sets a population target of 1.6 billion people by the year 2050.

Chinese officials, as they have for the past two decades, sought to suggest to the outside world that these targets and quotas will be achieved by "education" and "persuasion," rather than coercion and compulsion: The velvet tongue, rather than the mailed fist. As an example of the effectiveness of "education" and "persuasion," the *White Paper* reported that women were postponing childbirth. While in 1970 they gave birth to their first child at 20.8 years of age, by 1998 they were putting off childbearing until they were almost three years older, age 23.6, to be exact. But this claim is disingenuous. Women are giving birth later in the PRC not because officials have gently whispered in their ears, but because they are strictly forbidden to marry until age 23, and hustled off for an abortion if they become pregnant out of wedlock. Ah Fang would have given birth at 20, had she not been ordered to terminate her pregnancy. As it is, she will be 23 or older when she has her first (and perhaps her only) child.

*   *   *

Powerful images of China's teeming multitudes, dating back to the time of Marco Polo, are etched deeply in Western minds. The wandering Venetian found much to admire in Cathay's ancient greatness, civilization and art, but it was the sheer number of Chinese that left him astounded. Skeptical contemporaries gave him the mocking title "Il Milione" for the frequency with which he used this superlative to describe the populations of China's cities and provinces, the numbers of her civil functionaries, and the seemingly endless ranks of her men under arms.

But Marco Polo was, in this respect, a perfectly reliable witness. The world had never seen a more populous empire than the thirteenth-century Sung Dynasty of his acquaintance. It had a population of some 110 million occupying a continent-sized territory with a standing army of ... a million. It dwarfed contemporaneous Western states, such as the England of Henry II, in every respect. Moreover, it had been in existence, in one dynastic guise or another, for over 1500 years. China's population was already 60 million at the time of Christ and reached ever-greater peaks during later dynasties—80 million in the ninth-century Tang Dynasty, 110 million at the time of Marco Polo's sojourn, 200 million in the sixteenth-century Ming, 425 million in the nineteenth-century Qing. Throughout these long centuries, China's large population was rightly seen as an indispensable element of its national greatness and imperial power, both at home and abroad.

There is another, darker Western perception of China's population, dating back to the Mongol hordes of the non-Chinese Genghis Khan, which sees them "as a faceless, impenetrable, overwhelming mass, ir-resistible once loosed."[8] And a mass, it might be added, that was thought to be feverishly multiplying. If all of the Chinese people were formed up into a column five abreast, went a cocktail riddle popular in the 1920s, how long would it take the entire column to march past a fixed point? "Never!" was taken to be the correct answer. The column would turn out to be endless, because the Chinese would simply breed faster than they marched—or so it was wrongly supposed.[9] The image of China's population as a "yellow peril" was brought vividly to life again in the 1950s, when a sea of Chinese flooded across the Yalu River into Korea, and "human wave" attacks were reported by American troops. The lurid and hyperbolical reporting of China's "overpopulation problem" over the past twenty years arises in part from these same dark fears—and further incites them. In the view of the new Malthusians, China was a boiling pressure cooker of people, who at any time could explode beyond her borders in a human flood of illegal immigration—or conquest.

Supporting China's One-Child Policy

The controllers welcomed China's 1979 foray into population control with a mixture of euphoria and relief. Euphoria that the world's most populous nation was at last getting serious about its numbers. Relief because China would now dam up its seas of people before they could inundate the world. Not that they were content to stand idly by while the Beijing regime put the fix on one-fifth of humanity. No, they would roll up their sleeves and pitch in. They would help the design and implement a program that would turn China, everyone's brutish infant of overpopu-lation, into a poster child of family planning. China would become a model for other countries. Depressing the birthrate in China—important in itself—would in this way help them to further depress birthrates worldwide. It would move the controllers at the United Nations Popula-tion Fund (UNFPA) and elsewhere that much closer to their global goal, as stated by UNFPA Executive Director Nafis Sadik, of "achieving the lowest level of population in the very shortest time."[10]

No one stopped to think about China's abysmal human rights record. No one expressed concern that the Chinese government, in dictating how many children a couple might have, was violating parental rights. No one worried that, in enforcing the one-child policy, the government might resort to coercion, as it had done in past political campaigns. Everything—economic development, democracy and even human rights—would have to await the taming of her numbers.

Acting as if they were afraid that the Beijing regime might change its mind, the controllers hastily began helping to fund it. The largest grant came from the UNFPA, which would quickly become the major player in China; it ponied up a hefty $50 million over the first five years. The International Planned Parenthood Federation (IPPF) signaled its approval with a much smaller, but still significant, grant of $500,000. The money went to its Chinese affiliate that, IPPF reported with paternal pride, "organize[s] ... the family planning group which will formulate the birth plans."[11] The World Bank opened up its coffers as well, and by 1996 had loaned more than $22 billion to China.[12] All this international largesse, as economist Jacqueline Kasun has noted, comes at the expense of unsuspecting taxpayers in industrialized nations.[13]

Having funded the China program, population control advocates were soon chanting its praises, acclaiming its achievements, and even expressing approval of many, if not all, of its methods. The United Nations picked 1983, a year of unusually severe coercion inside of China, to present the first United Nations Population Award to the People's Republic of China. The decision was criticized in many quarters—Theodore W. Schultz, the respected American Nobel laureate economist, immediately resigned in protest from the UN Population Award advisory commission—but the United Nations was undeterred. As a family planning "high tide" ripped through the Chinese countryside, UN officials in solemn ceremony lauded China "for the most outstanding contribution to the awareness of population questions."[14] That same year the International Planned Parenthood Federation (IPPF) welcomed the Chinese Family Planning Association to full membership in the Federation, declaring the goals of the Chinese program *entirely consistent with its own.*[15] Commendations from the World Bank and the Better World Society of Washington, D.C. followed.[16] One wonders what the approximately 15 million young Chinese women who were aborted that year, perhaps 90 percent under coercive circumstances, thought of such accolades.

Talk of exporting the China model had already surfaced. Werner Fornos of the Population Institute, a fringe group closely tied to the UNFPA, declared in 1982 that the Chinese program was one that "the world should copy."[17] The World Bank, in its *Development Report 1984*, insisted that "voluntary" incentives "need be no more objectionable than any other taxes or subsidies," and then went on to describe the Chinese program in laudatory terms.[18]

As the 1980s progressed, the trickle of reports about coercion in China became a flood. Michele Vink wrote in the *Wall Street Journal* of women who were "handcuffed, tied with ropes or placed in pig's baskets" for their forced trips to the abortion clinics.[19] Christopher Wren reported in the pages of *The New York Times* that thousands of Chinese women were being "rounded up and forced to have abortions." He described women "locked in detention cells or hauled before mass rallies and harangued into consenting to abortions." He told of "vigilantes [who] abducted pregnant women on the streets and hauled them off, sometimes handcuffed or trussed, to abortion clinics," and of "aborted babies which were … crying when they were born."[20] Michael Weiskopf of the *Washington Post* in 1985 published a series of articles on the one-child policy which brought home to people in our nation's capital the human cost of the program. Elliott Abrams, then assistant secretary of state for human rights, ensured that the Chinese practice of forced abortions and sterilizations made its way into the State Department's *Country Report on Human Rights Practices*. With the press in the People's Republic of China speaking openly about the "butchering, drowning, and leaving to die of female infants and the maltreating of women who have given birth to girls," little doubt was left in the minds of reasonable people that China's population control program was synonymous with brutality and coercion.[21]

For my part, I published a best-selling book on rural China called *Broken Earth,* appeared on *60 Minutes* and other television shows, and lectured around the country, reporting on the forced abortions and sterilizations that I had witnessed.[22] Many people shared my outrage at these crimes, but I found the reaction of others strangely muted. Some in Congress and in the media, I was disappointed to find, were all too ready to excuse these acts in the name of fighting "overpopulation." As one of the leaders of the National Organization of Women put it to me, "I am personally opposed to forced abortion and sterilization but, after all, China does have a population problem." Others, sounding for all the world like the Chinese Communist Party officials I had interviewed in China, openly argued that, because China was a poor country, its people could not be allowed to have as many children as they wanted. A number actually applauded the Chinese model, and wanted to use it as a blueprint for other countries. "Limiting everyone to one child, even in the U.S., is a good idea," one said to me.

What I had thought was an open-and-shut case—who would defend the forced abortion of a woman eight months pregnant?—had turned out to be an open question, at least in the minds of some. A wild-eyed professor at California State University at San Luis Obispo became angry with me for even suggesting that moral considerations should enter into the equation. "Don't you see that the Chinese government *must* control childbearing under a state plan in order for China to develop!" he shouted in front of the 800 faculty and students who had gathered for my lecture. Lurking behind his utilitarian obtuseness was the misguided belief that the Chinese people in their numbers were the chief obstacle to China's prosperity.

Nothing, however, could match the enthusiasm of the professional population control movement. Their earlier actions—in praising, awarding and funding the program—had turned them into collaborators in the abuses that followed. Having praised and funded the program, they lacked the moral authority to criticize its shortcomings, even in private meetings with Chinese officials. But they really didn't seem to care. As long as China was "doing something" about its "overpopulation problem," they were onboard. Many, like the head of the Population Council, Bernard Berelson, had long wanted to go "beyond family planning" to massive government intervention to force down fertility.[23] Sharon Camp, then with the Population Crisis Committee, admitted that "the Chinese in many areas of China are able to put enormous pressure on a woman who is pregnant out of turn—and her family and her group—to terminate that pregnancy." But then she went on to say, "I am not at all convinced that there is widespread physical coercion in the Chinese program. And yet visiting Sichuan I do have to ask myself *if they have any other choice but to implement a strong program!*"[24] (italics added). The IPPF and its affiliates were more direct, continuing to offer fulsome praise of China's "successful" one-child policy and abstaining from any hint that this success was obtained under duress.[25] China was to be applauded, not condemned, for coming to grips with its population problem.

Parroting Chinese official denials, the controllers dismissed reports of forced abortions as "local aberrations" or, more commonly, refused to acknowledge them at all. Nor were they concerned that the one-child policy ran roughshod over traditional values and human rights. They rarely referred to the family planning "high tides" which periodically gripped the country. They avoided mentioning the "mass mobilizations" in which women are rounded up against their will to have IUDs inserted, undergo abortions, or be sterilized.[26] They turned a blind eye to the severe punishments visited upon women, like Li Aihai, who evaded the mandatory "surgeries," and bore children without government permission. What was important to them was that it was efficient, like Mussolini's trains.

China had taken a page out of the controllers' own playbook. How could they condemn China for actually *doing* what they had long advocated? Of course it was necessary for them to avert their eyes from the resulting carnage. It was too painful to watch. They had never thought through the political implications of what they were advocating or its possible cost in other important human values. They had been fixated by the numbers, like Dr. Richard Cash of the Harvard School of Public Health. After congratulating China's State Family Planning Commission on having "a very strong family planning program for many years," Dr. Cash urged China and its foreign supporters to continue their "very good work" and not allow the Chinese "people to slip back into having larger families."[27] The numbers were the thing. As long as births in China were headed in the right direction—namely, down—what did it matter how it was done?

The more criticism of the one-child policy grew, the more its foreign supporters rallied to its defense with a strange combination of threats and denial. Some warned darkly that other countries, if they could not get their birthrates down by voluntary means, would soon have to adopt compulsory family planning. Some singled out countries, like India, where the Chinese model should be adopted immediately. The denial crowd was led by UNFPA head Nafis Sadik, who made headlines in 1989 when she informed a CBS reporter that "the implementation of the policy [in China] and the acceptance of the policy is *purely voluntary.* There is *no such thing* as, you know, a license to have a birth and so on"[28] (italics added).

It is uncertain whether Sadik actually believed this. Chinese officials are of course at pains to reassure every Western visitor that the one-child policy is "purely voluntary," but every Chinese alive understands that the state has assumed regulatory power over reproduction. The state-run media regularly warns couples that they are not free to have as many children as they would like. The Jilin provincial newspaper in October 1993 reported that, according to the provincial birth control regulations, married couples "cannot *voluntarily* have children unless they obtain a child-bearing license"[29] (italics added).

The China Model

Two years later, in April 1991, Sadik made an equally breathtaking claim, gushing to a Chinese reporter that "China has every reason to feel proud of and pleased with its remarkable achievements made in its family planning policy and control of its population growth over the past 10 years. Now the country could offer its experiences and special experts to help other countries."[30] She added that "UNFPA is going to employ some of [China's family planning experts] to work in other countries and popularize China's experiences in population growth control and family planning."[31] This was no idle threat. When the UNFPA served as the "technical secretary" of Peru's infamous sterilization campaign a few years later, it brought in Chinese experts to, among other things, train the surgical teams in how to tie a woman's tubes assembly-line style.

Exporting the Chinese model in its entirety has proven difficult, since most governments are either unwilling or unable to bring all the child-bearing in their countries under state control. One of the few exceptions is Vietnam, whose political and economic system is almost identical to that of its giant neighbor to the north. Hanoi, with UNFPA assistance, has designed and is carrying out a population control policy that relies on targets, quotas, and coercive measures virtually identical China's to limit every couple to two children. "Communist Party members who have more than two face automatic expulsion and parents are often asked to pay the health and education costs of a third child," reports the BBC. "More serious sanctions include having land confiscated."[32] Such sanctions are serious, indeed. In a peasant society like Vietnam, a family's plot of land is often all that stands between it and starvation. Another consequence of the policy is that Vietnam, like China, has "one of the world's highest rates of abortion."[33] Even the *Population and Development Review*, as a rule no critic of family planning, reports that "women have been forced to use IUDs and have been forced to have abortions."[34]

This familiar litany of abuses has elicited nothing but praise from the UNFPA, which remains unabashedly eager to take credit for the forced reduction in fertility which has resulted. According to one U.N. document, "Although government policy bears the main responsibility for this achievement [Vietnam's falling birthrate], UNFPA's assistance in preparing for and supporting the policy reform provided necessary capacity and support for implementing it."[35] Omar Ertur, UNFPA country representative in Hanoi, gushed that "They [Vietnam's National Committee for Population and Family Planning] have been very successful.... They have achieved a tremendous reduction in a very short period of time."[36] "They" also, of course, performed a tremendous number of forced abortions and forced sterilizations in a very short period of time, but this presumably was not what the UNFPA had in mind when it honored Vietnam's population controllers with its 1999 "United Nations Population Award."[37] The UNFPA has of late taken to running "model county" programs in Vietnam, a dodge which, as in China, serves to insulate the organization from the charge that it is complicit in the widespread human rights abuses which abound in the country as a whole.[38]

Although the Chinese model has proven difficult to export in its entirety, that hasn't deterred the UNFPA and other population control organizations from imposing the program piecemeal on other countries. Governments have been encouraged by the UNFPA and other population control organizations to adopt Chinese-style (1) targets and quotas, (2) bribes and punishments, (3) organizational structures, and (4) promotional propaganda. Where these techniques have been successfully transplanted, they have given rise to systematic coercion, even in countries lacking a high degree of control. All that is required for this to happen, as John Aird has observed, is "a politically inert, uneducated, impoverished population and an established pattern of bureaucratic authoritarianism."[39] Quite a few countries in the developing world fit this description.

National Targets: China, in its effort to "control reproduction under a state plan," has been setting targets since the 1970s for all kinds of population indices. There is a target for total population, a target for the birthrate, and a target for actual numbers of babies born. There are targets for the population increase rate and for how much the population can increase in absolute numbers in a given year. There are even targets for how many third births can be allowed (few to none), and for the numbers of women who must be sterilized and contracepted. And of course the "one-couple, one-child" policy is itself a target for family size.[40]

Following China's lead, the UNFPA and other international agencies always insist that governments, at a minimum, set 10- or 15-year targets for family size and total population. Targets for such things as "number and percentage of contraceptive acceptors," or "numbers and percentage of women sterilized," are also pushed. Governments reluctant to set targets have been told by the World Bank and USAID that they will not receive grants and loans until they do.[41] Targets and quotas, it should be noted, were banned by the 1994 Cairo population conference on the grounds that they *always* lead to abuses, but this prohibition has been largely ignored by officials who claim that the numbers are only used for "planning purposes."

Bribes and Punishments for Officials: To keep its millions of population control cadres and officials on task and on target, China developed what it calls the "job responsibility system." Each year, officials at each level of government pledge in writing to their superiors that they will meet their assigned birth control targets and quotas. Those who do so receive public commendations and cash awards, and are slotted for advancement. Those who fail are publicly reprimanded and fined, and may even be demoted. Repeated failure ends in complete disgrace: Loss of Party membership and dismissal from one's post. Meeting targets is thus a career-maker—or breaker. No one should be surprised when Chinese officials pressure a pregnant woman into aborting an "over-quota" child, or lock up a mother of two until she "agrees" to sterilization. China's leaders certainly aren't: They designed the "job responsibility system" to ensure precisely this kind of outcome.[42]

Promoting the Chinese approach, international aid agencies such as the World Bank and the USAID often make continued assistance to developing countries contingent on their attainment of family planning targets.[43] National authorities, anxious over future funding prospects, then bear down on local officials, suggesting that assigned targets are to be attained by whatever means necessary, as happened in India. This approach has led Indian officials to compel submission to sterilization by withholding food rations, confiscating salaries, issuing strongly worded threats, and even resorting to the out-and-out use of physical force.[44]

The Chinese practice of giving local administrators public commendations and awards for their achievements has also led to abuses in places like in Bangladesh, the Philippines, Indonesia, and Vietnam. Even national goals that have been set (with foreign encouragement) "for planning purposes only" have encouraged compulsory measures when local officials are judged on how well they meet them.[45] Regional leaders in Indonesia may have imagined that they were setting targets for numbers of contraceptive acceptors in their areas for "planning purposes only," but when local officials were then held responsible for achieving them, massive abuses ensued.[46]

Bribes and Punishments for Families: Heavy pressure is brought to bear directly on families by a combination of bribes, threats, and punishments. Those who go along with the one-child policy are promised that their children will have preferential access to inoculations, education, and employment. Those who break the rules are not only denied such benefits, which adversely affects the welfare of their children, but are additionally threatened with extraordinarily heavy fines. According to regulations adopted in 1991 in Beijing municipality, the penalties for having a second child range from 5,000 to 50,000 yuan, and for having a third 20,000 to 100,000 yuan.[47] Considering that the average rural family earns less than 1,000 yuan a year, fines of such magnitude seem spectacularly out of proportion, until one realizes that their true purpose is to *deter* couples from continuing out-of-plan pregnancies and *submit* to abortions. As incomes have risen in China, so have the fines escalated as well, as recent reports indicate.[48] The fines are deliberately kept so high as to be virtually unpayable for many.

Chinese-style threats and fines have been adopted in Indonesia, for example, where in the 1980s Balinese Hindus who refused to use birth control were threatened with expulsion from their villages.[49] Even incentives can have the force of compulsion if they relate to vital necessities, as happened in Peru under the infamous sterilization campaign of dictator Alberto Fujimori.[50] Poor, hungry women were told that to qualify for free food, or to receive needed medical care, they must submit to sterilization. Similar abuses occurred in Bangladesh in recent years, where the Chinese model has explicitly held up as one to be emulated.[51]

Group Pressure Tactics: To further discourage couples from having children outside the plan, the Chinese government deliberately generates "peer pressure" against potential rule-breakers by means of group rewards and punishments. Heilongjiang province, for example, bowed to peasant desires for sons (and rising rates of female infanticide) by announcing in 1988 that it was partially relaxing the one-child policy in the villages, but *only* if everyone cooperated. Rural couples whose first child was a boy would still have to stop at one. Couples whose first child was a girl would get a second chance at a male heir, but on one condition: There could be absolutely no unauthorized births in their village.[52] Neighboring Liaoning province adopted a variant of the same policy, requiring that a village have no unauthorized births and all of its married women on birth control before it could qualify for second births. If even one illegal baby was born, all second births would be forbidden that year. The policy was said to have "strengthened group awareness" among Liaoning's peasants.[53] No doubt it did, for it forced families expecting legal second children to be constantly alert for women pregnant outside the plan. For if even a single slacker gave birth, then they would all have to have abortions. It is hard to imagine the intense hostility, even hysteria, that this policy would generate in a small, tightly knit rural community towards anyone who threatened to break the rules. No wonder the then-head of China's State Family Planning Council, Ms. Peng Peiyun, publicly praised this pressure tactic as a way of "tightening up" family planning work, recommending that it be implemented throughout the country.[54]

Similar tactics are used in the cities, where the one-child policy continues to be strictly enforced. Workers in a given factory or department are denied bonuses, awards, expansion plans, and other benefits if even one of their number has an unauthorized child. Women who get pregnant outside the plan are immediately ostracized by their fellow workers and put under tremendous pressure to abort.[55] As a result, as China demographer John Aird has observed, in urban China compliance with the one-child rule is almost total.[56]

These Chinese group pressure tactics have been put to very effective use elsewhere. In India, for example, some villages have been denied access to irrigation water at subsidized prices until they came up with the required number of sterilizations.[57] A new village well was promised to another village if "100 percent of eligible couples" would undergo sterilization; after the last vasectomy was performed, the well was dug.[58] Elsewhere on the subcontinent cash payments have been offered to all families in a village if 75 percent of the men would submit to vasectomy.[59]

Long-Term Contraception/Sterilization: From the beginning of the one-child policy, the Chinese authorities have followed a single, inflexible rule: Sterilize or implant an IUD in a woman after the birth of her first child; sterilize her after the birth of her second. The advantage for China's family planning officials of such methods is obvious: They no longer have to maintain constant surveillance over all women of childbearing age to make sure that they are not trying to start an unauthorized pregnancy or concealing one. In China the government-run clinics will remove an IUD on request only if it is causing severe side-effects, and then only if the woman agrees to use another birth control method, preferably a long-term implant like Norplant or an injectable like Depo-Provera. For a woman to remove her own IUD is defined as a criminal act. Those who wish to do so must rely on illegal operations that often involve dangerous methods and unsanitary conditions. Back-alley IUD removals, one might call them.

This component of the Chinese program has proven so successful in China that it is becoming a standard feature of family planning programs worldwide. This shift from contraceptives, such as birth control pills and condoms, that are controlled by the user, to more permanent measures—intrauterine devices, sterilization, and long-term implants and injectables—more easily imposed on the user, has been underway for two decades now. The result has been marked decrease in the freedom of women and couples in the developing world to decide for themselves the number and spacing of their children.

Women pressured into adopting such measures may change their minds later, but there is often little they can do about it, especially if the family planning clinics refuse to reverse the sterilization or remove the IUD, or charge exorbitant fees for doing so. In Bangladesh and Haiti women suffering from acute side-effects from Norplant implants accepted as part of an "experimental" program were reportedly told the device could not be removed.[60] Too poor to seek alternate medical care, they had no choice but to endure their debilitating chemical sterilization until the five-year implant had run its course.

Promotional Propaganda: China's state-controlled media has bombarded the Chinese for a quarter century with anti-people propaganda, to the point where many otherwise educated Chinese believe the Party when it claims that China's principal problem is too many people (rather than, say, absence of democratic rule, massive official corruption, lack of the rule of law, insecure property rights, etc.). Dissenting voices are not tolerated. In January 1994 two Chinese newspapers were reportedly punished for printing articles favoring second births and "opposing family planning."[61] Chinese censorship of this and related sensitive issues has actually tightened in recent years.

The Chinese are constantly told that the country's demographic situation is "grim," that economic progress is imperiled, and that even the food supply is in grave danger because of excessive population growth.[62] Not only does the government propaganda machine constantly churn out claims that population control is vital to China's continued economic development in the long run, it insists that even failing to meet *current* targets will mean social and economic ruin for the whole country. Thus does the propaganda help to justify coercion. Even if Chinese couples were not subject to compulsion where the bearing of children was concerned, the constant barrage of propaganda ("persuasion," in Chinese Communist parlance) would forge anti-natal fetters on their minds.

One-sided propaganda does not require a controlled press. In much of the world, all it requires is money. Even in democratic countries, including the United States, media discussion of population problems is dominated by the deep pockets of the anti-people movement. Literally tens of millions of dollars are spent each year by the movement to convince the world's press—and through them the world's people—of the gravity of the "population crisis." The UNFPA alone devotes 10 percent of its quarter-billon dollar budget, or approximately $25 million, to conjuring up specters of calamity and catastrophe. This headline-grab-

bing effort has paid off, as the U.S. media has repeatedly run with the
UNFPA bad news bears:

- "The United Nations yesterday asked people everywhere to pause July
  11 [1987] and contemplate the bleak future of Baby 5 Billion, the child
  whose birth will push the Earth's population over the 5 billion mark."
- "Nutrition levels are dropping and infant mortality may once again be
  on the rise." [1987] [Not true, as we will see in Chap. 5]
- "'The world's population is growing by three people every second. And
  unless this is curbed, most gains so far achieved and improving quality
  of life will be swept away,' the U.N. Population Fund said today." [Not
  true, as we will see in Chap. 5]
- "U.N. report warns of population 'catastrophes'."
- "U.N. says 4 billion will be living in hunger by the year 2050." [2001]
  [This is many times higher than the Food and Agriculture Organization
  (FAO) would claim or project.][63]

In the United States and other developed countries, the purpose of
such propaganda is to generate popular and political support, and hence
funding, for more population control programs. Even when these efforts
fail, as when the Bush administration announced in 2002 that it would
no longer fund the UNFPA, the major media accepted that organization's
sob story that it was an innocent victim of US abortion politics. The
incontrovertible fact that it was deeply involved in real abuses in China
was largely ignored.

In the developing world, as in China, such propaganda has a different
purpose: It is designed to directly affect couples' reproductive behavior
by predisposing them not to have additional children, and thus to help
the government meet national targets. As John Aird has noted, "[Such]
one-sided propaganda ... does not meet international standards for "freedom of information" and would not even if the contraceptive decisions
of individual ... couples were entirely voluntary."[64]

The UNFPA in China Today

The controllers' symbiotic relationship with Chinese-style family
planning continues. Thoraya Ahmed Obaid, newly-appointed executive director of the UNFPA, told a PRC journalist in January 2002 that
"China, having adopted practical measures in accordance with her current
situation, has scored remarkable achievements in population control. In
recent years, the UNFPA and China have carried out a series of favorable and positive cooperation with more than 100 cooperative items of
assistance established in the country."[65]

The most curious development occurred in 1998, when the UNFPA announced that it had been invited by the Chinese government to set up "model family planning programs" in 32 of China's counties, or county-level municipalities. Nafis Sadik, then-director of UNFPA, let it be known that the Chinese government had agreed to suspend the one-child policy during the next four years. In her words, "In the project counties couples will be allowed to have as many children as they want, whenever they want, without requiring birth permits or being subject to quotas."[66] In a later letter to the U.S. Congress about the new program, Sadik was even more specific. Within the UNFPA's 32 model counties, she said,

(1) reproductive health programs are fully voluntary;
(2) women are free to voluntary select the timing and spacing of their pregnancies;
(3) targets and quotas have been lifted;
(4) abortion is not promoted as a method of family planning; and,
(5) coercion does not exist.

Although her claim to have set up a "no-coercion zone" in China was later to be proved false by Population Research Institute investigators, it was by itself a remarkable, if backhanded, admission of the real state of affairs in China. For up to that point it had been the steadfast position of the Chinese government—and had been maintained by the UNFPA itself—that the one-child policy neither relied upon birth quotas and targets, nor required parents to obtain a birth permit prior to having a child. Also left unanswered was the question of why the Chinese government would abandon controls that had successfully driven down the birthrate for two decades? "The Government of China is keen to move away from its *administrative approach* to family planning to an integrated, client-centered reproductive health approach," the UNFPA sought to explain[67] (italics added). But the Chinese government did not have to be sold by the UNFPA or anyone else on the idea of replacing direct coercion with the more subtle forms of threats, bribes and propaganda that the controllers commonly employ to stop Third World families from having children. Senior Chinese family planning officials have always urged their juniors to employ such techniques to meet their quotas, reserving forced abortions and forced sterilizations for the truly recalcitrant.

We at PRI thought UNFPA's claims to have de-fanged China's family planning program extravagant. So in September 2001 we organized a team of investigators, led by paralegal Josephine Guy, to go undercover into a UNFPA "model county." After four days in Sihui County,

Guangdong province, Ms. Guy reported back that people had flocked to tell her about the abuse that they and their families has suffered as a result of still-coercive family planning policies. As she was later to testify before the International Relations Committee of the U.S. House of Representatives:

> We were told of efforts by many women to hide their pregnancies from government officials, in an attempt to escape forced abortion, so they could give birth to a child they desired. We were told of women having to hide their children, to escape retribution from officials for not having an abortion. We were told of the many so-called "black" children in the region who are born out of accord with local birth regulations. We were told of the punishments inflicted on those who wish to freely determine for themselves the timing and spacing of pregnancy.
>
> We were told of the non-voluntary use of IUDs and mandatory examinations so that officials can ensure that women have not removed IUDs in violation of policy, and the strict punishments which result from non-compliance with this coercive and inhumane policy.
>
> … The interviews we conducted were recorded in notebooks, on audio and video-tape, and additional photographic evidence was obtained. The abuses we documented during this investigation are recent, ongoing, rampant, and unrelenting. And they exist in a county where the United Nations Population Fund claims that women are free to determine the timing and spacing of pregnancy.
>
> At a location not far from [the UNFPA office], a woman testified that she became pregnant despite an earlier attempt by family planning officials to forcibly sterilize her. That attempt failed. She became pregnant, and was forcibly sterilized a second time by family planning doctors and officials. Had she refused, she told us on videotape, then family planning crews would have torn her house down.[68]

Everyone Ms. Guy spoke with had a story to tell—a sister who had been sterilized, a friend who had been forcibly aborted. People spoke of women who had gone underground to save their babies, and of family members arrested and homes destroyed in an effort to force them out of hiding. Young women told of how they had been ordered in for abortions, because they had conceived children before the legal age of marriage.[69] There is no voluntarism in Sihui, she concluded, despite UNFPA claims to the contrary.

On her last day in Sihui, Ms. Guy and her team set out to locate the office from which the UNFPA directs its "model family planning program." To her surprise, she was directed to the Sihui County family planning office, where she found the single UNFPA representative sitting in the midst of government family planners. The significance of this arrangement was immediately apparent: The Chinese government and the UNFPA were working hand-in-glove to enforce the one-child policy.

Thoraya Obaid ducked an invitation to testify at this same congressional hearing, lamely responding in a letter that UNFPA's China program is completely "voluntary" and does not "condone coercion." In an argument echoed by many of her camp followers, she suggested that UNFPA is a force for the good in China. In actuality, there is reason to believe that UNFPA's "model county" program may be making things worse, not better. Why? Because being designated a "model" anything in China brings with it not only increased benefits—in Sihui's case a grant from the UNFPA—but also increased scrutiny from the central government. Local officials in Sihui are undoubtedly under considerable pressure from on high to prove that the county is indeed a "model" in family planning. And how would they do so? Undoubtedly by obeying the rules to the letter, that is to say, by contracepting all women with one child, sterilizing all women with two, and aborting all women pregnant outside the plan. As one family planning victim told Ms. Guy, "Family planning policies involving coercion and force are stricter today than ever before."[70]

The Population Research Institute's investigation of China prompted the Bush administration to undertake one of its own, sending a three-member assessment team to the People's Republic of China in May 2002. The "official" nature of the visit constituted a tremendous handicap for the team, for it ensured that the Chinese state was able to monitor their comings and goings, and ensure that they did not come into direct contact with cases of coercion. Nonetheless, visiting one UNFPA "model county" the team discovered that women who have more than one child are hit with a crippling fine equivalent to two to three years' income. These "social compensation fees" are deliberately set high, the team concluded, in order to force mothers to have abortions.

The team also noted that UNFPA supplies computers and medical equipment to family planning offices engaged in coercive practices. "In the context of the PRC," the Bush administration concluded in a later review, "supplying equipment to the very agencies that employ coercive practices amounts to support or participation in the management of the program." Computers allow Chinese family planning officers "to establish a database record of all women of child-bearing age in an area and to trigger the issuance of 'birth-not-allowed' notices." UNFPA also helps to "propagate the government's distinction between legal births and out-of-plan births … [and] takes credit for posted documents that note that it is forbidden 'to prevent legal births'—thus bearing partial responsibility for disseminating the message that it is not forbidden for government employees to prevent out-of-plan births."[71]

On 21 July 2002 Secretary of State Colin Powell dropped the ax: "UNFPA's support of, and involvement in, China's population-planning activities allows the Chinese government to implement more effectively its program of coercive abortion. Therefore, it is not permissible to continue funding UNFPA at this time."[72] The $34 million appropriated by Congress for FY 2002, he went on, will go instead to Child Survival and Health programs. Powell called on the UNFPA to stop "support[ing] a program of coercive abortion," but the population control agency appears determined to mire itself even more deeply in the muck of China's program. The agency reacted to the cut-off in US funding by *expanding* its program in China from 32 to 42 counties. The new, multi-million dollar deal with China carried through 2007 and will probably be extended.

From 2003 on, the budget submitted by President Bush to Congress each year included $25 million for the UNFPA. This sum was intended to serve as an inducement to the UN agency to either withdraw from China, or to reform its program there. The UNFPA chose to do neither, and each year the State Department invoked the Kemp-Kasten Amendment to block the disbursement of these funds. This money, totaling $157 million by 2007, has been redirected to other purposes.[73]

The China Model

The UNFPA's support for China's one-child policy began in 1979, the year I first arrived in China. But our reactions to the unfolding campaign could not have been more different. It took me about six months to conclude that the forced abortions and forced sterilizations I was witnessing on the local level in Guangdong were not provincial aberrations, but part of a centrally inspired campaign of *coercion by design*. A quarter century later, the UNFPA not only refuses to pass judgment on the coercive aspects of China's program, it *denies* this fundamental, observable fact about life and death in China. Why? Even more importantly, why has it continued to praise, fund, and promote a coercive program in China *despite* overwhelming evidence of its compulsory character?

China's one-child policy constitutes a kind of acid test of the character of the population control movement, for it pits their beliefs against their principles. Here was a country they believed was desperately overcrowded and on the brink of disaster (it wasn't and isn't, as we shall see). Here was a country that, in solving its own "population problem," would simultaneously relieve "population pressure" throughout the globe—or so they believed. The problem was that China's forced-pace measures violated certain fundamental principles that the movement claimed to hold dear, namely, voluntarism and human rights, specifically the right of couples to freely determine the number and spacing of their children.

The population control movement has failed this test, sacrificing their principles (and, it must be said, their humanity) on the altar of their beliefs. They fell prey to the fallacy that China must reduce its numbers at all costs, even if fundamental human rights are systematically, even brutally, violated along the way. For if they won't condemn the forced abortion of women who are nine months pregnant, then there is no birth control measure they will not praise. If they will not reject the forced sterilization of a woman who desires more children, then there is no form of involuntary contraception they will not embrace. If they do not reject China's program as a great evil, then there is no population control program, however horrific, that they will not accept as good as long as the birthrate is falling. In the end, only the numbers count.

China is often portrayed in the media as an extreme case of population control, but what does that say about the UNFPA, the IPPF, and other international organizations that have stood shoulder-to-shoulder with Beijing all these years? What you see in China—the generous foreign funding and repeated endorsements from leading elements of the population control establishment, the promotion of China's program as a model for other "overpopulation" countries—suggests that, despite occasional twinges of discomfort occasioned by the more draconian manifestations of China's policy, there is essentially no difference between the Chinese state and its control-minded friends on population matters. They are joined at the hip.

The population controllers continued sponsorship of the "China model" also sends an unmistakable, if unspoken, signal to Third World governments. What else are they to conclude from this shameless embrace of China than:

- Moderation in pursuit of family planning is no virtue. The urgency of world population problems, in the view of international agencies, demands targets and forced-pace measures to reach them.
- Extremism in pursuit of population targets is no vice. Coercion will be viewed with tolerance, if not approval, by international agencies providing development assistance.
- International aid for family planning and other forms of development assistance will never be called into question for being too severe, *regardless of the level of human rights abuses*. (And its corollary: Funding *will* be in jeopardy if programs are seen as either too lax or as ineffective in reducing the birthrate.)

This message—that anything goes in the name of population control—is underscored each time the controllers extol China's one-child policy, as Thoraya Obaid did upon taking office in January 2001. Obaid "praised that (sic) over the past 20 years, China has seen notable achievements made in *population control* by implementing the family planning policy. It has thereupon played an active role in *curbing the population growth* across the world"[74] (italics added).

The only thing that really matters to the controllers, you see, is getting the birthrate down.

"Just do it," as Deng Xiaoping said.

And the controllers said, "Amen."

Notes

1. *Population and Development Review*, 1985, 119.
2. Josephine Guy, "Story of a Beautiful Baby Boy," *PRI Review* 11(4) (September-October 2001): 8-9.
3. Quoted in Josephine Guy, "Women and Child Abuse in China," *PRI Review* 11(4) (September-October 2001): 3.
4. The quote comes from Vice Premier Chen Muhua, who said in 1979 that "China is a socialist country. We should be able to control reproduction the same way that we control production under a state plan." See my *Broken Earth: The Rural Chinese* (New York: Free Press, 1983).
5. I have made periodic trips into China to assess family planning policies, have commissioned others to undertake such investigations, and have closely followed both official Chinese pronouncements and reports appearing in the specialized literature and the population press.
6. See the testimony of Gao Xiaoduan who, as a senior population control official in Fujian province, had systematically committed these and other abuses of human rights with the encouragement and support of her superiors. Following her escape from China, Mrs. Gao was invited by Cong. Christopher Smith (R-NJ) to testify before the Subcommittee on International Operations and Human Rights of the International Relations Committee. Gao Xiaoduan, "Forced Abortion and Sterilization in China: The View from the Inside," Subcommittee on International Operations and Human Rights, 10 June 1998 Human Rights in China: Improving or Deteriorating Conditions, Hearing before the Subcommittee on Africa, Global Human Rights and International Operations of the Committee on International Relations House of Representatives, http://commdocs.house.gov/committees/intl-rel/hfa27067.000/hfa27067_0.HTM#132. Also see my book, *A Mother's Ordeal: One Woman's Fight Against China's One-Child Policy* (New York: Harcourt Brace, 1993), for similar abuses.
7. John Aird, *Slaughter of the Innocents* (Washington, D.C.: AEI Press, 1990), 92.
8. Harold R. Isaacs, *Scratches on Our Minds: American Images of China and India* (New York: John Day, 1958), 63-64. Also quoted in my *China Misperceived: American Illusions and Chinese Reality* (New York: Basic Books, 1990), 18-19.
9. Given that China's population was roughly 500 million at the time, and assuming that the column marched at 3 miles an hour, it would take approximately 762 days, or a little more than two years for the entire column to pass under the arch.

10. The quote is from Nafis Sadik, the former executive director of the UNFPA, as quoted in Nicholas Eberstadt, "UNFPA: A Runaway Agency," *PRI Review* 12(3) (May-June 2002): 8.

11. International Planned Parenthood Federation, IPPF in Action (London: Typographic Press, 1982), 20. Quoted in Jacqueline Kasun, *The War Against Population,* Revised Edition (San Francisco: Ignatius, 1988), 122.

12. Bryan T. Johnson, "The World Bank and Economic Growth: 50 Years of Failure." (Washington, D.C: The Heritage Foundation, May 16, 1996), based on World Bank figures. Quoted in Kasun, *The War Against Population*, 122.

13. Kasun, *The War Against Population*, 122.

14. The respected American Nobel Laureate Economist, Theodore W. Schultz, resigned in protest from the U.N. Population Award advisory commission over the decision to reward China for coercion.

15. "Guojia jihua shengyu lianhehui Wu Kunhuang he Aluweihaier zhuren shuo: renmin xuanze Zhongguo de jihua shengyu shi renmin zijide xuanze" ("President Ng Khoon-Fong and Director Aluvihare of the International Planned Parenthood Federation say that China's family planning program is the people's own choice"), *Jiankang bao (Health Gazette)*, Beijing, 18 April 1983, 1.; and "Family planning measures hopeful," *China Daily* (Beijing), 4 May 1983, 3. Cited in John Aird, "The China Model," *PRI Review* 4(4) (July-August 1994): 1.

16. Kasun, *The War Against Population*, 122.

17. "China Daily wins global media award," *China Daily* (Beijing), 16 March 1982, 3. Cited in John Aird, "The China Model," 1.

18. The World Bank, *World Development Report 1984*, 160. Quoted in Jacqueline Kasun, *The War Against Population*, 124.

19. Michele Vink, "Abortion and Birth Control in Canton, China," *Wall Street Journal*, 30 November 1981.

20. Christopher Wren, "Chinese Region Showing Resistance to National Goals for Birth Control", *The New York Times*, 16 May 1982.

21. See my "Why are Baby Girls Being Killed in China?" *Wall Street Journal*, 30 November 1981.

22. See, inter alia, my *Broken Earth: The Rural Chinese* (New York: The Free Press, 1983), esp. Chapter 8; Michael Weiskopf, "One Couple, One Child," *Washington Post,* 7-10 January 1985.

23. Berelson, who headed the Population Council, from 1968 to 1974, thought that the population crisis so severe that "forced-pace measures" were necessary. In his article, "Beyond Family Planning," he proposed that massive government intervention was the only answer. See *PRI Review* 4(5) (September-October, 1994): 11.

24. Sharon Camp, *The Diane Rehm Show*, WAMU, 13 December 1991. See also "Population Crisis Committee OK's Coercion," *PRI Review* 2(2) (March/April 1992): 10.

25. The IPPF affiliate is the Japanese Organization for International Cooperation in Family Planning (JOICFP), which publishes *JOICFP News*, August 2000, September 2000.

26. John Aird, "The China Model," *PRI Review* 4:4 (July-August 1994): 1.

27. See "A Peoples' Project in China," *JOICFP News* (234) (December 1994): 6, as quoted in the *PRI Review* 4(2) (March-April 1994): 7.

28. Quoted in Christopher Smith, "Judging a Civilization," *PRI Review* 11(4) (September-October 2001): 8.

29. "Several regulations of Jilin province for the administration and management of family planning," *Jilin Ribao*, Changchun, 29 October 1993, Joint Publications

Research Service, no. 94010, 10 February 1994, pp. 19-20. Cited in John Aird, "The China Model," 3.

30. XINHUA-English, Beijing, 11 April 1991, Foreign Broadcast Information Service (FBIS), *Daily Report: China,* no. 91-071, 12 April 1991, 8-9; See also John Aird, "The China Model," 1.

31. Although Sadik did not know it at the time, the same month that she endorsed the Chinese model, Party leaders had ordered a new crackdown on out-of-plan births. Family planning officials throughout the country resorted to more direct forms of coercion, and the Chinese birthrate plummeted to unprecedented low levels. News of the crackdown finally broke in April 1993, embarrassing the UNFPA and other foreign supporters of China's "voluntary" program. Sadik, eager for the United States to resume funding her organization, aired the possibility of withdrawing from China. When the newly installed Clinton administration proved willing to resume US funding of the UNFPA in spite of its involvement in China's coercive program, all talk of withdrawal was dropped. See Nicholas D. Kristof, "A U.N. agency may leave China over coercive birth control," *The New York Times*, 15 May 1993, 1.

32. Owen Bennett-Jones, "Vietnam's Two-Child Policy," BBC, 8 November 2000. Also quoted in Doug Sylva, "The United Nations Population Fund: Assault on the World's People," Catholic Family and Human Rights Institute, 2002, 50-51.

33. "Vietnam Plans Law to Ban Tests on Sex of Fetus," *Reuters*, November 16, 2001. Also quoted in Doug Sylva, "The UNFPA," 51.

34. Daniel Goodkind, "Vietnam's New Fertility Policy," *Population and Development Review* 15(1), March, 1989. Also quoted in Doug Sylva, "The UNFPA."

35. "Capacity Building for Eradicating Poverty, an Impact Evaluation of U.N. System Activities in Vietnam 1985-1997" Also quoted in Doug Sylva, "The UNFPA."

36. Bennett-Jones, "Vietnam's Two-Child Policy." BBC, November 8, 2000. Also quoted in Doug Sylva, "The UNFPA."

37. UNFPA pamphlet, "Vietnam: Key Issues in Population and Development," Hanoi, 1999. Also quoted in Doug Sylva, "The UNFPA."

38. "UNFPA Supports Coercion in Vietnam," PRI Weekly Briefing, 1 February 2002.

39. John Aird, "The China Model," 2.

40. Ibid.

41. See, for example, Fred T. Sai and Lauren A. Chester, "The Role of the World Bank in Shaping Third World Population Policy", in Godfrey Roberts, ed., *Population Policy: Contemporary Issues* (New York: Praeger, 1990). Also see Betsy Hartmann, "Population Control as Foreign Policy," *Covert Action* 39 (Winter 1991-92): 28.

42. For example, according to Article 4 of the *Tianjin Municipality Regulations of Planned Birth*, which were promulgated on 15 April 1994, this major city in North China holds the heads of work units "duty-bound, authorized, and accountable" for meeting birth quotas set by their superiors. Xinnanliuxing Village of Dongpuhwa Township in Wuqing County, Tianjin, which has a population of 500, is allowed a quota of 5 children every two years. As Harry Wu comments, "If [officials] fail to [meet their quotas], they will lose their promotions and risk dismissal or punishment. This is the principal reason why Communist cadres at all levels resort to desperate, barbaric practices of forcing abortion and sterilization, and killing infants. Such a practice relates directly to the security of their jobs." See Harry Wu, "China's population policy," *PRI Review* 11:4 (September-October 2001): 7.

43. As discussed in Chapter Three, this contingency is written into "The U.S Foreign Assistance Act of 1961." Also see Betsy Hartmann, "Population Control as Foreign

Policy," *Covert Action* 39 (Winter 1991-92): 28.
44. John Aird, "The China Model," 2.
45. Donald P. Warwick, *Bitter Pills: Population Policies and Their Implementation in Eight Developing Countries* (Cambridge: Cambridge University Press, 1982), 203-204; Margot Cohen, "Success brings new problems," *Far Eastern Economic Review*, (Hong Kong, 18 April 1991): 48-49; Wardah Hafidz, Adrina Taslim, and Sita Aripurnami, "Family planning in Indonesia: the case for policy reorientation," *Inside Indonesia*, March 1992, 19-22; and Judith Banister, "Vietnam's evolving population policies," *International Conference on Population, New Delhi, September 1989,* (Liege: International Union for the Scientific Study of Population, 1989), 156-60.
46. Donald P. Warwick, "The Indonesian Family Planning Program: Government Influence and Client Choice," *Population and Development Review* 12:3 (September 1986): 453-490.
47. Cited in Tao-tai Hsia and Constance A. Johnson, "Recent legal developments in China's planned births campaign" (unpublished memorandum), 9 July 1991, 2. Beijing municipality includes extensive rural areas and populations. Quoted in John Aird, "The China Model," 3.
48. The Kaisernet reported on June 1, 2007, that fines had been increased in parts of Guangxi. See "Guangxi Province Residents Protest China's One-Child Policy, Call for Refunds of Fines." http://www.kaisernetwork.org/daily_reports/rep_index.cfm?DR_ID=45278. Accessed June 3, 2007. Increases are periodically reported in the foreign press, e.g., Damien McElroy, "China's One-Child Policy Fine Rises," *The London Telegraph*, 30 July 2002.
49. Donald P. Warwick, "The Ethics of Population Control," in Godfrey Roberts, ed., *Population Policy: Contemporary Issues.* (New York: Praeger, 1990), 26.
50. See Chapter 5.
51. In December 1991 the president of Bangladesh, welcoming a family planning delegation from China headed by Peng Peiyun, the Minister of China's State Family Planning commission, praised China's success in population control and expressed the hope that Bangladesh and China could learn from each other's experiences. XINHUA-English, Beijing, 9 December 1991, FBIS, no 910237, 10 December 1991, 20.
52. Haerbin radio, Heilongjiang Provincial Service, 20 April 1988, FBIS, No 88-82, 28 April 1988; Meng Fang and Chen Fenglan, "Heilongjiang sheng kaizhan cang wu jihua wai shengyu cun houdong qude chengxiao" (Heilongjiang Province carries out activities to create villages with no unplanned births and obtains results,") *Zhongguo renkou bao (ZGRKB)* (China Population News), Beijing, 7 October 1988, 2. Quoted in John Aird, "The China Model," 3.
53. Yin Su and Li Zheng, "Liaoning Kaizhan cangjian 'Jihua shengyu hege cun' quanmian quanche jihua shengyu xianxing zhengce" ("Liaoning carries out activities for establishing 'qualified family planning villages' " and "Implements the current family planning policy fully"), *ZGRKB*, 30 September 1988, 1. Quoted in John Aird, "The China Model," 3.
54. Peng Peiyun, "Guanyu 1989-nian de gongzuo" ("On the work in 1989"), *ZGRKB*, 24 February 1989, 1. Quoted in John Aird, "The China Model," 3.
55. For example, see the policy as described in a letter from a Chinese factory manager to a Chinese employee studying in the United States who had an unauthorized pregnancy that I quote in my article, "The long arm of 'one-child' China," *The Washington Post,* 10 April 1988, B4. See also my *A Mother's Ordeal: One Woman's Fight Against China's One-Child Policy* (New York: Harcourt Brace, 1993).

56. John Aird, "The China Model," 3.
57. Donald Warwick, 197-98.
58. Robert M. Veatch, "Governmental Population Incentives: Ethical Issues at Stake", *Studies in Family Planning* 8(4) (April 1977):100-108, quoted in Jacqueline Kasun, *The War Against Population: The Ideology and Economics of World Population Control*, revised edition. (San Francisco: Ignatius Press, 1999), 111.
59. Ibid.
60. UBINIG, "The price of Norplant is TK.2000! You cannot remove it" *Issues in Reproductive and Genetic Engineering* 4:1 (1991):46.
61. "Propaganda department tightens control on press," *Ming bao*, Hong Kong, 15 January 1994, FBIS, no. 94-011 (18 January 1994): 17.
62. These arguments are still being advanced despite the continuing growth of the Chinese economy in the high, single digits. China's grain production is reported to have increased by 50 percent between 1979 and 1993 while the population grew by less than 22 percent. The grain figures are given in XINHUA-English, Beijing, 16 September 1993, FBIS, no. 94-027, p. 37.
63. The headlines come from Nicholas Eberstadt, "UNFPA: A Runaway Agency," *PRI Review* 12(3)(May/June 2002): 1.
64. John Aird, "The China Model," 4.
65. *Peoples Daily*, March 2001, quoted in Christopher Smith, "Judging a Civilization," *PRI Review* 11(4) (September/October 2001): 8.
66. Letter from Nafis Sadik to Mr. Bill Richardson dated 7 January 1998 and quoted in "Aiding a Holocaust: New UNFPA Program Designed to Tidy Up One-child Horror," *PRI Review* 7(2) (March/April 1998):14. Of course, since the Founding Charter of the UNFPA says that "couples have the right to decide the number and spacing of their children," and given that China has from the inception of the one-child policy denied that right, the only honorable course of action for the UNFPA is to withdraw from China—but that it refuses to do.
67. Kirsten Trone, the UNFPA program director for China, quoted in "Aiding a Holocaust: New UNFPA Program Designed to Tidy Up One-child Horror," 14.
68. Josephine Guy, "Women and Child Abuse in China," Testimony before the Committee on International Relations of the U.S. House of Representatives, 17 October 2001. See also *PRI Review* 11(4) (September-October 2001):3. PRI also published a comprehensive investigative report entitled "UNFPA, China and Coercive Family Planning" (Front Royal, VA: Population Research Institute, 21 December 2001).
69. See the stories of Li Aihai and Ah Fang with which this chapter begins.
70. Josephine Guy, "Women and Child Abuse in China." See also *PRI Review* 11(4) (September-October 2001): 3.
71. "Analysis of Determination that Kemp-Kasten Amendment Precludes further Funding to UNFPA under Pub. Law 107-115," attachment to letter from Secretary Colin Powell to Patrick J. Leahy, chairman Subcommittee on Foreign Operations, Committee on Appropriations, US Senate, 21 July 2002.
72. Letter from Secretary Colin Powell to Patrick J. Leahy, chairman, Subcommittee on Foreign Operations, Committee on Appropriations, US Senate, 21 July 2002.
73. In 2004 the Crowley Amendment, which would have added $50 million for 2004 and an additional $50 million for 2005, was defeated.
74. *Peoples Daily*, March 2001, quoted in Christopher Smith, "Judging a Civilization," *PRI Review* 11:8.

4

Out of Africa: The Case of Nigeria

The combination of bribes, threats, and blandishments used to induce governments in the developing world to address their "population problem," or at least to allow foreign-funded groups to operate freely within their borders for the same purpose, defies simple description or generalization.

In some cases the population control proposals are relatively straightforward, as in 2000 when the UNFPA offered the government of Pakistan $250 million for accepting a national sex education syllabus for primary and secondary students in which both graphic sex ed and the benefits of population control would be prominently featured. According to the Pakistani Health Ministry, "The UN official [promoting the project] contended that if the children are imparted awareness on small families from an early age, it will help control population growth." Pakistan rejected the aid package because of the extraordinary conditions that the UNFPA imposed on the project. The UN organization not only demanded control over classroom sex education throughout the country, it also insisted on control over the budget out of concerns that previous money for "population welfare projects" had been "misspent."[1]

This bold attempt to hijack the Pakistani school curriculum is only unusual in that Islamabad successfully resisted—this time around—the attempt by the controllers to impose their own agenda on the country. More common is what happened in Bangladesh, where USAID programs met little opposition. By the early 1970s, USAID, in conjunction with other foreign aid agencies, had virtually taken over the health care system. US and foreign contractors were providing both the intellectual justification for the Health and Family Welfare Ministry's focus on population control, as well as the technical expertise needed to drive this work forward.

101

Of course, to mute local opposition, the pretense that Bangladesh still controlled its own population destiny was carefully maintained. For example, US officials were nowhere to be seen on July 11, 1996, when the Bangladeshi Health and Family Welfare Minister, Salahuddin Yusuf, publicly unveiled a seven-year plan (1997-2004) to reduce the country's population growth rate.[2] A week later the U.S. ambassador, David Merril, called on Minister Yusuf to congratulate him on this effort and pledge $200 million in support of this new effort. Lowering the population growth rate, Ambassador Merril told Minister Yusuf, was a wise course of action for Bangladesh because it would alleviate poverty, reduce hunger, secure democracy, and improve the general health of the population.[3] (We will examine the extravagant claims made on behalf of population control programs in chapters 7 and 8.) The press did not report that this course of action had been imposed on Bangladeshi by a phalanx of foreign aid donors, led by the United States.

How does this happen? The controllers are nothing if not persistent, seeking to gain entry into a country and influence over its family culture in multiple ways—through international institutions like the World Bank and the United Nations, through national ministries of health and education, through local schools and clinics, through the mass media, even through religion. How these multi-pronged attacks work in practice is best grasped through the medium of a case study.

I have chosen to present an example from Africa, simply because that continent has always loomed strangely large in the minds of those who have made the elimination of people their primary concern. Lightly populated relative to China, India, and Southeast Asia, the Dark Continent has nonetheless received a disproportionate share of attention over the decades. When Pentagon researchers in 1988 warned of a dramatic shift in power in coming decades, for example, they spilled much ink on Africa.[4] They worried that, by the early decades of the next century, Nigeria, Kenya, Ethiopia, Zaire, Tanzania, and South Africa would all rank among the top 25 nations in population worldwide, and that Nigeria, in particular, would move past the United States into third place. Although they conceded what has since actually transpired—that the AIDS epidemic might undercut their projections—they nevertheless concluded that US policymakers must energetically pursue programs to lower the African birthrate.

One of the best documented and most disturbing cases of population control imperialism comes from Nigeria. It is largely the work of Elizabeth Liagin, a researcher-journalist who has spent many years documenting how First World cash and clout was consciously and deliberately used to try to reshape the views of Nigerians on children, family life, and even religion. It is a story she knows from the inside, for she resided in Africa's most populous country for a decade, and raised her own family there.[5]

*   *   *

In the mid-1980s, officials with the U.S. Department of State and USAID mulled over the problem of Nigeria. For almost 20 years, they had tried to build a network of "family planning" services in oil-rich Nigeria, black Africa's most populous state. They had little to show for their efforts. The birthrate had remained high. Repeated controversies had erupted over the heavy-handed, even duplicitous methods used in the campaigns. The campaign had generated a seething suspicion of U.S. motives among ordinary Nigerians. But these U.S. officials remained convinced that there were already too many Nigerians, and they were determined to move ahead, whatever the cost, to cap its population growth.

One problem they had encountered was that a huge majority of Nigerians belonged to religious groups which rejected Western birth control methods on moral grounds. More than half of Nigeria's people, mostly those residing in the north of the country, professed Islam, while a substantial portion of the southern population were Catholic. The Catholic Church's prohibition of artificial contraception, having been recently restated in the papal encyclical, *Humanae Vitae,*[6] was scarcely amenable to local obfuscation or reinterpretation. Islamic teaching on the subject roughly paralleled that of Catholicism: Children were blessings from God while contraception, sterilization, and abortion are frowned upon. Islam, however, lacks a pope, and in the absence of a central, authoritative figure able to offer a final judgment on contraception the controllers saw an opportunity.

USAID embarked upon a project breathtaking in its cultural arrogance. Working, as is its wont on the population control front, through middlemen—the Futures Group, the Pathfinder Fund, and the Carolina Population Center[7]—the agency hired a Pentagon consultant to create texts suggesting that Islamic teaching approved of family planning.[8] These works were disguised as the product of research initiated by the Nigerian government, and were planted in Islamic colleges and universities throughout the country.

Carolina Population Center was involved in contacting prime contractors for this "Islam and Population Policy" project, in which capacity it sent a confidential proposal to Muhiuddin Haider at the Pathfinder Fund. In the proposal, dated 14 November 1986, the Center is careful to point out that the project was to proceed "exercising great caution," warning Haider that "Any tendency toward politicization in this matter might have serious effects." Reading the enclosed contract, one can appreciate the necessity for stealth, since it proposed to tamper with religious convictions held sacred by believers.

According to the contract, the objectives of the "Islam and Population Policy" project were to "motivate Muslim men and women to time and space births," to "help to disseminate *correct* concepts on Islam and family planning," and to promote "involvement by *Muslim leaders* with issues of population policy" (italics added). The activities described in the draft—including the publication of "a source manual for Muslim scholars" and a series of "carefully organized, small seminars"—were to be funded under USAID's "RAPID" program.

RAPID was a too-clever-by-half acronym for "Resources for Awareness of Population Impacts on Development," and was carried out through the Glastonbury, Connecticut-based Futures Group. Like other "policy development" programs funded by USAID, RAPID was intended to convince leaders in poor countries to formulate and implement national policies to reduce the birthrate.[9] This often meant in practice convincing the leaders of poor countries *to allow USAID population contractors like the Futures Group* and its employees and consultants to formulate and implement policies to reduce the birthrate.

That is certainly what happened in this case. According to the 1986 proposal, a Professor Abdel-Rahim Omran was to research and write an Islamic textbook, plan and participate in seminars, and assist in follow-up activities. Professor Omran taught epidemiology at the University of North Carolina until the mid-1980s, at which time he joined the staff of the Center for Development and Conflict Management at the University of Maryland.[10] The final version of the "Islamic" text he authored bears the title, *A Resource Manual on Islam and Family Planning with Special Reference to the Maliki School*. Prof. Omran is identified on the cover only as a "consultant to the Ministry of Health, Nigeria." No mention is made of his Pentagon connections, nor of the fact that he received $25,000 from Pathfinder in 1987 for preparation of documents on Islam and family planning, and another $57,000 between March and September of 1988 for "Islamic and population workshops."[11]

In late 1987, USAID decided to move ahead with an even more ambitious plan. On the table was a blueprint for an externally funded population control program in Nigeria, a huge, green-covered, two-volume document the size of a couple of big-city telephone directories. The final version, dated 9 July 1987 and designated "unclassified," described the soon-to-be implemented plan as "a major, innovative, and far-reaching endeavor ... designed to increase the acceptability and the practice of family planning by approximately four-fold in the most populous country of Africa." Its initial target was to recruit 2.5 million committed contraceptive users within five years. "At the end of the five-year project," it added, "80 percent of the population aged 15-45 will be informed of family planning concepts. Hopefully, smaller family norms will result."

Enormous obstacles stood in the way of this ambitious assault on Nigerian values and birthrates, the document went on to acknowledge. Fertility surveys suggested that the average Nigerian woman was likely to give birth to between six and seven children during her reproductive lifetime.[12] Even worse, from the State Department's point of view, Nigerian women had no sense of having "too many" children. USAID-funded fertility surveys showed that the average woman wanted between eight and nine children. In others words, a truly voluntary program of family planning, one based solely on facilitating the free will choice of Nigerian women where childbearing was concerned, would result in nothing less than a 25 percent *increase* in the national fertility rate. State and USAID had no intention of allowing this to happen, of course. Permitting Nigerian women to decide for themselves the number and spacing of their children was emphatically *not* what they had in mind.

The preference for large families runs deep in Nigerian culture, an appendix to the 1987 document noted, to the extent that the celebration of fertility is "ingrained in many rituals of life and even in daily greetings.... Nothing is more rewarding to most Nigerian women than to bear and raise children. Nothing can give a Nigerian man more pride than to be surrounded by an admiring crowd of family and children. They are not just a sign of his wealth and power; they are his wealth and power."

The report went on to note that the Nigerians are a religious people and that most object to Western birth control methods on moral grounds. In fact, a pair of World Bank consultants were cited in the report to the effect that opposition to Western birth control programs spanned the religious spectrum: "[P]oliticians, civil servants, and political activists all feel that the programs may run counter to the basic spiritual beliefs and emotions of African society."

Another section warned that political currents were equally unfavorable to an ambitious anti-natal program: "The political furor surrounding censuses in Nigeria reflect some of the political obstacles to family planning. Political groups, regions, and ethnic groups and religions vying for position all want to be numerous."

Past efforts to enlist African governments and leaders into promoting population control among their own people failed, the report said bluntly, because those embracing such activities in the past "have repeatedly been attacked on the grounds that population programs are a form of foreign intervention and that they are imperialist, neo-colonialist plots to keep Africa down." For this reason, "African governments have given either no leadership or uncertain leadership to family planning programs."

None of this really mattered to the elitists gathered around the table. The "spiritual beliefs and emotions" of the Nigerian people they regarded as mere superstition, the desire for large families as a false consciousness, and the unwillingness of African leaders to lead an anti-natal campaign as mere political cowardice. These considerations would affect their tactics, but not their overall strategy. The U.S. government had determined that Nigeria's population was growing too rapidly. For a whole host of reasons ranging from US national security (remember Nigeria's oil) to improving the health of Nigeria's women (women who have been sterilized do not die in childbirth), Nigerians had to stop having babies in such numbers. State Department officials were determined to seize the opportunity presented by Nigeria's economic slowdown to force the country's leaders to adopt a Western-dictated population policy.

Past Efforts in Nigeria

When a government self-consciously decides to intervene in the fertility of its own people, by adopting measures to encourage or discourage childbearing, it generally formulates a population policy, that is, a formal statement of its demographic intentions. Some European countries, as we will see in Chapter 8, have adopted population policies that are meant to *increase* the birthrate. Few nations have—voluntarily, at least—taken the opposite tack, one of declaring their birthrate excessive and establishing programs to drive it down. Yet this is precisely what developing countries are urged to do by the United States and its population allies, who are ready to apply significant financial and diplomatic muscle to force them to knuckle under. Nigeria was to prove more resistant than most, and so the arm-twisting was more intense and thus more evident.

Early efforts to get birth control devices into the reproductive tracts of the Nigerian people made little headway. The Family Planning

Council was set up under British colonial administration in the late 1950s. Groups such as London-based International Planned Parenthood Federation (IPPF), the Population Council in New York, the Ford Foundation, and the U.S. Agency for International Development (USAID) began to fund projects to set up clinics and popularize contraceptives. But there was no government policy explicitly favoring such activities, and no health ministry resources behind them. The clinics themselves were little more than curiosity shops to the Nigerians, odd reminders of the extremes to which the white world would go to realize their eccentric ideas about childbearing. Birthrates remained high. Following the 1970s oil boom that gave a huge boost to the national economy, they went even higher.

Efforts to create elite opinion in favor of a policy of population control began early. A directory of USAID's population assistance programs published in September 1968 noted conferences to discuss population issues, scholarships for Nigerian students to study demography, and a survey of population growth rates done under the auspices of the United Nations. But the very notion of limiting births generated tremendous opposition. "Opponents of population control range from the Catholic Church ... to the commissioner of economic development," said a 30 March 1972 cable from the U.S. Embassy in Lagos to Washington, which added that the Nigerian people "question the motives of externally supported family planning programs, and dismiss birth control as alien to Nigerian values."

The World Bank also played a key role. Created at the end of World War II to finance the reconstruction of Western Europe, it had, by the 1970s, become a major source of development funds for the developing world. With its leverage over fragile developing economies came the ability to impose domestic policies. The premise was simple: Any country wishing to borrow money from the World Bank was required, as a condition of credit, to present a realistic plan for economic development. After 1968, with Robert McNamara at the helm, the Bank insisted that each such plan include a population control component. While USAID was forbidden, at least during the Reagan and two Bush administrations from using population funds to perform abortions, or to lobby for their legalization, the World Bank faces no such restrictions.

What precisely is "The World Bank's Role in Shaping Third World Population Policy?" According to a World Bank "internal working paper" by the same name:

> Policy development is a *complex and sensitive process*. Efforts and techniques used to influence policy must be adjusted to be appropriate to the size, setting and political,

social, and economic environment of each country. One of the Bank's major strengths is *influencing policy development through policy dialogue*. This encompasses a wide range of activities: *informal and formal discussions with government officials* and pertinent program managers regarding population policy issues, population project design and implementation, sector and economic work, and the participation of high level government officials and managers in Bank-sponsored seminars[13] (italics added).

The author of this genteel description of the World Bank's strong-arm population tactics was none other than Fred T. Sai, the former head of IPPF. Sai was himself an African from Ghana, a black face used to break the bad news to African leaders that, if they wanted the money, they must not only accept but actually endorse population control programs. Thus was population "policy development" influenced by "policy dialogue" in practice. However indirect and "sensitive" were the "formal discussions" of which Sai speaks, the "informal discussions" must have provided an opportunity for this vulgar truth to be plainly stated to obdurate Africans.

Using these techniques, bank officials had successfully imposed population policies on a number of African nations in the 1970s and early 1980s. Now, in the mid-1980s, it was Nigeria's turn. Oil revenues were no longer sufficient to keep the Nigerian economy afloat. Its government, increasingly anxious for international assistance, was vulnerable. The World Bank moved in and, by its own account, it "helped lay groundwork for policy formation."[14]

Nigeria was a special case that required considerable effort, not only because it was the most populous country in Africa, but also because of its unstable political environment. The strategy was to create a shift in elite opinion towards family planning, in part to allay concerns of the leadership of a popular backlash. Besides recruiting "Nigerian consultants" who were paid with Bank funds, USAID brought in a special team from the Futures Group, a government contractor which works primarily with the Pentagon. The Futures Group teamed up with the Bank's consultants to train still more Nigerian "experts." These then fanned out across the country to explain to government officials, religious leaders, and other influential persons "why the government was developing a population policy." The effort to undermine the Islamic teaching on the immorality of contraception, recounted at the beginning of this chapter, was part of this effort. All of these activities, Sai confirmed, "helped pave the way for eventual approval of the policy."

The population policy was presented to officials not as a radical new departure—which it in fact was—but merely as a supplement to Nigeria's existing "national health policy." It was a modest proposal, they were told, that required nothing more than the inclusion of "family planning" in the larger health program.

"Family planning" was to be explained to Nigerian government officials, according to the 1987 State Department plan, in equally innocuous terms. It was to be described as a service to help couples "achieve their wishes" with regard to the prevention of "unwanted pregnancies" and the "securing" of "desired pregnancies," and to educate them about the "spacing of pregnancies" and limiting family size "in the interest of family health." The program and its methods, Nigerian leaders were assured, would be "compatible with [Nigeria's] culture and religious beliefs."

Such soothing language so grossly misrepresented the program that, under US legal standards, it might well be considered fraud. The program, of course, had absolutely nothing to do with helping the Nigerian people to achieve their desired family size (which may well have led to an increase in the birthrate, as we have seen). The 1987 plan listed a huge array of program activities that went far beyond what was culturally acceptable, much less permissible on religious grounds. The claim that the program would assist Nigerians in "securing desired pregnancies" was particularly ludicrous, since the entire thrust of the program was to *prevent* as many Nigerians as possible from conceiving and bearing children.

Nevertheless, in February 1988 Nigeria's Armed Forces Ruling Council approved an official population policy. Shortly thereafter, the head of the Council, General Ibrahim Babangida, signed a bilateral population agreement with the United States. The population policy officially took effect in April of that year; and the money began to flow. In addition to the promised loans, the World Bank committed $95 million specifically for family planning for the period 1987-90. The USAID kicked in $67 million. Other countries, UN agencies, and private foundations ponied up substantial amounts.

The 1987 plan had proposed a full-throated propaganda offensive in the mass media, in commercial entertainment, and at traditional gatherings. Johns Hopkins University, which in March 1988 signed a contract with USAID for nearly $15 million, took the lead in carrying out this highly sophisticated "population communication" campaign,[15] which was intended to undermine prevailing pro-natalist attitudes, and effect "significant attitudinal changes favoring smaller family norms."[16]

Family planning messages were integrated into "existing popular radio and television series," as well as into "variety shows and soap operas."

New radio and television programs containing an anti-natalist message were created and funded. Testimonials in support of family planning were solicited from "traditional and religious leaders," including Islamic leaders, and aired through local media outlets. "Islam and family planning" was the focus of a host of activities.

Popular singers were recruited to record anti-child lyrics for albums and jingles for commercials. What were termed "scholarships," but which could perhaps more accurately be called bribes, were to be awarded to journalists, publishers, and film makers to encourage their participation in, and support for, this media campaign. Thousands of "television, radio, film, and folk media programs and spots, and newspaper and magazine inserts in at least five languages" were produced and distributed. (The 1987 plan had called for 3,000 such interventions.)

Scores of "orientation symposia" were carried out for influential public and private sector leaders across the country, to explain to them the pressing need for family planning. Educators had a separate track of workshops, at which they were given ideological guidance in how to present the new anti-natal creed to their students. There were special conferences for key groups of opinion makers, such as journalists and publishers.

More direct action was carried out as well. Organizations were formed and secretly financed to give the appearance of "policy support" at the grassroots. Thousands of "motivational agents" were recruited and trained to advocate birth control. Public opinion polls, focus group studies, and "anthropological research" were carried out in order, in the words of 1987 plan, "to convince the greatest number of people" to practice family planning and create "a positive public atmosphere for the population program."

The 1987 plan, in the spirit of NSSM 200, had sternly dictated that all these activities were to be carried out in a way that disguised the involvement of the United States. The agreement between USAID and Johns Hopkins, as Jean Guilfoyle has noted, uses language more befitting "a Cold War 'black propaganda' operation than a development assistance project."[17] Johns Hopkins was instructed to "optimize the influence of its family planning messages" by ensuring that they are "conspicuously disseminated and distributed by familiar, credible, and multiple channels of communication." Local hirelings were to establish a beachhead for this invasion of foreign ideas; American government officials were to stay well out of the picture.

The Nigerians were to think that the tidal wave of anti-natal propaganda which had suddenly engulfed them was nothing more than a spontaneous sea change in local attitudes. But this was not to be. Lawrence Adekoya, a well-known Nigerian pro-family activist, was among those who noted that this population propaganda was "part of a planned escalation which has been well orchestrated.... For many months the public ha(s) been treated to the buildup of a preparatory and public-reaction-softening campaign. Hardly did any month pass without one foreign "expert" or representative of an international organization dropping a hint of how badly Nigeria was doing because of a purported population explosion. The latest item in the agenda of fear ... was that Nigeria was becoming the 13th poorest country in the world."[18]

The bilateral population agreement was no secret. And the propaganda offensive was so plagued with defections, corruption, and scandal that the identity of its principal backer, the United States, quickly became common knowledge. "We have incontrovertible information on an American plan to trim the size of the world to a manageable level," wrote Adekoya at the time. "In 1974 the U.S. government commissioned confidential study [NSSM 220] on the implications of population growth for 'US Security and Overseas Interests.' ... Nigeria was identified as one of the '13 key countries' in which there is 'special US political and strategic interest.' That document—which is now declassified but not widely known—suggests, among other things, the need to step up family-planning campaigns that would drastically reduce the fertility of women in developing countries."[19]

At the time, abortion was virtually unthinkable as an official family planning practice in Nigeria. In 1990, for example, the Planned Parenthood Federation of Nigeria (PPFN) came under attack for promoting the sale and use of "contraceptives" that were abortifacient in character. Its executive director issued a blanket denial, claiming in the December 1989 issue of PPFN's *Planfed News* that its methods do not induce early abortion and, further, that "they have been tested, verified and well documented in all developed countries as well as international agencies including the WHO and the IPPF." The article went on to say that PPFN "as an organization has never and does not encourage abortion" and does not have any long-term plan "to soften our deep set cultural values towards life, towards the eventual introduction of an abortion-on-demand legislation."[20]

Yet the legalization of abortion was a key goal of the population controllers and, in one sense, they could not have picked a better time to make their move. Nigeria was ruled by a military government, not a democratic one. Power was concentrated in the hands of a 28-member

Armed Forces Ruling Council headed by General Ibrahim Babangida. The Council had publicly promised that Nigeria would transition to a democracy before the end of 1992, but in the meantime exercised virtually absolute control. Elections were occurring in stages, with voting for new local and municipal leaders set for late 1991 and state elections scheduled for early 1992. No date had been set for the election of a new president and vice president. Even though neither Babangida nor his fellow generals showed signs of wanting to succeed themselves, many Nigerians were uneasy about the upcoming series of elections. They feared that a strenuous protest against the government, for whatever reason, might place them in jeopardy. All of this put the generals beyond the reach of the Nigerian electorate, which was overwhelmingly pro-life, and made them answerable only to themselves—and their foreign patrons.

On 22 August 1991, Nigerian Minister of Health Olikoye Ransome-Kuti, dropped a broad hint that the military government was preparing to legalize abortion, chiefly for demographic reasons. Ransome-Kuti stated that nearly half of Nigeria's population was under the age of 20, and that a high pregnancy rate among this group would create hardship for the country. This looming demographic crisis might make it necessary for Nigeria to resort to abortion. He also leaned on a favorite argument of Western abortion activists, arguing that current laws protecting the unborn merely drove women into the bloody hands of back-alley abortionists.[21]

Some members of the press braved the wrath of the generals to speak out. "Last year, we alerted the nation on the plans of the military to legalize abortion before they retire to the barracks," editorialized *The Leader*, a Catholic newspaper, on 15 September 1991. "Health Minister Professor Olikoye Ransome-Kuti's recent call on the government to legalize abortion clearly indicates that the plan is about to be consummated."[22]

The backlash grew when the World Bank, which is taken in many parts of the world to be synonymous with the United States, was accused of pressuring Nigeria into legalizing abortion. The evidence? Less than three months before, in May 1991, the World Bank had approved a $78.5 million loan for implementation of Nigeria's population policy goals. Moreover, the terms of the loan were particularly soft. The money was transferred in the form of IDA credits, which have a more lenient repayment schedule, and little or no interest.[23] As the World Bank admitted in its 1991 annual report, "This long-range project seeks to strengthen the institutional framework and expand the basis for undertaking a large-scale, intersectoral national population program over the coming decades in fulfillment of Nigeria's ambitious population policy goals."[24] To further sweeten the pot, a separate $70 million loan under the Bank's "population, health and nutrition" lending program was also conveyed to the Nigerian capital.

Of course, this was by no means the sum of Nigeria's indebtedness. By the end of the mid-1991 reporting period, Nigeria owed more than $6 billion to the World Bank.[25] An additional $319 million was approved by the International Monetary Fund (IMF) in the year ending April 1991.[26] Although the lion's share of these funds is not earmarked for a population-related purpose, they are all granted under the condition that the recipient country, in this case Nigeria, conform to World Bank policy prescriptions on a host of issues, including population control.

The UNFPA also expressed approval of Nigeria's actions by approving, in early 1992, a $35 million dollar grant to finance population activities in that country. The amount represented a 21% increase over the 1986-1990 period.[27]

Given that Nigeria's population policy was crafted in Washington, advanced by a whole phalanx of US-funded NGOs and international organizations and, in the end, rubberstamped by a military dictatorship, it seems a mockery to refer to it as a "Nigerian" policy at all. In fact, the World Bank was well aware that its $78.5 million population control loan to the current military dictatorship would likely be jeopardized by a return to civilian rule. The head of the International Development Association (IDA) explicitly warned Bank officers in a 1991 memo that Nigeria's population policy was a product of the "period of military rule" and the return to civilian rule would impose a significant "risk" of "transition." "Civilian politicians," it cautioned, would be "less likely to give high priority to an interventionist population policy."[28]

Nothing more clearly exposed the policy's exogenous roots than its ignominious end. General Ibrahim Babangida, the Nigerian dictator who originally approved the population policy and later legalized abortion, finally stepped down in November 1993. He was replaced by the popularly elected Mohammed Sani Abacha. President Abacha, beholden to the Nigerian people rather than to the population controllers, proved to be his own man. One of his first acts as head of state was to trash the detested bilateral population agreement with the United States.

*   *   *

Still, other population control organizations, such as the UNFPA, remained active in Nigeria. The UNFPA's 1996 *Inventory of Population*

Projects in Developing Countries Around the World,[29] the last such report available, outlines the agency's overall country strategy for Nigeria:

> The Governing Council approved $35 million for a five-year programme starting in 1992. The programme will: decrease maternal and infant mortality; achieve a lower population growth rate through the reduction of fertility by voluntary fertility regulation compatible with the social and cultural conditions of the country and the economic and social goals of the nation; enhance the status and condition of women and encourage their full participation as equal partners in the development process of the country; continue the population education programme for secondary schools and organized labor; and promote (IEC) [information, education and communication] campaigns for special target groups, with special emphasis on the promotion of Safe Motherhood; promote community and NGO [non-governmental organization] involvement in programme development, implementation, monitoring and evaluation.

This country strategy, which is typical of the strategies for all of the developing countries in which the UNFPA operates, suggests a broad-based program in which efforts to reduce maternal and infant mortality are given priority over the wholesale distribution of contraceptives for population control purposes. *But closer examination of UNFPA projects reveals that this is not the case.*

The *Inventory* provides details on UNFPA's 22 projects in Nigeria during the 1993-1997 time period. These include:

- Three community reproductive health service projects (with a strong emphasis on providing contraceptives, in particular condoms)—at a total cost of $840,482;
- Three contraceptive supply projects—total cost $6,151,000;
- Seven Maternal and Child Health/Family Planning projects, which consist of increasing the availability and accessibility of contraceptives—total cost $4,839,000;
- One "Safe Motherhood" project, which seeks to improve cooperation between traditional birth attendants and the medical staff in the communities—total cost $373,000;
- "Family Health Soap Opera Television Series"—total cost $658,000; and
- Seven projects designed to perform research and data analysis on population policies. These projects primarily include the collection and analysis of demographic data, cartography and census work, planning, and coordination, monitoring and evaluating various population programs—total cost $3,367,552.

Of the 22 Nigerian population projects, 14 are "grassroots" efforts, comprising the first four categories above. Of the total of $12,203,482 in expenditures on these fourteen projects, only three percent—the "Safe Motherhood" project—will have any lasting impact on maternal health.

The UNFPA effort in Nigeria, as in the developing world as a whole, is heavily weighted toward preventing pregnancy in order to, as its own country strategy suggests, "lower [the] population growth rate." However loudly the UNFPA trumpets the slight reduction in maternal mortality that follows from their massive campaigns to prevent pregnancy, it is clear that this reduction in maternal mortality is merely a secondary effect of its primary goal: to reduce the number of Nigerian babies born.

*   *   *

Upon Abacha's sudden death in June 1998, Major General Abdusalam Abubakar succeeded him as head of state. With the demise of popular politician and businessman Moshood Abiola a month later, the situation in Nigeria grew increasingly tense and uncertain. While the political environment is hardly yet ripe for renewed population intervention, the nation is almost certainly becoming more vulnerable.

*   *   *

This attempt to subvert Nigeria's indigenous culture was only extraordinary in its scale. These same methods, intended to produce dramatic changes in attitudes towards marriage, family, and children, have been used in dozens of countries worldwide. Although Nigeria ultimately rejected these programs, most countries, more economically vulnerable than that oil-rich state, have had to go along.

The population control movement of late has been inclined to admit its early years were fraught with abuses, as when the IPPF acknowledged in 2002 that "in the 1960s and 1970s less developed countries came under enormous pressure from the more developed to establish nationwide family planning programmes." At the same time, it claims that such strong-arm tactics are no longer used. Instead, it maintains that the less developed countries have seen the merit of fertility reduction programs and voluntarily adopted them. "By 1996 more than 90% of all developing countries, led by India, supported such programmes—albeit mainly for reasons of human rights, reproductive health, and gender equity rather than demographic concerns," continues to IPPF.[30] But while the justifications have varied over time, the pressure from donors on the less developed countries has remained a constant.

Notes

1.   "Pakistan may lose $250 million aid for not agreeing to sex education," *Pakistan Business Recorder*, 8 August 2000; "UN Attempts to "Buy" Pakistan and Impose

Population Control," Zenit, 16 August 2000; "UN Offers $250 Million to Pakistan if it Teaches Population Control," CWNews, 9 August 2000.

2. "Plan to Reduce Population Growth Rate: Yusuf," *The Bangladesh Observer* (Dhaka), 13 July 1996.

3. "New $200 m[illion] USAID package for Health Sector Likely," *The Daily Star* (Dhaka), 18 July 1996.

4. The study commissioned by the Office of Net Assessment in the Department of Defense and was published in abbreviated form by the Center for Strategic and International Studies in the spring 1989 issue of its publication, *Washington Quarterly*. "Global Demographic Trends to the Year 2010: Implications for U.S. Security," by Gregory D. Foster, *et al.* The study included information provided by the Futures Group, Johns Hopkins University, and other major players in the anti-people movement. Africa occupies a large place in the mental landscape of the controllers, even though it is still a relatively lightly populated continent. Pentagon researchers, worried about the accretion of power by increasingly populated African states, warned in 1988 that Nigeria would surpass both the United States and the USSR to become the third largest nation in the world in the first part of the next century.

5. An earlier version of this case study first appeared in the *PRI Review* as "Money for Lies," *PRI Review* 8(4) (July/October 1998):5.

6. *Humanae Vitae*, which is usually rendered "On Human Life," was issued by Pope Paul VI in 1968, and forbids all forms of artificial contraception. Natural Family Planning, on the other hand, is encouraged as a means of welcoming and, if need be, regulating births.

7. The Futures Group, according to the *Guide to Sources of International Population Assistance 1991* (New York: United Nations Population Fund, 1991), is a "private organization concerned with policy analysis, development and strategic planning" (p. 225). It works mainly with USAID and the Department of Defense. The Pathfinder Fund, which we have seen elsewhere in these pages, is a major recipient of funds from USAID's Office of Population, receiving tens of millions of dollars in multiyear contracts to provide birth control information and services to developing countries. According to USAID's Users Guide to the Office of Population, 1991, Pathfinder was then in the middle of a $67 million contract. The Carolina Population Center, located on the campus of the University of North Carolina, participated in the design phase of the $100 million Nigerian population control program financed through USAID's African Bureau. See USAID agreement no. 698-0462-C-000-7012-00, from 1987, with a budget of $56,184.

8. The following section is based on research carried out by Jean Guilfoyle and reported in her excellent article, "Islam and Family Planning" *PRI Review* 2(4) (July/August 1992):6-7, from which many of the below citations are taken.

9. The subcontract to Haider was written during RAPID's second contract with USAID, pithily called RAPID II. A 1991 directory of USAID population projects explains that the RAPID project is intended to "raise leadership of relationships between population growth and development and about the positive socio-economic and health effects of lower fertility." See *User's Guide to the Office of Population* (Washington, D.C.: USAID, 1991), p. 13. By then the Futures Group was on to RAPID III, which ran from September 1987 to September 1992, to the tune of $12,666,000. Much of USAID's population funding is expended in this sequential fashion to a core group of trusted population control surrogates, which are more properly considered quasi-governmental organizations than non-governmental organizations.

10. *Nations and Needs*, newsletter of the Center for International Development and Conflict Resolution, March 1985, 3.

11. Abdel R. Omran is also identified as a Pentagon contractor in a study by Gregory D. Foster *et al*, called "Global Demographic Trends to the year 2010: Implications for U.S. Security." *Washington Quarterly* (Washington, D.C.: Center for Strategic and International Studies), Spring 1989. The payments to Omran are recorded in "Overview of AID Population Assistance, FY 1989," Office of Population, April 1990, a computer database print, under section of "Subproject Level Activities," run date 4/5/90, 34 (Nigeria).
12. High infant and child mortality rates meant that many of those born would not survive until adulthood, of course.
13. Fred T. Sai and Lauren A. Chester, "The World Bank's Role in Shaping Third World Population Policy," Internal Working Paper of the World Bank, Washington, D.C., November 1990.
14. Ibid. See also Elizabeth Liagin, "Money for Lies," *PRI Review* 8(4) (July/October 1998):9.
15. Johns Hopkins University Population Communication Services project, AID contract no. 620-0001-C-00-8013-00 in the amount of $14,998,497. Cited in Guilfoyle.
16. This language is taken from a contract signed by the Washington-based Center for Development and Population Activities (CEDPA), a subcontractor in a highly specialized USAID "population communication" program in Nigeria run by Johns Hopkins University. See Jean Guilfoyle, "Islam and Family Planning," for details of the $1.4 million contract.
17. Jean Guilfoyle, "Islam and Family Planning," 6.
18. Lawrence Adekoya, "Nigeria objects," *PRI Review* 2(2) (March/April 1992):8.
19. Ibid.
20. Quoted in Jean M. Guilfoyle, "Abortion in Nigeria: U.S. Connection?" *PRI Review* 2(2) (March/April 1992): 6.
21. "Government may legalize abortion," *Nigerian News Digest*, 20 September 1991.
22. *The Leader* (Owerri, Nigeria), 15 September 1991, 1.
23. Jean M. Guilfoyle, "Abortion in Nigeria: W.S. Connection?" 7. See also footnote 9. The Nigerian case is also discussed by Barbara Akapo, "When family planning meets population control," *Gender Review*, June 1994, 8-9.
24. *World Bank Annual Report 1991*, 153.
25. *World Bank Annual Report 1991*, cumulative lending tables, 184.
26. *International Monetary Fund Annual Report 1991*, "stand-by and extended fund facility arrangements ... ," Table 11.3, 85.
27. "Gratis to Nigeria from UNFPA," *PRI Review* 2(2) (March/April 1992):9.
28. "Nigeria: Population Policies," International Development Association, 19 April 1991, 45. Cited in Jean M. Guilfoyle, "The United Nations' Civil Society," *PRI Review* 5(5) (July/August 1995): 4.
29. In recent years, as the controversy over population control programs has grown, the UNFPA has ceased publishing this compendium. Responding to an e-mail, the publications office at UNFPA informed me that they haven't published this since "1998 or 1999." They have no copies available of this publication, and it is not available on their website.
30. Egon Diczfalusy, "Population Growth: Too Much, Too Little, or Both?" *IPPF Medical Bulletin* 36(1) (1 February 2002):1.

Part II

The Hidden Costs of Population Control

5

Human Rights and Reproductive Wrongs

*Pharaoh said to his subjects, "Look how numerous
and powerful the Israelite people are growing,
more so than we ourselves! Come, let us deal
shrewdly with them to stop their increase; otherwise, in time of war they too may join our enemies
to fight against us, and so leave our country." Accordingly, taskmasters were set over the Israelites
to oppress them with forced labor ... Yet the more
they were oppressed, the more they multiplied and
spread. The Egyptians, then, dreaded the Israelites
and reduced them to cruel slavery, making life
bitter for them with hard work.... [Still] the people
... increased and grew strong. Pharaoh then commanded all his subjects, "Throw into the river
every boy that is born to the Hebrews...."*

–Exodus, Chapter 1, Verses 9-22 passim, New American Bible

*[Population control programs] treat the people
involved not as reasonable beings, allies facing a
common problem, but as impulsive and uncon-
trolled sources of great social harm, in need of
strong discipline."*

–Amartya Sen[1] Professor of Economics Harvard University

What happens when governments, often in response to pressure
from abroad, attempt to directly regulate the fertility of their people?
Both human rights and primary health care, it turns out, tend to suffer
setbacks. Urging governments to interfere in the intimate decisions of
couples concerning childbearing, as we will see in Chapter 5, does not
encourage limited government and the rule of law, but their opposite,
an intrusive bureaucracy and human rights abuses. Nor does concentrat-
ing scarce health care resources on fertility reduction programs lead to
improvements in the general state of health of a population, the topic of

Chapter 6. As Cambridge economist and Nobel-prize winner Amartya Sen has argued, by giving priority to "family planning arrangements in the Third World over other commitments such as education and health care," international policy makers "produce negative effects on people's well-being and reduce their freedoms."[2]

*   *   *

When the government sterilization team arrived in their little town of La Legua, Peru, Celia Durand and her husband, Jaime, looked at each other and shook their heads. Although Celia had considered a tubal ligation in the past, she had begun to hear rumors of women damaged or even killed during the national tubal ligation campaign. She had decided that she didn't want to be sterilized that way. *Maybe sometime later I will do it,* she told Jaime, *maybe in a hospital.* Certainly not in the little medical post down one of La Legua's bare earth streets, with its windows opened wide to the dust, insects, and the smells from the pigs and other animals rooting and defecating in the nearby streets and yards. Certainly not in the middle of a *Festivale de Ligaduras de Trompas* (Tubal Ligation Festival), as the banner hastily hung in front of the clinic declared, with the doctors in a hurry to cut, snip, and sew their way through a long line of patients.[3]

But then the campaign began in earnest. Ministry of Health "health promoters" descended upon her neighborhood, going door to door, house to house, pressing Celia and her neighbors to accept sterilization. Interviewed later, Jaime recalled the singular nature of their advocacy. It was sterilization or nothing. No other contraceptive method was offered. The *promoturas*, as they are called in Spanish, sought to allay Celia's fears about having the procedure done during the campaign. "Do it now," they told her. "You may have to pay [to have it done] later." Ligation is "easy," "safe," and "simple," they repeatedly reassured her. Nothing was said about possible side effects or risks. "All they told her was how easy it was, nothing more," Jaime said later.

And the *promoturas* were relentless. Again and again they came to the family's home, refusing to accept "no" for an answer. Celia finally gave in. She would come in the following afternoon, she agreed, to have the procedure.

Her mother, Balasura, continued to worry. The two even quarreled about it. "Don't go, daughter," Balasura remembers saying. "There is always time later." But Celia wanted the daily visits to end and, besides, the health promoters had convinced her that the procedure was safe and simple.

"Don't worry, mama, I will be back in a couple of hours," she said as she left for the post. That was the last time that her mother saw her alive.

Sometime during the procedure at the medical post, the surgeon caused enough damage to Celia that she slipped into a coma. Medical staff put off frantic visits from Celia's brother-in-law, mother and husband. Then, as her condition worsened, they finally transferred her from the post to a larger clinic in the nearby city of Piura. It did no good. Celia Durand died without ever regaining consciousness. The date was July 3, 1997.

*   *   *

The sterilization campaign had begun the year before. President Alberto Fujimori, elected to a second term in mid-1995, had wasted no time in legalizing sterilization as a method of birth control. He ordered the country's Ministry of Health, headed by Dr. Eduardo Yong Motta, to focus its efforts on family planning, specifically, on tubal ligations. To train Peruvian doctors and officials in how to structure and run a sterilization campaign, Dr. Motta brought in Chinese, Indian, and Colombian doctors who had carried out such campaigns in their own countries.[4] To monitor the success of the campaign, Fujimori himself set national targets for the numbers of sterilizations to be performed—100,000 in 1997 alone—and demanded weekly progress reports.

Mobile sterilization teams, a fixture of such campaigns, were soon being assembled in the capital city of Lima. These teams of doctors and nurses, who often had no prior training in obstetrics or gynecology, were hurriedly taught how to do tubal ligations, and then sent to the countryside to conduct a series of one- or two-week "ligation festivals." Prior to a team's arrival in an area local Ministry of Health employees would hang banners announcing the forthcoming "Ligation Festival," and fan out across the countryside to *captar* ("bring in" or "capture" in English) women for tubal ligations. The effort was focused on the poorer provinces, home to a high percentage of Peruvians of Indian descent.

The teams themselves operated under very tight time constraints. Organizers sought to get as many women as possible under the knife in as short a time as possible. Celia Durand's family discovered after her death that she had been the last of the 15 patients scheduled for that afternoon.[5] As soon as the last surgery was finished, the team moved out, heading for the next "Ligation Festival," providing no follow-up care.

How were tens of thousands of Peruvian women induced to submit to sterilization? In some cases, like Celia's, harassment by repeated home visits, along with false assurances of safety, was sufficient to bring them in. Those who resisted official "invitations" found that the encounters all too often turned ugly. Women in the Ayacucho region, which PRI investigator David Morrison visited in 1998 and again in 1999, routinely reported being subjected to harsh forms of verbal abuse. If they objected to sterilization, officials shouted that they were no better than "cats" and "dogs," or called them "animals" or "beasts." The women, mostly Quechua-speaking Indians, were repeatedly told how "ignorant" or "stupid" they were for wanting to have more children.[6]

Browbeating didn't work with everyone. Some had to be bribed with promises of government benefits, while still others were threatened with punishment unless they complied. Ernestina Sandoval, poor and badly in need of assistance after a string of weather-related problems cost her husband his job and then their home, was told about a government program that would help feed her family. When she went to enroll, however, she was told by officials that she would first have to undergo sterilization. "They told me I had to bring a card from the hospital saying I had been ligated," Mrs. Sandoval reported. "If I didn't agree to do this they wouldn't give me anything."

Maria Elena Mulatillo enrolled her daughter, a sickly child, in a food supplement program. Two months later government officials told her that, unless she agreed to a tubal ligation, her little girl could not continue in the food program. Maria refused and the officials followed through on their threat. There were no more monthly cans of protein powder for her daughter.[7] Using food to coerce a poor, hungry women into surrendering her fertility is bad enough, but there is something particularly despicable in threatening to let her children go hungry unless or until she agrees.

Why were doctors, nurses, and other officials so insistent? Because they themselves were being judged—and rewarded or punished—on the basis of the number of women they "captured." Dr. Hector Chavez Chuchon, president of the regional medical federation of Ayacucho, testified before the U.S. Congress that the central government was imposing sterilization quotas on medical workers throughout Peru. He produced Ministry of Health documents stating that each medical worker had to bring in (*captar*) two women for sterilization each month or risk losing their jobs.

"The Ministry of Health denies that there are campaigns and quotas for sterilizations," Dr. Chavez testified. "[But] doctors work under pressure from their superiors, are given quotas, and are subjected to other, more subtle, forms of pressure. It is also true that doctors work under very unstable employment conditions, and could easily lose their posts."[8] Peruvian officials neatly corroborated Dr. Chavez's testimony by summarily firing his wife, a government dentist, after he returned to Peru from his whistle-blowing expedition to the United States. He himself would have been terminated from his government posts had U.S. Congressman Christopher Smith (R, N.J.) not intervened. Maria Lopez, the administrator of a local medical sub-post, was also among those who went on record to say that she, and others like her, would be demoted or fired if their posts consistently failed to meet its family planning targets.[9]

Those who exceeded their quotas were routinely rewarded. Stories appeared in major Peruvian dailies, like *El Comercio* and *La Republica*, about "health promoters" who were rewarded with special prizes for bringing in more than their quota of women for sterilization. A young medical student by the name of Javier Chavez told PRI investigators that, while working with a group of "family planning promoters," whoever gained the most new "clients" in a month received a special bonus of 20 Peruvian *soles* (about US$6) and sports clothes.[10]

Doctors and nurses struggling to meet quotas or eager for bonuses often ignored the wishes of the women, simply refusing to take no for an answer. Sterilization during a caesarean section delivery—with or without the woman's consent—was a favorite tactic. Victoria Vigo Espinoza went into pre-term labor when she was seven months pregnant, and was rushed to the hospital on 23 April 1996. One of the first questions the obstetric nurse asked was "How many children do you have?"

"This is the third," responded the petite brunette, in considerable pain.

"Are you going to be sterilized?" the nurse then asked.

Victoria, worried about her unborn baby and with waves of pain washing over her body, didn't bother to answer. It had been difficult for her to conceive children because of an irregular menstrual cycle and infertility. She had only gotten pregnant this time after undergoing months of hormone therapy. Being sterilized was the last thing she was interested in. She scribbled her name on a consent form without reading it, thinking that she was giving her permission for a caesarean section, and was prepped for surgery.

When Victoria woke up the next day, her first thought was for her child. "Please bring my baby to me," she smiled at the nurse. Instead, the intern who had attended her surgery and the doctor on duty somberly filed into the room. Her son had died during the night, they told her.

Victoria burst into tears.

At this, the intern became agitated as well. "She is very, very sad because of her child's death," he said to the doctor. "Very sad," he repeated helplessly

"I want to go home now," Victoria finally choked out through her tears, struggling to sit up.

The doctor attempted to calm her down before she hurt herself. It was too soon after the surgery to release her. "You will have another child," he said softly.

"No, she won't," Victoria heard the intern whisper to the doctor. "She is ligated."

The intern came back later that afternoon, this time alone. "Have I been sterilized?" Victoria asked him directly.

"Yes, Ma'am," he responded. "The doctor performed a ligation on you." He hesitated for a minute and then added, "Forgive me. I feel guilty over what has happened."

Victoria left the hospital on the third day. "I felt completely defeated," she later testified. "I was depressed about never having more children, and went to see a psychiatrist to overcome my depression. And I still have faith that I may one day have more children."[11]

If agents of the state combed American communities, attempting to harass women into accepting sterilization, issuing verbal insults and threats to those who resisted, the outcry would be deafening. Add to this already volatile mix the kinds of bribes and sanctions that were imposed on Peruvian women and riots might well result. How many American women would quietly suffer the kinds of injuries, indignities, and coercion that the Peruvian state inflicted upon tens of thousands of women over the course of the mid-to late 1990?

Yet neither Peru nor China is an isolated case. Women in dozens of developing countries have suffered the kinds of human rights abuses reported in Peru's sterilization campaign, from lack of informed consent to out-and-out coercion. For the use of bribes, sanctions and bullying on both "acceptors" (women) and "promoters" (doctors, nurses, and other government agents) is commonplace in family planning programs, as are targets and quotas.

In Bangladesh, for example, a system of bribes was begun in 1976, with those who agreed to sterilization receiving a sum equal to about the week's earnings. In addition, women are given a *saree* and men a *lungi*. Such inducements may seem trivial compared to the gravity of permanently giving up one's fertility, but against a background of extreme poverty they loom large. Population control workers were assigned a monthly target of two sterilizations and one IUD.[12]

In El Salvador, hospitals, clinics and fieldworkers have been given monthly targets for the number of sterilizations they are to carry out, and women have been sterilized without their knowledge or consent.[13]

In South Africa under apartheid, black South African women were given Depo-Provera shots by health care workers who told them that the injections will "help their milk supply." Black women were often unable to apply for jobs unless they could present a family planning card showing that they were on some type of birth control.[14]

Vietnam has a two-child policy, but in other respects its rigorous laws on birth control could have been copied verbatim from its giant neighbor to the north. The country denies third children a birth certificate and offers a reward of $20 to women who have a hysterectomy. Punishment for having a third child exists across Vietnam, but it appears the policy, which began in 1985, is most strict among the subsistence farmers who make up the poorer echelons of society. Families who violate the policy are denied land to grow rice—and thus effectively starved—until they fall back into line. They are also fined about $80, a seemingly paltry amount that is in fact the equivalent of 10 months' income. The government encourages women to undergo a hysterectomy following the birth of her second child, a procedure to which approximately half of all village women have been subjected.[15]

Mexico has used similarly draconian methods to cut its birth rate. Following the passage of a national population law, the first in Latin America, in 1974, government doctors were told that they must either sterilize or insert an IUD in every woman who comes in to give birth. From the moment a woman in labor enters a government-run clinic, she is bombarded with questions about which method she wants: "temporary" (an IUD) or "definitive" (sterilization). Even if she rejects both, she is often ligated or has an IUD implanted anyway.[16]

Sometimes the deception is even more complete, as in the case of the mobile medical clinics of Guatemala. The clinics travel about the countryside offering free medical examinations to all comers, but those who take advantage of the offer often get more than they bargained for. Senora Flores went in for a free physical, but after the exam she began to hemorrhage. The bleeding and discomfort grew as the days passed. Finally, in desperation, she undertook a journey to the nearest town to see a doctor. He soon discovered the source of her troubles: An IUD had been secretly inserted in her during the medical examination, and it had

Table 5.1
Reproductive Rights and Wrongs

Country	Year	Type of Abuse	Sex Targeted
Australia[1]	Early 1990s	Use of still-experimental contraceptive	Women
Bangladesh[2]	1976 to Present	Bribes, targets, contraceptive experimentation	Women & Men
Brazil	Early 1990s	Illegal sterilization	Women
China	1979 to Present	Forced Abortion, forced sterilization, coercive measures, sex-selective abortions & infanticide, neglected babies in orphanages	
Costa Rica[3]	Late 1990s	Sterilization campaign	
Cuba[4]	Mid 1990s	Babies aborted to tilt infant mortality statistics	
El Salvador	1980s	Sterilization campaign, quotas	
Guatemala[5]	1980s to Present	Lack of informed consent	
Haiti[6]	Mid 1990s	Norplant experimentation without informed consent	Women
Honduras[7]	1993	Dangerous contraceptives given without informed consent	Women
India[8]	1970 to Present	Forced sterilization, sex-selection abortion, female infanticide	
Indonesia[9]	1990s	Forced sterilization	
Kenya[10]	1990s to Present	USAID focus on birth control replacing much-needed medical care	
Kosovo[11]	1999	Kosovo in need of medical supplies given abortion kits instead	
Morocco[12]	2002 to Present	Experimental methods, i.e., quinacrine sterilization	
Mexico[13]	1970s to Present	Sterilization campaign, quotas, lack of informed consent	
Netherlands[14]	1993	Parliament approves euthanasia	Men & Women
New Guinea	Early 1990s	Dangerous contraceptives pushed	Women
Peru[15]	Mid to Late 1990s	Forced sterilization, coercion	
Philippines	1970s	Lack of informed consent, bribes, quotas	
Russia[16]	1993 to Present	Use of raw materials from aborted babies	
Scotland[17]	2004	Teenage girls sterilized with Implanon without parental knowledge	

Table 5.1 (cont.)

Country	Year	Type of Abuse	Sex Targeted
Sri Lanka[18]	Late 1980s to Present	Sterilization campaign, bribes, quotas, "subtle coercion"	
South Africa[19]	Early 1990s	Lack of informed consent	Women
Thailand[20]	Early 2000s	HIV-positive women in sometimes forced to have abortions	
Tibet[21]	Early 1990s to Present	Racist-driven abortion/sterilization by Chinese	Women
United Kingdom[22]	2004 to Present	Evidence of forced-abortion trends, babies aborted because of birth defects	
United States	1927-1981	Eugenics laws allowing forced sterilization of those deemed "unfit"; 2001 FACE act allows for forced abortions in U.S.	Women & Men
Venezuela[23]	Late 1990s	Sterilization campaign	
Vietnam[24]	1990 to Present	Forced sterilization, bribes and sanctions, lack of informed consent	

Notes

1. *PRI Review* 2(1) (January/February 1992): 11.
2. *PRI Review* 1(5) (September/October 1991): 5.
3. *PRI Review* 10(1) (January/February 2000): 4.
4. *PRI Review* 5(6) (November/December 1995): 5.
5. *PRI Review* 10(4) (July-September 2000): 4.
6. *PRI Review* 6(3) (May/June 1996): 5; *The Human Laboratory* a documentary produced by BBC's *Horizon* series and aired in Britain (8 November, 1995).
7. *PRI Review* 3(5) (September/October 1993): 7; "Final report about the use in Honduras of the oral contraceptive Ovrette (Norgestrel) in lactating women," Honduran Medical Association (7 June 1993).
8. *PRI Review* 10(1) (January/February 2000): 4.
9. *PRI Review* 13(5) (September/October 2003): 14; Aphaluck Bhatiasevi, "Women 'often blamed' for virus," *Bangkok Post* (8 October 2003); *SPUC News* (9 October 2003).
10. *PRI Review* 7(2) (March/April 1997): 10; USAID Congressional Presentation FY 1997.
11. *PRI Review* 9(3) (April/May 1999): 1; United Nations High Commissioner for Refugees (UNHCR) and United Nations Population Fund (UNFPA), *Proceedings for the Second Preparatory Meeting on Reproductive Health in Refugee Situation,* Geneva: (April 5-6, 1995) 8.
12. *Yale Alumnae Review.*
13. *PRI Review* 5(5) (September/October 1995): 8; *San Francisco Chronicle* (3 September 1995): 1-2.

14. *PRI Review* 3(2) (March/April 1993): 11; Jerome Socolovsky, The Associated Press (10 February 1993).
15. *PRI Review* 7(2) (March/April 1998): 1; Bermudez, "Sterilization without consent," *Catholic World Report* (March 1998).
16. *PRI Review* 4(4) (July/August 1994): 15; *Stern*, 6 (1993).
17. *PRI Review* 14 (4) (July/August 2004): 14.
18. *PRI Review* 7(2) (March/April 1997): 14; "Study reveals dark side to Sri Lanka's population control," Interpress Service Colombo (19 December 1996).
19. *PRI Review* 2(5) (September/October 1992): 6; "Family Planning and Race in South Africa," *Women's International Public Health Network News* 11 (Spring 1992): 9.
20. *PRI Review* 13(5) (September/October 2003): 14; Aphaluck Bhatiasevi, "Women 'often blamed' for virus," *Bangkok Post* (8 October 2003); *SPUC News* (9 October 2003).
21. *PRI Review* 3(2) (March/April 1993): 10; *Children of Despair,* Report No. 3, compiled by Martin Moss for Campaign Free Tibet, introduction by Paul Ingram, 6,2.
22. *PRI Review* 14 (3) (May/June 2004): 6.
23. *PRI Review* 10(1) (January/February 2000): 4.
24. *PRI Review* 10(1) (January/February 2000): 4.

---

led to a severe case of Pelvic Inflammatory Disease (PID). The doctor removed the IUD, but warned her that, because of the damage to her reproductive system, she may never be able to have children.[17]

For sheer brutality the North Korean population control program cannot be outdone. The policy is even stricter for the millions of inmates of that country's gulag, where pregnancy is a crime and births are absolutely forbidden. One former prisoner reported that "While I was there, it was commonly known that pregnant women were taken to a hospital outside the camp for forced abortion and that babies born alive were killed. One day when we came back from our work outside the camp, prisoners told us that a police doctor had inspected the female prisoners in the morning and had found out that two of them were pregnant.... Both were ordered to run around the camp yard with a heavily loaded stretcher. The first woman had [a] miscarriage and collapsed. Then, two prisoners were ordered to kick the swollen belly of Kim Son-hi. She miscarried about one or two hours later...."[18]

China, Bangladesh, Guatemala, Pakistan, Cambodia, South Africa, Sri Lanka, Indonesia: The roll call of countries where human rights have been abused in the cause of limiting fertility is entirely too long. Many of these countries received U.S. funding for their programs, others were encouraged and financed by U.S.-funded international organizations. Many received both.

Table 5.1 lists the countries in which human rights abuses have been reported by the international media or in scholarly journals. This is obviously not an exhaustive list, since abuses occurring in remote rural areas of developing countries are often not reported at all.

Even the mildest of these crimes constitutes a serious offense against the dignity of women and men. For they have been seduced, in effect, by the lies of the anti-natalists. Those who have been sterilized under some form of duress have been violated in an even more fundamental way. They have been sexually assaulted by the population controllers, and have had not just their reproductive rights, but their very persons, violated. It is arguably a form of rape and, in the case of tubal ligation and vasectomy, it is permanent. In the developing world, sterilization is for all practical purposes irreversible.

Human rights are nonnegotiable, or they are not rights at all, merely privileges to be withdrawn at the whim of governments, international organizations, or both. Abuses of basic rights, such as the right to bear children, cannot be expunged by reference to any calculus of costs versus benefits, any more than comparable violations of other basic human rights can be explained away, excused, or justified by reference to a supposedly larger social good.

Yet many controllers, committed to their salvific mission, disagree. When demographer Richard Easterlin visited India as a member of a UN Family Planning Mission in 1969, he was told by a program administrator in Bombay that strong-arm tactics were being used in the slum districts to ensure that government vasectomy targets were met. When he expressed concern at this, the administrator responded, "Surely, the end justifies the means."[19]

The original promoters of fertility reduction programs neither condemned nor absolutely proscribed coercion, but merely suggested that it be "gradated." That is to say, the state is encouraged to apply the precise amount of coercion on the target population necessary to enforce compliance. As explained by Bernard Berelson and Jonathan Lieberson in the pages of the *Population and Development Review,* this means in practice that "The degree of coercive policy brought into play should be proportional to the degree of seriousness of the present problem and should be introduced only after less coercive means have been exhausted. *Thus, overt violence or other potentially injurious coercion is not to be used before noninjurious coercion has been exhausted*"[20] (italics added). Note that violent acts against women's (and men's) bodies are neither condemned nor absolutely proscribed; they are merely kept in reserve until such time that lesser forms of coercion have played out.

Some human rights groups are belatedly beginning to pay attention, although their complaints have often been ignored. Father R. W. Timm, C.S.C., who has been involved in human rights work in Bangladesh for three decades, was able to get the army out of the sterilization program in the mid-1980s after threatening to expose USAID.[21] The Human Rights Commission of the Mexican government in 2003 condemned the Ministry of Health's practice of sterilizing or contracepting women immediately after childbirth, although the practice continues. Both Amnesty International and Human Rights Watch have criticized forced abortion, especially in the Chinese context, but to no avail. Similar abuses have also received notice in the State Department's annual "Country Reports on Human Rights." Most importantly, the U.S. Congress in the late 1990s moved to proscribe some forms of coercion in U.S.-funded programs, and a few programs have been defunded as a result.

The Tiahrt Amendment

From the beginning of its population control programs in the 1960s, USAID has consistently referred to them as "voluntary." When the phrase "family planning" is used, for example, USAID customarily tacks the adjective "voluntary" onto the front of it. But the phrase often seems little more a clever marketing technique, a dodge designed to sell the program both to U.S. taxpayers and, even more importantly, to potential "clients" overseas. For many of these programs are not truly "voluntary" at all, but were cleverly designed to bribe, pressure, intimidate and manipulate poor women into changing their attitudes towards children and compromising their fertility.

By the late 1990s, USAID-funded "voluntary" programs in Peru and elsewhere had become so notorious for their bullying tendencies that the U.S. Congress felt compelled to intervene.[22] Congressman Todd Tiahrt (R-KS) took the lead in sponsoring legislation designed, in his words, to "define the term 'voluntary' to ensure that no participants are bribed or otherwise coerced regarding participation in certain family planning methods. Forced sterilization of some of the most vulnerable classes of women in foreign countries should not be occurring in U.S.-funded family planning programs."[23] His fellow legislators concurred, and on 22 October 1998 the Tiahrt Amendment was signed into law.

With the passage of this law, coercion became an unacceptable part of any population control program funded by the U.S. government. The Tiahrt Amendment is worth considering in detail, not only because the activities it forbids are a matter of historical record, but also because similar abuses continue to occur in dozens of family planning programs around the world, some funded by the United States, others not. In many countries, these forbidden practices *are* the sum and substance of the family planning program. The text of the amendment follows, with a brief analysis of each paragraph:

> *(1) Any voluntary family planning project [funded by the United States] shall meet the following requirements: (1) service providers of referral agents in the projects shall not implement or be subject to quotas, or other numerical targets, of total number of births, number of family planning acceptors, or acceptors of a particular method of family planning (this provision shall not be construed to include the use of quantitative estimates or indicators for budgeting and planning purposes);* [24]

Quotas, targets and other ways of measuring the success of family planning programs by the numbers of women sterilized or using so-called "modern" contraceptive measures date back to the time of Dr. Ravenholt, whose ambitious goal it was to tie the tubes of one-quarter of the women of the world. Quotas became commonplace in the 1980s. There is indisputable evidence from a broad array of countries that such quotas lead to coercion, as women are forced to use a specific method because project leaders need to meet a target or, more broadly, that women are forced to use one of several "modern methods" to drive up the contraceptive prevalence rate, that is, the percentage of women using a "modern" contraceptive.

Quotas have been officially out of favor since 1994, when the *Program of Action* of the International Conference on Population and Development (ICPD) officially condemned the practice. "Government goals for family planning should be defined in terms of unmet needs for information and services. Demographic goals, while legitimately the subject of government development strategies, should not be imposed on family-planning providers in the form of targets or quotas for the recruitment of clients," the ICPD document said.[25] In other words, family planning programs should be driven from below, by the "unmet needs" of ordinary people for their services, not by targets and quotas from above, set by governments and international organizations.

Old habits, however, die hard. USAID has continued with its top-down approach, as its regular budget requests to the U.S. Congress testify. Here, in clear, unambiguous language, is proof that USAID is not simply interested in diminishing preexisting "unmet need," but is actively seeking to drive up "contraceptive prevalence rates" *and setting targets for same.* USAID sought to justify its 1998 budget request for preventing births in Kenya by noting that:

Between 1984 and 1995, USAID was the lead donor to the Kenya national family planning program. Its financial and technical assistance has contributed to an increase in modern method contraceptive prevalence among women of reproductive age, from 9% in 1984 to 30% in 1995....[26]

The agency goes on to make clear that it will consider the family planning program in Kenya a success if "modern contraceptive prevalence" rises from 28% in 1996 to 31% in the year 2000.

Quotas remain common in many, if not all, family planning projects which USAID funds around the world. In fact, a USAID contractor, Management Services for Health, runs a program called the Family Planning Management Development Project, whose purpose is to train clinic personnel to achieve targeted increases in the contraceptive prevalence rate in the given region.[27] The pretense that such numbers are merely intended "for planning purposes" cannot disguise the reality—to which USAID turns a blind-eye—that they are understood as targets for contraception or sterilization at the local level, thus giving rise to abuses.

(2) The project shall not include payment of incentives, bribes, gratuities, or financial reward to (A) an individual in exchange for becoming a family planning acceptor; or (B) program personnel for achieving a numerical target or quota of total number of births, number of family planning acceptors, or acceptors of a particular method of family planning;

The use of bribes or payments either in exchange for participation in population control programs or as incentives for workers in such programs to bring in more "acceptors" is a longstanding and well-documented abuse. Bribes offered to women for accepting sterilization or contraception have included everything from saris and clothing for children in India to food in Peru, radios and other small electronic equipment in parts of India and Africa, and money in Bangladesh, Pakistan, and other places. This provision makes it illegal for family planning programs to offer women money, goods, or anything else in exchange for using contraceptives or agreeing to be sterilized.

Family planning workers have often been rewarded for bringing in a certain number of women. In India, for example, family planning workers who bring in women for sterilization (in assembly-line fashion) collect bonuses if they meet their quota, and extra prizes if they exceed their quota. This provision means that family planning workers cannot be offered money, food, clothing, electronics, household goods, medical care, toys for their children, airline tickets, or anything else as a reward for getting women to accept family planning or for meeting a target or quota.

(3) The project shall not deny any right or benefit including the right of access to participate in any program of general welfare or the right of access to health care, as a consequence of any individual's decision not to accept family planning services.

Making various types of government benefits and programs available to only those who agree to use a so-called "modern contraceptive method" also has a long and ugly history. In the 1970s, an Indian government program restricted business licenses to those companies in which a given percentage of male employees had agreed to vasectomy. In Indonesia, government housing was promised to those who accepted contraception. And as discussed above, the Peruvian government ejected children from a government-sponsored nutritional supplement program if the mother refused sterilization. In Bangladesh, women whose families were driven from their homes by flooding were told they would not receive international humanitarian assistance, that is, food, water, blankets, and tents, until they submitted to sterilization.

(4) The project shall provide family planning acceptors comprehensible information on the health benefits and risks of the method chosen including those conditions that might render the uses of the method inadvisable and those adverse side effects known to be consequent to the use of the method;

Few women in the developing world are told honestly, completely, and in a language they can understand about the various methods of contraception and sterilization that are being urged on them. What passes for "informed consent" is often little more than a short, one-sided sales pitch for a particular method, with no mention of the warnings or adverse medical consequences that may follow. Misleading language is often used to name or describe it. Sterilization, for example, is invariably referred to as Voluntary Surgical Contraception, an Orwellian description for a procedure that is neither truly voluntary nor reversible for the poor on whom it is urged. Outright lying about a method is not uncommon. And what is one to call the practice of giving reading materials on a method to a woman who is illiterate, and then asking her to give her written consent.

Nothing is more dishonest than the practice, common in Mexico, Guatemala, and other countries, of sterilizing or contracepting women without their foreknowledge or consent. Mexican government hospitals, according to a 2003 report from the Human Rights Commission of the Mexican government, routinely sterilize or insert IUDs into women delivering their second or third child without their foreknowledge or consent and sometimes, even over their objections, *immediately after giving birth.*

(5) The project shall ensure that experimental contraceptive drugs and devices and medical procedures are provided only in the context of a scientific study in which participants are advised of potential risks and benefits;

Women in the developing world have often been used as guinea pigs in trials of particular population control devices, drugs or methods. In Bangladesh and Haiti women were invited to come into clinics for a free five-year contraceptive which, they told, had few side effects. They were not told that they were part of a test of a then-unapproved device called Norplant, which is surgically inserted under the skin and which chemically sterilizes a woman for five years. When the implants caused adverse medical consequences—bleeding, blood clots, loss of vision, and in a few cases complete blindness—the women had no recourse. The clinics, which had been paid to insert the device, responded to pleas for their removal by saying that there were no funds to pay for their removal, only their insertion.[28] The attitude of those directing this study, which was funded by the Population Council, is summed up in the words of "cooperating gynecologist" Dr. Kohinoor, who said "95% of our clients belong to the very poor class. They are responsible for giving birth four or five times. Since they cannot remember to take birth control pills every day, long-acting contraceptives are much better for them.... In order to have a good thing there is always a price to pay. If two or three women die—what's the problem?"[29]

Women in other countries have been sterilized in quinacrine trials. A quinacrine hydrochloride tablet is injected into the uterus, where it promptly dissolves into hydrochloric acid. The resulting chemical burn scars the openings of the fallopian tubes shut, preventing conception. In Vietnam a woman named Nan was one of approximately 100,000 who were sterilized in this fashion. The trial went forward without even the barest pretense of informed consent. Nan was simply ordered to report to the clinic at her state-run factory for a gynecological exam. Only after the "exam," when she was lying on the examining table in extreme pain, did she realize that the doctor had hurt her. She had been sterilized with quinacrine without her consent.[30]

In these and similar cases around the world, international norms for human involvement in drug trials were simply ignored. Results from both allegedly scientific studies are still being cited as justification for an increased use of each method. This portion of the amendment seeks to disallow that particular practice.

Population Control Paternalism

The temptation by elites to apply what Amartya Sen calls "strong discipline" to groups whose burgeoning numbers are seen as a threat goes back to the very beginning of recorded history. The Book of Exodus tells the story of the ancient Hebrews who, though enslaved in Egypt, saw their population grow dramatically in just a few generations. Pharaoh felt threatened by this increasingly numerous religious minority, and devised a plan to check their numbers. Every boy child born to the Hebrews, he decreed, must die.[31]

Few programs today are as deliberately callous as this, although the family planning programs of present-day China and North Korea come close. But all resemble ancient Egypt's in that they are simply imposed on the population by a tiny elite, without a popular referendum or even a semblance of democratic debate. Benevolent dictators like China's Deng Xiaoping and Peru's Alberto Fujimori are encouraged by the international population control movement to believe that, in limiting the fertility of those peoples under their control, they are acting in their countries—and the world's—best interests. The certainty inspired by this superior wisdom drives such leaders and their subordinates to run roughshod over all opposition, be it individual or institutional.

Fujimori and his officials, for example, were so convinced of the rightness of the sterilization campaign that for years they lied to the Peruvian people about its very existence. Appearing before the Peruvian Congress in 1998 to answer concerns about sterilization abuses, Marino Costa Bauer, then Fujimori's minister of health, denied to this democratically elected body reports of abuses, denied reports of targets and quotas, and even denied the existence of the sterilization campaign itself, which by then had been underway for three years.[32] Fujimori's presidential health advisor, Dr. Eduardo Yong Motta, was another who dismissed reports of forced sterilizations and deaths as exaggerations or outright lies. When asked about the death of Celia Durand and the sterilization of Victoria Espinoza, the short, pudgy doctor was curt, even dismissive. "These things could not have happened," he bluntly asserted during an interview with PRI investigator David Morrison on 29 January 1998, sending the suffering of these and countless other women down the memory hole.

The deep-seated paternalism of the Fujimori regime towards ordinary Peruvians, and especially towards women, came through loud and clear during the course of this interview. "Health workers are like educators," Yong Motta explained at one point. "They are with the people. They know what the people think and what the people need." What the people need, he made clear, was to stop having children. "Women in Peru have too many children," he asserted.

Yong Motta's anti-natal bias was apparently homegrown. "I come from a large family," he revealed early. "I am one of ten children. My father, also a doctor, was tired all the time. He had to work very hard merely to provide his children with an education. It was a very sad situation.

Many children bring many problems." Yong Motta sounded for all the world as if he wished the Peruvian government had sterilized *his* mother after, say, the birth of her second child.

It is a doctor's responsibility to convince the patient to do what is best, Yong Motta went on. Even if that meant making repeat visits to her house? he was asked. Absolutely, he responded. If the Ministry of Health did not do the campaigns house-to-house, he asserted. "women would not come." Why does the government insist that women accept sterilization in preference to, say, Depo-Provera? Sterilization is preferable, Young Motta said bluntly, because "a woman might forget to come in for her shot or *might not want to*" (italics added). Do targets for ligations exist? "Of course the campaign has targets; if not how would we know how we are doing."[33]

Although the overall goal of the campaign was to reduce the birthrate, the Peruvian sterilization campaign was aimed at specifically at women. Targets were set in terms of tubal ligations, not vasectomies. Women were visited in the home, not men in the workplace. It was the women, not the men, who were threatened with ejection from government programs.

This sort of gender profiling, as it might be called, was not limited to Peru in the late nineties, but is found almost everywhere that a rigorous family planning program is in place. With very few exceptions, such as India in the mid-1970s, women have been the targets of choice (see Table 5.1). Nearly all of the human rights violations documented over the past few decades have involved women—women being forcibly aborted, sterilized, and contracepted, women being bribed or punished into compromising their fertility, women being used a guinea pigs for the development of new forms of sterilization or contraception, women being denied access to full and complete information about the medical risks and consequences of family planning procedures.

A self-declared feminist, who worked for the Office of Population at USAID during the Clinton years, once assured me that coercion was not a problem now that they had, as she put it, "gotten rid of all of the men." Leaving the misanthropic implications of her comment aside, evidence coming in from the field suggests that abuses against women continue, despite the departure of the strident Dr. Ravenholt.

Genocide in the Andes?

Today's population control programs resemble pharaoh's campaign against the Hebrews in another way as well, for they always target the "others." In Fujimori's Peru, a woman was never more a likely candidate for sterilization than if she were brown-skinned, poor, and a non-native speaker of Spanish. In a real sense, at the grassroots, the Peruvian sterilization campaign pitted the "haves"—the largely urban descendants of Francisco Pizarro's *conquistadores,* against the "have-nots"—the largely rural descendants of the ancient Incas. The majority of the sterilization teams were sent to the *altiplano,* or the Andean mountain valleys, and the majority of the sterilizations were done on the Quechua-speaking inhabitants of those regions. This concentration on the impoverished *Indios,* living a hardscrabble existence on mountain plots, was why these crimes are rightly termed genocide.

This was confirmed when the elections of late 2000 brought a new president, Alejandro Toledo, and a reform-minded Congress into the capital.[34] Both the Ministry of Health, under the leadership of newly appointed Dr. Carbone, and the Peruvian Congress began to systematically collect information on the origins and direction of the sterilization campaign. The Congress authorized the formation of an investigative commission, called the "Voluntary Surgical Contraception Commission" (Anticoncepcion Quirurgical Voluntaria, or AQV in Spanish), headed by Dr. Chavez Chuchon. After a four-and-a-half month-long investigation, the AQV Commission submitted its final report, which was accepted by the Human Rights Commission of the Peruvian Congress by unanimous vote on 10 June 2003.[35]

The AQV Report didn't pull any punches. Over the course of the nineties, it reported, the Ministry of Health of President Fujimori sterilized 314,605 women, of whom 90 percent were pressured or tricked into having the operation.[36] Fujimori's campaign had "carried out massive sterilizations on designated ethnic groups, benefiting other ethnic or social groups which did not suffer the scourge with the same intensity … the action fits the definition of the crime of Genocide." The AQV Report reminded legislators that according to the Peruvian Penal Code, Article 319, "Whoever intentionally seeks to destroy totally or partially any national, ethnic, social or religious group by …. carrying out measures designed to prevent births within the group…. shall be sentenced to at least 20 years in prison." It concluded by making a "Constitutional Indictment against Alberto Fujimori, Marino Costa Bauer …. Eduardo Yong Motta [and others] for the alleged commission of crimes against Individual Liberty, against Life, Body and Health, of Criminal Conspiracy, and Genocide…."[37]

If there is anything that speaks to the covert racism that drives many population control programs, it is that those in power never target themselves for fertility reduction. Indeed, regardless of how high the birthrate is among those who resemble us in race, ethnicity, religion, caste or status, we tend to applaud. But the fertility of the "others," however many or however few children they actually average, is almost always viewed as a threat, and slated for selective reduction.

Indigenous peoples are invariably at risk when a family planning program gets underway. The Vietnamese government, for example, has been aggressively sterilizing the Hmong peoples of the mountains, also known as the Montagnard tribesmen, since the beginning of its two-child policy. Although Hanoi claims that the Hmong are subject only to fines and incentives, evidence gathered by Montagnard expatriates living in the United States suggests otherwise.[38] In remote mountain areas, such as parts of Quang Nam County, they report that entire Hmong villages have seen their women forcibly ligated. That the Hmong have been singled out is perhaps not surprising. Not only does the historical animosity between the Hmong and Vietnamese peoples run deep, the Hmong earned the lasting enmity of the Hanoi regime by fighting on the side of the United States and South Vietnam during the Vietnam War. The current population control measures against them can be seen as a continuation of that war by other means.

As the Vietnamese example suggests, peoples on the "wrong" side of an ethnic divide often bear the brunt of family planning programs. The Indian Ocean island state of Sri Lanka has had a tubal ligation campaign in place since the late 1980s. Health workers "concerned only with meeting official [population] targets," in the words of researcher Padma Kodituwakku of the Colombo-based Women and Media Collective, bribe and coerce women into undergoing sterilization at government-run clinics. Women are promised 500 rupees (about US$12.50) if they undergo a tubal ligation. But members of Sri Lanka's Tamil minority come under extra pressure, Kodituwakku found. Health workers, who are nearly all majority Sinhalese, use "subtle coercion" to force minority women to agree to the operation to stop them from having a third child. In every case she investigated the Tamil woman was made to feel guilty for already having two children. They were called "ignorant and irresponsible breeders," among other epithets. Sri Lanka's birth rate is already among the lowest in Asia, but the birth rate of a despised and rebellious minority—the Tamil Tiger guerilla movement has been active for years—can never be low enough, it seems.[39]

The People's Republic of China is going to great lengths to reduce the next generation of Uyghurs, a Turkish Muslim people whose historical homeland, East Turkistan, now falls within the borders of the People's Republic of China. (The Chinese term for East Turkistan is Xinjiang or "New Border.") Beijing's public posture of "ensuring a steady growth in minority population" and "improving the quality of minorities" is merely a cover, Uyghur sources say, for a brutal campaign of abortion, sterilization, and contraception against Uyghur women, especially in rural areas. Every year, according to eyewitness accounts, mobile family planning teams are sent out to the countryside to conduct mass abortions and sterilizations. In one incident, a woman about to deliver twins was instead aborted when authorities learned that she already had one child. Those arrested for practicing their faith are also reportedly sterilized.[40]

In Serbia, the regime of Slobodan Milosevic had long been alarmed by the high birth rate of ethnic Albanians in Kosovo. A century ago Serbs had been in the majority, but they were now outnumbered, badly, by ethnic Albanians. A "demographic bomb" was ticking there, warned the Serbian Ministry of Family Affairs in an official 1998 report. Later that same year, Milosevic's Minister of Family Affairs, Rada Trajkovic, was even blunter, disdainfully referring to Albanian women as "child-bearing machines." By then the Serbian Army had been dispatched to forcibly remove ethnic Albanians from within Kosovo's borders by any means possible, a program of ethnic cleansing that NATO would eventually put a stop to. Little noticed in the fray, the UN Population Fund set up shop in the Kosovo capital of Pristina in early 1999. UNFPA spokesman Alex Marshall later admitted that the Milosevic regime had in December 1998 "invited" UNFPA into Kosovo—and only Kosovo out of all the territory that it controlled—to conduct "reproductive health" assessments and to follow them up with "regular programs."[41]

The local press in Kosovo was up in arms over this new threat to Kosovars, who had already suffered so much. The Kosovopress news agency reported that "Milosevic's regime worked on developing a variety of genocidal tools against the Albanian population of Kosovo, including reproductive health practices."[42] PRI investigator Josipa Gasparic discovered one such tool in the newly opened office of the UNFPA: A manual entitled *How to Change the Mentality of Kosovar Women*.[43] It is instructive to imagine the outcry if Adolf Hitler had invited a population control organization into Poland to help "control" the reproduction of "undesirables" in that country. Was indicted war criminal Slobodan Milosevic's invitation to the UNFPA to target ethnic Albanians with a "reproductive health" campaign all that different?

One of the largest and most violent sterilization campaigns the world has ever seen—and one of the few to focus almost exclusively on men—occurred in India from 1975-77. The campaign began when President Indira Gandhi, encouraged by the United States, declared a "population emergency" in mid-1975.[44] New Delhi issued an edict: "Where a state legislature ... decides that the time is ripe and it is necessary to pass legislation for compulsory sterilization, it may do so." The days of friendly foreign workers handing out boxes of contraceptives to equally congenial Indian villagers were over. Indian government officials were assigned vasectomy quotas, and were denied raises, transfers and even salaries, until they had met them. The government referred to its tactics as "compul-suasion"—a word chopped up out of compulsion and persuasion—but the emphasis was definitely on force. Hard numbers are difficult to come by, but upwards of 6.5 million men may have been given vasectomies, many against their will, before the campaign ground to a halt the following year in the face of massive popular protests. Official reports put the death toll at 1,774, but the actual total was probably higher.[45] Given that a vasectomy is, surgically speaking, a relatively simple procedure, this high death rate suggests that many men suffered from subsequent infections that went untreated.

It is commonly thought that the reason the campaign inspired such fierce resistance—there was rioting in the streets of India's major cities and the government of Indira Gandhi was eventually brought down—was that it had targeted men. But this is only part of the story. The rioters were mostly made up of two groups, one despised for reasons of religion, the other for reasons of caste. For it had not taken Untouchables and Muslims long to discover that, while the vasectomy campaign was being led by high-caste Hindus—Brahmans and the like—it was members of their own groups who were going under the knife. Singled out for decimation, they rioted to show their acute displeasure.

Who Is Responsible?

It is rare for a family planning program to be called off merely because people object to the way it is being pursued, even in countries like India that enjoy a tradition of democratic governance. Such campaigns have never reflected the popular will in any event—I am unaware of any people ever freely voting to impose fertility controls on themselves (as opposed to "others")—and only rarely have they been truly national initiatives. Instead, they have been encouraged, orchestrated and, more often than not, imposed from abroad. Recall that in November 1976, as the Indian sterilization campaign was getting underway, World Bank president Robert McNamara called on that country's minister of family planning "to congratulate him for the Indian government's political will and determination in popularizing family planning."[46] Loans followed.

But as India's vasectomy campaign ended and Indira Gandhi's popularity plummeted so, too, did Peru's Ligation Festivals cease as the end of Alberto Fujimori's second term approached. Fujimori fled into exile in Japan shortly after leaving office, as human rights and corruption charges against him mounted. Once the AQV Commission was constituted and began its work on the origins and direction of the sterilization campaign, it was soon clear that he and his subordinates, Costa Bauer, Yong Motta and others, had not acted alone. Rather they had been encouraged, aided and abetted in their campaign by outside agencies, chiefly USAID and UNFPA. The *AQV Report* charged that:

> The population policy followed by the Peruvian government was induced and financed by international organizations, namely USAID and UNFPA. These restrictive [population] policies from outside the country carried with them not only financing but also demographic objectives which translated into targeted reductions in the fertility rate of Peruvian women, emphasizing those in our poor areas. In particular, this international aid included medical and surgical instruments to carry out sterilization and a variety of contraceptives. ...
>
> The presentation of Dr. Jorge Parra Vergara, former Director of the Program of Reproductive Health and Family Planning shows clearly that the majority of the sterilizations were closely related with the larger financial amounts from USAID ...
> ... in 1993 the United States basically took charge of the national health system of Peru ... The bilateral accord of 1993 that put the United States in such advantageous position, known as 'Project 2000,' was signed by the Peruvian and American authorities in September 1993 and was effective for seven years, ending in 2000. An examination of this document shows that USAID-Peru, the office in Lima of USAID, was for all practical purposes in control of the Peruvian health sector, before and during the years that the abuses took part. ...
> Although on paper the [sterilization campaign] was a task of the Peruvian government, USAID put great emphasis in the training of officers and personnel of the Health Ministry.

In other words, the AQV Commission charged, USAID funded, planned and managed (albeit indirectly, through proxies) the sterilization campaign, to the point of even providing the actual surgical instruments used. When these charges were made public in mid-2002, USAID predictably went into paroxysms of denial.

But is it mere coincidence that Timothy Wirth, Clinton's assistant secretary of state for population and the environment, paid a special visit to President Fujimori in mid-1995, just as the sterilization campaign was getting underway in earnest? The parallel with McNamara's earlier visit to India is striking. Wirth not only shared McNamara's apocalyptic views on population, he came to Lima bearing gifts.[47] The director of the USAID office in Lima, George Wachtenheim, soon announced that more U.S. funding was on the way:

> … $15 million, half of which goes to the government and the other half to the [family planning] NGO Manuela Ramos, with whom we are working in 'punctual' areas [poor ethnic enclaves with relatively high fertility], such as Puno, Ayacucho and Apurimac…. the birth rates have been brought down from 3% to 2%[48] in the country [of Peru], which is impressive, but in rural areas the figures are seven children per woman [sic]. *It is necessary to fight on, focusing on these [rural] areas* [italics added].[49]

Wachtenheim's comments were made in 1996, a time when the sterilization campaign was already well underway, generating what the *AQV Report* calls "hundreds of complaints regarding the absence of informed consent as called for in Peruvian law." His public celebration of past reductions in the birth rate, and militant exhortations for more of the same, could only have been taken by the Fujimori regime to mean that the United States fully approved of its methods.

Certainly senior Peruvian officials impatiently rejected the suggestion that the United States did not approve of their campaign. The presidential health advisor, Dr. Eduardo Yong Motta, told PRI in 1998 that "USAID is disqualified from objecting to the methods used because it has been helping in the family planning program from the first."[50]

Yet when Peru's sterilization campaign became the subject of a congressional hearing, and began to garner negative publicity in the pages of publications like the *New York Times*,[51] USAID began furiously backing and filling. It not only disclaimed all responsibility for what was happening in Peru, it sought to paint itself as a vigorous opponent of all campaigns, targets and quotas. Mark Schneider, USAID's assistant administrator for Latin America and the Caribbean, appeared before the House International Relations Committee to distance USAID from any involvement in Peru's sterilization campaign. He stressed to legislators at the 25 February 1998 hearing that USAID "in no way" approved of the use of quotas in family planning programs in Peru or anywhere else. On the contrary, he maintained that "As soon as USAID became aware of the government of Peru's move toward quantitative targets for sterilization and campaign strategy, US officials communicated strong concerns about the potential for distortions to the government."

This posturing may have been useful for publicity purposes, but the evidence suggests that the only "strong concern" USAID had earlier communicated to the Peruvian government was that the birthrate come down as fast and as far as possible. Nor did USAID, once it was aware of these abuses, suspend—even temporarily—its aid to Peru's population control program. Money, contraceptives and sterilization equipment continued to flow into Peru in a steady stream, further confirming in a very concrete way that what Peru was doing had USAID's blessing.[52]

Now, however, Mr. Schneider announced to the U.S. Congress startling news: The Peruvian government had agreed to immediately halt its sterilization campaign. Moreover, he went on, that government had promised to clarify to health workers that there are no targets for sterilization, and to implement a comprehensive monitoring program to ensure compliance with informed consent procedures.[53]

Why did the sterilization campaign come to such a sudden and ignominious end? Why, at least on paper, were informed consent procedures being hastily put in place? Obviously because USAID, whose actions in support of the campaign were coming under congressional scrutiny, had in turn put pressure on the Peruvian Ministry of Health to call off the dogs of sterilization. It must be noted, the Peruvian Ministry of Health *did exactly as ordered.* The number of tubal ligations performed in the National Family Planning Program dropped dramatically, falling from 88,518 in 1997 to 21,384 in 1998.[54] Recall the words of the *AQV Report:* "USAID-Peru ... was for all practical purposes in control of the Peruvian health sector, before and during the years that the abuses took part."

The evidence suggests that USAID could have successfully intervened at any point to stop the sterilization campaign. If the agency had been truly concerned about abuses, as it later claimed to be, then why didn't it do so? Was it because many in the agency actually applauded Fujimori's effort to realize the Ravenholt ideal, and sterilize large numbers of women of childbearing age?

Birth Control by the Numbers

Even Mr. Schneider's denunciation of Peru's "quantitative targets" rings hollow. USAID then as now continues to rely on quantitative targets in its budget requests to Congress. In 1998 the agency told Congress that the country of Guinea will have a population program which pleases USAID if its contraceptive prevalence rate—the percentage of women of reproductive age who have been chemically or surgically sterilized—moves from two percent in 1992 to five percent in 2001.[55]

Even Uganda, whose women may reasonably want more children to replace those lost during the civil war, is expected to see contraceptive prevalence rise from 13.25% in 1995 to 25% by 1999 if its program is to be called a success.[56] USAID pretends that it throws these numbers around merely for "planning purposes," but if defining "success" in terms of population percentages is not a target, then nothing is.

Even more troubling, USAID trains those in charge of family planning programs in both governmental and non-governmental organizations to evaluate success (and failure) by the numbers. This is done in part through the Family Planning Management Development (FPMD) project, a multi-million-dollar USAID program administered by a USAID surrogate called Management Sciences for Health (MSH).[57] Its publication, *The Family Planning Manager* is chock full of advice and case studies, and the emphasis is on the numbers.[58]

In an article entitled "Using National and Local Data to Guide Reproductive Health Programs," the *Manager* frankly instructs readers to set up "indicator panels" to monitor the "effectiveness of your reproductive health program."[59] And how is *effectiveness* defined? By the number and percentage of women of reproductive age who are using "modern contraception," that's how. (See Figure 5.1.)

The article goes on to list other "recommended local reproductive health indicators"—"percentage of new contraceptive acceptors; percentage of continuing contraceptive users; contraceptive method mix; number of referrals for long-lasting or permanent contraceptive methods." *What is striking about this list is that each and every one of these indicators has to do with disabling as many reproductive systems as possible, preferably permanently.* The claim that family planning programs are primarily designed to help women have healthy pregnancies and healthy babies is a tale told for the gullible.

Nothing more clearly illuminates the real goal of family planning programs than this narrow definition of "reproductive health." For according to this definition, the higher the percentage of women who have been surgically and chemically sterilized, the better their collective "reproductive health" is judged to be. This leads to the perverse result that a population enjoying perfect "reproductive health" would be unable to reproduce at all!

The case study in the same issue of the *Manager* is an even more open exhortation to targets. Misleadingly entitled "Tracking the Progress of Reproductive Health Services in the Highland District," it approvingly describes how a team of family planning workers sets targets for the

Figure 5.1
"Acceptors" of "Modern Methods"

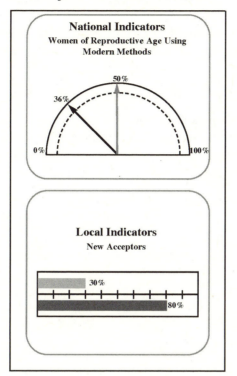

"Acceptors" of "Modern Methods" is how
The Family Planning Manager
recommends evaluating programs.

number of "new contraceptive acceptors" in their district during the
coming year.[60] The first quarter target for "new contraceptive acceptors" is set at 212, while the "year-end objective" is 650. Model charts
included in the text provide squares for recording "progress during the
first quarter."

Elsewhere, *The Family Planning Manager* frankly admits: "If family planning clinics paid as much attention to keeping existing clients
as to trying to enroll new ones, they could achieve a greater impact on
contraceptive prevalence with less effort and at lower cost. *Yet, clinic
managers are continually pressured to increase numbers of new acceptors*" (italics added).[61]

USAID's continuing reliance on targets has the effect of turning poor
women in developing countries into mere ciphers. Millions of women

have been confronted by government officials and health workers who view them not as human beings but as a means of reaching a target, or as numbers to be entered into a grant report. Abuses follow, such as the sterilization of women who are past menopause. This doesn't reduce the birthrate one iota, of course, but it does produce one more check mark on a chart.

Fujimori's "Technical Secretary": The UNFPA

The United Nations Population Fund also played a major role in the Fujimori sterilization campaign, "bringing not only special financing but also demographic goals, for the focalized reduction of the Peruvian population." Furthermore, according to the *AQV Report:*

> International aid proposed to the Peruvian government concentrated preferentially on meeting demographic objectives, especially after the inauguration of the government of ex-President Alberto Fujimori. These [democratic] objectives were incorporated into the National Population Program of 1991-1995. In unprecedented fashion, this national legislation gave the Technical Department of that Program to an international organization, the UNFPA.[62]
>
> The United Nations Population Fund (UNFPA), known for its support of population control in developing countries, took charge. For that end, the UNFPA act[ed] as [the campaign's] Technical Secretary, working in coordination with the National Population Council."[63]

The UNFPA's response to these very specific charges that it played a key role in the sterilization campaign has been to offer vague assurances that it never, ever does anything improper. UNFPA Chief of Media Services Alex Marshall blandly asserted following the release of the report that "All our programmes are consistent with national sovereignty and international human rights standards." He was so anxious to put some distance between the UNFPA and recent abuses that he denied that the organization in fact had anything to do with fertility reduction at all: "We do not espouse 'population control,' or in fact any ideology about population."[64] This laughable assertion is, of course, belied by the organization's very name. The UN Population Fund was founded in 1969 to deal with the imagined crisis of "overpopulation," and continues today to measure the success of its country programs by how fast fertility rates decline.

There is reason to believe that, in the case of Peru, the UNFPA leadership knew precisely what its operatives were up to. In 1999 the organization commissioned an investigation by Peruvian scholars into its involvement in the sterilization campaign. It refused to publicly release the resulting report, however, presumably because it shows the organization in a bad light. This was certainly the conclusion of the Peruvian media, which reported that the investigation concluded that UNFPA did bear some responsibility for the campaign.

The Peruvian *AQV Report* provides the clearest evidence yet that foreign agencies design, fund, and help manage family planning campaigns, even those that involve substantial and ongoing human rights abuses. Not surprisingly, it has come under fierce attack by USAID, UNFPA, and their surrogates. According to Anne Peterson, the former assistant administrator of USAID's Bureau of Global Health, the *AQV Report* "cannot be substantiated," is of questionable "veracity," and has been "officially discredited," "publicly repudiated," and "formally rejected."[65] These are extraordinary remarks to make about an investigative report signed by three members of the Peruvian Congress and which has been officially accepted by the Human Rights Commission of that same democratically elected body.

One final note: Local "haves" can and do adventitiously target local "have-nots" in family planning programs, as the targeting of *Indios* in Peru demonstrates. But the irony of such targeting is that the local elites themselves are targets. For such population programs, in the largest sense, are intended by the global "haves" of the world to control the global "have-nots." This includes local elites in developing countries. However these may in turn seek to turn the program to their own political, racial, ethnic, or religious advantage, or imagine that they are part of some global ruling class, they, too, are targets. Some local elites may convince themselves, as Fujimori apparently did, that they are serving their own interests. But they are serving the interests of their unacknowledged masters as well.

"Overpopulation" Ideas Have Consequences

Population control was not imposed on China by the West, as it was imposed on smaller, weaker countries, but that doesn't absolve the West of all responsibility for the one-child policy and its attendant abuses. Not only did Western-funded organizations like the UNFPA, IPPF and others lend China their enthusiastic support but, as recent research by Susan Greenhalgh and others makes clear, the intellectual impetus for the policy came from the West.[66] Vaporous 1960s ideas about population growth and resource depletion had explosive real-world consequences a decade later and half a world away. The core ideas underlying the one-child policy, it turns out, came from Western "science," more precisely from the notorious 1974 Club of Rome study that asserted we were breeding ourselves to extinction.

The Limits to Growth computer simulation, carried out by a group of MIT-based systems engineers, predicted that the world would come to an end by about 2070 if population growth continued.[67] The authors saw "no other avenue to survival" than population control, which was "the only feasible solution" to mankind's dilemma.[68] The book's conclusions lent themselves to hype which, it turned out, was precisely what the Club of Rome wanted. A public relations firm was hired, a press conference was organized, and the book was released with great fanfare. Scary stories sell, and this one sold a frightening four million copies, injecting the book indelibly into the world's consciousness.

The stage was now set for Song Jian, a systems control specialist for China's state-owned defense industry, to visit Europe in 1978. He might as well have come from another planet. Like other Chinese intellectuals, he had been isolated from the outside world for decades, and was desperately eager to catch up on developments. During his trip, as he later wrote, he "happened to learn about the application of systems analysis theory by European scientists to the study of population problems with a great success. For instance, in a "Blueprint for Survival" published in 1972, British scientists contended that Britain's population of 56 million had greatly exceeded the capacity of the country's ecosystem to sustain it. They argued Britain's population should be gradually reduced to 30 million, namely, a reduction by nearly 50 percent ... I was extremely excited about these documents and determined to try the method of demography" (typographical errors in original).[69] He had been to the future, or so he thought. In his baggage when he returned to China was a copy of *The Limits to Growth*.

Although Song Jian had no way of knowing it, what he thought was cutting-edge systems analysis was little more than a scientific hoax. The data were incomplete and sometimes inaccurate, its methodology was flawed, and it assumed—wrongly—that scientific and technical advances would cease.[70] In Julian Simon's words, "*The Limits to Growth* has been blasted as foolishness or fraud by almost every economist who has read it closely or reviewed it in print."[71] But the most decisive refutation of the study came from the Club of Rome itself, which two years after its publication suddenly "reversed its position" and "came out for more growth."[72] The Club's founder, Italian industrialist Aurelio Peccei, offered a remarkable explanation for this about-face: "*Limits* was intended to jolt people from the comfortable idea that present growth trends could continue indefinitely."[73] In other words, they rigged the study in order to dupe people into demanding population control.

In Song Jian they captured their most important convert ever, for through him their little caper impacted the lives of over a billion people—and continues to do so down to the present day. Borrowing the strident rhetoric of the Club of Rome report, he popularized the notion of a world in crisis: "Facing the rapid increase in population, countries everywhere are watching developments with grave concern."[74] He regurgitated its scary scenarios of ecological devastation, applying these specifically to China:

> As population increases, forests are chopped down. Now forest coverage is about 30 percent worldwide; in China that figure is only 12 percent.... In our country there is only 1.5 mu [one-sixth of an acre] per person.... The decrease in forest area, arable land per person, lack of food supplies, lack of protein, increase in pollution, and the use of natural resources are growing with the increase in population.... However, the expendable power of nature's stability is limited. To guarantee future generations adequate or good survival conditions, we cannot exceed our limit on taking natural resources or use a method that destroys the balance and stability of the ecosystem.[75]

He reinforced his rhetoric with eye-catching charts showing China's population remaining low for 4,000 years then, in Greenhalgh's phrase, "spiking up terrifyingly" to 1 billion by 1980.[76] No mention was made of recent, dramatic declines in the birth rate.[77]

Other experts jumped into the debate, arguing that not only China's ecology, but also its economy, was collapsing under the weight of its gargantuan population. Population growth was said to be responsible for every conceivable economic ill, from rising levels of unemployment and poverty to falling levels of labor productivity and investment. China, it seemed, faced a population crisis of enormous proportions which, if left unchecked, would shatter any hope of ever joining the ranks of the developed nations. Nothing less was at stake than the country's drive for wealth and global power, warned Vice Premier Chen Muhua in the pages of the *People's Daily*: "In order to realize the Four Modernizations, we must control population growth in a planned way.[78]

Once the Chinese leadership had been, to use Club of Rome terminology, jolted into accepting the idea that population growth was sabotaging the nation's modernization, they were ripe for a radical solution. After all, the future of the Chinese nation hung in the balance. As Susan Greenhalgh has demonstrated, it was Song Jian, armed with a computer simulation right out of the pages of *The Limits to Growth*, who offered one.

After returning from Europe, Song set out to replicate the economic and ecological projections he had stumbled across in Europe, this time with China as the subject. He formed a research group comprised of two other systems control specialists, one economist, and himself. Using newly available computer technology, the Song group first set out to calculate China's "optimal" population in the year 2080. Making the same kinds of highly questionable assumptions as their Club of Rome mentors, using data that were even more fragmentary, they calculated that the optimal population in 2080 would be between 650 and 700 million people. This figure, which was roughly two-thirds of China's 1980 population, they proposed as the goal of any birth control program.[79] China's "only choice" was to reduce the population down to this level, Song maintained, borrowing the *Limits* language. There was simply "no other way," "no other choice."[80]

In order to determine the level of fertility control necessary to reach this goal, the group next projected future population growth under different childbearing schemes: 3.0, 2.3, 2.0, 1.5, and 1.0. The first three they rejected out of hand. If the people were allowed to continue to bear children at the 1978 rate—a total fertility rate of 2.3—they calculated that the population would grow to 2.12 billion in 2080. Even if the TFR were forced down to 2.0, there would still be 1.47 billion Chinese alive after a century. These schemes "obviously cannot be adopted," they said. The seriousness of the population crisis required sterner measures. Limiting women to an average of 1.5 children produced the kind of population reduction they were looking for. Under this scenario, the number of Chinese would decline to 777 million by 2080, within striking distance of their "optimum population" of 650-700 million. Under their final scenario, in which every couple would be limited to one child by 1985, the population would plummet to only 370 million, well below the optimum.[81]

The Song group was well-connected, and soon after completing their computer simulations they were able to present them to top Communist Party and government leaders. These were reportedly "very impressed with the science and the numbers."[82] As well they might be. The presentation by the Song group confirmed one of their most cherished beliefs, namely, that Western science and technology, appropriately applied to the Chinese context, would be the salvation of their nation. As Greenhalgh writes, "The attitude towards everything foreign was close to idolatry. This was to have fateful consequences."[83] Western "science", or at least one odd brand of it, had become the core of Chinese policy.

The computer simulation presented by the Song group—perhaps the first that senior Chinese leaders had ever seen—must have been greeted with not only awe but also relief. Here was welcome confirmation that "overpopulation," rather than, say, economic mismanagement or political turmoil, was the true source of China's backwardness. Not only had the Song group used Western "science" to identify the problem, it had used those same techniques to devise a plan to save China from the flood of people that threatened to inundate it. Scientific and technological modernization, named by Paramount Leader Deng Xiaoping the most important of his Four Modernizations, was paying off. How proud they must have been that their own scientists, using the latest in Western "science," had so precisely calculated China's "optimum population." That Song's group was even able to offer precise advice on fertility levels and future population numbers was an added bonus. The leadership had few qualms about regulating the fertility of its subjects—it had done worse over the previous three decades—but Song's insistence that Western "science" left them "no other choice" made the decision easy.

The only question was whether to adopt the 1.5 child per family policy preferred by the Song group, or to impose an even more restrictive one-child-per-family policy. The leadership in the end rejected the 1.5 children option, apparently fearing that the peasants would then push for two or more.[84] When Song's study was later published in the *People's Daily* on 7 March 1980, it was edited to read that the 1.5 child per family policy would be "disadvantageous to our country's four modernizations … and to the raising of the people's standard of living." The one-child-per-couple policy, which results in a population much smaller than the supposed optimum, was described as "a comparatively ideal scheme for solving our country's population problem."[85]

Publication in the official party organ, the *People's Daily*, meant that the policy had received the imprimatur of the Communist Party and was therefore beyond further discussion and debate (such that there is in China). Six months later, in mid-September 1980 the one-child policy was formally ratified by the third session of the Fifth National People's Congress. From then on it was set in stone. On this terrible altar hundreds of millions of mothers and children have suffered and died, sacrificed for a scientific fraud.

The flagrant intellectual dishonesty of the Club of Rome's *Limits to Growth* report had striking real-world effects in China, having metamorphosed into the one-child policy and, as such, proven fatal to a considerable number of Chinese women and baby girls.[86] It may be that the Club of Rome merely wanted to shock the Western world out of its complacency about population growth, but tens of millions of Chinese baby girls, and no few women, have died in earnest.

The Party, for its part, was happy to blame China's "overlarge population" for all of China's problems and backwardness, since this distracted the people from its own errors of the preceding three decades. Population growth became an all-purpose villain in the official press, blamed for everything from declines in labor productivity to sagging economic growth. If only *you* wouldn't have so many children, the Chinese Communist Party continues to chide the people even today, *we* could achieve wealth, power and glory for China in a few years.

As the China case puts in stark relief, the real danger to men, women and children of the developing world is not "overpopulation" at all, but rather alarmist notions of overpopulation.[87] The notion that people are somehow social, ecological and economic nuisances is a pernicious one, predisposing governments to treat their own citizens as a form of pestilence. Instead of trying to lift their poor out of poverty, governments instead try and reduce their numbers. Authentic economic development is neglected, human rights abuses abound, and everyone's freedoms are put at risk. Population control encourages domestic tyranny of a very personal and deadly sort.

Notes

1. Amartya Sen, "Population: Delusion and Reality," *New York Review of Books*, 22 September 1994, 71. Also quoted in "The United Nations Population Fund: Assault on the World's People," Catholic Family and Human Rights Institute, 2002, 67.
2. Amartya Sen, "Population: Delusion and Reality," *New York Review of Books*, 22 September 1994, 71.
3. This account of the Peruvian sterilization campaign is taken from David Morrison, "Cutting the Poor: Peruvian Sterilization Program Targets Society's Weakest," *PRI Review* 7(2) (March/April 1998):1.
4. Alexandro Bermudez, "Sterilization without consent," *Catholic World Report*, March 1998.
5. The record for the most tubal ligations in the shortest amount of time is held by an Indian sterilization team, which reported ligating 48 women in 128 minutes, for an average of less than three minutes per operation from start to finish. James Miller, "The Disassembly Lines," *PRI Review* 7(4) (July/August 1997):9.
6. David Morrison, "Tiahrt Violations! USAID Continues to Fund Family Planning Programs in Peru, Despite Verifiable Abuses," *PRI Review* 10(1) (January/February 2000):7.
7. David Morrison, "Cutting the Poor: Peruvian Sterilization Program Targets Society's Weakest," *PRI Review* 7(2) (March/April 1998):5.
8. "A Doctor Speaks Out: What Happened to Medicine when the Campaign Began?" Statement of Dr. Hector Chavez Chuchon to the Subcommittee on International Operations and Human Rights of the House International Relations Committee, 25 February 1998, as reprinted in the *PRI Review* 7(2) (March/April 1998):.

9. David Morrison, "Tiahrt Violations!" 12.
10. Ibid., 13.
11. "Sterilized after giving birth," Statement of Victoria Vigo Espinoza to the Subcommittee on International Operations and Human Rights of the House International Relations Committee, 25 February 1998, as reprinted in the *PRI Review* 7(2) (March/April 1998):9.
12. Studies in Family Planning, 1991. See also, "Bangladesh Sterilization Incentives," *PRI Review* 1(5) (September/October 1991):5.
13. *The London Observer*, 1 April 1984. See also, *The Demographic, Social and Human rights consequences of U.S. Cuts in Population control funding: A Reassessment*, (Front Royal, VA: Population Research Institute, 1996), 5.
14. Brian Clowes, "Coercive Birth Control: Examining Antinatalist Thought and Action," *Yale Journal of Ethics* (Fall 1995). Dr. Clowes carried out research on population control activities during an August-September 1995 visit to Cape Town, Johannesburg, and Soweto, South Africa.
15. "Vietnam's Two-Child Policy," *PRI Review* 5(5) (September/October 1995):7.
16. "Mexican 'Family Planning' by Force," *PRI Review* 5(5) (Sept/Oct 1995):7. "Family planning by force," *San Francisco Chronicle*, 3 September 1995, 1-2.
17. *Know Your Rights: Women, Family Planning and U.S. Law*, (Front Royal, VA: Population Research Institute, 1998), 9-10.
18. PRI *Weekly Briefing*.
19. Quoted in Karl Zinsmeister, "Supply-Side Demography," *PRI Review* 3(4) (July/August1993):9.
20. Bernard Berelson and Jonathan Lieberson, "Government Efforts to Influence Fertility: The Ethical Issues," *Population and Development Review*, December 1979, 609. The Population and Development Review is one of the flagship journals of the population control movement.
21. Personal communication, 24 February 2007. Father Timm wrote, "I can cite many abuses in the family planning program involving the US officially. [In 1985] we got a rumor that the Army was doing forcible sterilization among tribals on the northern border and that eight women had died. I sent Alo D'Rozario ... to investigate ... The Army had come a month before and met the Union Council chairmen and told them to prepare a list of women who had three or more children. If they didn't show at the appointed times their husbands would be taken for vasectomy and they wouldn't get the lungi and Tk 150 which were given for sterility purposes and to compensate for work lost. The previous month the govt. health centre in Haluaghat Upazila has sterilized 18. Army did 550 in two weeks. I immediately went to USAID, the funder of the program and spoke to Dr. John Neponek ... the head of the program. I told him if they didn't get this stopped immediately their name would be mud throughout the world by the next week. He asked for a little time to investigate and they verified everything I had told him. The US ambassador called President Ershad and told him they wouldn't get another [penny] if they didn't get the Army out of there, *quamprimum*. They did and the Army has been out of family planning ever since."
22. The information uncovered by PRI in Peru led directly to the passage of the Tiahrt Amendment. The Tiahrt Amendment defined coercion to include those very abuses that were rampant in the Peru sterilization campaign—quotas, targets, bribery, and lack of informed consent. Some of these practices had earlier been criticized by the Programme of Action that was adopted at the 1994 Cairo Conference, but without effect. United Nations, *"Programme of Action" of the 1994 International Conference on Population and Development*, Cairo, Egypt, 18 October. A/CONF.171/13 (New York: United Nations, 1994), see paragraph 7.12.

23. "Congress to USAID: Stop the Abuse," *PRI Review* 8(4) (July/October 1998):1.
24. Congressman Todd Tiahrt, HR 4569, amendment no.38, *Congressional Record*, 105th Cong., 2d session, 1998, 144, no.123: H7922; also quoted in "Congress to USAID: Stop the Abuse." 4-5.
25. *Program of Action,* International Conference on Population and Development (Cairo, Egypt: United Nations Population Fund, 1994:), Chapter 7.
26. USAID FY1998 Budget Presentation for Kenya found at http://www.info,usaid.gov/pubs/cp98/afr/countries/ke.htm.
27. David Morrison, "Family Planning by the Numbers," *PRI Review* 8(2) (March/April 1998):10.
28. "Stoppage of Nor-plant Use Demanded, *The Morning Sun* (Dhaka), 1 January 1996, 7. "Who Cars if a Third World Woman Dies?" *The Daily Star* (Dhaka), 6 February 1996, 5. Also, *Know your Rights!*
29. Farida Ahktar, "Norplant the Five Year Needle," *Issues in Reproductive Engineering* 3(3):221-8. See also Jean M. Guilfoyle, "USAID: Enabling 'The Piper's Tune'," *PRI Review* 2(6) (January/February 1993):4.
30. *Know your Rights!*
31. Exodus 1:22, *The New American Bible* (New York: Catholic Book Publishing Co), St. Joseph Edition.
32. David Morrison, "Cutting the Poor," 6.
33. David Morrison, "Interview with Eduardo Yong Motta," *PRI Review* 7(2) (March/April 1998):4-5.
34. The Peruvian Constitution limits a president to two terms, and a last-ditch effort by Fujimori to amend the constitution to remove this restriction failed. He was not eligible to run again.
35. A majority of the Health Committee of the Peruvian Congress, after intense lobbying by population control organizations named in the report, voted against accepting the report in late 2002. The Human Rights Commission, unencumbered by ties to foreign-funded family planning programs, passed it unanimously.
36. Peruvian Ministry of Health, "Number of Tubal Ligations," 12(4) *PRI Review* (July/August 2002):16.
37. Subcommittee Investigating the Persons and Institutions Involved in Voluntary Surgical Contraception, *Final Report Concerning Voluntary Surgical Contraception During the Years 1990-2000.* (Lima, Peru: Congress of Peru, June 2002).
38. The Montagnard Foundation, "Vietnam Ambassador Admits Sterilization of Montagnard Hill Tribes: Crime of Genocide: Imposing measures to prevent births," Press release, August 2001. See also Steven W. Mosher, "UNFPA Supports Coercion: Vietnamese are Victims of UNFPA," *PRI Review* 12(1) (January/February 2002):3.
39. "Sri Lankan Population Atrocities," *PRI Review* 7(2) (March/April 1997):14.
40. Yemlibike Fatkulin, testimony before the International Relations Committee of the U.S. House of Representatives, October 17, 2001. See also Yemlibike Fatkulin, "The Plight of the Uyghur People," *PRI Review* 11(4) (September/October 2001):10-11.
41. Taped interview with Alex Marshall, 9 August 1999.
42. Kosovopress, "New Proof of Serb Plans to Use Reproductive Health as a Genocidal Tool," 20 July 1999.
43. Steven W. Mosher, "When Family Planning is Ethnic Cleansing," *PRI Review* 9(5) (August/September 1999):2.
44. For U.S. involvement, see Bernard Berelson's *Beyond Family Planning* and Chapter Four of this book.
45. Robert Whelan, *Choices in Childbearing: When Does Family Planning Become Population Control?* (London: Committee on Population & the Economy, 1992), 29.

46. Karl Zinsmeister, "Supply-Side Demography," 9.
47. Wirth, for example, led the effort at the 1994 Cairo population conference to impose worldwide targets for population growth, a dangerous enterprise that was only narrowly defeated by the countries of the developing world and the Vatican. Wirth, a former Colorado senator, went on to head Ted Turner's UN Foundation, the primary purpose of which is to fund population control programs.
48. Wachtenheim here presumable is referring to the population increase rate, not the birthrate.
49. George Wachtenheim, remarks given at reproductive health conference. Lima, Peru, 1966. Quoted in *Final Report Concerning Voluntary Surgical Contraception During the Years 1990-2000,* Subcommittee Investigation of Persons and Institutions Involved in Voluntary Surgical Contraception, June 2002.
50. David Morrison, "Interview with Eduardo Yong Motta," 4.
51. Calvin Sims, "Using Gifts as Bait, Peru Sterilizes Poor Women," New York Times, 15 February 1998, section 1.
52. According to *El Peruano*, which serves as the equivalent of the *Federal Register* for Peru, the Peruvian government approved donations from USAID to its family planning NGO, AB Prisma, totaling roughly US$5.3 million, or about 32,000 pounds of contraceptive drugs and devices, for the year 2000. See also, USAID, US Embassy, Lima, Peru, "Improved Health, including Family planning, of High-Risk Populations," 10 January 2000. http://ekeko.rep.net.pe/usa/aidsale.htm.
53. Mark Schneider, USAID Assistant Administrator for Latin America and the Caribbean, Testimony before the House International Relations Committee, Subcommittee on International Operations and Human Rights, 25 February 1998. See also, David Morrison, "Tiahrt Violations!" 6. Schneider also testified that the Peruvian government would (1) welcome investigations by the Peruvian Ombudsman's Office of complaints received, and would respond to any additional complaints from the public; (2) implement a 72-hour "waiting period" for people who choose tubal ligation or vasectomy, which would occur between the second counseling session and surgery and (3) require health facilities to be certified as suitable for performing surgical contraception [sterilization] to ensure that no operations would be done in makeshift or in substandard facilities.
54. Peruvian Ministry of Health, "Number of Tubal Ligations," 16.
55. USAID FY1998 Budget Presentation for Guinea found at http://www.info,usaid,gov/pubs/cp98/afr/countries/gn.htm.
56. USAID FY1999 Budget Presentation for Uganda found at http://www.usaid.gov/pubs/cp99/afr/ug.htm. Accessed 1 May 2007.
57. USAID paid Management Sciences for Health over $7.5 million through late September 1997 to create FPMD. USAID Office of Procurement, *Contracts and Grants and Cooperative Agreements with Universities, Firms and Non-Profit Institutions Active During the period October 1, 1995-September 30, 1996.*
58. FPMD is meant to help "national and local family planning programs and organizations to develop their capability to successfully plan and manage sustainable family planning programs Family Planning Management Development Project, "About FPMD," http://www.msh.org/fpmd/main/about.htm. Accessed 2 May 2007.
59. Judy Seltzer and Stee Solter, editors, "Using National and Local Data to Guide Reproductive Health Programs," *The Family Planning Manager* 6(2) (Summer 1997).
60. Seltzer and Solter, editors, "Tracking the Progress of Reproductive Health Services in the Highland District," *The Family Planning Manager* 6(2) (Summer 1997).

61. Dick Roberts, Promboon Panitchpakdi, and Benjamin Loevinson, editors, "Using Information on Discontinuation to Improve Services" *The Family Planning Manager* 2(3) (May/June 1993).

62. *Subcomision Investigadora de Personas e Instituciones Involucradas en las Acciones de Anticonception Quirica Voluntaria,* June 2002. (Hereinafter *AQV Report*) (AQV, AQV@congreso.gob.pe).

63. *AQV Report,* See also *PRI Review* 12(4) (July/August 2002):12.

64. UNFPA letter dated July 2002, signed by Alexander Marshall, UNFPA Chief of Media Services.

65. Anne Peterson, USAID Bureau for Global Health, letter to Seven Mosher, dated 7 January 2003.

66. Tien, H. Yuan, "Demography in China: From Zero to Now," Population Index 47(4):683-710; Tien, China's Strategic Demographic Initiative (New York: Praeger, 1991). In this section I draw upon Susan Greenhalgh, "Science, Modernity, and the Making of China's One-Child Policy," *Population and Development Review* 29(2) (June 2003).

67. D. H. Meadows *et al., The Limits to Growth: A Report for the Club of Rome's Project on the Predicament of Mankind.* (New York: Universe Books, 1972).

68. Meadows et al. 1974: 196; "The Only Feasible Solution" is the title of Chapter 9 of the second volume of the report, *Mankind at the Turning Point* by Mesarovic, Mihajlo, and Eduard Pestel. *Mankind at the Turning Point: The Second Report to the Club of Rome* (New York: E.P. Dutton, 1974).

69. Song Jian, "Systems Science and China's Economic Reforms," in *Control Science and Technology for Development,* Yang Jiachi, ed., (Oxford: Pergamon, 1986), 1-8. Quoted in Susan Greenhalgh's "Science, Modernity, and the Making of China's One-Child Policy." 170.

70. As a demonstration of the significance of its error, these rules were used to predict the period 1870 to 1970 from the basis of what was known in 1870, and the computer predicted that the world would come to an end before 1970, in part because of the inability to control the massive amounts of horse manure. This can stand as an apt commentary on the whole enterprise. See Robert Sassone, *Handbook on Population*, Fifth Edition (Stafford, Virginia: American Life League, 1994), 6.

71. Julian Simon, *The Ultimate Resource.* (Princeton: Princeton University Press, 1981), 286. See, *inter alia*, Cole, H.S.D., Christopher Freeman, Marie Jahoda, and K.L.R. Pavitt, eds., 1973. *Models of Doom: A Critique of The Limits to Growth.* (New York: Universe, 1973).

72. *Time* magazine, 26 April 1976, 56; *New York Times*, 14 April 1976.

73. *Time* magazine, 26 April 1976.

74. Song Jian, "Population Development—Goals and Plans," in *China's Population: Problems and Prospects*, Liu Zhen, Song Jian *et al*, eds.,(Beijing: New World Press, 1981), 25-31. Cited in Greenhalgh, "Science, Modernity, and the Making of China's One-Child Policy," 173. Note that this English-language publication came out several years after Song had begun circulating these same ideas inside of China.

75. Song, "Population Development—Goals and Plans," 26. See also Song Jian. 1999 [1980]. "Cong xiandai kexue kan renkou wenti" (Population problems from the perspective of modern science), in Song Jian, *Song Jian kexue lunwen xuanji* (Selected scientific papers of Song Jian). (Beijing: Kexue Chuban She, 1999) 552-553. Originally published in *Guangming Ribao*, 3 October 1980. Quoted in Greenhalgh, 174-175.

76. Song Jian, Chi-Hsien Tuan, and Jing-Yuan Yu. 1985. *Population Control in China: Theory and Applications.* (New York: Praeger, 1985), 2. Also cited in Greenhalgh, 173.

77. Chinese figures of the time showed that the years 1971-79 saw the natural increase rate fall by half, from 23.4 to 11.7, and the crude birthrate decline by almost as much, from 30.7 to 17.9. Tian, H. Yuan, 1981. "Demography in China: From Zero to Now," *Population Index* 47(4):683. Quoted in Greenhalgh, 173.

78. Chun Muhua, "In order to Realize the Four Modernizations, We Must Control Population Growth in a Planned Way," *Renmin Ribao* (People's Daily), 11 August 1979, 2. The "Four Modernizations" was Deng Xiaoping's plan to modernize China's science and technology, military, industry, and agriculture by century's end.

79. Song, "Population Development—Goals and Plans," 28-30. Cited in Greenhalgh, 179.

80. Ibid, 31. Cited in Greenhalgh, 182.

81. Song Jian, Tian Xueyuan, Li Guangyuan, and Yu Jingyuan, "Concerning the Issue of Our Country's Objective in Population Development," *Renmin Ribao* (People's Daily), 7 March 1980.

82. Greenhalgh, 184.

83. Greenhalgh, 171-172.

84. Greenhalgh, 184.

85. Song Jian *et al*, "Concerning the Issue of Our Country's Objective in Population Development," 37. Cited in Greenhalgh, 181.

86. Susan Greenhalgh, "Science, Modernity, and the Making of China's One-Child Policy," *Population and Development Review* 29(2) (June 2003). The author seems intent to shield the Club of Rome in particular, and the overpopulation school in general, from any responsibility for what has happened in China, although the body of her text makes it clear that this is where some responsibility lies. She is also at pains to deny that those who naively imported the notion of a "population crisis" into China should be held responsible, even though it was they who convinced senior leaders to adopt a policy that was inhumane on the face of it, and became even more so as it was operationalized. One appreciates the necessity of protecting one's informants—she interviewed the principal Chinese players in the course of doing her paper—but surely some apportioning of responsibility is appropriate under the circumstances. The author, for whatever reason, fails to reach the conclusions demanded by the evidence she has amassed. Perhaps she doesn't believe in the existence of free will, but rather that they were merely reacting to their environment, following orders, or fated. This, of course, is perilously close to the Eichmann defense of "Befehl ist Befehl."

87. The environmental movement's recent emphasis on "sustainable development" continues to fuel China's misguided policy. Sustainable development first entered the global vocabulary at the 1992 UN Conference on Environment and Development in Rio de Janeiro, Brazil. As we will see in Chapter 6, much of the discussion at the so-called "Earth Summit" centered around Agenda 21, an ambitious 40-chapter plan for fundamentally altering the world's priorities away from economic growth and towards preserving at all costs the natural environment "for future generations." Agenda 21 called on governments to make "[a]n assessment ... of national population carrying capacity" and enact programs to reduce fertility to replacement level or below. China, which speaks of continuing the one-child policy to 2050, is carrying out this agenda with a vengeance.

6

Population Control While People Die: Undermining Primary Health Care

> *Our health sector is collapsed. Thousands of the*
> *Kenyan people will die of malaria, the treatment*
> *for which costs a few cents, in health facilities*
> *whose shelves are stocked to the ceiling with mil-*
> *lions of dollars worth of pills, IUDs, Norplant,*
> *Depo-Provera, and so on, most of which are sup-*
> *plied with American money.*
> –Stephen Karanja, M.D. Former Secretary, Kenyan Medical Association[1]

> *"Children and women are to be the Trojan Horse*
> *for dramatically slowing population growth.*
> –James Grant U.N. Children's Fund (UNICEF)[2]

Each year at least 1.5 million people—or about one every 20 seconds—die of malaria.[3] Yet USAID spends only $10 million to reduce the death toll from this deadly disease, a pittance compared to the hundreds of millions of dollars it pours into fertility reduction programs in the developing world.[4] While family planning devours aid budgets, this old killer stalks the poor—and their children.

Malaria's Medical Burden

Emily Adekoya, eight years old, had seemed in good health when she left for school that last morning. But at noon she spiked a fever and began trembling uncontrollably, the unmistakable signs of a malarial attack. Her parents carried her to a local clinic but, with no malarial tablets on hand, there was little the director could do but advise the parents to take her back home and wait for the disease to run its course. This didn't take long. Emily had contracted cerebral malaria or *falciparum*, as it turned out, a particularly lethal form of the disease. By late afternoon, she was dead.

161

Her death was entirely avoidable. There is no mystery, from a medical point of view, about how malaria spreads or how it kills. Unlike HIV/AIDS, whose origins, prevention and treatment are matters of controversy, malaria is among the best known of human parasitic diseases, having been exhaustively studied for over a century. Its origins (as a mosquito-borne protozoa), its methods of treatment (by quinine and related drugs), and its courses of prevention (drain swamps and eradicate mosquitoes) are well understood.

As any medical textbook will report, the infective cycle begins when a female mosquito belonging to the genus *Anopheles* bites a person already carrying one of four species of protozoan parasites belonging to the *Plasmodium* family. Along with the blood she ingests come tiny malarial cells called gametocytes. These migrate to the mosquito's mid-gut where, over a period of about 12 days, they sexually produce sporozoites, which are the cells responsible for infecting humans and which migrate to the mosquito's salivary glands. When the malarial-infected mosquito bites a new host a large number of the sporozoites mingle with the saliva and enter the person's bloodstream, where they move quickly to infect liver cells. There, over about 10 days, they reproduce and mature into cells called merozoites. These, in turn, reenter the bloodstream, where they infect and kill red blood cells by appropriating the host cell's critical hemoglobin for their own asexual reproduction. A microscope reveals this microbiological assault in dramatic detail. Ellen Shell writes of seeing "greatly enlarged photographs" which capture malaria parasites "pouring from the ghostly white hulks of dead blood cells like soldiers fleeing a scorched earth spree."[5]

Now, during the final stage of the cycle, they massively infect other cells. At the same time, they produce huge numbers of gametocytes to await introduction into a new mosquito. It is here that the unwilling human host suffers the fever, shakes, anemia—and often death—that malaria brings.

Although the differences between the species of *Plasmodium* appear relatively minor, their disease impact is not. *P. falciparum* is both the most dangerous of the four and, tragically, the one most resistant to the current range of anti-malarial drugs. *Falciparum* has the ability to alter the surfaces of the blood cells it infects to make them sticky. As soon as cells are infected, they tend to adhere to the walls of surrounding blood vessels. The resulting blood clots can interrupt the blood flow to parts of the brain and other vital organs, causing strokes, heart attacks, and other health problems.

Ellen Shell writes movingly of the toll that the dreaded *falciparum* takes on children. In one clinic near Dakar, Senegal, she found that every child admitted was under treatment for cerebral malaria. The "full-blown cases" she described as looking "terrible": "Their eyes were unfocused under half-closed lids, and they lay absolutely still. Scientists aren't sure, but they believe that cerebral malaria causes brain damage in about 10 percent of cases and it is estimated that an additional 10 to 50 percent of cases result in death."[6] But even this, like less fatal forms of malaria, is treatable *if* appropriate drugs are available and *if* they can be administered to the children in time, conditions which can often not be met. It was cerebral malaria that killed young Emily.

The overall magnitude of the malaria problem is mind-boggling. According to the World Health Organization (WHO), over 2 billon people, roughly 40% of the world's population, are "at risk" for malaria because they live in one of the 90 countries where the disease is considered endemic. There are 300 to 500 million *confirmed* cases of malaria in the world each year plus an additional number of cases, thought to be substantial, that go undiagnosed or unreported. As far as the number of deaths is concerned, 1.5 million is a very conservative figure. WHO admits that the actual figure may be double or triple this. Difficult conditions, primitive communications, and lack of reliable equipment make the actual number difficult to estimate, says WHO, which is content to estimate deaths worldwide at somewhere *between* 1.5 and 2.7 million. But even this figure, the agency freely admits, does not include the number of people for whose deaths malaria is a primary—although not causative—agent, such as mothers weakened by malaria who die during childbirth. One-third of the total is infants and small children under the age of five.

Few regions are completely free of malaria, but the disease has something akin to a stranglehold on Africa. Of the one million malaria deaths each year, 75% are African children under the age of five.[7] The drag on Africa's already faltering economies is substantial. To direct expenditures for treatment and prevention must be added the indirect cost of productivity lost. WHO estimated Africa's loses to the GDP at US$12 billion every year,[8] but even this seems low given the huge numbers infected and the utterly debilitating nature of the disease.

It is a shortsighted parasite that kills its host. The vast majority of malarial victims survive (unlike their HIV counterparts), even if their infection is left untreated. Children in Africa who have survived bouts of infection are said to be "immune" from the disease once they reach the age of five. But their so-called "immunity" should not be taken to mean, as it customarily does, that their bodies have developed such a resistance to the malaria sporozoites that these can never again mount a successful invasion. Rather it means their body has *surrendered* to the parasite in return for its *promise* not to kill them, at least not directly.

Being "immune" from malaria in Africa actually means that you are anything but: You will be regularly assaulted by the disease for the rest of your life, each time left alive enough to recover and play host for the next parasitical round—so long as your weakened state does not cause you to die from something else first. Every malarial attack means hundreds of thousands of parasites sucking as much as a quarter pound of hemoglobin out of your blood cells in a matter of hours, killing them in the process. In America this would be the equivalent of a significant—a very significant—blood donation. But malaria, unlike the local blood bank of the Red Cross, does no weight, health or other screening. Everyone, even small children, loses a pint or more of blood whether they can afford to or not. And many lose them at such a rate that they are continually anemic. Bernard Nathan, a physician working with malarial patients in Kenya, reports that "one in twenty" children in the villages surround his clinic are so anemic that "if their blood were tested in the United States they would be rushed to a hospital for emergency transfusions."[9]

Although numbers are sketchy and hard to come by, the general consensus among epidemiologists and public health officials seems to be that the world's malarial problem is growing worse. One close study of published data found that malaria, across Africa, accounts for 40 percent of fever cases and up to 24 percent of fever cases that end in death. Even though only between 8 and 25 percent of Africans with malaria were actually able to go to a doctor for their illness, malarial cases still accounted for between 25 and 50 percent of all admissions to African health services. The growth in the number of malaria cases across the continent ranged from a "low" of 7.9 percent to a high of 21.0 percent.[10] In Zambia, cases per 1000 people have risen from 167.5 in 1982 to 355.7 in 1994.[11]

In sum, malaria's medical impact is so great in Africa that it negatively affects every other aspect of health, including reproductive health. The benefits to be gained from eradicating this pestilence are almost incalculable. One study recently conducted in Gambia suggests, in the words of Ellen Shell, "that control of malaria seems to bring about a radical reduction of mortality from all causes."[12] Given that there are literally hundreds of millions of individuals who have been wounded and weakened by the disease, that conclusion seems self-evident.

Consider the problem of maternal mortality. There are no reliable statistics for the actual number of women dying in childbirth in the developing world. So let us, just for the sake of argument, accept the perhaps exaggerated estimate of 600,000 sometimes advanced by the family planners. A geographic analysis of the mortality distribution suggests that more than a third of these deaths can be attributed to complications from malaria, particularly among women entering pregnancy already anemic. This means that, if malaria were eradicated, 200,000 fewer women would die in childbirth each year. Compared with this great life-saving project, the claim of the family planners—that their anti-pregnancy programs reduce maternal mortality by roughly 4,000 for every $100 million they spend—fails to impress.[13]

Then there is the problem of low-birth-weight babies, who are at greater risk of disease and death. In countries where malaria is endemic, some twenty to forty percent of babies are born with low birth weight, an average of 469 grams lower than average in one study.[14] Anemic mothers, not surprisingly, produce low-birth-weight babies. Eradicate malaria from a population where it is endemic, and the percentage of high-risk births will plummet. The family planners suggest that their anti-pregnancy efforts, by reducing the total number of births, also reduce the number of low-birth-weight babies. Once again, as in the case of maternal mortality, they adventitiously lay claim to a side effect—an unintended consequence, really—of their main program. A direct approach would be far more efficacious. Dramatically improve the health of African mothers by freeing them of the curse of malaria and you will dramatically improve the health of their babies.

Finally, there is a clear relationship between malaria and miscarriage. Anemic mothers miscarry roughly a third of their pregnancies. Malaria thus operates as a population control mechanism by directly reducing the birth rate.

Given the massive numbers of deaths from malaria, one would think that its eradication would have consistently been a top priority of U.S. foreign aid. Not so. The rapidly falling line in Figure 6.1 represents USAID's faltering commitment to the fight against malaria, from $50 million in 1985 to a mere $10 million in 1994. This money has disappeared as a result of shifting priorities, chief among them population control. Compare the $10 million spent on malaria in 1994 to the over $400 million spent on fertility reduction programs that same year.

Figure 6.1
USAID's Shrinking Malaria Budget

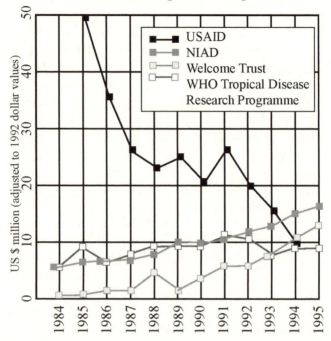

Given this disproportion—the kindest word I can think of under the circumstances—it is not surprising that many Africans have grown cynical about America's purposes. "Malaria keeps Africa down," one African leader told Shell, "and that is where the world wants us to be." Others were even more frank, declaring that "population control, not disease control, is USAID's central mission in Africa."[15] Listen to Dr. Stephen Karanja, an obstetrician/gynecologist and past secretary of the Kenyan Medical Association: "USAID has targeted Kenya for depopulation at the expense of the integral development of its people."[16]

Undermining Primary Health Care

As the malaria story suggests, when the population controllers move into a poor country like Kenya or Peru, primary health care invariably suffers. Government health officials and local medical associations are first co-opted by highly prized opportunities for advanced training overseas, or offered generous gifts (read: bribes) of office equipment or limousines. Once a country's medical establishment has agreed to make "family planning" a priority, national health budgets tend to be spent disproportionately in this area.

At the same time, fertility reduction programs funded by such groups as USAID, UNFPA, and IPPF are set up. Generously funded by local standards, such programs become magnets for scarce local medical resources. Local doctors, attracted by the higher wages, abandon primary health care in favor of "family planning." Local health care clinics are transformed into "family planning" stations, where the only readily available medical care involves contraception, sterilization, and abortion. On a 1997 trip to Kenya, Dr. Mary Meaney discovered an ill woman lying by the side of one of the country's many poor roads. Alarmed by her condition, Mary and her companion drove this woman to the nearest government hospital, five hours away by car. There they found no doctor—and precious little of anything else. In the pharmacy, Meaney recorded, there were "no gloves, no syringes, no vitamins, no basic medical supplies ... [nothing] but *75,000 condoms from USAID*"[17] (italics added).

The predictable result of this diversion of resources is the rapid erosion of primary health care. "Our health sector is collapsed," Kenya obstetrician Stephen Karanja says simply, opening his hands in a gesture of hopelessness. "Thousands of Kenyan people will die of malaria, the treatment for which costs a few cents, in health facilities whose shelves are stocked to the ceiling with millions of dollars worth of pills, IUDs, Norplant, Depo-Provera, and so on, most of which are supplied with American money."[18]

Dr. Karanja knows whereof he speaks. As a newly appointed district medical officer in the late eighties, he was shocked to discover that his foreign-donated medical stores consisted *solely* of anti-natal pills, drugs, and devices. "I was eager to fight disease," he told me, "and they wanted me to fight against my own people. A mother brought a child to me with pneumonia, but I had not penicillin to give the child. What I have in the stores are cases of contraceptives." He locked up the "useless" stores for which there was no demand and didn't reopen them for three years, by which time the expiration dates had passed and everything had to be discarded.[19]

Many kinds of medical equipment and supplies, of course, have a multitude of uses. Surgical instruments, for example, can be used to perform a tubal ligation and to repair an umbilical hernia with equal ease. The problem, Dr. Karanja found, was that the donors had put strict conditions on the equipment they provided, stipulating that they could only be used for family planning purposes. "Special operating theaters fully serviced and not lacking in instruments are opened in hospitals for the sterilization of women," he noted. "While in the same hospitals, emergency surgery cannot be done for lack of basic operating instruments and supplies."[20] Dr. Karanja himself asked to use these operating rooms but was turned down. These theaters," he notes, "are being used and equipped today, everyday, every week, everywhere and especially in Kenya and for one purpose only—for sterilization. These have drugs, have instruments of all types, but if any woman, if any children, if any member of the family needs emergency surgery, there are no gloves, there are no instruments. You can't perform operations because there is no equipment, no materials. The operation theater isn't working. But if it is for a sterilization, the theater is equipped."[21]

Dr. Karanja decided to form a group of reform-minded doctors—he calls them "Young Turks"—who were determined to turn the situation around and restore the health care system. His leadership led to his election as the secretary of the Kenyan Medical Association. The only supplies in the Kenyan Medical Association warehouse, he quickly ascertained after he took control of the organization, were the same kinds of pills, drugs and devices he had seen in the countryside. They suffered the same fate as his earlier stores.

It did not take long for the combined political (and financial) clout of USAID, the British aid agency, and other foreign donors to put down this uprising by the natives. Dr. Karanja was voted out of office, and the Kenyan Medical Association was once again under the control those who enjoyed the foreign trips, limousines, and other perquisites provided by foreigners, and who shared—or at least pretended to share—their views on Kenya's "population problem." The health care system was once again distorted into a vehicle for providing family planning, and health care providers sidetracked into narrow, anti-natal specialties.

Such is the state of medical care in many developing countries, where generously funded family planning programs have become a magnet for local personnel, resources, and official attention, leaving primary health care programs to "collapse," in Dr. Karanja's words, from official inattention or outright neglect. Where they have not collapsed, they have been co-opted, as in the area of maternal and infant health. Dr. Karanja explains: "The contraceptive movement has taken over all the maternal/child health facilities where we used to educate our people on simple hygiene, on nutrition, on simple preventive measures that our people could use to help themselves and to prevent disease. Now, 90 percent of all the education taking place in these facilities is indoctrination into contraception."[22]

Population control programs do not bolster primary health care; they compete with it for personnel and resources. Indeed, more often than not, especially in very poor countries vulnerable to outside manipulation, such programs *out compete, overwhelm, and subsume primary health care to their own purposes.* The "opportunity cost", as the economists say, of this redirection of medical resources can be counted in human lives. How many Kenyans die of easily preventable diseases because health clinic personnel are paid to endlessly lecture women on the need for smaller families and have no time to teach basic hygiene?

The case of Peru is instructive. Once President Fujimori, under foreign pressure, had made family planning his number one priority, the Ministry of Health underwent what one high-ranking insider called in Spanish a "transformacion"—a complete makeover, as it were. It wasn't so much that the Fujimori administration or foreign donors provided new money for the sterilization campaign, he said, at least not at first. Existing resources were simply commandeered and reprogrammed. The family planning component of the ministry's portfolio moved up from being merely one among eight or nine other health programs to being the first and "most publicized." And within the family planning program itself, sterilization became the first and "most publicized" birth control method.[23]

Dr. Raul Cantella, director of an independent research institute in tropical diseases, told the author that the predictable result of this concentration of medical resources on sterilization was a startling rise in the incidence of infectious disease throughout the country, and in the death rate. These deaths stem directly from the misallocation of medical resources and personnel to the sterilization campaign. "The Fujimori regime lied about the increase in the incidence of malaria and other diseases," according to Dr. Cantella. "They put out false statistics. But now we know that the numbers climbed during the late nineties."[24]

How many additional deaths are we talking about? Dr. Cantella puts the number of additional deaths from malaria, typhoid, and typhus in the hundreds.[25]

The human cost of the sterilization campaign was thus much higher than the dozen killed, thousands wounded, and the tens of thousands coerced in the campaign itself.[26] To these figures must be added the hundreds who died because the doctors who might have treated them were off doing tubal ligations, and the drugs that would have cured them were not available from a Ministry of Health obsessed with meeting quotas. The opportunity to save these lives was lost because of the sterilization campaign.

In the case of Bangladesh, the continuing push of key foreign donors to co-opt the Ministry of Health for population control purposes has resulted in five major reorganizations of that institution since independence in 1971, with each shake-up giving family planning a higher priority in the scheme of things. By 1983 family planning had achieved bureaucratic equivalence—and functional dominance—over primary health care. What had come to be called the "Ministry of Health and Population Control" was divided into two bureaus, the first concerned itself with family planning and Maternal and Child Health (MCH), the second with all other health services. Local clinics offer other services in addition to family planning but, as Betsy Hartmann has demonstrated, family planning dominates. "The shift towards greater integration of the two [types of services] stems in part from the emphasis on sterilization and the IUD, which require clinical infrastructure," Hartmann writes. "While the population program has benefited from the use of medical facilities and personnel, basic health care has suffered. ... The blind drive for 'cost-effective' population control has not only distorted the family planning system, but severely undermined health delivery."[27]

To be sure, not all government-sponsored family planning programs are as all-consuming as Bangladesh's or Peru's, but they all come with what economists call an "opportunity cost." This is the benefit foregone when resources are used for one purpose rather than another, in this case, for family planning rather for primary health care. The highest population control "opportunity costs" are being paid at present in Africa, in the painful coin of not just malaria and other tropical diseases but, above all, in millions of cases of Acquired Immune Deficiency Syndrome, or AIDS.

AIDS in Africa

For the first time since the Black Death in the Middle Ages, a disease is sending whole nations into absolute demographic decline. AIDS—Acquired Immune Deficiency Syndrome—was first recognized in the late 1970s. In the years since, some 25 million people have died of the disease.[28] Yet the deadly virus continues to spread with horrifying rapidity in many parts of the world. Today, approximately 42 million people are infected with HIV worldwide, with most of these residing in Africa and the Caribbean. Millions die each year, yet transmission rates in many countries are so startlingly high that the AIDS pandemic continues to claim even more millions of new victims. While over three million died of AIDS in 2002, for example, five million more were newly infected that year.[29] AIDS has rightly been called the worst public health crisis since the bubonic plague.

The epicenter of the plague is sub-Saharan Africa. Of the 45 countries classified by the UN Population Division (UNPD) in 2000 as "highly affected," 35 were located in this region of the world.[30] Sub-Saharan Africa is home to 70% of the adults infected with the virus, and to 80% of the children. In the Republic of South Africa, for example, over 13% of the total population—or more than one in every eight people—is infected with HIV.[31] Those infected will, barring life-extending retroviral treatment, all be dead within a decade.

AIDS raises the death rate, shortens life spans, and may, in "highly affected" countries, reduce the overall population. When the UN Population Division began in the late nineties to examine the demographic impact of AIDS, especially in Africa, they were startled by what they found. AIDS was dramatically shortening life spans, especially in the 35 "highly affected" countries. By 2015 average life expectancy will drop to only 48.3 years, or *6.5 years less* than it would have been without mortality associated with AIDS. The impact of AIDS over longer time periods is even more pronounced, as the disease cuts an ever wider swath through generations to come. There will be 300 million fewer Africans alive in 2050 because of deaths from AIDS.[32]

Numbers alone fail to convey the enormous social devastation wrought by AIDS, which leaves millions of broken families and orphans in its wake. Dr. Karanja estimates that about four million out of Kenya's population of 28 million, or one in seven people, were infected with HIV by 2002. "But these are not just nameless, faceless statistics," he hastened to add. "They are human beings, people's children, mothers, fathers, and brothers and sisters. They are the soul of the nation. The number of AIDS orphans currently roaming the poverty-scarred Kenyan landscape is estimated at 1.5 million. These are children who need care, shelter, education, guidance, love affection and upbringing but who are growing up without a parental presence."[33]

This continent-sized tableau of infection, death, and looming societal collapse is in large part a consequence of the very AIDS programs that were supposed to prevent it from happening in the first place. Two decades ago, acting on early reports from experts that HIV/AIDS in Africa was exclusively a sexually transmitted disease, USAID made an error that would prove fatal to many Africans. HIV/AIDS prevention programs, it decided, would be incorporated—or "integrated" in USAID's phrase—into existing family planning programs. The same clinics, condoms, and safe sex message used to lower the birthrate could also be used to prevent the spread of HIV/AIDS, or so the agency fantasized. This gadget-based approach has resulted in more HIV/AIDS, not less. It is not that the cure was worse than the disease so much as the cure *was* the disease.

The re-use of dirty needles—used in injecting contraceptives, for example—is responsible for many of Africa's HIV infections. Other family planning procedures, such as Norplant implantation and abortion (euphemistically called "post-abortion care") by manual vacuum aspirator (MVA) may also provide an opportunity for the virus to enter and infect a woman's body. The condom worship that characterizes family planning programs is not without its drawbacks as well. The accompanying "safe sex" message creates a false sense of security that may encourage promiscuous behavior on the part of those who have been led to believe that condoms provide absolute protection against HIV.

Africa's primary health care system, already weakened by parasitical family planning programs, is completely unable to cope. Clinics, although well supplied with Depo-Provera, IUDs, and condoms, lack health care essentials such as needles, syringes, rubber gloves, and disinfectant. Medical equipment, such as syringes and manual vacuum aspirators, cannot be properly disinfected before it is reused. The local blood supply may be tainted, turning a simple transfusion into a death sentence. Almost all who seek treatment are turned away. A doctor in rural South Africa describes his frustration, saying, "We have no medicines. Many hospitals tell people, you've got AIDS, we can't help you. Go home and die."[34]

When the history of the AIDS epidemic is written, the population controllers and those who fund them will go down as the chief villains of this dark page in human history. The research team of David Gisselquist, Stephen Potterat, and their colleagues concluded in 2003 that *two-thirds* of the HIV/AIDS in Africa results from injections with infected needles or other medical exposures to infected blood.[35] Even if the population controllers and their clinics are responsible for only a tiny fraction of this number, as their defenders are now claiming, this would still lay millions of deaths at their doorstep. If AIDS is killing Africa, then the population controllers must be indicted as accomplices.

A Heterosexual Epidemic Assumed

Not long after AIDS was discovered in Africa, well-placed and influential experts wrongly concluded that heterosexual sex was driving the spread of the disease. In a prominent 1988 article in *Science*, Piot *et al.* wrote that "Studies in Africa have demonstrated that HIV-1 is primarily a heterosexually transmitted disease and that the main risk factor for acquisition is the degree of sexual activity with multiple partners, not sexual orientation."[36] That same year the World Health Organization's (WHO) Global Program on AIDS circulated estimates that 80% of HIV infections in Africa was due to heterosexual transmission, 10.8% was from mother-to-child transmission, 6% from blood transfusions, 1.6% from contaminated medical injections and other health care procedures, and 1.6% from male homosexual activity and injection drug use (IDU).[37] Similar estimates emerged from Zaire's National AIDS Control Program and the United States Centers for Disease Control at that time.[38] By mid-1989, an overview of global HIV epidemiology by leading AIDS experts at the Fifth International Conference on AIDS did not even mention medical injections as a risk for HIV.[39]

Epidemiological evidence to the contrary, which pointed to poor medical practice as the cause, was misrepresented or simply ignored. As Gisselquist and Potterat note, "The consensus among influential AIDS experts that heterosexual transmission accounts for 90% of HIV infections in Africa .... has suppressed inquiry and dissent. Hence, from 1988 the consensus has been self-reinforcing, as researchers in Africa ... have often assumed sexual transmission without testing partners, without asking about health care exposures, and when conflicting evidence nevertheless emerges—such as infected adults who deny sexual exposures to HIV—routinely rejecting it."[40]

Science moves by paradigm shifts. And once a new paradigm is accepted by a critical mass of researchers, it is simply *assumed* to be correct. This is especially true when the new paradigm becomes the basis for lucrative research grants and programs. Driven by this paradigm, and tempted by the millions available to those who validate it, researchers have taken ever more extreme positions. A special series in *The Lancet* on Africa's HIV/AIDS epidemic averred that most infections are from heterosexual intercourse, while "blood transfusions, injections with infected needles, and scarification are thought to represent *only a few* infections"[41](italics added). According to the World Health Organization, which is very much part of the international AIDS establishment: "current estimates suggest that more than 99% of HIV infections prevalent in Africa in 2001 are attributable to unsafe sex."[42] 99%!

On what evidence were these sweeping conclusions based? After an exhaustive review of the literature, Gisselquist and Potterat say: "We have been unable to locate any document—from the 1980s or later—that describes a process to estimate a 90% sexual contribution to Africa's HIV epidemic from empirical studies of risk factors for HIV."[43] So where did the "consensus" come from?

AIDS, Ideology, and Institutional Interests

Several, though by no means all, of the very early studies done in Africa found that AIDS was associated with promiscuity, principally involving prostitutes and those who patronized them.[44] One study found that of seven Rwandan women with AIDS, three were practicing prostitutes.[45] Another reported that 58 African men with AIDS symptoms had averaged 32 different sex partners a year.[46] Some AIDS experts seized on these studies to argue that Africans were simply incapable of being anything other than promiscuous where sex was concerned.[47] Africa was breeding a heterosexual epidemic because Africans, alone among all the peoples of the earth, were having too much sex with too many partners in circumstances that were too risky; or so they imagined.

This ugly racial stereotype—to call it by its proper name—has no basis in reality. Africans, as it happens, report no more partners than Americans do. And America, of course, does *not* have a heterosexual AIDS epidemic. "Levels of sexual activity reported in a dozen general population surveys in Africa are comparable to those reported elsewhere, especially in North America and Europe," summarize Gisselquist, Potterat and company. "Perhaps more importantly, there appears to be little correlation with the level of risky sexual behavior shown in these surveys and the epidemic trajectories observed in these countries."[48]

But many groups welcomed the prospect of a heterosexual epidemic, be it in Africa or anywhere else. AIDS activists promoted the idea in their press releases and promotions, rightly calculating that it would bring what had become known as "the gay disease" into the mainstream. Deceased homosexual activist Randy Shilts wrote in his account of AIDS in America that "Nothing captured the attention of editors and news directors like the talk of widespread heterosexual transmission of AIDS."[49]

The "discovery" of a heterosexual AIDS epidemic in Africa was also a great boon for the multibillion dollar industry that was growing up around HIV/AIDS research, treatment and prevention programs, bringing much new public and private money into the fight. "[I]t was in the interests of AIDS researchers in developed countries," write Gisselquist and Potterat, "—where HIV seemed stubbornly confined to [male homosexuals, intravenous drug users], and their partners—to present AIDS in Africa as a heterosexual epidemic."[50] Congress began to write ever larger checks—$194 million in 1999, $1billion in 2003, and so on—for AIDS in Africa. In his State of the Union address on January 28, 2003, President George W. Bush committed $15 billion over the next five years, including $10 billion in new money to "turn the tide against AIDS."[51]

USAID bought into the notion of a heterosexual epidemic early, and by 1984 had decided to piggyback its HIV/AIDS programs onto preexisting family planning programs. Organizations applying for funding for such "integrated" programs—so-called because they brought together HIV prevention *and* pregnancy prevention under the same roof—may have been encouraged to emphasize the sexual transmission of HIV in their grant proposals and reports. But they probably didn't need much in the way of persuasion. USAID's little gaggle of family planning surrogates simply followed the money.

Although this may look like AIDS profiteering on the part of the population controllers, there were real convictions in play here. Nearly everyone in the foreign aid community shared the belief that Africa was "overpopulated," and that both the world and Africa would be a better place if fewer African babies were born.[52] In order to drive down the birthrate, family planning programs relied upon the promotion and distribution of condoms and contraceptives through their USAID-funded clinics. The idea of a heterosexual epidemic was naturally appealing to those who ran such programs. If "unprotected" sex was driving up *both* the birth rate *and* the HIV/AIDS rate, then their integrated clinics were the perfect answer to both problems. Condoms worn to prevent HIV infections would also prevent conceptions.

The condom strategy also had the endorsement of American AIDS experts. The spread of HIV/AIDS had been slowed in the U.S. and Europe by targeting high-risk groups like gay men and intravenous drug users with a pro-condom campaign. It could be stopped in the general population, they argued, by means of the same kind of campaign. The availability of what seemed like a ready-made *solution* to sexually transmitted HIV/AIDS helped to further solidify the consensus that this was at root the *problem.*

Armed with these beliefs, USAID set out to expand its social marketing program throughout Africa, emphasizing the dual protection offered by condoms against both pregnancy and HIV/AIDS. In the African country of Mali, for instance, the aid agency developed a television ad campaign to promote condom use based on a pair of villagers who go to the big city. Songalo, the exemplary character, follows the advice of a village elder to always be prepared for the dangers and the pleasures of the world as he sets off to explore the delights of the city. He arms himself with "Protector" condoms in order to avoid getting his wife pregnant on his infrequent visits home and to guard himself from HIV/AIDS and other sexually transmitted diseases as he regularly visits prostitutes. Thanks to latex, he lives a long and happy life. His less-astute counterpart seals his doom by ignoring the advice of the same village elder and failing to use "Protector" condoms on his brothel forays. In short order, he contracts HIV/AIDS, impregnates his wife, infects her with HIV/AIDS, and dies in misery. USAID proudly reported on this effort in its monthly magazine, *Frontline*, under the title, "Mali Media Campaign on Target."[53] Such was USAID's advice to young African men (and women) facing the deadly epidemic.

These campaigns, carried out in country after country, were based on the assumption that African HIV/AIDS was sexually transmitted. The alternative was literally unthinkable, at least to family planning functionaries. For if AIDS was *not* spread by risky sex, then that meant that risky medical procedures were to blame. This potentially implicated anyone and everyone who was doing any kind of health care in Africa, from those running family planning clinics to those carrying out immunization programs. Public health officials tended to downplay the danger of contracting HIV/AIDS from unsafe injections because they didn't want people to start avoiding them altogether. Gisselquist and Potterat write that "health professionals in WHO and elsewhere worried that public discussion of HIV risks during health care might lead people to avoid immunizations. A 1990 letter to *The Lancet,* for example, speculated that 'a health message—e.g., to avoid contaminated injection materials—will be misunderstood and that immunization programs will be adversely affected.'"[54] New family planning clients would become more difficult to find and targets for tubal ligations and IUD insertions more difficult to fill.

In short, Western public-health experts and government scientists, who are supposed to be neutral observers concerned only with facts, read into the African situation their own biases against population in general and the African population in particular, and their own agenda in favor of family planning and immunizations. In their haste to conclude that HIV was being spread by promiscuous African men and women, these experts ignored and misinterpreted contrary evidence.

How HIV Is Transmitted through Health Care

Gisselquist and Potterat reexamined all the evidence on African AIDS transmission available through 1988, before what they call the "premature closure of the debate" led researchers to simply *assume* (rather than test for), a heterosexually driven epidemic. What they found, in their review of 22 separate studies, is startling:

- Injections were more highly associated with HIV than sex. "Published epidemiological evidence from 1984-88 in Africa shows higher average crude PAFs [population attributable fractions, a measure of risk] associated with injections than with measures of sexual exposure."[55]
- Most of those infected with HIV were in a long-term monogamous relationship. "Although some adults may have under-reported numbers of sexual partners, the consistency of the evidence suggests a large majority of HIV infections in non-promiscuous adults, and little concentration in the general population according to sexual activity."[56]
- Those of higher socioeconomic status have higher rates of HIV than those of lower status. "Since STDs [sexually transmitted diseases] have long been associated with lower socioeconomic and educational attainment, it was at least equally plausible that associations between high status and HIV pointed to differences in health care rather than sexual behavior."[57] That is to say, the more "health care" one was exposed to, the greater one's risk of developing HIV.
- Clinic attendance was associated with HIV. "Comparison of HIV prevalence and incidence in STD clinics with prevalence in general population studies suggests that risk for HIV infection was associated with clinic attendance."[58]
- Infants were medically infected with HIV. "High rates of HIV infections in children that could not reasonably be attributed to vertical [that is, mother-to-child] transmission."[59]

What is the actual percentage of HIV/AIDS cases in Africa that are attributable to sex? While the WHO and others were glibly repeating their 90 to 99 percent guess-estimates,[60] Gisselquist and Potterat actually crunched the numbers. The figure they came up with was startlingly low, in the range of 25 to 35 percent.

They went on to calculate the actual *rate* at which sex was spreading HIV/AIDS in Africa. Based on numbers of partners reported in African surveys, and factoring in the generally accepted probability of transmission for penile-vaginal sex (about one in 1000[61]), their result further undermined the heterosexual transmission theory. *It was only about a third of what would be needed to fuel the exploding African epidemic.*

Over the years, increasingly frantic efforts have been made to salvage the theory of a heterosexual epidemic, and many researchers have seized upon the idea that sex in Africa is somehow exceptional. How exceptional? Well, some have speculated that in Africa—and only in Africa—a single act of intercourse with a casual partner is sufficient to transmit HIV.[62] That this transmission rate is *one thousand times higher* than the generally accepted probability of heterosexual transmission left them untroubled. The theory of a heterosexual epidemic *demands* hypersonic transmission rates. Other speculations—higher rates of anal intercourse, lower frequency of circumcision, infection with sexually transmitted diseases (STDs), etc.—are similarly unencumbered by data.[63]

The elephant in the drawing room is unsafe injection. "A growing body of evidence points to unsafe injections and other medical exposures to contaminated blood as pathways that have not yet been adequately addressed," note Gisselquist and Potterat.[64] The risk of infection with the HIV virus from a contaminated medical injection—which has been estimated at one in 30—is *33 times higher* than the risk from heterosexual sex.[65]

Where do Africans experience such exposures? To answer this question, we must look to existing HIV/AIDS and population control programs and, specifically, to how these have been "integrated" in internationally funded clinics all over Africa.

Deadly Combination: USAID AIDS/SRH Integration

Believing that both HIV and pregnancy were a result of "unprotected" sex, and determined to reduce the incidence of both, USAID decided in 1984 to adopt what it called an "integrated" approach. HIV/AIDS programs would be piggybacked on existing population control programs (also called "family planning" programs or, more recently, "sexual and reproductive health"—or SRH—programs). The two problems would be attacked simultaneously, out of the same clinics, with the same staff, and utilizing the same equipment. This decision was made at a time when the numbers of those infected with HIV in sub-Saharan Africa could still be counted in thousands, rather than millions.

In the years following, other countries followed suit, combining HIV prevention with population control in the clinics funded through their own foreign aid programs. The integrated approach received a further boost in 1994, when it was endorsed by the UNFPA-sponsored Cairo Conference on Population and Development. The UN Global Fund for

AIDS, established in 1998, similarly funds integrated HIV/SRH clinics, as they are called. Integrated AIDS/SRH programs are thus the "gold standard" in HIV prevention.

USAID alone has spent over $2.3 billion in its "fight against the global AIDS pandemic,"[66] with the lion's share of this money going into integrated programs. Like any well-funded program, the integrated AIDS/SRH approach to AIDS relief has its strident supporters, chiefly USAID's major "family planning" NGOs like Population Services International, Family Health International (FHI), and Pathfinder International. These have adopted and aggressively promoted the integrated AIDS/SRH model, and in return receive tens of millions of dollars from U.S. taxpayers each year to provide HIV/AIDS services through their existing programs.[67] International Planned Parenthood Federation, which expects to be a major beneficiary of increased international spending on HIV/AIDS, has launched a major public policy campaign to preserve the AIDS/SRH integrated paradigm for AIDS relief.[68]

Family planning NGOs hoping to be on the receiving end of an AIDS grant from USAID—or anywhere else, for that matter—are well-advised not only to adopt the integrated approach, but also to tout its effectiveness. So we find Population Action International (PAI), a USAID-funded population control group, averring that "Prevention efforts need to promote the *integration* of sexual and reproductive health services, including *family planning*, maternal health care, and *STI/HIV prevention* and care, especially for young people. In the absence of a vaccine, preventive measures such as sexual health education and provision of condoms that provide dual protection from both *sexually transmitted infections (STIs) and unwanted pregnancies* remain the most effective and affordable interventions for *slowing the HIV pandemic*" (italics added).[69]

This is whistling past the graveyard. The HIV pandemic in Africa is accelerating, not slowing down. The number of HIV cases in sub-Saharan Africa continues to rise exponentially. Since USAID began its integrated programs over 2.3 billion dollars ago, the number of people infected with HIV/AIDS globally has increased more than one-thousand-fold, going from 43,000 in 1987, to over 14 million by 1995, to a total of about 60 million today, with an ever increasing percentage of these cases in sub-Saharan Africa.[70] As spending rises to record levels, so does the number of people infected each year. Family Health International, another USAID-funded NGO, admits as much: "[W]ith the HIV-positive population still expanding, the annual number of AIDS deaths can be expected to increase for many years."[71]

The reason why the integrated AIDS/SRH approach hasn't slowed the spread of HIV in Africa is because most HIV/AIDS cases on that continent are *not the result of sexual contact at all*. Rather they are the result of contact with HIV through dirty needles and other substandard, invasive medical procedures. More to the point, they are the result of the kinds of things—Depo-Provera and other injections, Norplant insertions, IUD implantations, tubal ligations, and Manual Vacuum Aspiration (MVA) abortions—that are done to women at integrated AIDS/SRH clinics. The implications of this are sobering. Could the very programs undertaken to stem the HIV/AIDS pandemic be contributing to its spread?

The first thing that must be said about integrated clinics is that they bring both seropositive (HIV positive) and seronegative (HIV negative) patients into the same setting, and subject both to the same kinds of invasive medical procedures. The possibility of HIV transmission by contaminated instruments is thus an ever-present danger, one that can be averted only by taking the strictest care. Yet substandard medical practices are common in Africa's chronically under-funded, understaffed, and poorly equipped clinics, conditions which the single-minded focus of foreign aid donors on family planning has done little to alleviate.

This is not mere speculation. There is empirical evidence linking HIV/AIDS transmission directly to African clinics that provide sexual and reproductive health care. Gisselquist and Potterat found that those who attended STD clinics were at greater risk of HIV infection:

> Comparison of HIV prevalence and incidence in STD clinics with prevalence in general population studies suggest that risk for HIV infection was associated with clinic attendance. In two STD clinics in Rwanda, HIV prevalence in attendees was four to nine times higher than in controls (general population samples). Among STD outpatients in Zambia in 1985, HIV prevalence in those reporting previous attendance at an STD clinic was 37% compared to 23% for first-time attendees. In another study in Zambia, 15% of HIV-negative STD patients seroconverted within two years. Among men attending an STD clinic in Nairobi in 1986-87 after recent contact with prostitute women, 8% seroconverted within an average of 15 weeks of follow-up.[72]

Brewer and his team found an increased risk of HIV infection among women who received reproductive health care at African clinics. As they write: "A higher HIV prevalence has been observed in women seen in prenatal, postpartum, and induced abortion settings than in their community counterparts. In a number of studies, there appears to be a discrepancy between the observed prevalence in women undergoing reproductive medical care, and the prevalence that would be observed in such a group from heterosexual transmission alone."[73] In plain English, clinic attendance seems to have condemned some mothers to an untimely death; a fact which the AIDS establishment would sooner eat ground glass than admit.

The "Exclusionary Mentality" of the Clinics

HIV/SRH clinics began life as anti-people establishments, and a population control mentality often still prevails. Clinics are still judged by the numbers—how many Norplants they implant, sterilizations they perform, and doses of Depo-Provera they inject. They, in turn, are out to maximize the number of "acceptors." Their HIV/AIDS arm concentrates, in the area of prevention, on pushing condoms to all comers. The only "safe sex" behavioral change that many clinic workers are taught to work for is correct and consistent condom usage, not abstinence. Individuals who practice abstinence do not need implants, injections, or condoms, of course, which makes them less profitable to process, and success that much harder to claim.

Some USAID-funded groups operate programs that, on paper at least, include an "abstinence education" component. The trouble is that abstinence is often only a fig leaf for the promotion of condoms and abortifacient contraceptives. Population Action International, for example, openly promotes a condoms-first approach to AIDS relief.[74] The "AIDS awareness" educational programs of PAI and other groups use clever marketing techniques and slogans to promote a lifestyle that contributes to the sexual transmission of AIDS. Some international abortion groups, such as IPPF, go even farther, explicitly denigrating abstinence and its role in AIDS prevention.

Family Health International describes at length its sex-education programs for school children,[75] its clean needle exchange programs, and its promotion of condom use among teens and adults throughout the developing world—anything and everything, it seems, except abstinence.[76] In Kenya, the local FHI program barely touches on abstinence before passing quickly to the marketing and distribution of condoms and oral and injectable contraceptives for women and teenagers. Even women who say that they practice abstinence are treated as potential "acceptors" and encouraged to accept contraception. Neither the risks of contraceptives nor the benefits of abstinence are discussed.[77]

Dr. Njai, who runs the family planning clinic at the Kenyatta National Hospital, is an advocate of abstinence as the only sure protection against HIV/AIDS. He finds it troubling that abstinence is not only not seriously taught in Western-funded HIV/AIDS "peer education" programs, but in practice is subtly discouraged. Such programs occasionally mention abstinence as "an effective way to prevent AIDS," he says, but always with the mocking coda that, "since abstinence is difficult for some people, condoms should always be worn." The corrosive effect of such "reproductive health" education on the attitudes of the young is predictable. Dr Njai tells his students of cases of people getting AIDS even while using condoms, but finds them indifferent or even hostile to the message. When he goes on to speak of abstinence as the only certain protection against HIV/AIDS, his students scoff and laugh. They treat the matter as a joke, even though they themselves are dying of the disease. Six out of every ten, Dr. Njai estimates, are already infected with the HIV/AIDS virus.[78] Like many Africans, they are paying for their HIV/AIDS "peer education" with their lives.

USAID speaks loftily of preventing HIV/AIDS by seeking a "common ground" between faith-based groups that reject abortion, population control and casual sex, and its long-time surrogates that promote these same practices.[79] But how can groups which are driven by an ideology that denies the possibility of self-control where sex is concerned, like Planned Parenthood, possibly take abstinence seriously? And how can groups concerned with population control ideology endorse an approach—Natural Family Planning—which allows women to take control of their own fertility? The more elaborate and sophisticated their HIV/AIDS education programs become, the more they openly mock abstinence, whether as a defense against AIDS or as a form of family planning.

There is a parallel here with the Immigration and Naturalization Service, or INS. Before its restructuring in 2003 as the U.S. Citizenship and Immigration Services (CIS), the INS was an agency in conflict. Its paramount mission was to serve as America's gatekeeper, admitting legal immigrants while barring the door to illegals. At the same time it was charged with adjudicating, through its network of immigration courts, the claims of the thousands of individuals who sought political asylum in the United States each year. Many of these had entered the country without a valid visa, and were, at least until they formally applied for asylum, illegal immigrants. And here was the rub.

The institutional culture of the INS was defined by its gatekeeper function, which produced an exclusionary mentality among its employees. Asylum applicants, who were in the United States under questionable circumstances, were not natural objects of sympathy. Some suggested that they had trouble getting a fair hearing as a result.[80]

The population control movement suffers from the same kind of "exclusionary mentality," albeit writ on a global scale. It wants to restrict entry to the Planet Earth, as it were, by preventing new human beings from coming into existence. Women who want children are automatically suspect. Concepts such as abstinence, fidelity and Natural Family Planning, which have no population control component, do not get a fair hearing.

Natural Family Planning or NFP, in the view of the movement, suffers from the gravest defect. For unlike sterilization or Depo-Provera, NFP cannot be reliably used to check a woman's fertility. In fact, since NFP allows a woman to decide for herself the number and spacing of her children, women—in Nigeria, for example—may use it for a pro-natal purpose. But the population control movement is not in the business of allowing women to carelessly populate the world by freely expressing their fertility.

The bias of the anti-natalists against abstinence has arguably cost millions of lives. Among other things, it has blinded them to the success of Uganda, virtually the only country in Africa that has held the line against AIDS. In the late 1980s Ugandan President Yoweri Museveni learned that hundreds of thousands of Ugandans, including a third of his army officers, were HIV-positive. He launched the much-vaunted ABC program, whose initials stand for "Abstain," "Be Faithful," and "Use a Condom"—in that order. Museveni mobilized Ugandan government officials and the private sector to promote a message of sexual purity via official speeches, school curricula and billboards. "Zero grazing outside of your own field," was one popular slogan. The impact was immediate, with the number of Ugandans who reported having a casual sexual partner declining from 30 to 20% over the first six years of the program, from 1989 to 1995. HIV/AIDS rates plummeted. At the same time that the pandemic was burning through other African populations, Uganda's HIV-prevalence rate fell from 21.2% in 1991 to only 6.2% by 2000.[81] This stunning success cannot be solely attributed to the drop in recreational sex. For the abstinence message not only kept Ugandans out of their neighbor's bedrooms, it kept them out of family planning clinics as well. The medical transmission rate probably fell even faster than the sexual transmission rate did.

Many health experts readily admit that Uganda owes its success in combating AIDS to abstinence. "Uganda's outstanding success really has American heads turning," said Dr. Milton Amayun, World Vision's HIV/AIDS international program representative. "Experts in the U.S. are starting to see the value of teaching people to limit their sexual relationships within the context of marriage."[82]

The AIDS establishment, on the other hand, studiously ignored the Ugandan example for as long as it could. Then, when word of Uganda's success became too well known to ignore, it sought to explain away the data. The surveys were faulty, or the analysis was flawed. Abortion and family planning groups argued that it was condom use, not abstinence, that was driving the decline in HIV prevalence in Uganda. Planned Parenthood and its research arm, the Alan Guttmacher Institute (AGI), claim that increased condom use in Uganda, between 1995 and 2000, "is likely to be a significant contributing factor" in lowering Uganda's HIV rate. "Abstinence ... is not a significant factor," they scoffed.[83] Susan A. Cohen, writing in *The Guttmacher Report*, says "contrary to the assertions of social conservatives, that the case of Uganda proves that an undiluted 'abstinence-only' message is what makes the difference, there is no evidence that abstinence-only educational programs were even a significant factor in Uganda between 1988 and 1995."[84]

The relationship between increasing abstinence before marriage and fidelity within marriage, on the one hand, and lower rates of HIV prevalence, on the other, is too striking to be ignored or explained away, however. Abstinence has also resulted in lower levels of STDs and thus in fewer clinic visits (and injections). Uganda receives relatively less amounts of USAID injectable contraceptives than many other African nations. Uganda's falling HIV prevalence rate may be related not just to lower sexual transmission of the disease, but to lower medical transmission as well.

One thing is certain, however. By ignoring the evidence that abstinence, not condoms, is the key to stopping the AIDS epidemic in Africa, the population controllers have been able to siphon hundreds of millions of dollars away from effective HIV/AIDS programs into their own anti-natal efforts.

The Victimization of Women

An examination of HIV/AIDS statistics by region and by gender reveals a curious anomaly where women are concerned. In areas of the world where the primary means of transmission is *assumed* to be heterosexual sex, such as sub-Saharan Africa, North Africa and the Middle East, and the Caribbean, the majority of HIV-positive adults are women. The United Nations Programme on HIV/AIDS (UNAIDS) and the World Health Organization have recently called attention to this disparity in their *AIDS Epidemic Update*. In sub-Saharan Africa, for example, they report that 58% of those who have HIV/AIDS are women.[85] In the younger age groups the disparity is even higher: "[O]verall about twice as many young women as men are infected in sub-Saharan Africa. In 2001, an estimated 6-11% of young women aged 15-24 were living with HIV/AIDS, compared to 3-6% of young men."[86]

These results are surprising because they appear to contradict what we know about human sexual behavior. Cross-culturally, men are more promiscuous than women. They have more sexual partners before marriage and higher rates of marital infidelity. Moreover, some of their number patronize prostitutes, who are a prime vector for AIDS transmission. These are all behaviors that expose men to a greater risk of sexually contracting HIV/AIDS.

"Why do young African women appear so prone to HIV infection?" asks UNAIDS and WHO. Their answer (which of course assumes that HIV is sexually transmitted) is that African women are forced by circumstances to have sex with HIV positive men: "Women and girls are commonly discriminated against in terms of access to education, employment, credit, health care, land and inheritance... [R]elationships with men (casual or formalized through marriage) can serve as vital opportunities for financial and social security, or for satisfying material aspirations. But, in areas where HIV/AIDS is widespread, they [men] are also more likely to have become infected with HIV. The combination of dependence and subordination can make it very difficult for girls and women to demand safer sex (even from their husbands) or to end relationships that carry the threat of infection."[87]

This explanation—that African women are infected by rapacious men—may be convincing to the radical feminist mind, but it completely begs the question. Why does HIV in Africa disproportionately strike women?

Perhaps the answer lies in the medical transmission of HIV/AIDS. The public health sector in many African countries has simply collapsed. African clinics are short of almost everything, from vaccines and malaria tablets to rubber gloves and needles. Little, if any, care is available to African men and women ill with malaria and other tropical diseases. Medical equipment, such as syringes, surgical instruments, and manual vacuum aspirators, cannot be properly disinfected before being reused. The local blood supply is unreliable.

The one exception to the generally dismal state of primary health care in Africa is Western-funded sexual and reproductive health programs that target women. African medical workers are taught (and paid) to emphasize reproductive health procedures (contraception, sterilization, and abortion), often to the near exclusion of primary health care. Otherwise poorly equipped clinics are kept well-stocked with Depo-Provera, IUDs, and condoms. Recall the plaint of Dr. Karanja, that "Thousands of the Kenyan people will die of malaria whose treatment costs a few cents, in health facilities whose stores are stacked to the roof with millions of dollars worth of pills, IUDs, Norplant, Depo-Provera, most of which are supplied with American money."[88]

Is it mere coincidence that the same groups that are targeted for invasive procedures are disproportionately afflicted with AIDS? I think not. Women and girls account for such a high percentage of HIV/AIDS victims in Africa because they are infected during procedures designed to disable their reproductive systems and prevent them from conceiving or bearing children. To paraphrase UNAIDS, it is the dependence and subordination of women to clinic personnel—often the only available source of health care for themselves and their families—that makes it very difficult to demand safe medical care, and to end medical relationships that carry the threat of infection.

Dirty Needles, Tainted Vials, and the Spread of HIV/AIDS

Among the population control procedures that may have directly contributed to the spread of HIV/AIDS in Africa among women are the reuse of injection equipment and multidose vials of injectable contraceptives such as Depo-Provera, or other medications used for STD treatment and antenatal care. Women visiting African clinics are rarely tested for HIV before being given injections and the likelihood that needles and syringes will be reused is high. Many of these clinics are filthy and drug use is largely unregulated.

The World Health Organization has belatedly recognized that disposable syringes—an all-plastic syringe with a separate steel needle—are not thrown away in the developing world, but reused again and again, with all the risks that this entails.[89] Warns the WHO: "Reuse of syringes and needles in the absence of sterilization exposes millions of people to infection. Syringes and needles are often just rinsed in a pot of tepid water between injections. In some countries the proportion of injections given with syringes or needles reused without sterilization is as high as 70%."[90] Elsewhere, the WHO reports that syringe/needle reuse "is most often reported" in sub-Saharan Africa and Asia, and speculates that half of all syringes and needles on these continents are reused.[91]

These ballpark estimates may strike readers as high. To me they seem unrealistically low, for two reasons. First, as anyone who has ever been in an African clinic can testify, practically every kind of medical device is in short supply. Few clinic staff are going to throw away a perfectly serviceable needle and syringe just because these have been used once, whatever the "Western experts" say. Even if they did, these disposable syringes and needles are unlikely to actually find their way into a land-fill. Armies of ragpickers stand in the way. Those syringes and needles recovered from the trash are sold on the black market to untrained lay practitioners who reuse them.[92] Or as WHO delicately words it, "In developing countries, additional hazards occur from scavenging on waste disposal sites and manual sorting of the waste recuperated at the back doors of health-care establishments."[93]

The second reason why needles and syringes are unlikely to be thrown away has to do with the mystique surrounding injections in the developing world, which has led to massive increases in the number of "sticks" there. The residents of the developing world receive an estimated 16 *billion* injections each year, a number that is well beyond reason.[94] The WHO has condemned this practice, noting that "In certain regions of the world, use of injections has completely overtaken the real need, reaching proportions no longer based on rational medical practice. In some situations, as many as nine out of ten patients presenting to a primary healthcare provider receive an injection, of which over 70% are unnecessary...."[95]

Out of the total of 16 billion injections given outside the developed world each year, let us assume that one in four, or 4 billion, are given to sub-Saharan Africans. This works out to a staggering 10 million injections a day across the continent. Needless to say, this number of injections vastly exceeds the number of new syringes and needles that are available from all sources. The sheer magnitude of the number of injections given suggests that each available syringe and needle is not only reused, but that it is reused until it is literally "worn out," that is, until the plunger no longer seals against the inside of the syringe or the needle breaks off.

Where does the limited supply of needles and syringes that are available come from? Some are introduced into Africa through immunization programs. But the principal source is injectable contraceptives, chiefly Depo-Provera, which is a staple of family planning programs across Africa. In the case of Depo-Provera, a progesterone-based contraceptive which acts by inhibiting ovulation and implantation, intramuscular injections are required every three months to ensure continued sterility.

What kind of numbers are we talking about? From 1994-2000, USAID provided 41,967,200 units of Depo-Provera into the developing world, at a cost of over $40 million.[96] From the inception of the program, according to Dr. Jim Shelton, senior reproductive health advisor for USAID, the U.S. aid agency has only shipped single-dose vials.[97] These vials come in packages which contain, in the words of one advertising poster, a "complete injection kit for convenience." An injection kit is a plastic syringe equipped with a steel needle. Both of these devices are reusable and, as noted above, are in fact reused, in the impoverished African context, countless times.

Another source of needles and syringes is the UNFPA, which boasts of being the largest supplier of contraceptives in the world. In the case of Depo-Provera this is undoubtedly true. The UNFPA provided about 12 million doses of Depo-Provera in 1992 and 20 million doses in 1994, including shipments for the World Bank.[98] By way of comparison, USAID delivered only 1 million doses in 1994 between August, when U.S. program shipments began, and December of that year. Other countries, such as Great Britain, also purchase substantial amounts of Megastron (Depo-Provera).

The lion's share of these shipments is bound for Africa. Depo-Provera (or its sister drug, Megastron) is a major component of foreign-funded family planning programs in Africa. USAID sends more units of Depo-Provera to Africa, to countries such as Mozambique, Tanzania and Nigeria, than to any other part of the world. Although the UNFPA is less open about the destination of its contraceptives, the UN agency does admit to spending more money on its African programs than elsewhere. The evidence suggests that spending by other agencies follows the same pattern. For example, in a project funded by the European Development Fund, the government of Kenya imported 3 million one-dose vials of Megastron, along with an equal number of separately packed disposable syringes and needles, in March 2003.[99]

Given the WHO's concerns about unsafe injections, one might think that USAID and other foreign donors would make every effort to restrict the use of injection equipment to trained medical personnel only. The opposite is actually the case. In its eagerness to contracept Africans, USAID funds social marketing giveaways of needles and syringes to as many women as possible. Throughout Africa, Depo-Provera kits are available over-the-counter at a nominal, subsidized price from dilapidated "pharmacies," corner grocery stores, and even makeshift stands for private use in completely unsupervised settings.[100] In Kenya, for example, the program is run by PSI Kenya, which proudly advertises that the injection kits are "Manufactured in Belgium by Pharmacia and Upjohn, and distributed by PSI Kenya." PSI stands for Population

Services International, one of the principal recipients of USAID family planning/population stabilization funds.[101]

What happens to the millions of needles and syringes recklessly distributed to the general public in this way? Bear in mind that these devices have been given to individuals with no medical training whatsoever. The germ theory of disease is a mystery to them. They are utterly clueless where the sterilization or disposal of contaminated medical devices is concerned. It is safe to assume that virtually all of these "disposable" syringes and needles are not disposed of at all, but reused again and again and again.[102]

How many Depo-Provera "injection kits" have been shipped to sub-Saharan Africa over the past decade from all sources? Again, exact numbers are not available, but the UNFPA and the World Bank have probably averaged close to 10 million kits a year; the United States providing something less than 2 million, with assorted other organizations and donor-countries adding a few hundred thousand here and there. Since the early 1990s, perhaps 100 million Depo-Provera syringes and needles have been put into circulation in Africa.[103] During this same decade, something like 40 billon injections have been given to Africans, and the AIDS epidemic simply exploded.

This is not the place to attempt a detailed calculation of the number of HIV/AIDS cases that have resulted from unsafe injections. But a rough calculation will suggest the dimensions of the problem. If we assume that each needle and syringe is used 10 times on a population in which 1 in 10 women are seropositive, and further that the injection transmission risk is 1 in 30, then there will be one seroconversion for each six syringes and needles distributed. This would result in 15-20 million new cases of HIV/AIDS over the past decade.

In a belated recognition of the possible role played by tainted needles and syringes in the transmission of AIDS, USAID has modified the injection kits in recent years. The first change came late in 2002 and involves the replacement of the previous reusable syringe with an "auto-disable syringe." The plunger on this type of syringe can only be pulled back once, to aspirate the contents of Depo-Provera vial. Once the plunger is depressed, in injecting the drug intramuscularly into the woman, the plunger cannot be withdrawn a second time. The second change, which was accomplished in May 2003, was the replacement of the standard needle size with a needle size unique to the Depo-Provera syringe. Because it is a unique size, the new needle cannot be attached to any other syringe than the one to which it is originally attached.

These changes constitute a tacit admission of the dangers of providing reusable injection equipment in circumstances where poverty and over-the-counter distribution to all comers makes their reuse not merely likely, but virtually certain. But don't expect a *mea culpa* from USAID any time soon.

Norplant, Sterilizations, and Blood Transfusions

Another population control procedure that may serve as a vector for nonsexual transmission of HIV is Norplant implantation. Norplant consists of six small flexible capsules made of Silastic tubing and filled with a synthetic progesterone, levonorgestrel.[104] The capsules are surgically placed under the skin on the inner side of a woman's upper arm. Then, five years later, after all the progesterone has leached out, the capsules are removed, again surgically. This is not always an easy task, since by this time the capsules are often completely surrounded by tough fibroid tissue. Dr. Anthony Levantino, an obstetrician-gynecologist who has inserted Norplant in dozens of women, says of the removal, "You have to dig—and I mean really dig—to locate and remove the capsules."[105]

The Population Council, which holds that patent for Norplant, claims that extensive clinical trials, involving some 55,000 women from 46 countries, have proven both the safety and the efficacy of Norplant. These trials, however, did not take into account the risk of HIV infection that women are exposed to in both the insertion and removal process, especially in an African setting. Nor did they factor in the increased risk of contracting HIV that results from using any progesterone-based approach to contraception, from Norplant and Depo-Provera, to birth control pills. A 1996 study conducted by researchers at the Aaron Diamond AIDS Research Center in New York and supported by the World Health Organization found an elevated infection rate among monkeys who were given subdermal progesterone implants and also found that the vaginal epithelia of the monkeys with the implants were "significantly reduced." The Aaron Diamond Study thus confirms that the presence of progesterone likely thins the vaginal wall and thus makes it far more vulnerable to infection by STDs or HIV during intercourse. More recently, a study published in the journal *Sexually Transmitted Disease*, found that the use of Depo-Provera increases the risk of contracting STDs by a factor of three.[106]

Sterilizations, also encouraged in population control programs, provide an additional vector for infection. Neither tubal ligation nor vasectomy has ever been popular or common in Africa. Of the reported 222 million individuals who have been sterilized worldwide, only 1% resides in sub-Saharan Africa.[107] Still, despite the limited numbers, the relatively primitive conditions under which these operations are performed probably ensure that the HIV transmission rate is relatively high.

Blood transfusions, often required in surgical procedures, are another major, though unquantifiable, risk. The World Health Organization's Global Program on AIDS circulated estimates in 1988 that 6% of the HIV infections in Africa were due to blood transfusions. Dr. Stephen Karanja concurs: "If a woman requires a blood transfusion, I wait until the last possible minute, because a blood transfusion is often a death sentence." Still, when one weighs the various risk factors, as Gisselquist and Potterat have, "[the data] point to injections—not blood transfusions—as the main health care risk."[108]

Manual Vacuum Aspirators, Abortion, and the Transmission of HIV/AIDS

There is another crude and dangerous operation, beloved of the population controllers, that undoubtedly infects its share of African women. This is the widespread practice of performing abortions with hand-held suction abortion syringes under the guise of "menstrual regulation" or "post-abortion care."

Since at least 1991 a company known as International Products Assistance Services (IPAS), an offshoot of the Planned Parenthood Federation of America, has been manufacturing and distributing these syringes, generally referred to as manual vacuum aspirators or MVAs, to countries in Africa and elsewhere. An MVA consists of a long plastic tube attached to a large syringe. The model in current use, called the "IPAS Double-Valve Aspirator," contains a 60cc aspirator, or syringe, to which plastic cannulae [tubes] sized 4-12mm can be attached "for use in uterine evacuation for several clinical indications." The tube is inserted into the cervix, and the plunger on the syringe is pulled back by hand to suction out the contents of the uterus. "Aspirator holds evacuated tissue for easy examination," IPAS assures the user.[109]

This operation, known in many African clinics as simply "the procedure," is the most common form of abortion in Africa. It is performed without anesthesia, up to and beyond 16 weeks gestation. A Marie Stopes International (MSI) clinic operator in Kenya told a PRI investigator that the procedure *can* be performed up to 20 or 24 weeks gestation "if the technician is brave." But, he warned, "the women tend to cry."[110] No doubt. Attempting to extract a second-trimester fetus 12 to 14 inches in length and weighing 1 to 2 pounds using a cannula with a maximum diameter of only 12 millimeters (roughly 1/2 inch) must be a daunting—and gruesome—prospect for all concerned.

In the context of the HIV/AIDS epidemic in Africa, MVA abortions hold a significant risk of infection. First, the forcible dilation of the cervix can cause abrasions. Second, despite IPAS's assurance that "The flexible design [of the polyethylene plastic tube] can reduce the risk of uterine perforation," some risk remains, especially as the gestational age of the fetus to be aborted increases. Third, the "whistle cut" or "scoop" opening near the end of the tube can also scrape or nick the uterus.

Women visiting African clinics are rarely tested for HIV before being given an MVA abortion, and the syringes and the tube used for this procedure will almost certainly be reused in the days following. In fact, the MVA and its detachable tubes were designed with reuse in mind, and the manufacturer touts this as a selling point. "Reusable aspirator results in very low per-procedure cost," IPAS writes. The warning that follows this boast—written in fine print, of course—requires some explanation:

> In the United States, the cannulae are strictly single-use. Where reuse is *required* and local regulations allow, the cannulae must undergo sterilization or high-level disinfection before reuse[111] (italics added).

Why are the cannulae "strictly single-use" in the United States? Because plastic is notoriously hard to sterilize, that's why. So why would reuse ever be *required,* especially in overseas settings like Africa where it is highly unlikely that the requirements laid down by the manufacturer for "sterilization or high-level disinfection" of these plastic tubes could be met? Because IPAS knows that its principal clients, which are USAID grantees and other agencies that purchase this abortion equipment for shipment to Africa, are supplying far too few cannulae for the number of abortions that are being performed.

It is difficult to estimate the likelihood of transmitting the HIV virus by means of an infected MVA and cannula. Given the trauma and bleeding associated with the procedure, however, the transmission efficiency is probably as high as or higher than that of an injection, which is 1 in 30. In 1997 the World Health Organization estimated that in sub-Saharan Africa there were 4,400,000 unsafe abortions performed each year, leading to 32,800 cases of maternal mortality.[112] If the number of MVA abortions performed annually is in this range, then these hand-held suction abortion syringes may be a prime vector of HIV/AIDS transmission, infecting hundreds of thousands of women each year.

While some HIV-positive women may be aborted by clinic personnel who do not know their HIV status, others may be specifically targeted for this procedure precisely because they have the disease. There is credible evidence that, in some countries, abortion is being used as a means of AIDS prevention. The UN's World Health Organization (WHO) has condoned and promoted this method of preventing the mother-to-child transmission of AIDS, writing that "Access to safe abortion and counseling to ensure informed decision making and consent by the women, should be part of the services" (for pregnant HIV positive women).[113] Pathfinder International promotes manual vacuum aspiration, as part of so-called post-abortion care (PAC), in the Caribbean and South America and elsewhere. With the support of IPPF, Pathfinder has integrated MVA abortion into HIV/AIDS projects designed to prevent mother-to-child HIV/AIDS transmission. The International Planned Parenthood Federation performs abortions and promotes AIDS/SRH integration.[114]

The HIV/AIDS epidemic is also being used by some to justify the legalization of abortion, on the grounds that the best way to prevent mother-to-child transmission is to end life *in utero*. A conference in Haiti, entitled "A quest for legislation for protecting public health and the rights of people living with HIV/AIDS," provided a forum for advocates of aborting HIV victims. As one participant, a Haitian lawyer, asserted, "To deny a woman the right to undergo abortion, when we know that the risks of transmission of the virus to the baby at birth are very high, would be to deny her the freedom of choice."[115]

But is the risk of mother-to-child transmission (MTCT) as high as he suggests? MTCT can occur during pregnancy, at the time of delivery, and after birth through breastfeeding. According to the World Health Organization, "Based on a compilation of studies, it is estimated that MTCT rates, without any anti-retroviral intervention, range from 15 to 30% in the absence of breastfeeding, to 25 to 35% if there is breastfeeding through 6 months and to 30 to 45% if there is breastfeeding through 18 to 24 months."[116] Delivery techniques can further reduce the rate of mother-to-child transmission, as can anti-retroviral therapy. Even without these kinds of special interventions, only one of every four or five babies born to seropositive mothers will be seropositive at birth. Most newborns of HIV/AIDS mothers do not carry the virus. Should all be terminated because some fraction of their number will contract the disease?

MVA abortion as "AIDS prevention" constitutes an absolute betrayal of trust. It is population control masquerading as HIV/AIDS prevention. It harms women, eliminates their unborn children on specious grounds, and further contaminates medical devices that will be used on subsequent, HIV negative patients.

Condoms and "Safe Sex"

Over the past 20 years, HIV/AIDS prevention programs have centered on the large-scale distribution of condoms. These have been combined with "safe sex" propaganda campaigns aimed at convincing the public that putting a layer of latex between sexual partners can guarantee protection against infection by the HIV/AIDS virus by keeping body fluids from commingling. Population Services International, a USAID-funded group, uses aggressive and ubiquitous advertising campaigns to flood the media with a pro-condom message. These "safe sex" campaigns involve, using PSI's own martial language, a constant "barrage of radio spots and films shown on television, in cinema halls, and on [PSI's] fleet of mobile film vans" all extolling the perfect protection afforded by condom usage.[117]

But the "safe-sex" approach, designed to induce a "behavioral change" (wearing a condom), has not been effective in reducing the incidence of HIV/AIDS. A study published in *The Lancet* and reported in the *AIDS Weekly* found that promoting safer-sex made no difference in a Ugandan intervention trial.[118] Numerous studies, on the other hand, have repeatedly shown that promoting abstinence and being faithful to a single sexual partner resulted in significant declines in HIV incidence in Uganda.

On the macro level as well, there is no evidence that throwing boat-loads of condoms at the epidemic has had a significant impact. Over the course of the nineties, USAID shipped approximately 5 billion condoms abroad.[119] Billions of others came from the UN Population Fund, the UK's Overseas Development Agency, and other providers. Yet, despite this flood of condoms into the developing world, the rate of HIV/AIDS infection continued to grow at startling rates. The number of victims increased one thousand-fold, from just over 40,000 in 1990 to over 40 million in 2000. Why was this?

Condoms obviously cannot protect one against unsafe injections, as we have seen. But the scientific evidence suggests that they have also been oversold as a defense against sexually transmitted diseases as well. The National Institutes of Health (NIH) in 2001 published a comprehensive review of the scientific evidence on condom effectiveness.[120] Citing a study by Davis and Weller, NIH concluded that condoms, even if consistently and properly used, only provide an 85% reduction in the risk of contracting HIV/AIDS.[121] This is far from being the perfect protection promised by the "safe sex" propaganda funded by USAID. Even paved with condoms, the road to promiscuity still leads to death.

This was strikingly illustrated by a graph that appeared in, of all places, the IPPF's own *Medical Bulletin*. The author, Willard Cates Jr., designed the graph to illustrate his point that condoms reduce the risk of HIV infection by about 70% if they are used "consistently and correctly." "Clearly sexual abstinence will eliminate all the risk," wrote Cates. "But if we plot abstinence and condoms on the same graph, we see that use of condoms reduces by approximately 70% the total risk between unprotected sex and complete sexual abstinence."[122]

But Cates passes over in silence what also leaps out of the graph: That even the perfect condom user will eventually, inexorably contract HIV/AIDS as surely as if he had injected the HIV virus directly into his bloodstream.

Figure 6.2
Risk (of contrcting HIV) vs. Exposure (the number of sexual encounters)

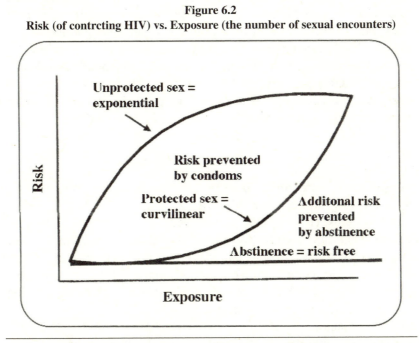

Risk (of contracting HIV) vs. Exposure (the number of sexual encounters). Note how the right side of the ellipse ("protected sex") rises to meet the left ("unprotected sex") at a point which represents 100% risk.

The failure of condoms to provide perfect protection against HIV/AIDS is also suggested by studies of condom use for the prevention of pregnancy. Approximately 3% of couples who reported using condoms consistently and correctly (considered "perfect use") are estimated to experience an unintended pregnancy during the first year of use.[123] If sperm can find their way around the latex barrier, then so, presumably, can the AIDS virus.

To further complicate matters, the presumed protection resulting from using a condom may perversely lead to behavioral changes that completely negate the protection. For example, individuals who believe that consistent and correct use of condoms provides near-absolute protection against HIV/AIDS may engage in recklessly promiscuous behavior that they would otherwise avoid. Why? Because they have been led to believe that, by practicing "safe sex," they are immune from contracting the disease. In this way, the rate of HIV/AIDS transmission may not be reduced at all by the "safe sex" message, but may actually increase over time.

An article in *The Lancet*, the premier British medical journal, suggested that a condom-based approach, by creating a false sense of security on the part of users, had not only failed to stop the spread of AIDS, but had actually exacerbated the problem. The authors drew a parallel with the seat belt law, which had been projected to dramatically decrease the number of traffic fatalities. Instead, the number of deaths remained roughly the same, as drivers took risks they previously would have avoided because they *felt* safer wearing a seat belt. Perhaps this is one of the reasons why, despite massive shipments of condoms overseas, the rate of HIV/AIDS infections continues to grow.[124]

Conclusion

Population control undermines primary health care. It diverts scarce resources away from pressing public health concerns, and often gives rise to new concerns. The neglect of primary health care in Africa has allowed malaria to come back with a vengeance, and is arguably responsible for allowing HIV/AIDS to reach epidemic proportions. The billions of dollars that have been poured into population control programs could have saved millions upon millions of lives, *if* it had been used to improve the general health of the population.

The Africans are not blind to their predicament. While AIDS is ravaging their continents and threatening to decimate the populations of country after country, they see the donors of the developed world, led by USAID, continuing to spend hundreds of millions of dollars on thinly veiled "population stabilization" efforts. Already many Africans, particularly those more educated and politically aware, uneasily note how prominent and well-funded "reproductive health" programs are in comparison to other forms of U.S. foreign aid. Shell reports speaking with noted African opinion makers who told her that many Africans "assume that the West considers malaria a necessary evil."[125] They see that family planning programs instituted to reduce fertility rates have actually contributed, in various ways, to the spread of AIDS. Is it any wonder that African leaders are beginning to denounce such programs as racist and even genocidal? Africans can perhaps be forgiven for wondering if their AIDS epidemic (not to mention their malaria one) was an intended consequence, for it was surely an avoidable one.

No one outside of Africa would say that the population control movement deliberately undertook to spread a fatal illness in Africa, but their blindness to the dangers posed by their devices, their heedless zeal for reducing fertility, and their ransacking of primary health care for their pet project, borders on the criminally negligent. And there is a callousness about their comments that suggests that, in their heart of hearts, they're not overly disturbed about the rising mortality rates anyway.

Former USAID official Edwin Cohn illustrated the anti-people mindset of some in the organization when he said that "better some people should be sick with malaria and spread the job opportunities around. In fact, people in the Third World would be much better off dead than alive, and riotously reproducing."[126]

Asked about the demographic impact of HIV/AIDS, Sharon L. Camp, former vice president of the Population Crisis Committee, responded with studied insouciance: "I asked what level of infection rate it would take for AIDS to increase death rates to equal birth rates in Africa today—which are very high—*not that I would propose doing that by any means*—but just to get a sense of what the rising mortality of AIDS would be. The answer was 50 percent of all the urban world's men and women, adults and children!"[127] (italics added).

The professional distance that Camp was able to maintain from the real-world suffering of millions of victims of AIDS may strike one as unfeeling but, she is, after all, one of the spiritual descendants of Parson Malthus. Dedicated Malthusians down to the present day have always coldly accepted (if not warmly embraced) pestilence as a way of, as Ebenezer Scrooge put it, "reducing the excess population."

Those taking such an arid and abstracted view of human suffering and death fail to realize that, by condoning high mortality rates, they are working at cross purposes to their anti-natal goals. Just as the natural reaction of a woman suffering a miscarriage is to conceive a "make-up" baby as quickly as possible, so the natural reaction of a human population suffering high mortality rates is high fertility rates. Jared Diamond, the author of *Guns, Germs and Steel: the Fates of Human Societies,* has correctly pointed out:

> High infant mortality rates and short adult lifespans resulting from preventable diseases such as malaria, AIDS, cholera and parasitic infections are a major cause of poverty—and paralyze whole economies in multiple ways. First, they sap the productivity of workers, who are often sick and die young; *second, they stimulate high birth rates, because parents expect many of their children to die.* The result is that much of the population is too young to work and women can't join the workforce because they are busy raising children. All those things make countries unattractive to investors. The biggest economic success stories of recent decades have been Hong Kong, Mauritius, Malaysia, Singapore and Taiwan, all of which invested heavily in public health and say their GNPs rocket *as* child mortality *and* family size plunged and as worker lifespans lengthened (italics added).[128]

In the real world falling mortality causes behavioral changes that lead to declining fertility. It always has.

Notes

1. Dr. Stephen Karanja, "Health System Collapsed," *PRI Review* 7(2) (March/April 1997):10.
2. World Bank 1993 International Development Conference, Washington, D.C., 11 January 1993, 3. Also quoted in *PRI Review* 4(5) (September-October 1994):9.
3. "Malaria: avoidable catastrophe?" *Nature,* 10 April 1997.
4. In June 2005, President Bush launched the President's Malaria Initiative (PMI). He pledged to increase U.S. malaria funding by more than $1.2 billion over five years to reduce deaths due to malaria by 50 percent in 15 African countries and challenged other donor countries, private foundations, and corporations to help reduce the suffering and death caused by this disease. PMI is a welcome correction to the overweening emphasis on population control that characterized USAID global health programs for 40 years. See http://www.pmi.gov/.
5. Quoted in David Morrison, "Pop Control While People Die," *PRI Review* 7(6) (November/December 1997):5.
6. Ibid.
7. Roll Back Malaria (World Health Organization, "Children and Malaria," http://www. rbm.who.int/cmc_upload/0/000/015/367/RBMInfosheet_6.htm. Accessed March 14, 2007.
8. Roll Back Malaria (World Health Organization), "Malaria in Africa," http://www. rbm.who.int/cmc_upload/0/000/015/370/RBMInfosheet_3.htm. Accessed March 14, 2007.
9. Quoted in Ellen Shell, "Resurgence of a deadly disease," *The Atlantic Monthly,* August 1997.
10. Brinkman, "Malaria and health in Africa: the present situation and epidemiological trends," *Tropical Medicine and Parasitology,* November 1991.

11. Ettling and Himonga, "Impact of malaria on Zambian children," *Zambian Health Information Digest,* April-June 1995. Also cited in Morrison, "Pop Control While People Die," 8.

12. Shell, "Resurgence of a deadly disease," *The Atlantic Monthly,* August 1997.

13. The Alan Guttmacher Institute (AGI) estimated that if $190 million were cut from the family planning budget, 8,000 more women will die in pregnancy and childbirth, and that 134,000 more infants will die as a result of an increase in high-risk births." Alan Guttmacher Institute, "Estimate of the Number of Additional Abortions, Maternal Deaths and Infant Deaths Resulting from a 35% Cut in USAID Funding for Family Planning for All Countries Excluding China," 6 March 1996. See also, *Innocents Betrayed: A Side of Family Planning the White House Does Not Discuss.* (Population Research Institute, 1997) We point out that the figures advanced by AGI are not based on hard statistical data and may, for reasons having largely to do with abortion ideology and fundraising, be inflated.

14. Larkin, "Congenital malaria in hyperendemic area," *American Journal of Tropical Medicine and Hygiene,* November 1991. Also cited in Morrison, "Pop Control While People Die," 5.

15. Shell, "Resurgence of a deadly disease," *The Atlantic Monthly,* August 1997.

16. Dr. Stephen Karanja, "Population Control—The Kenyan Perspective," unpublished paper, 2 August 1997.

17. "More health care undermined …", *PRI Review* 8(4) (July/October 1998):14.

18. Karanja, "Health System Collapsed," 10.

19. Ibid., 11.

20. Ibid.

21. Interview with Dr. Stephen Karanja, published under the title of "The Sword of Damocles: Population Control and AIDS Destroy African Families" in the *PRI Review* 10(5) (October/December 2000):9.

22. Ibid.

23. David Morrison, "Cutting the Poor," *PRI Review* 7(2) (March/April 1998):5.

24. Interview with Dr. Raul Cantella, March 2001.

25. Ibid.

26. Several thousand of the women sterilized will suffer in future years from ectopic pregnancies, a condition which, if undiagnosed or left untreated, can lead to death. Dr. Herbert Peterson and other researchers with the U.S. Centers for Disease Control in Atlanta, Georgia, have determined that roughly seven out of every 1000 women who undergo sterilization will have an ectopic pregnancy in later years. In an article published in the *New England Journal of Medicine* (13 March 1997), Peterson reported that a study of almost 11,000 women revealed that the possibility of ectopic pregnancy persisted even as long as a decade after sterilization and was twice as high in women who were sterilized under 30 years of age. "All women undergoing this procedure should be informed that ectopic pregnancy may occur long after sterilization," Peterson recommended. The 300,000 Peruvian women sterilized, many of whom were in their twenties, including some in their very early twenties, were not so warned.

27. Hartmann, 234.

28. USAID, Global Health, "HIV/AIDS: Frequently Asked Questions," http://www.usaid.gov/pop_health/aids/News/aidsfaq.html#deaths.

29. UNAIDS, "AIDS Epidemic Update," December 2002, 6.

30. United Nations Population Division (UNPD), 2000 Revision, Part One. Highlights of the 2000 Revision, III, "The Demographic Impact of HIV/AIDS", 12, "highly affected" designated countries with 2% of overall population infected with AIDS;

Angola, Benin, Botswana, Burundi, Burkina Faso, Cameroon, Central African Republic, Chad, Congo, Cote d'Ivoire, Democratic Republic of the Congo, Djibouti, Eritrea, Ethiopia, Gabon, Gambia, Ghana, Guinea-Bissau, Kenya, Lesotho, Liberia, Rwanda, Sierra Leone, South Africa, Swaziland, Togo, Uganda, United Republic of Tanzania, Zambia, Zimbabwe.

31. Ibid.
32. Ibid., 13.
33. Dr. Stephen Karanja, "Kenya, A Country of Graves," *PRI Review* 12(3) (May/June 2002):4.
34. Quote is from President George Bush's "State of the Union Address" of January 28, 2003. White House, Office of the Press Secretary, "The President's State of the Union Address," The United States Capitol, Washington, D.C., 28 January 2003.
35. This brilliant meta-analysis of African AIDS studies should be read by all concerned about the future of the African peoples. In the first part, the authors propose that "existing data can no longer be reconciled with the received wisdom about the exceptional role of sex in the African AIDS epidemic." In the second, they discuss "how health care transmission of AIDS in Africa was ignored" in previous studies. In the third and final article, they estimate the actual percentage of HIV/AIDS cases in Africa that was transmitted heterosexually, as opposed to medically. The meta-analysis by Gisselquist, Potterat, and their colleagues, was published in three parts in the March 2003 issue of a respected peer-reviewed journal, the *International Journal of STD & AIDS*. The three studies are Brewer, David D., Brody, Stuart, Drucker, Ernest, Gisselquist, David, Minkin, Stephen F., Potterat, John J., Rothernberg, Richard B. and Vachon, Francois, "Mounting Anomalies in the Epidemiology of HIV in Africa: Cry the Beloved Paradigm," *International Journal of STD & AIDS,* 2003, 14:144-147; Gisselquist, David, Potterat, John J., Brody, Stuart, and Vachon, Francois, "Let it be Sexual: how Health Care Transmission of AIDS in Africa was Ignored," *International Journal of STD & AIDS,* 2003, 14:148-161; and Gisselquist, David, and Potterat, John J., "Heterosexual Transmission of HIV in Africa: An Empiric Estimate," *International Journal of STD & AIDS,* 2003, 14:162-173.
36. Piot, P., Plummer, F.A., Mhalu, F.S., Lamboray, J.L., Chin, J., Mann, J.M., "AIDS: An International Perspective," *Science,* 1988, 239:573-9.
37. Chin, J., Sato, P.A., Mann, J.M., "Projections of HIV infections and AIDS cases to the year 2000. Bulletin, WHO, 1990, 68:1-11. Homosexual activity among males is sometimes referred to as "men who have sex with men", or MSM for short.
38. N'Galy, B., Ryder, R., "Epidemiology of HIV Infection in Africa," *Journal of Acquired Immune Deficiency Syndrome,* 1988, 1:551-8.
39. Piot, P., Laga, M., Ryder, R., *et al.*, "The Global Epidemiology of HIV Infection: Continuity, Heterogeneity, and Change, *"Journal of Acquired Immune Deficiency Syndrome,* 1990, 3:403-12.
40. Gisselquist, *et al*, "Let it be Sexual ... ," 148.
41. Buve, A., Bishikwabo-Nsarhaza, K., Mutangadura, G., "The Spread and Effect of HIV-1 in Sub-Saharan Africa," *The Lancet,* 2002, 359:2011-17.
42. World Health Organization (WHO), "The World Health Report 2002: Reducing Risks, Promoting Healthy Life." Geneva: WHO, 2002. After the Gisselquist-Potterat studies came out, WHO hastily convened a meeting of experts who denounced them. At the same time, however, they raised their estimate of medical transmission to 2.5 percent. This means, in round numbers, that they admit that at least a million cases of AIDS were caused by dirty needles.
43. Gisselquist, *et al.*, "Heterosexual Transmission of HIV in Africa," 162.

44. Quinn, T.C., Mann, J.M., Curran, J.W., Piot, P., "AIDS in Africa: an Epidemiologic Paradigm." *Science,* 1986, 234:955-63.

45. Van de Perre, P., Rouvroy, D., Lapage, P., *et al.* "Acquired Immune Deficiency Syndrome in Rwanda," *The Lancet,* 1984, ii: 62-65.

46. Clumeck N, Van de Perre PH, Rouvroy D, Nzaramba D., "Heterosexual promiscuity among African patients with AIDS." *New England Journal of Medicine*, 1985, 310:492-7.

47. Others have commented how "the role of sexual promiscuity in the spread of AIDS in Africa appears to have evolved out of prior assumptions about the sexuality of Africans." Packard, R.M., Epstein, P., "Epidemiologists, Social Scientists, and the Structure of Medical Research on AIDS in Africa," *Social Science and Medicine,* 1991, 33:771-83.

48. Brewer, *et al.*, "Mounting Anomalies in the Epidemiology of HIV in Africa: Cry the Beloved Paradigm." *International Journal of STD & AIDS,* 2003, 14:144-147. 145.

49. Shilts, Randy, *And the Band Played On: Politics, People, and the AIDS Epidemic* (New York: St. Martin's Press, 2000), 513.

50. Ibid., 158.

51. "Fact Sheet: The President's Emergency Plan for AIDS Relief," January 29, 2003, http://www.whitehouse.gov/news/releases/2003/01/20030129-1.html.

52. Gisselquist, David, *et al.*, "Let it be Sexual ... ," 158.

53. USAID, *Frontline*, 1995 (5).

54. Gisselquist, *et al*, "Let it be Sexual ... ," 158.

55. Ibid., 154.

56. Ibid., 152.

57. Ibid., 153.

58. Ibid., 154.

59. Ibid., 153.

60. Gisselquist, *et al.*, "Heterosexual Transmission of HIV in Africa," 171.

61. Royce, R.A., Sena, A., Cates, W. Jr., Cohen, M.S., "Sexual Transmission of HIV," *New England Journal of Medicine,* 1997, 336:1072-8.

62. Auvert, B., Ballard, R., Mertens, T., *et al.* "HIV Infection Among Youth in a South African Mining Town is Associated with Herpes Simplex Virus-2, Seropositivity and Sexual Behavior," *AIDS,* 2001, 15:885-98.

63. Gisselquist *et al.*, "Heterosexual Transmission of HIV in Africa," 171.

64. Ibid.

65. Drucker, E.M., Alcabes, P.G., Marx, P.A., "The Injection Century: Consequences of Massive Unsterile Injecting for the Emergence of Human Pathogens," *The Lancet,* 2001, 358:1989-92.

66. "USAID: Leading the Fight Against HIV/AIDS," http://www.usaid.gov/pop_health/aids.

67. Population Services International, "HIV/AIDS," www.psi.org_program/hiv_aids.html. Family Health International, "Reproductive Health Service Integration," www.fhi.org/en/aids/wwdo/wwd23.html.

68. IPPF, AIDS Summary, "Integration of HIV/STI Prevention into SRH Services," ww.ippfwhr.org/publications/serial_issue_e.asp?PubID=20&SerialIssuesID=90.

69. Population Action International (PAI), Fact Sheet, "How Reproductive Health Services and Supplies Are Key to HIV/AIDS Prevention," http://www.populationaction.org/resources/factsheets/FactSheet18_AIDS.htm.

70. By 1987, over 43,000 AIDS cases in 91 countries were reported by the World Health Organization (WHO), "AIDS diagnosis and control: current situation:

report of a WHO meeting," WHO Regional Office for Europe, Munich, March 16-18, 1987, 2. Two years later, in 1989, 145 countries reported cases of AIDS. The World Health Organization estimated over 400,000 AIDS cases globally, almost ten times more than when USAID began its "war against AIDS." USAID estimates that more than 60 million people have been infected with HIV since the pandemic began, USAID, Global Health, "HIV/AIDS: Frequently Asked Questions," www.usaid.gov/pop_health/aids/News/aidsfaq.html. In 1991, estimates for the number of people worldwide infected with HIV/AIDS began at 5 million, over 100 times more than when USAID began its "war against AIDS," modeled on AIDS/SRH integration and centering on the condom. By the end of 1993, at which time USAID was funding abortion groups, the estimated number of HIV/AIDS cases was 14 million HIV infections, WHO, 1995, "Global Programme on AIDS, Progress Report 1992-1993", 2, UNAIDS. Since 1994, the AIDS/SRH integrated programs were promoted globally, and abortion as a method of reducing AIDS transmission has failed. From 1993 to 1999, the number of AIDS infections had more than doubled to an estimated 33 million people, UNAIDS. At present, an estimated 50 million people are infected.

71. FHI-avert.org, Global statistical information and tables, 2002, www.avert.org/globalstats.htm.
72. Gisselquist, *et al*, "Let it be Sexual … ," 154. Lest it be thought that clinic attendees brought their HIV with them, Gisselquist, *et al.*, go on to write that "Reported differences in HIV prevalence between clinic patients and controls and before and after STD treatment exceed differences in general population studies between persons with and without a history of STD."
73. Brewer, *et al.*, 145. They cite an earlier study by Gisselquist, D., Rothenberg, R., Potterat, J., *et al.*, "HIV Infections in Sub-Saharan Africa not Explained by Sexual or Vertical Transmission," *International Journal of STD & AIDS,* 2002, 13:657-66.
74. PAI, "The "ABCs" of HIV/AIDS Prevention," www.populationaction.org/resources/publications/condomscount/ABCs.htm.
75. FHI, "Policy and Advocacy in HIV Prevention," http://www.fhi.org/en/aids/aidscap/aidspubs/handbooks/bccpol.pdf).
76. FHI, "Technical Services: HIV prevention for drug-using populations," http://www.fhi.org/en/aids/wwdo/wwd13.html.
77. "Provider checklists for reproductive health services," *Family Health International*, 2002, http://www.fhi.org/en/fp/checklistse/chklstfpe/englishchecklists.pdf.
78. "Kenya Report," unpublished document, Population Research Institute, March 2003. The report is based on interviews conducted by PRI investigators in the Kenyatta National Hospital in Nairobi, Kenya, in January 2003.
79. USAID, "The ABC's of HIV Prevention,"
80. The INS was first subject to review by the Office of Asylum Review, set up in the Justice Department outside of the INS, and finally, this function was taken entirely away from the INS altogether. The restructuring moved the asylum application and review process from INS, now called Citizenship and Immigration Services (CIS), control. AIDS programs should be taken out of the hands of the population control movement, and put into the hands of those who do not have an "exclusionary" bias towards people.
81. USAID, "The ABC's of HIV Prevention," http://www.usaid.gov/pop_health/aids/News/abcfactsheet.html.
82. Uganda's "ABC" Approach to AIDS Proven Effective, http://www.worldvision.org/worldvision/pr.nsf/stable/update_uganda_52902.

83. "Flexible but Comprehensive: Developing Country HIV Prevention Efforts Show Promise," *The Guttmacher Report*, October 2002.

84. Susan A. Cohen, "Beyond Slogans: Lessons from Uganda's Experience with ABC and HIV/AIDS," *The Guttmacher Report*, December 2003, 2.

85. "AIDS Epidemic Update," Joint United Nations Programme on HIV/AIDS, UNAIDS/World Health Organization (UNAIDS/WHO), December 2002, 6.

86. Ibid., 19.

87. Ibid., 19.

88. Dr. Stephen Karanja, "Health System Collapsed," *PRI Review*, 7(2) (March/April 1997): 4.

89. WHO, "Wastes from Health-Care Activities," Fact Sheet No. 253, October 2000, 2, www.who.int/inf-fs/en/fact253.html.

90. WHO, "Safety of Injections: Misuse and Overuse of Injection Worldwide," Fact Sheet No. 231, April 2002, www.who.int/inf-fs/en/fact231.html.

91. WHO, "Safety of Injections: Facts & Figures," Fact Sheet No. 232, October 1999, 2, www.who.int/inf-fs/en/fact232.html.

92. WHO, "Safety of Injections: Misuse and Overuse of Injection Worldwide," 1.

93. WHO, "Waste from Health-Care Activities," 2. In the same document, WHO reports that "public health authorities in West Bengal, India, have recommended a shift to reusable glass syringes, as the disposal requirements for disposable syringes could not be enforced." In the absence of proper disinfection procedures, this would obviously not address the problem of medical infection by injection.

94. Ibid. This WHO estimate includes injections given in "transitional" countries, i.e., former members of the Soviet bloc.

95. Ibid.

96. Numbers are from the Population, Health and Nutrition Projects Database (PPD), http://ppd.phnip.com. PPD is a computer-based information system managed by the Population, Health, and Nutrition Information Project on behalf of USAID's Center for Population, Health and Nutrition. See also *PRI Review,* 13(1) (January/February 2003): 5.

97. Personal Communication with the author, March 2003.

98. "New Era for Injectables," *Population Reports,* 23(2) (August 1995). http://www.infoforhealth.org/pr/k5/k5.pdf   Accessed on 3 November 2007.

    Like most UN agencies, the UNFPA is extremely secretive about its operations. According to *Population Reports*, DMPA (Depo-Provera, Megastron) makes up three-quarters of UNFPA shipments of injectables, and NET EN (another injectable contraceptive) one-quarter. Thus in 1994 UNFPA shipped enough injectables for about 4.6 million woman-years of use. Deliveries of DMPA by the International Planned Parenthood Federation increased from 336,000 doses in 1991 to 735,000 in 1994. Deliveries of NET EN increased from 305,000 in 1991 to 438,000 in 1994. It is unclear whether the UNFPA, International Planned Parenthood Federation (IPPF), or other suppliers ship only single-dose vials, with an equal number of syringes and needles, or whether they sometimes provide the drug to end-users as multi-dose vials, with the associated risk of contamination and HIV transmission that reusing the vials entails.

99. Ministry of Health of the Government of Kenya, "Procurement of Progestagen-only Injectable Contraceptives," Undated, 37 pages, http://europa.eu.int/comm./europaaid/tender/date/AOF343239.pdf.

100. The provision of "injection kits" with Depo-Provera would not eliminate this risk. Clinics where nearly everything except contraceptives are in short supply would be tempted to cannibalize or reuse whatever injection equipment was available.

101. Encouraging the self-injection of drugs which, in the United States, can only be administered by a health care professional, raises additional questions. A number of serious warnings are listed by the manufacturer including "delay in spontaneous abortion," "fetal abnormalities," "thrombotic disorder" (blood clots), "ocular disorders" ("a sudden partial or complete loss of vision"), and "lactation" (the passing of the drug through breast milk to nursing infants). Cf. Physicians Information for Depo-Provera (medroxyprogesterone acetate injectable suspension), "Important Product Information," www.depo-provera.com/index.asp.

No reference is made to these dangers in the standard "bilingual patient information leaflet" handed out in Kenya, for example. The "leaflet"—a single 3½" by 8" sheet—answers the question, "Is Megastron [another brand name for Depo-Provera] Safe?" by saying only: "Yes, it is safe for use. Severe side effects, like heavy bleeding is unusual. Some women may experience missing periods or spotting, but there is no need for undue concern." No mention here of birth defects, blood clots, or blindness. Taking Depo-Provera while not under a doctor's care renders women vulnerable to potentially deadly or disabling side effects. As Dr. Stephen Karanja has commented, "I see women coming to my clinic daily with swollen legs—they cannot climb stairs. They have been injured by Depo-Provera, birth control pills, and Norplant. I look at them and I am filled with sadness. They have been coerced into using these drugs. Nobody tells them about the side effects, and there are no drugs to treat their complications. In Kenya if you injure the mother, you injure the whole family" (Stephen Karanja, "Health System Collapsed," 11). To the extent that follow-up care is received, and involves injections, then these women are put at additional risk of exposure to HIV.

102. Taking Depo-Provera while not under a doctor's care also renders women vulnerable to potentially deadly or disabling side effects. Moreover, to the extent that follow-up care is received, and involves injections, then these women are put at additional risk of exposure to HIV.

103. Immunization programs are another primary source of injection equipment which can, and undoubtedly is, being reused and abused in the African setting.

104. Norplant was until 2002 manufactured by Wyeth-Ayerst, a division of American Home Products. Although Wyeth-Ayerst has ceased production, the device is still being manufactured for use in developing countries by a Finnish firm. The Population Council holds the patent for Norplant.

105. "Norplant Alleged to Cause Blindness," *PRI Review* 6(3) (May/June 1996):5-7, 11.

106. "Media Reports: Depo-Provera is hazardous to your Health," PRI Weekly Briefing, September 7, 2004.

107. *Contraceptive Sterilization: Global Issues and Trends* (Engender Health: New York, 2002), see esp. Chapter 2, "Sterilization Incidence and Prevalence."

108. Gisselquist, *et al.*, "Let it be Sexual: How Health Care Transmission of AIDS in Africa was Ignored," 151.

109. http://www.ipas.org/english/products/mva.

110. Where abortion is legal, MVA abortion is advertised as such. Where abortion remains illegal, MVA abortion masquerades as "post-abortion care," or PAC. Women are aborted under the pretense that they are simply receiving "menstrual regulation," or that they are being treated for the "complications of unsafe abortion." IPAS itself indicates that the device is customarily used for performing abortions, not post-abortion care, when it says that "The sac remains intact [inside the aspirator] for confirmation of evacuation." A Marie Stopes International (MSI) clinic operator in Kenya told a PRI investigator that, because abortions are "technically illegal" in Kenya they are done under the euphemism of "post-abortion care" or PAC. Officials

of USAID-funded family planning groups in Kenya also told PRI that PAC is widely promoted in U.S.-funded family planning programs in Kenya. MSI, UNFPA and USAID-funded NGOs collaborate to promote MVA use throughout Kenya.

111. Ipas, "Manual Vacuum Aspiration (MVA)," Flexible Karman Cannulae, http://www.ipas.org/english/products/mva/cannulae.html, "Ipas flexible Karman cannulae (size 4mm-12mm) are made of the highest-quality medical grade polyethylene plastic, offering optimal flexibility, strength and durability. The flexible design can reduce the risk of uterine perforation. They are individually wrapped and are sterilized with ethylene oxide gas, remaining sterile as long as the wrapper is intact or until the expiration of the three-year shelf life."

112. *Unsafe abortion: Global and regional estimates of incidence of mortality due to unsafe abortion with a listing of available country data*, Third Edition, 1997, World Health Organization, "Chapter 4: "Estimating Regional and Global Incidence of, and Mortality Due to, Unsafe Abortion." See esp. Table 2, "Global and regional annual estimates of incidence and mortality, unsafe abortions, United Nations regions, 1995-2000." Since IPAS is a "Partner" of the WHO, these estimates presumably do not include the millions of abortions performed by MVA.

113. WHO, "Pregnancy and HIV/AIDS," Fact Sheet No. 25, June 2000, www.who.int/inf-fs/en/fact250.html. See also WHO, "Human Rights, Women and HIV/AIDS," Fact Sheet No. 247, June 2000, which speaks, in the context of "human rights issues relating to mother to child transmission" of HIV, of termination of the pregnancy, www.who.int/inf-fs/fact247.html.

114. Pathfinder International, "Comprehensive Family Planning and Reproductive Training Curriculum," February 1998, http://www.pathfind.org/pf/pubs/module11.pdf. International Planned Parenthood Federation of America, *Advancing Sexual and Reproductive Health in the America, AIDS Summary*, No. 5: "Strengthening Integrated Services: Prevention of STD/AIDS in Primary Health Care in Bahia and Ceará: Strategies for Impact, Institutionalization and Sustainability," February 2002, 8. See also IPPF, AIDS Summary, http://www.ippfwhr.org/publications/serial_article_e.asp?PubID=20&SerialIssuesID=90&Article ID=179.

115. *The Panos Institute, Medianet Bulletin*, News from the Caribbean: "Haiti: A quest for legislation for protecting public health and the rights of people living with HIV/AIDS," October 1999, by Ronald Colbert, Adapted by Jan Voordouw of the Panos Institute, http://www.panosinst.org/Island/IB17E.shtml.

116. "Breastfeeding and Replacement Feeding Practices in the Context of Mother-to-child Transmission of HIV: An Assessment Tool for Research," World Health Organization, Department of Reproductive Health and Research, WHO/RHR/01.12, 1.

117. Population Services International, "Bringing Mass Media to Rural Populations through Mobile Video Vans," PSI flyer, November 1994.

118. Anatoli Kamali, "Interventions for HIV prevention in Africa," *The Lancet,* 2003, 361(9358):633. See also *AIDS Weekly*, March 10, 2003, 16.

119. USAID, *USAID Highlights*, 6:4, 1989; USAID, Population, Health and Nutrition Projects Database. Note: the volume of USAID condoms shipped overseas is likely smaller than that of the UN Population Fund, which boasts of being the largest international supplier of condoms.

120. "Scientific Evidence on Condom Effectiveness for Sexually Transmitted Disease (STD) Prevention," *National Institute of Allergy and Infectious Diseases*, National Institutes of Health, Department of Health and Human Services, July 20, 2001.

121. Davis, K.R., and Weller, S.C., "The Effectiveness of Condoms in Reducing Heterosexual Transmission of HIV," *Family Planning Perspectives,* 1999, 31(6):272-279.

122. Cited in "Condoms limited vs. HIV," PRI Review 7(3) (May/June 1997):13.
123. Trussell, J., "Contraceptive Efficacy," in Hatcher, R.A., *et al.*, (eds.) *Contraceptive Technology*, 1998, 17th revised ed. (Ardent Media, New York, NY), 779-844. Also cited in "Scientific Evidence on Condom Effectiveness for Sexually Transmitted Disease (STD) Prevention," 10.
124. J. Richens, J. Imrie, A. Copas, "Condoms and seat belts: the parallels and the lessons," *The Lancet* 355(9201) (29 January 2000): 400-403.
125. Shell.
126. Quoted in Robert S. Desowitz, *The Malaria Capers* (New York: W. W. Norton and Co., 1993).
127. Sharon Camp, radio interview. Cited in the *PRI Review*. Camp currently heads the Alan Guttmacher Institute.
128. Jared Diamond, "Why We Must Feed the Hands that Could Bite Us," *The Washington Post,* 13 January 2002.

Part III

The Myriad "Benefits" of Population Control

7

The Illusory Benefits to Donor Countries

"Whatever your cause, it's a lost cause unless we control population."
–Population Crises Committee[1]

The great harms done to humanity by population control are, in the view of its advocates, completely overshadowed by a higher imperative: The need to protect us, collectively, from "breeding ourselves to death."[2] Population growth is apocalypse now, and compunctions about human rights cannot be allowed to stand in the way of the paramount need to "control the flood of humanity that threatens to engulf the earth."[3]

Those who enlisted in this crusade sought various ways to convict the unenlightened of the urgency of their cause. Without population controls, they predicted, "schools, churches, colleges, hospitals, museums, libraries, community chests, heart funds, and conservation will inevitably be swamped by too many people."[4] Food would run out, famine would ensue, farmland would erode, land for recreation would shrink, natural resources would be exhausted, energy would be in short supply, and pollution would cover the face of the earth. "Whatever your cause is, it's a lost cause without population control," was—and is—a frequent theme of their publications."[5]

But population control would not merely avert disasters like long lines at libraries. It would also, we were told, confer (at least on those of us who survived the controllers) a myriad of benefits. The security-minded spoke of preserving the global economic, political, and military dominance of the United States. Believing in "cradle power," and worried about the demographic decline of the West, they sought to engineer a baby bust among more prolific peoples. By keeping the numbers of have-nots down, they would both preserve American access to strategic raw materials and prevent the rise of other great powers. Committed secular humanists rejected such concerns as mere chauvinism, but nonetheless advocated a reduction in human numbers. This would not only benefit human beings, they argued with the peculiar broadmindedness of their kind, but *all* species, not to mention Mother Earth herself. Both Earth-firsters and America-firsters joined together in an unlikely coalition to urge the developing world, for its own good, to get with the program. The road to economic success, these countries were told, was paved with condoms and contraceptives.

The claimed benefits of population control thus divide themselves rather naturally into two classes: (1) the supposed benefits to the funding countries and (2) the supposed benefits to the countries on the receiving end of these programs. We will examine these claims in the following two chapters.

> *Therefore the ruler of men desires to have more*
> *people for his own use.*
> *The ruler loves the people because they are useful.*
> *–Guan Zhong (c. 730 B.C.-645 B.C.) The Book of Master Guan, Chapter 16*[6]

> *[W]orld population growth is likely to contribute,*
> *directly or indirectly, to domestic upheavals and*
> *international conflicts that could adversely affect*
> *U.S. interests. Population growth will also reinforce*
> *the politicization of international economic rela-*
> *tions and intensify the drive of [less-developed*
> *countries] for a redistribution of wealth and of*
> *authority in international affairs.*
> *–The Central Intelligence Agency, 1977*[7]

Population and National Power

Few in the ancient world would have taken exception to Master Guan's dictate that the astute ruler "desires to have more people." Writing seven centuries before the birth of Christ, the founder of Chinese statecraft saw clearly the benefits of population growth. "An extensive territory, an affluent economy, a teeming population, and a strong army—these are the foundation of the hegemon-king," he advised would-be rulers.[8] Others concurred.[9]

Living in a world of small producers, these writers could easily observe that nearly all wealth was created by human activity. A rock was not wealth until it had been hewn by human hands into a building block for the king's palace or a lowly stone hut. Copper ore was not wealth until it had been discovered, extracted, smelted, and worked into lamps and bowls. A tree was not wealth until it had been felled, sawed, planed, and fashioned into a table, a bed, or other useful article.

Vital, thriving civilizations have ever been densely populated. As Samuel Johnson said to Boswell in 1785, "men, thinly scattered, make a shift, but a bad shift, without many things…. It is being concentrated which produces convenience."[10] Understanding this, the prime object of rulers and governments throughout human history has been to attract and increase the number of their people. Prince Potemkin, knowing the czar's inspector general would not be impressed by an unpeopled wilderness, constructed his famous faux villages to deceive him into thinking that his fief was peopled and, hence, prosperous.

The historical record suggests that the great civilizations of Greece and Rome emerged as great powers following a period of rapid population growth. Their eventual declines were preceded by a lengthy period of population decline that hollowed out these once-powerful empires and made them vulnerable to foreign invasion. In China, too, periods of dynastic exuberance and expansion were marked by rapid population growth, while population declines coincided with dynastic decay and collapse.

Even today, recognizing the essential link between population and wealth, many countries in the developed world have adopted pro-natal policies intended to boost the birthrate. Most European countries have put in place what the Austrians call *Kindergeld*, or "child money," a system of monthly state subsidies to parents to help defray the cost of raising children. The United States itself allows income deductions for dependents and generous child tax credits to more efficiently reach the same end. But the U.S., aided by many of its European allies and Japan, follows a very different policy abroad, seeking to discourage real or imagined potential competitors from having children.

Barren Thy Neighbors

Late twentieth century Westerners, mostly of European stock, have made a determined effort to reduce the inhabitants of less developed countries. But unprecedented this effort is not, for in the history of mankind there have been many other such efforts. The earliest recorded population control program occurred in ancient Egypt, when the pharaohs of old, haunted by the increase in the enslaved but prolific Hebrews, decreed that the sons born to every Hebrew family should die.

Much closer to our own age is an example of population control that should make every American cringe. It turns out that the modern effort of the United States to render potential competitors barren is freighted with historical irony, *for this was precisely the same policy that was*

*adopted by Great Britain vis-à-vis the American colonies in the years
leading up to American independence.* The rules made by England in
the mid-1700s—no new blast furnaces in the American colonies, no
settlements beyond the Allegheny mountains—were driven ultimately
by alarm over America's burgeoning population.

Britain's colonies in North America were home to only 250,000 settlers in the year 1700. Over the next fifty years, however, that number
doubled, and then doubled again. Of this remarkable natural increase
Benjamin Franklin noted in 1751 that "[T]here are supposed to be now
upwards of one million of English souls in North America (though it
is thought scarce 80,000 have been brought over sea), and yet perhaps
there is not one fewer in Britain, but rather many more, on account of
the employment the colonies afford to manufacture at home. This million doubling, suppose but once in twenty-five years, will, in another
century, be more than the people of England, and the greatest number
of Englishmen will be on this side of the water....."[11]

London's fear that the center of gravity of the English-speaking world
would one day shift across the Atlantic was accepted by thoughtful men
in both countries. By the eve of the American Revolution, the population
of the 13 colonies had surged again to 2.4 million. Edward Wigglesworth,
professor of divinity at Harvard, assured his fellow Americans in 1775
that, whatever the outcome of the thirteen colonies' bid for independence,
the astonishing growth in American numbers ensured that they would
inherit the mantle of empire by 1825.[12]

Great Britain's efforts to curb the runaway population growth in its
colonies included no direct restrictions on childbearing, but rather a pano-
ply of regulations that was clearly intended to keep them underpopulated
and dependent upon the mother country. This was such a serious matter
that the signers of the Declaration of Independence, Benjamin Franklin
among them, included it in their formal list of charges against "the present King of Great-Britain." Under their "History of repeated Injuries and
Usurpations, all having in direct Object the Establishment of an absolute
Tyranny over these States," we find the following charge:

> He [King George III] has endeavoured to prevent the Population of these States;
> for that Purpose obstructing the Laws for Naturalization of Foreigners; refusing to
> pass others to encourage their Migrations hither, and raising the Conditions of new
> Appropriations of Lands.[13]

The efforts of the British elite to keep the rustics from the colonies
few and weak were so much resented that they helped incite a revolu-

tion. How distressing that the country that rebelled against the "injury and usurpation" of population control should now inflict an identical injury on others, usurping their right to have children out of a misguided national chauvinism. Given our own history, how could Americans fail to understand the burning resentment that many in developing countries feel towards us today as a result of these policies?

We saw in Chapter 2 that the history of family planning was less one of beneficence than brutality. The primary reason for this is that such programs find their roots not in American compassion but fear. Like Great Britain two centuries ago, we fear the developing world's growing population, fear economic competition for scarce resources, and fear social unrest leading to hostile regimes or spilling over our borders.

National Security Study Memorandum 200 (NSSM 200)

As the populations of developing countries began to grow after World War II, alarm bells sounded in the heads of many in the national security establishment. Their reading of history had convinced them that great numbers meant great power. Katherine and A.F.K Organski, writing in 1961, gave voice to this fear when they wrote: "World power ... is passing from the West, for the largest nations lie in the East. If, as seems likely, these lands complete their own industrialization successfully, their size alone guarantees to them a place that Western nations cannot rival."[14] "[P]opulation is, indeed, a nation's greatest resource."[15] Demographic projections, showing population spiking in the developing world, combined with falling birthrates in Europe, were viewed with foreboding. Hushed discussions in the corridors of power followed.

When the U.S. birthrate, robust until the early 1960s, headed south a few years later, these discussions quickly took on an increasing urgency. One of the first official expressions of concern was a classified National Security Council memorandum dated 10 August 1970. This memorandum, signed by President Richard Nixon's national security advisor, Henry Kissinger, stated that "The U.S. should recommend that the UN Fund for Population Activities undertake a study of *world population problems and measures required to deal with them, as a top priority item* in the Second Development Decade"[16] (italics added). The significance of this directive lies less in its substance—the UNFPA had been created two years before to do precisely what Kissinger was now suggesting it do—than in its source. The lead security agency of the U.S. government, the National Security Council, had gone on record as expressing concern about population growth in the developing world, making it clear that it viewed population control as a top priority.

As the Rockefeller Commission began its series of public hearings on the population question in the early 1970s, Henry Kissinger, ordered the National Security Council (NSC) to carry out its own secret analysis of the same question. The resulting document, called National Security Study Memorandum 200 (NSSM 200), represented the considered opinion of not merely the NSC, but the entire security, intelligence, and foreign affairs establishment of the U.S. government, including the CIA, the Pentagon, the National Security Agency (NSA), and the State Department.[17] The 250-page report was marked confidential—for good reason, as we will see below—and remained unknown outside of the U.S. government until it was declassified in 1990.

NSSM 200 was briefly mentioned in Chapter 1, but this seminal document in the history of American population control efforts deserves a closer look. The preoccupation of the U.S. security establishment with population growth—seen as a threat to U.S. security and economic interests—stands here revealed. At the same time, NSSM 200 is a blueprint for preserving the global economic, political, and military dominance of the United States. Believing that people mean power, and worried about the demographic decline of the West, these practitioners of *realpolitik* unapologetically sought to engineer a fertility decline among more prolific peoples. And they were fully prepared to deceive other countries into doing so with spurious arguments.

The NSSM 200 generally eschews the apocalyptic prose of writers like Paul Ehrlich and Hugh Moore—it was, after all, drafted by a committee of bureaucrats—but its numbers are no less inflated. "If present fertility rates were to remain constant, the 1974 population of 3.9 billion would increase to 7.8 billion by the year 2000 and rise to a theoretical 103 *billion* by 2075"[18] (italics added). Even the so-called medium variant projected that world population would reach 6.4 billion by 2000 and 12 billion by 2100. The population problem was even worse than these numbers would suggest, the report went on. Not only was the world's population increasing by over 2% a year, this *population growth rate* was still accelerating, or so it claimed. The bottom line for NSSM 200 was this: "The rate of [world population growth] is increasing and between two and a half and three and a half billion [people] will be added by the year 2000, depending partly on the effectiveness of population growth control programs."[19]

None of these assertions were true. *Contra* NSSM 200, the population growth rate was already beginning to decelerate at the time the report was written, and it has slowed dramatically in the years since. From

peak annual population increases of 2.07% during the period 1966-
1970, it had fallen to 1.33% by 1996-2000, and is expected to reach zero
population growth sometime between 2040 and 2050, not continue to
increase indefinitely. And the world's population in 2000 was actually
only 6 billion, not the 6.4 billion, much less the 7.8 billion, projected.
The population increased by only 2 billion from 1975 to 2000, or half
a billion *less* than the lowest projection assumed in NSSM 200. As
we discussed in Chapter 1, this was a one-time increase. The world's
population will never double again. Rather it will peak at 8 to 9 billion
around mid-century, and then begin to fall.

But this was 1974. Having conjured up this flood of humanity, what
consequences did these "secret" agencies foresee for America? In a
chapter entitled "Minerals and Fuels," NSSM 200 argues that "The lo-
cation of known reserves of higher-grade ores of most minerals favors
increasing dependence of all industrialized regions on imports from
less developed countries." The United States, in particular, is vulnerable
because "the U.S. economy will require large and increasing amounts
of minerals from abroad, especially from less developed countries....
That fact gives the U.S. enhanced interest in the political, economic, and
social stability of the supplying countries."[20]

Rapid population growth is a security threat because it leads to disrup-
tions in the supply of materials needed for the U.S. economy:

> In the extreme cases where population pressures lead to endemic famine, food riot,
> and breakdown of social order, those conditions are scarcely conducive to system-
> atic exploration for mineral deposits or the long-term investments required for their
> exploitation.... Whether through government action, labor conflicts, sabotage, or
> civil disturbance, the smooth flow of needed materials [to the United States] will be
> jeopardized. Although population pressure is obviously not the only factor involved,
> these types of frustrations are much less likely under conditions of slow or zero
> population growth.[21]

The report, which was written during the height of the Cold War, also
warns darkly of "disruptive foreign activities," a veiled reference to the
efforts of the Soviet Union and China to promote communist revolutions
and recruit client states:

> It seems well understood that the impact of population factors on the subjects already
> considered—development, food requirements, resources, environment—adversely
> affects the welfare and progress of countries in which we have a friendly interest and
> thus indirectly adversely affects broad U.S. interests as well. The effects of population
> factors on the political stability of these countries and their implications for internal
> and international order or disorder, destructive social unrest, violence and *disruptive*

foreign activities are less well understood and need more analysis. Nevertheless, some strategists and experts believe that these effects may ultimately be the most important of those arising from population factors, most harmful to the countries where they occur and seriously affecting U.S. interests[22] (italics added).

In other words, if the peasant hordes of Asia, Africa, and Latin America were allowed to multiply, their search for social justice might lead them to communism. This would limit America's access to strategic minerals and other raw materials, both directly through the action of hostile regimes, and indirectly because of greatly expanded local consumption. How were these consequences to be averted? "Wherever a lessening of population pressures through reduced birth rates can increase the prospects for ... stability, population policy becomes relevant to resource supplies and to the economic interests of the United States."[23]

The blunt Dr. Ravenholt, who was serving as population czar at the time NSSM 200 was circulated inside the government, put the matter in language that anyone could understand:
   Population control is needed to maintain the normal operation of United States commercial interests around the world. Without our trying to help those countries with their economic and social development [by instituting population control programs], the world could rebel against the strong United States commercial presence. The self-interest thing is a compelling element. If the population explosion proceeds unchecked, it will cause such terrible economic conditions abroad that revolutions will ensure. And revolutions are scarcely ever beneficial to the interests of the United States.[24]

Thus was population control declared to be a weapon in the Cold War. The immediate result was a huge jump in population control spending by the United States and its allies. Dozens of countries around the world were targets, especially those that were considered to be vulnerable to communist insurrection, such as Thailand and the Philippines, and those sitting on top of valuable metals, including the nations comprising the southern tier of Africa. Population control, by preserving our access to strategic raw materials and slowing the spread of communism, would supposedly eliminate future threats to U.S. national security.

The underlying aim was far more ambitious, however. Salted throughout NSSM 200 and other government publications are veiled references to another, wider, geostrategic goal: Using population control to prevent the rise of other great powers, and by this means to preserve the America's global primacy in arms, wealth, and all-around geopolitical muscle.

I, for one, do not take exception to the *end* of American primacy, only to the *means* advocated by NSSM 200. We need make no apology for striving to maintain America's global primacy, in my view, because it brings with it important advantages for Americans. Moreover, the benign American order, by generally promoting prosperity, political develop-ment, and international peace, carries benefits for the wider world as well. Americans are not mistaken when they believe that their country is, on balance, a force for good in the world. As Samuel P. Huntington has written, "A world without U.S. primacy will be a world with more violence and disorder and less democracy and economic growth than a world where the United States continues to have more influence than any other country in shaping global affairs. The sustained international primacy of the United States is central to the welfare and security of Americans and to the future of freedom, democracy, open economies, and international order in the world."[25]

The problem is that the positive international role for the United States *envisioned by* Huntington is not the least evident in NSSM 200. Instead of promoting freedom, it encourages governments to intervene, even violently, in the most private decisions of families. Instead of encouraging democracy, it imposes population control on sovereign nations. Instead of promoting open economies it hobbles economic growth by reducing human numbers. In short, real freedoms are sacri-ficed to forestall imagined future events—instability, unrest, violence, insurrection, famine, food riots, and so on. In so doing, NSSM 200 promotes violence, weakens democracy and hinders economic growth. The road down which we would take the developing world is the road to serfdom—to use Friedrich Hayek's phrase—and this is a path that benefits neither it nor ourselves.

Darkness always hates the light. It is not surprising that the originators of this report wanted it kept secret, or that they wanted it implemented by agencies one step removed from the U.S. government. The involve-ment of what were called "multilateral" agencies, the study reasoned, would help to conceal the U.S. role and purpose in implementing such programs.[26] "It is vital that the effort to develop and strengthen a com-mitment on the part of the LDC [less-developed countries] leaders not be seen by them as an industrialized country policy to keep their strength down or to reserve resources for us by the 'rich' countries."[27] In other words, both the U.S. involvement *and its goals* were to be concealed behind a façade of multilateralism.

The study also advised the United States to use its leverage with international financial institutions to promote policy change in the tar-geted countries. Here remember that the first NSC Memo to deal with population issues came out in the summer of 1970, the same year that the World Bank made its first population control loan, a $2 million credit to Jamaica.[28] This is not to say that the NSC "ordered" the World Bank to make this loan, but rather that the two organizations were moving in tandem on the population issue, with the NSC adding the weight of its national security argument to the other pressures on the World Bank to fund such programs. Four years later, in 1974, the NSC was pleased to report that the World Bank was continuing to make "progress:"

> The World Bank group is the principle [sic] international financial institution providing population programs. However, the Bank's policy prevents it from financing consumables such as contraceptives and other family planning commodities. This restricts its ability to finance population projects with its available funds. At present a high level outside consultant group is evaluating the Bank's population programs. This evaluation and our review of it should help provide a clearer picture of what improvement there might be in the Bank's role and activities in the population field.[29]

The NSC was not disappointed. The panel, headed by Bernard Berelson of the Population Council and reliably pro-population control, not only recommended that the bank "loan" money for contraceptives and other family planning paraphernalia, but that it work to develop "more satisfactory relationships" with donors such as the United States. The bank should also "include population considerations on a substantial and consistent basis in its economic reports, particularly with regard to key countries, and ... reach for collaboration with population policy units in key countries."[30] As NSSM 200 had recommended, the U.S. population program was becoming more sophisticated, especially in its use of surrogates.

The "key countries" targeted by NSSM 200 for population control were those likely to grow into regional powers, those rich in natural resources, or both. Brazil, which "clearly dominates" Latin America in demographic significance, has the potential, the report suggested, to exert its influence far beyond its borders. Its expanding population suggests a "growing power status for Brazil in Latin America and on the world scene over the next 25 years."[31] In Africa, Nigeria was singled out: "Already the most populous country on the continent, with an estimated 55 million people in 1970, Nigeria's population by the end of this century is projected to number 135 million.[32] This suggests a growing political and strategic role for Nigeria, at least in Africa south of the Sahara."[33]

Such programs could not be imposed upon developing countries without the consent of their leaders. "Development of a worldwide political and popular commitment to population stabilization is fundamental to any effective strategy," the study noted. "This requires the support and commitment of key LDC [Less Developed Countries] leaders. This will only take place if they clearly see the negative impact of unrestricted population growth and believe it is possible to deal with this question through governmental action."[34]

NSSM 200 was formally adopted as U.S. foreign policy by National Security Decision Memorandum 314 (NSDM 314), which was signed on 26 November 1975 by Kissinger's successor as national security advisor, Brent Scowcroft, on behalf of President Gerald Ford. A follow-up report, issued in 1976 by the Interagency Task Force on Population Policy for the Under Secretaries Committee of the NSC, asks—and suggests answer to—some disturbing questions:

- Would food be considered an instrument of national power? (Yes.)
- On what basis should such food resources then be provided? (To countries with population control programs in place.)
- Will we be forced to make choices as to whom we can reasonably assist, and if so, should population efforts be a criterion for such assistance? (Yes.)
- Are mandatory population control measures appropriate for the U.S. and/or others? (Maybe.)
- Is the U.S. prepared to accept food rationing to help people who can't/won't control their population growth? (No.)

The hint that strong-arm tactics may be necessary both at the international and the national level is underlined by a virtual endorsement of coercion in another section:

> Population programs have been particularly successful where leaders have made their positions clear, unequivocal and public, while maintaining discipline down the line from national to village levels, marshalling government workers (including police and military), doctors and motivators to see that population policies are well administered and executed.... In some cases, strong direction has involved incentives such as payment to acceptors for sterilization, or disincentives such as giving low priorities in the allocation of housing and schooling to those with larger families. Such direction is the *sine qua non* of an effective program.[35]

The NSC report might have been describing the enforcement mechanism of China's population control policy, which even in the 1970s already relied upon a "well-administered and executed" program of limits on family size and mandatory sterilization after three children to eliminate excess births. While passing over China's obvious reliance on coercion in silence, the report did find overall trends in its program to be "encouraging." "Encouraging" was also used to describe the programs of two other countries now well known for abuses, Indonesia and India.

At the time, India was in the midst of its infamous sterilization campaign, in which 6.5 million men were vasectomized.[36] The United States, which had for years pushed the Indian government to do more about its "population problem," quietly applauded when President Indira Gandhi declared a "population emergency" in mid-1975. World Bank President Robert McNamara visited the Indian Ministry of Health and Family Planning in November 1976, at the height of the campaign, to congratulate the Indian government on its "political will and determination."[37]

The NSC, while secretly commending India's program, strongly cautioned against public praise. "We recommend that U.S. officials refrain from public comment on forced-pace measures such as those currently under active consideration in India ... [because that] might have an unfavorable impact on existing voluntary programs."[38]

The Indian sterilization program was in fact wildly unpopular, especially among untouchables and Muslims, and riots followed. As I mentioned in Chapter 5, the rumor (later verified as fact) had spread that the Hindu majority was deliberately targeting low caste and minority groups for sterilization in an effort to reduce their numbers. Such an obvious and callous display of racial and religious bigotry should have elicited condemnations from the United States and other Western countries concerned about human rights. But the U.S. State Department not only applauded the policy—hence the NSC caution—it encouraged its surrogates, like McNamara, to reward it with loans. After all, how could we possibility condemn India for carrying out within its borders a policy that we were implementing on a global scale? For was not our population policy designed to curb the fertility of our own version of low caste and minority groups—the poor Africans, Latinos, and Asians of the world?

The 1976 report also recommended ways to silence the rising chorus of developing world criticism directed at the new U.S. foreign policy. To answer the charges of cultural imperialism, locals were to be hired to flak the new population programs. To avoid the appearance of neo-colonialism, U.S. population control funding was to be routed through international organizations like the UNFPA, as was done in China, or to private groups like the IPPF and Family Health International. And, first and foremost, U.S. officials were never to use phrases like population control or birth control.

All of these recommendations were the result of lessons learned in the early years, when "made-in-America" population policies generated massive public outrage in a number of countries. In 1967, for example, the Kenyan government, with strong encouragement from Washington and London, adopted a National Family Planning Program drawn up by the Population Council. The resulting firestorm was described by Donald Warwick in his book, *Bitter Pills: Population Policies and Their Implementation in Eight Developing Countries*:

> Critics soon charged that Kenya's efforts at population control were colonialism in economic clothing and might even have genocidal intent. The Catholic Archbishop of Nairobi claimed that there was no population problem in Kenya, for there were vast lands yet to be inhabited. Oginga Odinga, once Kenyatta's vice-president, stated during parliamentary debate on the health budget: "We oppose family planning and don't even want to hear of family planning in Africa."... Others criticized the speed with which the Population Council report had become national policy, especially without public hearings or debate.... Before long, key figures pulled back from their espousal of family planning.[39]

Grace Ogot, a well-known Kenyan writer, was among those who viewed foreign-funded family planning programs with suspicion: "Colonialism is still fresh in the minds of East Africans and it would, therefore, not be difficult to interpret the foreign experts' enthusiasm as a kind of neocolonialist trick to keep the African population down." Oginga Odinga, as the country's opposition leader, bluntly charged that the African people were already being systematically "eliminated from a sparsely populated continent and ... birth control would only speed up this trend."[40]

Warwick concludes that "The early emphasis on population control proved disastrous as it conjured up images of a white plot to limit African numbers..."[41] But the issue runs much deeper than merely a poor choice of words. A reasonable person, reading NSSM 200, might well conclude that "a white plot to limit African numbers" was exactly what was afoot. How else is one to interpret its repeated linking of U.S. national security interests in Africa with population control?

In any event, the population controllers learned their speech lessons well. By the mid-1970s, the NSC was cynically advised U.S. officials to pretend a complete lack of interest in anything resembling population control: "[A]void the language of 'birth control' in favor of 'family planning' or 'responsible parenthood,' with the emphasis being placed on child spacing in the interests of the health of child and mother...."

The programs themselves were also to be repackaged. To disarm critics in the developing world, population control programs were to be represented as "reproductive health care," "maternal health care," and even "child survival" programs. As one USAID-funded group advised at the time, population projects that "focus too narrowly on family planning as a solution" raise suspicions among host country officials. The solution they went on to propose is still in use today: Population projects were to be "Integrate[d] ... with maternal and child health care delivery."[42] A ruse by any other name is still ... a ruse.

The leaders and the people of newly independent states initially had little use for this new wave of secular missionaries or the anti-natal religion they preached. As in Kenya and Nigeria, they suspected that a new and insidious form of cultural imperialism was being unleashed on them by their former colonial masters. Had they known that they were the object of an anti-natal campaign drafted at the highest levels of the U.S. government—that is, had they known of the existence of a document called NSSM 200—perhaps they would have barred the condom bearers entirely. But the assault on their sensibilities was too subtle and too diverse to summon such a direct response. Some of their countrymen, quietly recruited to serve as the public face of these new programs, began suggesting that population control was a good thing. Anti-natal propaganda, paid for by Western agents, began to appear in their newspapers. International organizations, like the UNFPA and the IPPF, set up shop in their capital city. A delegation from the World Bank quietly suggested, without the least tone of threat or intimidation in their voices, that their country's latest loan request seemed to be incomplete because it lacked reference to a national population policy.

The men who so carefully elaborated a rationale for population control, developed an overall strategy for its prosecution, and even elaborated disinformation to use on the demographic battlefield were not monsters, of course, as monstrous as their project appears in retrospect. Far from being extremists of one kind or another, Henry Kissinger and his colleagues comprised some of the best and brightest minds in government service. But theirs were minds in thrall to the myth of overpopulation, stunted by the modern worship of statistics, and proud that their utilitarian calculations of the national interest were totally unencumbered by morality.

The End of the Cold War

The collapse of the Soviet Union in 1990 abruptly removed the chief competitor to American primacy from the world stage. Struggling to rise from the ruins was a rump Russia that could claim, at best, regional power status. The world communist movement, having lost its core state and chief sponsor, was reduced to the struggling outposts of North Korea,

Cuba, Vietnam and, perhaps, Mugabe's Zimbabwe. (China was not *really* communist, or so the story went.) Communist ideology, which had such cachet in parts of the developing world a few years before, virtually overnight came to seem a synonym for an archaic system of government despotism practiced by a handful of weak, failing regimes. This tectonic shift in international relations reduced the threat of "disruptive foreign activities" (read: Moscow-sponsored insurrections) to insignificance.

The sudden preeminence of the United States did not, however, provide an occasion for a general reconsideration of the population control project. For it had by then become part of the received wisdom in U.S. national security circles that maintaining the influence and reach of the United States required reducing population "pressure" in the developing world. No sooner had it arrived in Washington than the Clinton administration ramped up population-control spending, including a five-year, $75 million handout to IPPF, defending the increase in national security terms. In Somalia, where U.S. troops were then embroiled, the "core" of the crisis was "overpopulation." So said J. Brian Atwood, the newly appointed head of USAID, who neglected to mention that Somalia is one of the least populated countries on earth, with only 7 million people scattered across an area the size of Texas.[43]

At the 1994 UN Conference on Population and Development in Cairo, Egypt, the Clinton administration pushed strongly, albeit unsuccessfully, for global population targets. Responding to criticism from Republican congressional leaders, then-Secretary of State Warren Christopher responded in terms of U.S. national security. "Population and sustainable development are back where they belong in the mainstream of American foreign policy and diplomacy," Christopher said. Population pressure "ultimately jeopardizes America's security interests.... It strains resources. It stunts economic growth. It generates disease. It spawns huge refugee flows, and ultimately it threatens our stability."[44]

Population control would help to slow the emergence of future competitors, and extend the American century well into the next millennium. Population Council researcher Peter Donaldson writes that, "In the case of population-related foreign assistance, it is clear that senior government policy makers in the United States and other guardians of American culture and interests held a worldview that was threatened by the rapid growth of the Third World."[45] The *worldview* in question, with which the environmentalist Donaldson is not in sympathy, is the determination that the U.S.-dominated status quo shall continue. The *threat* can be summed up in two words: differential fertility.

Low population growth in the West, combined with high fertility in the developing world, could produce a dramatic shift in the balance of power in coming decades, warned Pentagon researchers in 1988.[46] "Declining fertility rates will make it increasingly difficult for the United States and its NATO allies ... to maintain military forces at current levels," they wrote. "In contrast, exceptionally high fertility rates in most LDCs [lesser developed countries], if not matched by a commensurate growth of jobs, could lead to expanded military establishments in affected countries as a productive alternative to unemployment... military establishments may have built-in momentum to capitalize on unused manpower for purposes of both internal and external security."[47]

To maintain U.S. military dominance (conceived in simplistic terms as merely a matter of numbers), the researchers advised "U.S. strategic planners" to place population control at the top of the nation's security agenda by embarking a kind of reverse cradle competition: "[P]ay serious attention to population trends, their causes, and their effects... do those things that will provide more bang for every buck spent on national security... anticipate events and conditions before they occur. [Policy makers] must employ all the instruments of statecraft at their disposal (development assistance and population planning every bit as much as new weapon systems). Furthermore, instead of relying upon the canard that the threat dictates one's posture, they must attempt to influence the form that threat assumes."[48] In other words, if our armies are shrinking because of falling birthrates, then we must ensure—through anti-natal programs—that the armies of our potential competitors shrink apace.

By 1991 the population surge in the Third World was beginning to slow, as most of these countries began their demographic transitions from high fertility to low fertility. Yet they were still high enough to inspire Darwinian fears that these faster growing populations would eventually displace slower growing ones. Demographer Nicholas Eberstadt, speaking at a U.S. Army Conference on Long-Range Planning," soberly noted that:

> [V]irtually all current population projections anticipate comparatively slow population growth in today's more developed regions (Europe, the Soviet Union, Japan, North America and Oceania) and comparatively rapid growth for the less developed regions. *If these trends continue for another generation or two*, the implications for the international political order and the balance of world power could be enormous. ... Such trends speak to pressures for a systematically diminished role and status for today's industrial democracies. Even with relatively unfavorable assumptions about Third World economic growth, the share of global economic output of today's

industrial democracies could decline. With a generalized and progressive industrialization of current low-income areas, the Western diminution would be all the more
rapid. Thus, one can easily envision a world more unreceptive, and ultimately more
threatening, to the interests of the United States and its allies. ... The population and
economic-growth trends described could create an international environment even
more menacing to the security prospects of the Western alliance than was the Cold
War for the past generation[49] (italics added).

Jean-Claude Chesnais, a leading French demographer, undoubtedly
had in mind his own aging country when he wrote in 1990 that "The
abrupt and massive changes in world population distribution resulting
from the *demographic trends of the next few decades* will lead to a
reshaping of the world political geography whose general outline can
already be foreseen. Young powers will emerge, basing their strength
in large part on their population size and the stimulus it creates, and old
powers will fade as their populations decline"[50] (italics added).

All of this, a mere 15 years later, seems a little overblown. While
Europe's demographic implosion has continued apace, fertility rates in
the developing world have fallen farther and faster than anyone was predicting a short time ago. The population projections of the UN Population
Division and the U.S. Census Bureau are regularly revised downward,
and whole continents are approaching zero population growth. The
population train is grinding slowly and inexorably to a halt, and recent
cohorts of newborns are outnumbered by their older siblings. The global
baby boom is over.

Peering into the face of this new demographic reality, population
alarmists strained to see new dangers to U.S. security. They found it in
the large cohort of young people, over a billion strong, who will come
of age over the next 10-20 years.

The Vertical Invasion of the Barbarians

As Robert Bork has noted, "Every new generation constitutes a
wave of savages who must be civilized by their families, schools, and
churches. An exceptionally large generation can swamp the institutions
responsible for teaching traditions and standards."[51] Judge Bork was
speaking in reference to the havoc wreaked in American universities
by Baby Boomers in the 1960s. But history is replete with examples of
youth movements, Samuel Huntington has reminded us, including the
Protestant Reformation. "Historically, the existence of large cohorts of
young people has tended to coincide with such movements ... A notable
expansion in the proportion of youth in Western countries coincided

with the 'Age of the Democratic Revolution' in the last decades of the eighteenth century... The proportions of youth rose again in the 1920s ... providing recruits to fascist and other extremist movements."[52]

It is the coming wave of savages, one billion strong, the population controllers argue, that we must fear. For as this torrent of young people inundates the developing nations of the world, a flood of instability, terrorism, and immigration will follow. The security literature is filled with references to the youth bulge, which is inevitably portrayed as a destabilizing element to be dreaded, rather than a demographic opportunity to be grasped.[53] Huntington, for example, dwells at length on the youth bulge in Muslim countries, relating it to the threatening rise of Islamic fundamentalism in Iran, Algeria, and other Middle Eastern states, and predicting further such threats as the percentage of 15-24-year-olds peaks in countries like Saudi Arabia, Pakistan, and Syria in the years to come.[54]

But not necessarily. Nineteenth-century Europe experienced a population increase of "dizzying rapidity"—in Ortega y Gasset's phrase—between 1800 and 1914: "For that rapidity means that heap after heap of human beings have been dumped on to the historic scene at such an accelerated rate, that it has been difficult to saturate them with traditional culture."[55] This historical increase in the European population was what "Rathenau called 'the vertical invasion of the barbarians.'"[56] Yet the result of this particular invasion was not a century of sustained protest, instability, reform, revolution, or terror. The political impact of these large cohorts of youth was blunted by strong families, by increased opportunities for education, by strong and settled religious sentiment, by the job opportunities provided by successful industrialization and—the last resort for the ambitious or malcontented—emigration to the New World, Australia or New Zealand. This suggests that if the mediating institutions are strong, then the youth, however many there are, will be well enculturated. If the mediating institutions are weak then the youth, however few there are, will remain insolent barbarians, ready to challenge the existing order. And if the mediating institutions are Wahabist mosques, where violence against Jews and Christians may be encouraged, then all bets are off, regardless of the birthrate.

Besides, if the youth bulge in Muslim countries is our principal concern, then what is the point of contracepting would-be terrorists who have already been born? Will the accompanying propaganda campaign urge them to "Make Love, Not Terror"? It didn't work with the Sixties generation, which was happy to engage in university-encouraged sterile sex, but continued taking to the ramparts in protest. And it won't work now, but merely whet the sexual appetites of real Islamic terrorists in anticipation of the 72 black-eyed virgins who, they have been told, await them in paradise.

Ultimately, the population project comes down to preventing an echo boom. That is to say, the controllers promise to ensure, in return for our money, that the global baby boomers of the past two decades do not reproduce their numbers a few years hence. But this is unlikely to be the case in any event. Given the pace at which the less-developed world is urbanizing and modernizing, and given rising levels of education, especially among girls, the echo boom is unlikely to be more than a distant demographic rumble.

How Not to Win the War on Terror

In the aftermath of September 11, the population controllers offered their own unique prescription for winning the war on terror. They would disseminate Depo-Provera, IUDs, and condoms to Muslim communities worldwide, thus eliminating would-be terrorists before they are born. This is, as the Chinese say, "picking up a rock only to drop it on your own foot." While population control programs may lower the number of babies born, they also give birth to anger and resentment. This is why USAID goes to such great lengths lower its own profile by laundering its family planning money through international organizations and NGOs. Adding one more grievance against the Great Satan to an already long list of injuries may make it easier, not more difficult, to recruit suicide bombers in the Middle East and elsewhere.

Dinesh D'Souza has cogently argued the "Cultural Left" has "fostered a decadent American culture that angers and repulses traditional societies, especially those in the Islamic world, that are being overwhelmed with this culture."[57] Moreover, it is "waging an aggressive global campaign to undermine the traditional patriarchal family and to promote secular values in non-Western cultures." Thus the Left is, in D'Souza's view, partly responsible for the rise of Islamic terrorism against the West.

The Cultural Left, without apology for its relentless promotion of abortion, sexual promiscuity, homosexuality, divorce and other "rights" at home and abroad, has dismissed his book out of hand. If you want to talk culpability for terrorist attacks, people like Michael Moore say, it was America's "lust for oil" and "neo-colonialism" that were responsible. These ridiculous assertions—America doesn't import its oil from semi-colonies, like China does from Sudan, but buys it on the open market—have nonetheless hardened into Leftist dogma.

The Right, which might have been expected to embrace D'Souza's thesis, has reacted coolly as well. Libertarians, who in general have little time for tradition, are unlikely candidates for cross-national coalitions in support of the natural family or life. Even cultural conservatives, who may be just as angered and repulsed by what they see issuing from Hollywood and their television sets as a devout Muslim, are skeptical.

Many, such as Robert Spencer, believe that terrorism is latent within Islam. Spencer argues that statements made by Mohammed about Christians and Jews, the whole notion of jihad that he set in motion, and the historic relegation of non-Muslims to dhimmi, or second-class, status, all contain the seed of violence, which can sprout at any time. Islamic expansionism, which several times took it into the very heart of Europe, occurred many centuries before America, much less the Cultural Left, even existed.

But it is possible to agree that radical Muslims hate us based on their reading of the Koran, and at the same time acknowledge that the recent and widespread antipathy towards America among Muslims in general gains strength from other currents as well. In pointing out that the Cultural Left's unceasing advocacy of practices like abortion and divorce that raise hackles in the Muslim world, D'Souza has illuminated an important truth.

Most Americans don't understand that this advocacy is not merely an incidental byproduct of the private sector, but is part and parcel of our foreign aid program. If Egyptians, for example, chose to patronize trashy Hollywood productions noteworthy primarily for their sex, violence, and bad language, then they have no grounds for complaint. But when Iraqi youths turn on their radios and listen to the vulgar lyrics of rap songs broadcast into their country by Radio Sawa, paid for by U.S. taxpayers, then we as a people can rightly be blamed.

The worst abuses, as we have seen, are found in government-funded population control programs. The United States, both directly and through international institutions like the World Bank, has been exporting various social pathologies into relatively innocent and untouched corners of the Muslim world for going on 40 years now under the guise of "family planning" and "reproductive health." Billions of dollars a year are being poured into programs that promote abortion, fund coercive sterilization and contraceptive campaigns, reach into the schools with pornographic sex education programs, fund anti-family and anti-child radio and television programs, undermine primary health care, and encourage governments to intrude into the private lives of their citizens.

Such programs create bitter resentment in Muslim and non-Muslim countries alike.

Let me be clear: It is not because women in the West have abortions and premarital sex that bin Laden and his pals attacked us. They were bent on violence in any case. But the promotion by the United States and other "modern democracies" of abortion, divorce, adultery, and premarital sex in Muslim countries cannot help but generate sympathy and new recruits for those who would attack the "Great Satan." One can understand the resentment of even moderate Muslims when Western-funded population controllers come knocking at the door of their houses, bearing their human pesticides and insisting that their wives be rendered sterile. Or their righteous anger when their young child arrive home from school with a pornographic sex education booklet, funded by a grant from USAID. It is no accident that U.S.-funded medical clinics are targeted by the Taliban in Afghanistan, since they are seen as promoting contraception, sterilization, abortion, and sex education, all activities which are anathema not just to the mullahs, but to village elders as well.

If our foreign aid programs have been hijacked by the Cultural Left, what is to be done? D'Souza writes that, "As conservatives, we should export our America. That means introducing in places in Iraq the principles of self-government, majority rule, minority rights, free enterprise, and religious toleration. But we must stop exporting the Cultural Left's America. That means we should stop insisting on radical secularism, stop promoting the feminist conception of the family, stop trying to promote abortion and 'sex education,' and we should try and halt the export of the vulgar and corrupting elements of our popular culture."

One can deplore the burka and at the same time recognize that we as a nation are doing deliberate violence to the values and family structure of developing countries. If we want to win the war on terror, we'd better stop making enemies in this way. The population controllers have it exactly wrong: This is how *not* to win the war on terror.

Immigration

The population controllers claim that their overseas programs benefit the United States by helping to curb immigration. Whether or not immigration, on balance, helps or harms the United States is, for most observers, an open question. The benefits, at least over the short term, seem to be fairly evenly matched with the costs, but grow over time. Not for the family planners, however, who long ago concluded that immigration brought into the United States people who were largely of inferior stock, a prejudice given new life by their latter-day fixation on keeping the total number of Americans down. This bias against immigrants is implicit in Warren Christopher's claim that population growth "spawns huge refugee flows," as well as in his proposed remedy of population control.

The original eugenicists were unhappy when southern Europeans began emigrating to the United States in large numbers and began funding birth control clinics in immigrant neighborhoods. The acquisition of Puerto Rico and other Caribbean territories following the Spanish-American War gave rise to a new fear (with very modern overtones), that the next wave of immigration would not come from Europe at all, but from the south. Donald Critchlow, in his book *Intended Consequences*, has ably documented how Puerto Rico was turned into a population control laboratory, and why.[58] The territorial governor, James R. Beverly, publicly declared in 1932 that "sooner or later the question of our excessive population must be faced," and that the question was not just the quantity of the population but its quality.[59] Birth control was incorporated into the federal relief program in Puerto Rico in 1932, despite local laws prohibiting such activities. A government economist on a fact-finding mission to the island reported back to Washington that "Our control of the tropics seems to me certain to increase immigration from here and the next wave of the lowly ... succeeding the Irish, Italians and Slavs ... will be these mulattos, Indians, Spanish people from this south of us. They make poor material for social organization, but you are going to have to reckon with them."[60] As Donald Crichtlow writes, "Emigration from the island in the immediate postwar years seemed to give added urgency to the island's population problem. One Rockefeller Foundation officer noted that Puerto Ricans were 'flooding New York City at a rate of 1500 a week with many of them getting on the relief rolls within a month after they arrive here.' He viewed birth control in Puerto Rico as a 'technical' and 'social' problem."

The impetus for population control in Mexico and Central America arose from the same motive—to reduce the number of potential migrants to the United States. More recent anti-immigrant groups, such as Federation for American Immigration Reform (FAIR) have close ties to the population control movement. They wish to ban all immigration, legal and illegal, in order to stop U.S. population growth. They believe that push factors, namely, population growth, high population density, and the like, are driving people out of developing countries and into the

United States. Population control, by reducing these push factors, can help curb immigration into the United States.

Writing in *World Policy Journal*, Professor Saskia Sassen noted that "Even a cursory review of emigration patterns reveals that there is no systematic relationship between emigration and what conventional wisdom holds to be the principal causes of emigration" namely "overpopulation, poverty, and economic stagnation." [61] This Columbia University specialist in urban planning went on to say that: "Population pressures certainly signal the possibility of increased migration." Yet such pressures "Whether measured by population growth or population density are not in themselves particularly helpful in predicting which countries will have major outflows of emigrants, since some countries with rapidly growing populations experience little emigration (many central African countries fall into this category), while other countries with much lower population growth rates (such as South Korea), or relatively low population density (such as the Dominican Republic), are major sources of migration." [62] Once again, the population controllers' superficially plausible claims fail to pass empirical muster.

What is responsible for international migration? Professor Sassen's article reviewed "other intervening factors," such as, "the establishment of political, military, and economic linkages with the United States, patterns of foreign investment, mobilization of large numbers of women into wage labor, the 1965 liberalization of the U.S. immigration law, the 'unfading image' of the U.S. as the land of opportunity, and changes in labor demand in the U.S." According to Sassen, U.S. immigration policy should not persist in viewing immigration as a "problem whose roots lie in the inadequacy of socioeconomic conditions in the Third World" and should recognize that "the United States, as a major industrial power and supplier of foreign investment, bears a certain amount of responsibility for the existence of international labor migrations." [63]

It is beyond the scope of this book to discuss how many immigrants should be allowed into the United States. But it should be evident to the reasonably minded that the best way to stop illegal immigration is not by eliminating potential immigrants before they are born, but by encouraging authentic economic development in Mexico and other Latin American countries. If Mexico is an economic basket case, then its people will seek employment in El Norte, regardless of what the birthrate is. A booming Mexican economy, on the other hand, could absorb all the energies of Mexico's young, while fueling development farther south as well. And, regardless of how well Mexico is doing, the United States will remain a magnet for the extraordinarily ambitious, as the land of extraordinary opportunity.

Backlash

One would think that both conservatives and liberals would be embarrassed by a project which is based on such questionable assertions as "[W]orld population growth is likely to contribute, directly or indirectly, to domestic upheavals and international conflicts that could adversely affect U.S. interests."[64] And what cloistered view of the national interest can produce such facile predictions as "Population growth will also reinforce the politicization of international economic relations and intensify the drive of [less-developed countries] for a redistribution of wealth and of authority in international affairs."[65] Both of these quotes are from a declassified CIA document, but similar language abounds in the security literature.

In other words, it is precisely because countries are growing in wealth, economic power, and political stability that American interests are threatened. You might think that we should rejoice that Mexicans, Colombians, and Brazilians are living under democratic regimes that look out for the interests of their people, but you would be scoffed at by the practitioners of *realpolitik,* who apparently believe that you can only stay on top by keeping others down. Survival of the nastiest, so to speak.

It is particularly schizophrenic for conservatives, who profess to believe in the magic of the market, encourage the spread of freedom, and oppose "big government," to at the same time espouse population control. What more grandiose government project can there be than to try and remake the fundamental unit of society, the family, by wrongly dictating the number of children born into it? This is the nanny state run amuck. And surely the more robust the global economy is, the more everyone, including Americans, will benefit. The stumbling economies of overcontracepted, underpopulated countries make a poor market for American goods and services.

Such views are not only a misreading of where America's interests lie, they are a misunderstanding of what America means. A rising tide lifts all boats, President Reagan famously remarked. The population enterprise has the effect of hulling the boats of our neighbors. This sabotage has not escaped their notice. As we saw in Chapter 6, people in the developing world often view these programs as intrusive, ethnocentric, and self-serving. That their chief backer is the United States is no secret, and reflects badly on us as a country and as a people. The old stereotype of the ugly American is reinforced, and so too is resentment of our often dominating presence overseas. Those who concern themselves with U.S. national security should take note.

In the run up to the Cairo Conference on Population and Development, an effort was made to get the developing world's scientific bodies—the national and regional academies of science—to endorse population control. The Declaration on Population had been drafted by the U.S. National Academy of Sciences, the Royal Society of London, the Royal Swedish Academy of Sciences and the Indian National Science Academy, and was presented at an international meeting of scientists held in New Delhi, India. The statement urged governments to establish an "integrated policy on population and sustainable development" and urged "zero population growth within the lifetime of our children." Zero population growth was described as essential for "dealing successfully with humanity's social, economic and environmental problems." Population technologies were to be integrated within a broader program of "reproductive health services," gender equity, and the provision of clean water and sanitation.

The African Academy of Sciences (AAS) not only refused to sign, it issued a formal rebuttal disputing the contention that zero population growth and low economic growth ("sustainable development") were desirable goals: "For Africa, population remains an important resource for development, without which the continents' natural resources will remain latent and unexploited." As far as gender equity was concerned, the statement went on to say that most Africans see "marriage as important both for companionship and for procreation.... The contribution of the North to Africa's population predicament must be acknowledged in any suggestion as to how that situation is to be confronted."[66]

This reasoned response masks the anger and resentment against the United States that our efforts to drive down the birth rate overseas more commonly produce. Zimbabwean parliamentarian Ruth Chinamano told the House that the distribution of "condoms and other contraceptives are a way of wiping out Africans.... Africa is not overpopulated." She went on to warn that "Whites want blacks to be less. Every action by developed countries since the days of slavery was for their own economic gain. We should view foreign prescription with suspicion."[67]

What does it matter that the peoples of Africa, Asia, and Latin America don't love us, the skeptic might ask, if population control programs have rendered them too weak in numbers to do anything about it? It matters because even from the standpoint of sheer numbers, such programs often backfire. To see how shortsighted these calculations are, one need look no further than the case of China. There one of the chief demographic consequences of population control, aside from the slowing of population growth itself, has been the development of an enormous imbalance in the sex ratio. The potential for aggression stemming from this huge, surplus population of males should not be underestimated.

Conclusion

Given the vast sums that are pumped into population control programs each year, one would naturally expect donors to demand a correspondingly high return on their investment. But while the controllers attempt to *publicly* justify their programs in a myriad of ways—as saving the environment, promoting economic development, and raising the status of women—the "return on investment" that they are actually looking for is higher "contraceptive prevalence rates," greater numbers of tubal ligations and, ultimately, the arrival of fewer African, Asian and Latin American babies. This is how they measure success.

It has not escaped the notice of those on the receiving end of population control programs that the chief financial backers of such programs, aside from the United States itself, consist of the white nations of northern Europe. The UNFPA, for example, draws its chief support from Germany, the Netherlands, Canada, and the Scandinavian countries—Norway, Denmark, Sweden and Finland. All of these are dying countries and some, especially Germany, have a racist past.[68] Japan, another country that annually allocates large sums of money for population control, would seem to add an Asian face to this line-up of white ones. But in this regard, as in so many others, Japan is merely following the lead of the United States. The Land of the Rising Sun is also noteworthy for its strong sense of racial superiority over its East Asian neighbors.

Underneath the shifting alibis so glibly offered by the population controllers lurk contentious questions of race and power. For the truth is that many see the very existence of large numbers of Africans, Asians, and Latin Americans as intrinsically undesirable. Here it is enlightening to note that those most likely to be targeted by family planning activities are precisely those who resemble family planners least: the poorer, darker populations of the developing world.

The anti-people movement views with alarm the prospect of larger populations in the developing world and perceives associated changes in balance of power, control over natural resources, and increased migration as a threat to its own security. Population control has less to do with helping others up, than with keeping others down ... and out. This is nothing less than a recrudescence of Social Darwinism. Or, as Margaret Sanger so memorably put it, more from the fit, fewer from the unfit.

Notes

1. The Population Crises Committee ran this ad in *Time, Fortune, Harper's, Saturday Review, The New York Times*, and other publications in late 1969.
2. The phrase appeared, among other places, as the title of Hugh Moore's biography. See Lawrence Lader, *Breeding Ourselves to Death* (New York: Ballantine Books, 1971).
3. The phrase appears in the same ad, but can be found in various permutations in all of the writings of the anti-people cult.
4. Ibid.
5. The group, Negative Population Growth, for instance, frequently uses the slogans, "Any cause is a lost cause without population control," and "Any cause is a lost cause without a reduction in population." *PRI Review* 3(5) (September/October 1993):9.
6. *The Book of Master Guan (Guan Zi)*, Chapter 15. Quoted in Zhengyuan Fu, *China's Legalists: The Earliest Totalitarians and Their Art of Ruling* (Armonk, New York: M.E. Sharpe, 1996), 50.
7. Central Intelligence Agency, "Political Perspectives on Key Global Issues," March 1977 (declassified, in part, January 1995), 4, cited in Elizabeth Liagin, *Excessive Force: Power, Politics and Population Control* (Washington, D.C: Information Project for Africa, 1995), 27.
8. *The Book of Master Guan (Guan Zi)*, Chapter 15. Quoted in Zhengyuan Fu, *China's Legalists,"* 39.
9. Garret Hardin quotes Han Fei, another Chinese Legalist, as saying that "In ancient times, people were few but wealthy and without strife. People at present think that five sons are not too many, and each son have five sons also and before the death of the grandfather there are already 25 descendants. Therefore people are more and wealth is less; they work hard and receive little. The life of a nation depends upon having enough food, not upon the number of people." Garret Hardin, *Population, Evolution, and Birth Control* Second Edition (San Francisco: W. H. Freeman, 1964), 18. This was definitely a minority view among the Legalists, who believed, as Zhengyuan Fu notes, that "Without a teeming horde of docile subjects the ruler has no one to be recruited into his army and no one to work in the fields and shops ..." Fu, 39. Ancient writers in the West also recognized the danger of depopulation to society. The Greek historian Polybius (204-122 B.C.) wrote, "One remarks nowadays all over Greece such a diminution in natality and in general manner such a depopulation that the towns are deserted and the fields lie fallow. Although this country has not been ravaged by wars or epidemics, the cause of the harm is evident: by avarice or cowardice the people, if they marry, will not bring up the children they ought to have. At most they bring up one or two. It is in this way that the scourge before it is noticed is rapidly developed. The remedy is in ourselves; we have but to change our morals." Robert de Marcellus, "A Foundering Civilization," *The Human Life Review*, Winter 2001.
10. Quoted in Jane Jacobs, *The Death and Life of Great American Cities* (New York: Vintage Books, 1961), 200.
11. Benjamin Franklin's seminal demographic work, "Observations Concerning the Increase of Mankind," from which this quote is taken, was first published in 1751.

It has been widely quoted, including by Garrett Hardin in *Population, Evolution, and Birth Control*, 20.

12. Robert V. Wells, *Revolutions in American Lives: A Demographic Perspective on the History of Americans, Their Families, and Their Societies* (Westport, CT: Greenwood Press, 1982), 80-81, and Robert Wells, *Uncle Sam's Family: Issues in and Perspectives on American Demographic History* (Albany: State University of New York Press, 1985), 30-37. Quoted in Allan C. Carlson, "Sexuality: A Litmus Test for Culture," *The Family In America* (The Howard Center), May 2003, 4.

13. *The Declaration of Independence* of the United States of America. The relative importance of this charge is suggested by the fact that it is listed near the beginning of a list of 27 charges, in seventh place, to be exact. Only the British Crown's refusal to pass necessary laws (charges 1-3) and its harassment and dissolution of state legislatures (charges 4-6) precede it.

14. Katherine Organski and A.F.K. Organski, *Population and World Power* (New York: Knopf, 1961), 251.

15. Ibid., 3.

16. National Security Decision Memorandum 76, August 10, 1970. Quoted in Elizabeth Liagin, *Excessive Force,* 111.

17. The full title of the document is *Implications of Worldwide Population Growth for U.S. Security and Overseas Interests*, National Security Study Memorandum 200 (Washington, D.C., National Security Council: 1974).

18. "Highlights of Current Demographic Trends," *NSSM 200.*

19. NSSM 200 did offer a third projection in the section entitled "Highlights of Current Demographic Trends." "If replacement levels of fertility were reached by 2000, the world's population in 2000 would be 5.9 billion and at the time of stability, about 2075, would be 8.4 billion." But this possibility, which roughly approximates what has actually happened in the past quarter century, was generally ignored in the discussion which followed.

20. "Minerals and Fuels," Chapter III, NSSM 200.

21. Ibid.

22. "Implications of Population Pressures for National Security," Chapter V, NSSM 200. While the report argues that population growth adversely affects economic development, food supply, resources, and the environment, we will see in Chapter 8 that this is not necessarily the case.

23. "Minerals and Fuels," Chapter III, NSSM 200.

24. Dr. Thor Ravenholt, Director of the Office of Population, USAID. Quoted in "Population Control of Third World Planned: Sterilization Storm in U.S.," *Evening Press* (Dublin), 12 May 1979, 9.

25. Samuel P. Huntington, "Why International Primacy Matters," *International Security* 17 (4) ((Spring 1993): 68-83. Quote on page 83.

26. NSSM 200, 106, 113-4, 149.

27. NSSM 200, 81.

28. See Steven W. Sinding, *Strengthening the Bank's Population Work in the Nineties* (Washington, D.C.: World Bank Population and Human Resources Department, Working Paper WPS 802, November 1991), 31.

29. NSSM 200. 10-11. Since the panel consisted of committed members of the international population control establishment, there was little doubt as to what its recommendation would be. The chairman was Bernard Berelson, president emeritus and senior fellow at the Population Council. The other four members of the panel were Dr. Frederick T. Sai, then assistant secretary general of the IPPF, A. Chandra Sekhar of the Ministry of Health and Family Planning in India, Goran Ohlin, a professor

of economics at the University of Uppsala, and Ronald Freedman, a professor of sociology at the University of Michigan's Population Studies Center.

30. "Final Report of the External Advisory Panel on Population," August 1976, 51.
31. NSSM 200, 22.
32. Nigeria's actual population in 2000, according to UNFPA, was 111.5 million, testifying once again to the propensity of the population alarmists to exaggerate. (UNFPA, *The State of the World Population 2000: Lives Together, Worlds Apart: Men and Women in a Time of Change.*)
33. NSSM 200, 21.
34. NSSM 200, 11.
35. "Report of the Interagency Task Force on Population Policy for the Under Secretaries Committee of the NSC," National Security Council, 1976,
36. Robert Whelan, *Choices in Childbearing: When Does Family Planning Become Population Control?* (London: Committee on Population & the Economy, 1992), 29.
37. Whelan, 29. Originally appeared in the *New Scientist*, 5 May 1977.
38. "Report of the Interagency Task Force on Population Policy ..."
39. Donald P. Warwick, *Bitter Pills: Population Policies and Their Implementation in Eight Developing Countries* (Cambridge: Cambridge University Press, 1982), 14.
40. Both quotes are from Donald Warwick, *Bitter Pills*, 98.
41. Ibid., 14-15.
42. Leonard H. Robinson, Jr., "Report to Africa Bureau, Office of Regional Affairs, Agency for International Development," Battelle Human Affairs Research Centers, 6 November 1981, 15.
43. John M. Goshko, "Planned Parenthood Gets AID Grant," *Washington Post*, 23 November 1993, A12-13.
44. "Christopher defends U.S. population programs," Reuters, Washington, D.C, 19 December 1994. Also quoted in "Shades of National Security Study Memo 200!" *PRI Review* 5(1) (January/February 1995):8.
45. Peter J. Donaldson, *Nature Against Us: The United States and the World Population Crisis 1965-1980.* (Chapel Hill, NC: University of North Carolina, 1990), 74.
46. The study commissioned by the Office of Net Assessment in the Department of Defense and was published in abbreviated form by the Center for Strategic and International Studies in the Spring 1989 issue of its publication, *Washington Quarterly.* "Global Demographic Trends to the Year 2010: Implications for U.S. Security," by Gregory D. Foster *et al.* The study included information provided by the Futures Group, Johns Hopkins University, and other major players in the anti-people movement.
47. Ibid., 6.
48. Ibid., 24.
49. Nicholas Eberstadt, "Population Change and National Security," *Foreign Affairs* 70(3) (Summer 1991):115-121. Quote at 117.
50. Jean-Claude Chesnais, "Demographic Transition Patterns and Their Impact on the Age Structure," *Population and Development Review* 16(2) (June 1990):327-336.
51. Robert Bork, *Slouching Towards Gomorrah* (New York: HarperCollins, 1997). 21.
52. Herbert Moeller, "Youth as a Force in the Modern World," *Comparative Studies in Society and History*, 10 (April 1968), 237-260; Lewis S. Feuer, "Generations and the Theory of Revolution," *Survey* 18 (Summer 1972):161-188.

53. The youth bulge is a demographic bonus that can help jumpstart development, as we will see in Chapter 8.
54. Samuel P. Huntington, *The Clash of the Civilizations and the Remaking of World Order* (New York: Simon & Shuster, 1996), 116-120.
55. Jose Ortega y Gasset, The Revolt of the Masses (New York: W. W. Norton, 1957), 50-53.
56. Ibid.
57. Dinesh D'Souza, *The Enemy at Home: The Cultural Left and Its Responsibility for 9/11* (New York: Doubleday, 2007). See also "How Not to Win the War on Terror," PRI Weekly Briefing, 15 March 2007.
58. Donald T. Critchlow, *Intended Consequences: Birth Control, Abortion, and the Federal Government in Modern America* (Oxford, Oxford University Press: 1999), esp. 36-41.
59. Ibid., 36.
60. Ibid., 37.
61. Saskia Sassen, "America's immigration 'problem'," *World Policy Journal* 4(4) (Fall 1989):811-832. Also quoted in "Conventional wisdom challenged," *PRI Review* 3(5) (September/October 1993):8.
62. Ibid.
63. Ibid.
64. Central Intelligence Agency, "Political Perspectives on Key Global Issues," March 1977 (declassified, in part, January 1995), 4, cited in Elizabeth Liagin, *Excessive Force: Power, Politics and Population Control* (Washington, D.C: Information Project for Africa, 1995), 27.
65. Ibid., 27.
66. "Science academies call for global goal of zero population growth," *Nature* 386 (4 Nov 1993). J.K. Egunjobi, head of programs at AAS, was the author of the statement. Besides Africa, scientists from Ireland, Spain, Georgia, Armenia, Japan, Argentina, Italy, and the Vatican refused to sign.
67. "Zimbabwe MP says condom use plot….," Reuters, 16 December 1994.
68. "Norway, Sweden and the United States are rated highest in commitment to world population assistance in 1991," *International Family Planning Perspectives* 19(4) (December 1993):155.

8

"We're from USAID, and We're Here to Help"

"Southerners will never publicly admit that they would like to see the Negro population decrease, but they do point to the poverty that could be avoided."

–Gunnar Myrdal, 1944[1]

"[I]t is more likely that one ingenious and curious man may rather be found among 4 million than 400 persons. ... And for the propagation and improvement of useful learning ... they are best promoted by the greatest number of emulators."

–William Petty, 1682[2]

Like some white Southerners in Gunnar Myrdal's mammoth study of race relations in the United States, the population controllers will never publicly admit that they would like to see the Indian (or Brazilian, or Nigerian) population *decrease*. It would make them wildly unpopular in New Delhi (or Brasília, or Abuja) if they publicly expressed concern that the growing number of Indians (or Brazilians, or Nigerians) would threaten the interests of their donors, or the globe as a whole. Rather, they "point to the poverty that could be avoided" by forestalling millions of new births.

Thus they assure officials in developing world capitals that controlling their numbers will stimulate their country's economic growth, jumpstart industrialization, and speed their entry into the first rank of nations. Think of the social services you *won't* have to provide, and the jobs you *won't* have to create, these officials are told. Think of the millions of new homes, thousands of new schools, hundreds of new hospitals, and so on, you *won't* have to build.

239

These arguments have a certain superficial plausibility, especially to government types with fixed horizons, and they have been around for a long time. The first study linking population growth to economic backwardness was produced by the Brookings Institution in 1928. Entitled *Puerto Rico and Its Problems*, it argued that one important obstacle to developing the island, which had been under U.S. administration since the Spanish-American War, was its growing population. The territorial governor, James R. Beverly, interjected the issue into the island's politics by declaring in early 1932 that "sooner or later the question of our excessive population must be faced," adding fuel to the fire by adding that the question was not just one of quantity, but of population quality as well. Puerto Rican nationalists responded by denouncing U.S.-funded birth control programs, then in their infancy, as part of an imperialistic plot designed to keep the island weak and subjugated. It was lesson in salesmanship that the burgeoning population control bureaucracy would never forget.[3] Thereafter they would attempt to recruit local elites to front for their programs.

This proved to be more difficult than they perhaps imagined. The great wave of decolonialization which swept the world in the 1950s and 1960s created dozens of newly independent states in the hands of nationalistic—often violently nationalistic—leaders. Such men had little use for this new wave of secular missionaries or the anti-natal religion they preached. It seemed to many that a new and insidious form of cultural imperialism was being unleashed on them by their former colonial masters. Had developing world leaders known of the existence of *National Security Study Memorandum 200*, perhaps they would have barred the contraceptive bearers entirely.

"It creates a very disagreeable impression," wrote the great French demographer Alfred Sauvy, "to see people who are white, European, or of European origin, trying to sow the seeds of sterility in populations that are about to escape from under their domination...."[4] Heavy-handed suggestions about limiting family size and contraceptive give-away schemes were not well received by many developing world leaders, and led to bitter complaints against the United States and European nations.

What happened in Honduras is typical. In 1995 USAID published a report called "Honduras Today and Tomorrow." The demographic section of the report started off innocently enough, recounting how the country's population had risen from 1.2 to 4.4 million from 1945 to 1988, and estimating the current population at 5.5 million. At present growth rates, the report went on, Honduras would have a population of some 14.6 million people by 2025. USAID characterized this situation as "dangerous."

Many Hondurans were upset by this characterization, but it was the prescription that followed that set off the explosion. For the agency's report suggested that limits were needed on the size of families. More specifically, it advocated a two-child policy and the establishment of an effective birth control campaign, and promised that thus restricting the number of babies born would provide a boost for economic development.

Honduran President Carlos Roberto Reina reacted immediately, declaring that "The answer to the alleged population explosion must not be the suppression of life in the bellies of mothers. It is the family's decision how many children they want to have."[5] The Catholic Church in Honduras condemned the proposed two-child policy in even stronger terms, as "demographic terrorism." The Latin American bishop's conference also weighed in, with the council's president, Bishop Oscar Andres Rodriguez, accusing USAID of "promot[ing] a [form of] imperialism disrespectful of the dignity and sovereignty of a people."[6]

U.S. diplomats attempted to defuse the situation by saying that it was not the intention of USAID to promote the idea of "drastic birth control," but merely "family planning."

This is kind of scenario which has been repeated in dozens of countries over the past thirty years. Nina Chowdbury, writing in the Bangladesh *Daily Star*, described "family planning" and "women's rights" as old funding favorites which "reflect the Western obsession" to check the population of the developing world.[7] Zimbabwean MP Ruth Chinamano told that country's parliament that the distribution of "condoms and other contraceptives are a way of wiping out Africans. ... Africa is not overpopulated." She went on to add that "Whites want blacks to be less. Every action by developed countries since the days of slavery was for their own economic gain. We should view foreign prescriptions with suspicion."[8]

Our anti-natalist foreign policy is dangerous geopolitically precisely because it generates such deep seated suspicions of our motives and widespread resentment of our actions, as we discussed in Chapter 7. Now I, for one, am fairly certain that the ranks of the population controllers are not dominated by racists. I am even willing to concede that they act out of a genuine (but mistaken) conviction that what they are doing is in the best interests of humanity. But what matters here is not how I view their motives, but how these are perceived by their intended "beneficiaries." Clearly, many Zimbabweans, Puerto Ricans, Filipinos and others are not happy about being targeted by programs whose patent purpose is to deny them children. It is not hard to understand how the actions of Dr. Ravenholt's minions (see Chapter 2) in the Philippines and elsewhere constitute an enduring archetype of the Ugly American abroad: Imagine the outrage among Americans if the government of the Philippines started airdropping boxes of condoms on small towns in the Midwest.

The initial reaction of most leaders in the developing world was to reject such programs. To overcome this resistance to programs that were rightly suspected of being racist, imperialist, and neocolonialist in origin, the controllers used a variety of tactics. Sometimes, as in the case of Nigeria discussed in Chapter 4, they had to be bribed or bullied into accepting the programs on pain of losing foreign aid. Native population experts were trained, put on the payroll, and used to indigenize anti-natal projects. Other times they were won over by sophisticated arguments touting the economic and political benefits of smaller families. Shocked and awed by the spectacular array of charts and graphs presented by these foreign "experts," who used Powerpoint presentations that put Chinese systems engineer Song Jian's simple computer model to shame, developing world leaders sometimes bought into the notion that population control is the way out of poverty and towards economic growth and social stability.

But while figures don't lie, liars do figure. To the modern instrumentalist of the ends-justify-the-means type, a lie told in the service of the good cause is hardly a lie at all. And what greater good can a committed population controller imagine than saving the world by reducing the birth rate abroad, all the while keeping his funding flowing generously through the population control pipeline at home?

I consider below the two principle arguments used to sway developing world leaders in favor of population control programs, namely, that population control leads to (1) economic growth and (2) social stability.

Does Population Control Lead to Economic Growth?

Malthus's dismal theorem—that population growth will outstrip food supply—has spawned a vast number of equally dismal corollaries. Population growth has been said to hinder economic development because it increases consumption, reduces savings, and diminishes the stock of land and other capital per capita. Overwhelming transportation, communication, and power grids, it sets additional roadblocks in the way of progress. Moreover, by straining schools, a growing population is said to reduce the quality or amount of education that children receive, thus lowering productivity. All of these arguments implicitly assume that production, what we might call earning opportunities, is fixed. In the grim calculus of the population controllers, when a calf is born in Kenya, national wealth goes up; when a child is born, it goes down.

In 1958 Ansley J. Coale and Edgar Hoover plugged some real-world numbers into these Malthusian speculations and came up with some startling results: If India lowered its birthrate, its per capita income would nearly double over the next thirty years. But if Indian fertility rates remained high, income would only increase by a meager 40 percent.[9] Coale-Hoover model—the first real economic-demographic model for Less Developed Countries (LDCs)—virtually demanded birth control programs as the price of progress.

The problem with Coale-Hoover model was that its findings were driven by unreasonable assumptions. As the late Julian Simon wrote, "[T]he main Coale-Hoover model simply *assumed* that the total national product in an LDC [Less Developed Country] would not be increased by population growth for the first thirty years, either by a larger labor force or by additional productive efforts."[10] If a fixed GNP is divided by an increasing number of consumers—the heart of the model—then per capita consumption will head south "by simple arithmetic," in Simon's phrase. This is hardly a surprising result.

Despite these shortcomings, the Coale-Hoover model had enormous impact. It neatly meshed with nascent anti-natal attitudes stemming from national security, radical feminist, and environmental concerns. Even more importantly, it provided a compelling economic rationale for population control that could be presented to foreign leaders. According to Phyllis Piotrow's historical account, "the Coale-Hoover thesis eventually provided the justification for birth control as a part of U.S. foreign aid policy."[11] This came about through the efforts of one Philander Claxton, Jr., who became special assistant to the secretary of state for population matters in 1966. As the highest-ranking State Department official involved in population matters, Claxton at once prepared a lengthy memo.

> ... adopting completely the Coale-Hoover thesis [that population growth retards economic growth]. ... Claxton argued that the U.S. government must move from reaction and response to initiation and persuasion. ... by the time the paper reached the Secretary of State's desk, it had already achieved part of its purpose. All the appropriate State Department and Aid bureaus had reviewed, revised, commented, added

244   Population Control

to, and finally cleared the document. The rest of its purpose was accomplished when Rusk agreed to every single one of Claxton's ten recommendations.[12]

The Coale-Hoover model, with all its shortcomings, had become official U.S. foreign aid policy, the theoretical basis of subsequent efforts to convince leaders of developing countries to limit their peoples' birthrates. "For the good of your own country," we inveighed foreign leaders, "You must stop your people from having so many children." This view is still seconded by the major media in the United States and Europe today. A typical editorial in the 3 June 1989 *Washington Post* says that "in the developing world ... fertility rates impede advances in economic growth, health and educational opportunities."[13]

The classic—and still perhaps the most comprehensive—refutation of these "overpopulation shibboleths" comes from Simon himself. In his seminal book, *The Ultimate Resource*, he begins by debunking the notion that a higher birthrate invariably reduces per capita income: "It is well documented that men work more if they have more children—and so do women, after their children are no longer young."[14]

Nor does the savings rate, vital to continued economic development, necessarily go down as additional children are born. While acknowledging that an additional child is a burden on the family's income, Simon speaks of "an opposing effect. With more children, parents may forgo some luxuries in order to save for the children's future needs—for example, a college education."[15]

The presence of children encourages families to think and plan ahead in other ways that increase family income as well. And, especially in a society based on subsistence agriculture, children become economic assets at an early age, assisting their now more industrious parents in the clearing of new land and the construction of irrigation systems. "Population growth stimulates this extra labor," writes Simon, "and hence adds to a community's stock of capital."[16]

The conventional view of the effect of population growth on transportation nodes, communication networks, power grids, and the educational system is straightforward Malthus. A fixed inventory of goods and services is divided among more people, implying less transport, communication, power or education per person. But such simple Malthusian pie-sharing ignores mankind's most common response to the needs of a growing population: We alter apparently fixed conditions by expanding the inventory of goods and services available. A community with more children is generally going to hire another teacher, not begin rationing downward the years of education that each student will receive.

Over the longer term, more people equates to more progress. Indeed, the whole material history of the human race may be summed up in the observation that human beings create more than they destroy. How this works is not difficult to understand. Population growth, by increasing the demand for raw materials and finished products, creates scarcities and drives up prices. These price rises lead people to seek new sources or substitutes for raw materials, and cheaper ways of manufacturing goods. The end result of this creative process—if it is not stultified by interference from corrupt or communistic regimes—is that the price of both raw materials and finished products falls, leaving humanity better off at greater numbers than it was at fewer. In truth, we discover more natural resources each year than we use.

As the late Julian Simon has so poignantly reminded us in his classic work, *The Ultimate Resource*, "It is a simple fact that the source of improvements in productivity is the human mind [and] … it seems reasonable to assume that the amount of improvement depends on the number of people available to use their minds."[17] This has been understood since at least the time of British economist William Petty, whose 1682 comment about the blessings of a large population opened this chapter. People are not just mouths, they are minds as well.

If population growth *was* a drag on development one would expect to find that countries with burgeoning populations would be experiencing slower per capita income growth. But Julian Simon, and his collaborator, Roy Gobin, found that there was no correlation between the two variables.[19] Population density, on the other hand, does tend to produce higher rates of economic growth. Simon and Gobin plotted the growth rate of per capita income vs. population density (see Figure 8.1). They found that the higher the population density, they greater the annual growth in per capita income.

While not yet prepared to stand with Simon on the economic merits of *more* people, most of his long-time adversaries now prefer to duck the argument altogether. For example, in the run-up to the Cairo Conference, the Overseas Development Council was asked by the World Bank and The Rockefeller Foundation to make the best case for population control possible on the basis of current research. The editor of the resulting two-volume work, Robert Cassen, declares at the outset that his population experts will offer Clinton administration policymakers "broader and more balanced understandings of the relationship between population and development" than was possible during the "significant retreat" from population issues of "the Reagan and Bush years."[20]

Figure 8.1
Economic Growth Rates Related to Population Density in LDCs 1960-1965

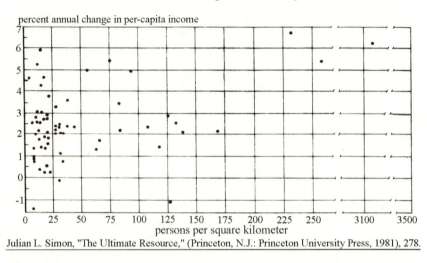

Julian L. Simon, "The Ultimate Resource," (Princeton, N.J.: Princeton University Press, 1981), 278.

Yet, despite this bold assertion, Cassen wastes no time in jettisoning the macroeconomic rationale for population policy altogether, admitting that "the available evidence from empirical studies does not clearly show that population growth exerts a negative influence on development"[21] and "Macroeconomic arguments now take a back seat in the debate about development and population."[22] Although Cassen doggedly maintains—after four *decades* of research—that "[T]he issue of whether per capita economic growth is reduced by population growth remains unsettled,"[23] even some of his contributors part company with him on this point. Allen Kelley, for instance, writes that:

> The contradictions in the mind of Malthus still confront many analysts and policymakers in the population field, those whose feelings, impressions, and personal certainties about the negative effects of population growth *are not supported by a careful sifting of the facts*[24] (italics added).

Robert Engelman of Population Action International is another population activist who, like Cassen, wants to have it both ways. At a forum organized by the Ethics and Public Policy Center, Engelman first conceded that "the link between economic growth and population [control programs] is not well established." But he nonetheless went on to argue that "most of those who work in the population field or make policy in the area generally accept the link on the simple logic, intuition, personal experience—and substantial documented evidence.... I've seen no evidence that … rapid population growth in any country acted in any fashion as a multiplier of the GNP."[25]

But what about the Army report, prepared by Nicholas Eberstadt and published in the Summer 1991 edition of *Foreign Affairs*, which concluded that the developing world had benefited tremendously from population growth? Between 1900 and 1987, Asia's population tripled, yet its per capita income increased more than three-fold during the same years. In Latin America, the statistics proved even more impressive. Population increased nearly seven-fold, while per capita output was up an incredible 500 percent. In other words, the region's total wealth has multiplied 35 times over since the start of the 20th century.[26]

Here we should allow the late Julian Simon, who convincingly debunked the conventional wisdom about "the negative effects of population growth," the last word:

> Do additional people increase the scarcity of land? In the short run … of course they do. The instantaneous effect of adding people to a fixed stock of land [or other capital] is less land to go around. But … after some time, adjustments are made; new resources … are created to augment the original stock. And in the longer run the additional people provide the impetus and the knowledge that leave us better off than we were when we started.[27]

A Tale of Two Populations

Explorers had discovered a vast, lightly inhabited continent, rich in natural resources. These early settlers, with land available for the clearing, multiplied rapidly, discovered as they went that these spacious skies contained vast reserves of wood, coal, and iron. A beneficent climate produced bountiful crops, without the need to build labor-intensive irrigation networks. Amber waves of corn and wheat began to stretch westward.

But the settlers, numbering 3 million or so, were firm in their conviction that the continent's greatest resource was … people. They enshrined this belief in their founding documents, in which human life, in all its abundance, was affirmed as the first inalienable right. Marriage was universal and fruitful, immigration brought in millions more, and the population grew rapidly.

By the turn of the next century the population stood at 76 million, and those same amber waves of grain now stretched two-thirds of the way across the continent. The average life span had climbed from 30 or so to 47, reflecting declining infant mortality. The Standard and Poor's composite index was 6.2.

But the best was yet to come. The population boomed over the next century, as did life-spans, scientific innovation and entrepreneurial activity. By 1990 the population had reached 270 million, the average life span was 77, and the Standard and Poor Index had reached 1,430, some 231 times its mark a century before.

Comparing the America of 1900 with the America of 2000, as the U.S. Census Bureau did in its *Compendium for the Millennium*, confirms the link between population and prosperity.[28] As America entered the new millennium, the report makes clear, America has never been so populous, productive and healthy. America's farmland, thanks to the ingenuity of tens of thousands of scientists and the hard work of millions of farmers, continues to set records in yield per acre and total yield. New scientific discoveries have paved the way for longer, healthier lives, and have helped cut death rates in half from 17.2 people per 1,000 per year in 1900 to 8.6 per 1,000 per year in 1997.

Few countries have such auspicious beginnings, and it is tempting to ascribe America's success to the extraordinary natural abundance that greeted the European colonists. But that same abundance had, after all, greeted the very *first* Americans: Those who had come in waves across the Bering land bridge some 10 to 15,000 years before. Once they had eliminated North America's large mammals, they spent the intervening millennia surviving as hunter-gatherers or, at best, planting corn in small slash-and-burn plots. Their numbers were limited to a few million. The lesson taught by these two successive waves of immigration is that there is no fixed carrying capacity, no fixed level of natural resources, no predetermined limits to what peoples might do given the same natural environment. Aside from the level of technology, in which the European colonists had a great advantage, the preeminent factors in the American success story were the enterprise, initiative, and risk-tolerance of a growing and energetic population determined to prosper.

Is there any doubt that Americans would be worse off today if Rockefeller's Commission on Population Growth had its way and the population of the United States had been "controlled" to 170 million or so? Or if the ideology of Negative Population Growth had prevailed and our population was cut to its supposed "ideal carrying capacity of the U.S." of 90 million? As Julian Simon wrote, "To me it seems reasonably plain that our ancestors bestowed benefits upon us through the knowledge they created and the economies of scale they left us, and if there had been fewer of those ancestors the legacy would have been smaller."[29] It is worth keeping this in mind when speculating about whether life today and in the future would be better if there were fewer people alive *today*.

My second example of the primacy of population in development is a small island, possessing no natural resources to speak of. In 1840 it had been home to a mere 2,000 people, who eked out a precarious living in the surrounding bays and inlets as fishermen. A little over a century later this island, along with an adjacent peninsula, held almost a million people, most of whom made a good living, by Asian standards, in foreign trade and manufacturing.

Thereupon the island faced a grave population crisis, brought on in part by high birthrates and in part by a revolution in a neighboring country. A tidal wave of humanity was set in motion and, as desperate refugees came pouring across the border by the hundreds of thousands, they simply overwhelmed the existing infrastructure. The government painted a grim picture of these times:

> Virtually every sizable vacant site … was occupied, and when there was no flat land remaining, [people] moved up to the hillsides and colonized the ravines and slopes which were too steep for normal development. The huts were constructed of such material as they could lay hands on at little or no cost—flattened sheets of tin, wood-ened boarding, cardboard, sacking slung on frames…. Land was scarce even for the squatters and the huts were packed like dense honeycombs or irregular warrens at different levels, with little ventilation and no regular access. The shacks themselves were crowded beyond endurance…. Density was at a rate of two thousand persons to an acre in single-story huts. There was, of course, no sanitation.[30]

These words appeared in a Hong Kong government report, which went on to assert that nearly everything—education, medical care, even food and water—was in critically short supply. The root of their difficulties was, to government officials, obvious: "The problem of a rapidly increasing population lies at the core of every problem facing the administration." Many observers predicted that Hong Kong's "state of supersaturation," to use American journalist John Robbins phrase, was a prelude to disaster.[31] Only massive Western aid, declared a UN official, could stave off an overpopulation apocalypse.

Yet local government officials, despite publicly fretting about their "population problem," refrained from attempting any forced reduction in fertility. Heir to a *laissez faire* tradition—even collecting survey data had once been frowned upon because it was thought to lead to obnoxious social engineering—the government busied itself provided basic services. As for ordinary Hong Kong Chinese and their newly arrived cousins from across the border, they merely set about, in their hard-working, energetic, and resourceful way, making a living. Within a relatively short time, this massive infusion of human capital began to pay substantial dividends, as the scale of economic activity began to expand even faster than the population.

By the time I arrived in Hong Kong in 1972, a mere twenty years later, the Hong Kong squatter slums were largely a thing of the past. Incomes had doubled from the dark days of the 1950s, and the British colony was in the midst of a general Asian economic boom that would carry first Japan and then the Four Tigers (Hong Kong, Singapore, Taiwan, and South Korea), into the ranks of the developed nations. Indeed, as its population surged to six million in the 1990s, the colony's per capita gross domestic product grew even faster, until it surpassed that enjoyed by the citizens of Mother England. All this from a largely barren rock—and the fecund intelligence of a large number of ingenious human beings.

"Development is the Best Contraceptive"

As these examples suggest, population control is ultimately out of synch with history. Neither West nor East required government-mandated family planning programs during its period of rapid demographic and economic growth. (One can only imagine the public outcry if anything along the lines of a state-mandated condom distribution program had been attempted in Victorian England.) Yet developing world leaders are not told these obvious truths from our own history and experience. Instead, they are misled into thinking that lowering their country's birth rate will jumpstart economic development. "Look at us," we say. "We have small families and are wealthy."

What we do not tell them is that this argument slyly reverses cause and effect. Declining fertility in the West was not the cause of economic development, but rather its unintended consequence. Moreover, it had a significant downside, and was resisted by a number of European governments, largely to no avail.

Most economists will agree that "economic development is the best contraceptive." Coercive population control programs aside, the other factors leading to reduced fertility are closely related to economic development, namely, urbanization, industrialization, and female participation in the work force. As a nation's economy develops, young people tend to marry later and to postpone childbirth. Even for those who remain in the countryside, the advent of modern agricultural technology, basic health care, and pension programs cause a marked drop in the birthrate. Farmers who enjoy these benefits don't feel the need to have as many children to work the fields, to ensure that some children survive, or to take care of them when they are old and infirm. As the quality of life of the people goes up, the birthrate goes down.

Even Indira Gandhi, who directed India's infamous sterilization campaign of the mid-1970s, moved away for forced-pace measures later in life. Observing that the birth rate in Kerala and the more advanced states of the Indian south was falling naturally, she rethought her position. By 1984 she could be quoted as saying that "The very best way of inducing people to have smaller families is more development. Where we have highly industrialized areas or much better education or even much better agriculture, we find automatically families tend to grow smaller."[32]

Does Population Control Lead to Social Stability?

Another corollary of Malthus's dismal theorem is that rapid population growth gives rise to all manner of social instabilities. Civil unrest and even civil war feeds on large cohorts of young people, or so the population controllers tell us, and population imbalances can even lead to cross-border conflicts and all-out war. So it is that we tell developing world leaders that "excessive" population growth is a security threat to their regimes, warning that chaos will erupt if they do not reduce the numbers of young people. Dictators, especially, for whom the maintenance of civil order, and hence their own position, is a top priority, are intrigued by the notion that they can buy stability by lowering the birth rate.

The notion that wars have their roots in the unrestrained growth of population contains echoes of Hitler's cry for "Lebensraum" for the German people, not to mention the belief of the Japanese militarists of the 1930s that the high population density of the home islands justified the conquest of new lands. That is to say, it is not based on science but on racist mythologies propagated by self-serving political elites.

Julian Simon, who surveyed the literature on population and war, concluded that "the data do not show a connection between population growth and political instability due to the struggle for economic resources. The purported connection is another of those notions that everyone (especially the CIA and the Department of Defense) knows is true, and that seems quite logical, but has no basis in factual evidence."[33]

While population control programs have little effect on social stability, they clearly encourage tyranny. The list of countries that have had violently abusive population control programs (see Chapter 3) is dominated by dictatorships, communist and otherwise. Think here of China under Deng Xiaoping and his successors, the Philippines under

Ferdinand Marcos, Indonesia under Suharto, Nigeria under Babangida, Egypt under Mubarak, North Korea under Kim Jong-il, and so on.

It is easy to see why the UN Population Fund, USAID, and the World Bank have been more successful at convincing dictatorships than democracies to adopt aggressive population control policies. In a dictatorship power is concentrated in the hands of a few, rather than dispersed as in a democracy, making it relatively easy to identify and approach key decision makers. Lacking a broad base of popular support, such regimes are often extraordinarily vulnerable to international pressure. Once the "supreme leader" and his inner circle come around to the view that babies are an obstacle to economic growth (or to foreign aid), action tends to follow immediately. No time is wasted in noisy, messy, and potentially embarrassing (to donors and recipients alike) public and parliamentary debates. Population control agencies, like invasive viruses, can quickly implant themselves in the machinery of government and turn it to their purposes. Witness the UNFPA serving as the "technical secretary" of Peru's sterilization campaign, helping to mobilize all of the resources of the Peruvian Ministry of Health to this end.

If it were just a matter of the controllers using repressive regimes to achieve their population goals, that would be bad enough. But the problem is compounded by the aggressive population control programs themselves, *which encourage further repression.* That is to say, repressive governments are not only more likely to adopt population control policies in the first place, but they also become even more repressive as they implement them.

Population control programs constitute an assault on liberty because they deny couples their natural right to decide for themselves the number of children that they wish to bear and raise. Moreover, they represent a retreat from the ideal of government of the people, by the people, and for the people. Rather, they are invariably imposed *by* the government *on* the people. Such programs work at cross-purposes to the most important goal of U.S. foreign policy, a goal which is emphatically not shared by the UNFPA: the promotion of democracy.

Human rights abuses, as we have seen in Chapter 3, have occurred in dozens of different countries around the globe. This pattern of systematic and widespread abuse did not occur by chance, but is the inevitable outcome of convincing governments that population growth inhibits economic development, creates poverty, underlies conflict, and so on. These wrongheaded ideas, and the urgency with which they are propounded, lead local leaders to approve inhumane programs of family planning coercion.

Fertility as an Excuse for (Economic and/or Political) Failure

The population controllers blame poverty, hunger, health problems, housing shortages, transportation problems, lack of education, unemployment, overcrowding, and a host of other problems on overpopulation. Yet many of the continuing problems of the developing world are clearly the result of the failure of governments to abide by the rule of law, respect property rights, and provide basic services. Plagued by misrule and corruption, it is hard for any country to develop.

How convenient for developing world leaders to have a prestigious foreign theory—overpopulation—that allows them to shift the blame for their own failures onto the people. Helpful foreigners will even fund expensive propaganda campaigns that exculpate them and their officials for failing to guard against corruption, build an adequate educational system, or fairly administer justice. The country's principal "problem," the people will instead be told, is that the birth rate is too high. This lets everyone, except mothers, off the hook.

In the West we have a name for such deception: It is called blaming the victim.

Notes

1. Gunnar Myrdal, *An American Dilemma: The Negro Problem and Modern Democracy*, 2 vols. (New York: Harper and Row, 1944), 179.
2. William Petty, *The Economic Writings of Sir William Petty*, Ed. By Charles Henry Hull, 2 vols. (Cambridge: Cambridge University Press, 1899), 474.
3. Annette B. Ramirez de Arellano and Conrad Seipp, *Colonialism, Catholicism, and Contraception: A History of Birth Control in Puerto Rico* (Chapel Hill, N.C.: University of North Carolina Press, 1983), 26-34.
4. Alfred Sauvy, "Le « Faux Problème » de la Population Mondiale," *Population* 4(3) (July/September 1949): 447-462.
5. "USAID Targets Honduras Population," *PRI Review* 5(6) (September/October 1995):9. See also IPS, Tegucigalpa, 7 September 1995.
6. Ibid.
7. Nina Chowdbury, Bangladesh *Daily Star*, 17 April 1995. Cited in Jean Guilfoyle, "The United Nations' Civil Society," *PRI Review* 5(5) (July/August 1995):4.
8. "Zimbabwe MP Says Condom Use Plot," Reuters, 16 December 1994.
9. Ansley J. Coale and Edgar M. Hoover, 1958. *Population Growth and Economic Development in Low-Income Countries* (Princeton: Princeton University Press, 1958).
10. Julian Simon, *The Ultimate Resource* (Princeton: Princeton University Press, 1981), 189.
11. Phyllis Piotrow, World Population Crisis, (Westport, CT: Praeger, 1973), 15.
12. Ibid, 124.

13. "Mr. Bush's Population Policy," *Washington Post*, 3 June 1989, A14.
14. Julian Simon, *The Ultimate Resource* (Princeton: Princeton University Press, 1981), 189.
15. Ibid.
16. Ibid.
17. Ibid., 197.
18. William Petty, *The Economic Writings of Sir William Petty*, Ed. By Charles Henry Hull, 2 vols. (Cambridge: Cambridge University Press, 1899), 474. Quoted in Simon, 197.
19. Julian L. Simon and Roy Gobin, 1979. "The Relationship between Population and Economic Growth in LDC's" In Julian L. Simon and Julie deVanzo, eds., 1979, *Research in Population Economics*. Vol. 2 (Greenwich, Conn.: JAI Press, 1979).
20. Robert Cassen et al, *Population and Development: Old Debates, New Conclusions* (New Brunswick, NJ: Transaction Publishers, 1994) and Robert Cassen with Lisa M. Bates, *Population Policy: A New Consensus* (Washington, DC: Overseas Development Council, 1994).
21. Cassen, *Population Policy*, 2.
22. Ibid., 16.
23. Ibid., 15.
24. Ibid., 124.
25. Robert Engelman, "A Response," Edited by Michael Cromartie, *The Nine Lives of Population Control* (Grand Rapids: Erdmann's, 1995), 40.
26. Nicholas Eberstadt, "Population Change and National Security," *Foreign Affairs*, Summer 1991.
27. Simon, *Ultimate Resource*, 237.
28. U.S. Census Bureau, *1999 U.S. Census Bureau Statistical Abstract:Compendium for the Millennium* (December 1999).
29. Simon, *Ultimate Resource*, 268.
30. Quoted in William McGurn, "Population and the Wealth of Nations," *First Things* 68 (December 1996):22-25.
31. John Robbins, *Too Many Asians* (1959). Quoted in McGurn.
32. Quoted in Karl Zinsmeister, "Supply-Side Demography," *PRI Review* 3(4) (July/August 1993):11.
33. Julian Simon, "Population Growth is Not Bad for Humanity," *PRI Review* 3(6) (November/December 1993):4-5. See here the masterly study of war in history by Quincy Wright (1968), the work on recent wars by Nazli Choucri, *Population Dynamics and International Violence* (Lexington, MA: Lexington Books, 1974), and Gary Zuk's study of Europe between 1870 and 1913, "National Growth and International Conflict: A Reevaluation of Choucri and North's Thesis," *Journal of Politics* 47 (1985): 269-281.

9

From Population Control
to Pro-Natal Programs

*The answer to anyone who talks about the surplus
population is to ask him, whether he is part of the
surplus population; or if not, how he knows he is not.*
  –G. K. Chesterton "Introduction" to 'The Christmas Carol'."
    Illustrated London News, 14 February 1925.

The population control programs of the past half century, born in
the dark fear of "the unchecked growth in human numbers," have been
a quiet but profound disaster for the poor and marginalized half of humanity. Hundreds of millions of poor women (and men) have had their
fundamental rights—i.e., to control their own reproductive systems and
to determine the number and spacing of their children—grossly violated.
An even larger number have had their overall well being compromised
as resources have been drained away from primary health care programs,
with some succumbing to HIV/AIDS and other epidemics. While the
cost of such programs in terms of human lives and suffering has been
all too real, the promised benefits have proven largely illusory. Is the
United States more secure, the global environment better protected, and
the world wealthier today because of population control programs? The
evidence presented here suggests not.

The idea of controlling human fertility "for the good of the state and
its people," as Beijing is fond of saying, is a 20th-century anachronism.
It deserves to be as thoroughly discredited as Marxist-Leninism, and for
the same reason: It is at heart a philosophy of state coercion. In its more
extreme manifestations in China and elsewhere, it has given rise to terror
campaigns. But even in its mildest guises, it encourages a technocratic
paternalism that effectively subjugates individual and familial fertility
desires to the wishes of the state.

255

Ending these programs will be far from easy. Movements that have billions of dollars, thousands of paid promoters, and tens of thousands of unpaid advocates at their disposal do not, unfortunately, march off quietly to their graves, however harmful to humanity they have proven to be. Nor can we expect that the controllers, like old soldiers, will simply fade away as birthrates continue to fall. Elena Zuñega, director of Mexico's National Population Council, told me that her personal goal is to drive Mexico's Total Fertility Rate (TFR) down to 1.85, a number that would cause the population of our southern neighbor to shrink over time. Like Zuñega, many of the more zealous just can't wait to go negative. News of dying populations reenergizes many advocacy groups precisely because they want to drive humanity's numbers down to one or two billion. Effecting such radical reductions in the world's population would, of course, keep the movement's regulars fully employed for a couple more centuries, not to mention virtually mandating a global one-child policy.[1] Those who continue to shout hard-line sixties slogans like "all causes are lost causes unless we control population growth"[2] are not out of touch with the changing demographics; they are emboldened by them.

Still, the programs have become controversial enough that some controllers have taken to speaking in code. Instead of baldly asserting that people are the enemy of the environment, for example, the initiated bandy about phrases like "sustainable economics." Still other controllers, mostly on the operational side, have opted for whole new identities as "reproductive health" workers. These justify their programs in terms of lowering maternal and infant mortality, when in fact their activities are geared to temporarily or permanently disabling as many reproductive systems as they can gain access to.

As always, the most important battles to be fought lie in the realm of ideas. The President could best serve the cause of truth by formally repudiating the two foundational documents of the war on people discussed in Chapter 7: *National Security Study Memorandum 200* and the *Report of the Commission on Population Growth and the American Future.* As we have seen in the course of this book, these reports from the early to mid-1970s are not only out of date, they also neglect the importance of human capital to development, ignore the centrality of the family, and failed to anticipate the cliff over which birthrates would cascade.

But refuting the arguments of the controllers, as I have attempted to do in this book, is only the first step. The brilliant Julian Simon may have won every argument he had with Paul Ehrlich—as in my opinion he did—but the population control juggernaut rolls on. The entire edifice of institutions, policies, and programs that has grown up around these failed twentieth century ideas must be consigned—to paraphrase a failed twentieth century ideologue—to the dustbin of history.

Get the United States Out of Population Control

A presidential administration concerned about ending human rights abuses in, and protecting women and families from, population control programs could order the USAID Global Health Bureau to take the following steps immediately:

- Invite recognized human rights groups to monitor its ongoing population control programs for violations of the Tiahrt Amendment, the Mexico City Policy, and other laws protecting women and families. Currently, client satisfaction surveys are conducted by The Population Council and other groups that have a vested interest in continuing these programs;
- Put in place a standard investigative protocol that would be automatically invoked when a violation of U.S. law or human rights conventions has been reported.[3] The absence of such a protocol has meant that past investigations, when undertaken at all, have often been desultory, incomplete, or pro forma;
- Cease relying upon the misleading concept of "unmet need for contraception" to determine the quantity of contraceptives to ship;
- Redesign the Demographic and Health Survey to elicit direct responses about women's health needs, and to use these responses, in conjunction with epidemiological data, to redesign health care programs to meet such needs;
- Accept Natural Family Planning (NFP) as a "modern method of contraception," and thus commit a significant portion of family planning funds to the promotion of this safe and natural method;
- Close the Population Office of USAID, the one-time home of the infamous Dr. Ravenholt and an anachronism whose chief purpose of late has been inventing rationalizations for continuing failed family planning programs in dying countries. Any legitimate demographic research questions that arise in the conduct of USAID's business can be addressed by the International Division of the U.S. Bureau of the Census, whose budget should be increased for this purpose, and whose prescriptions will not be tainted by a need to justify continued family planning funding;
- Undertake a long overdue reevaluation of the entire "population explosion" thesis. This could be initiated by the assistant secretary of state for population, refugees, and migration, as was the previous iteration in the mid-1960s, and take a fresh look at the numbers;
- Announce that, as the current Congressional mandate for population control is terms of "population stabilization," that henceforth developing countries with birthrates at or below replacement will be receiving

"family planning" assistance to increase, not decrease, their birth rate;
- Include notice of family planning abuses in the State Department's annual "Country reports on Human rights."[4] This has been done in the case of China, North Korea and Vietnam, but abuses in other countries have received little notice.

The U.S. Congress, acting in conjunction with the administration, could take several further steps to end human rights abuses in population control programs and respond to the real needs of women and children around the world:

- The U.S. Congress should cease appropriating funds designated for international family planning and/or population stabilization. Available funds should be transferred into primary health care, where they can be used to save lives.[5]
- The U.S. Congress should amend foreign aid legislation to remove "population stabilization" in its many guises ("family planning," "reproductive health," etc.) as a condition of foreign aid. The focus of U.S. aid should be on the provision of primary health care, as well as on programs that create the material and political infrastructure for economic growth and democratization.
- The United States should withdraw from the UN Population Fund. Ideally, the UNFPA, the creation of Rockefeller and his cronies, should simply be disbanded. Whatever legitimate health functions it performs can be transferred to the World Health Organization, UNICEF, or other international organizations. Some small programs, like that instituted to address the problem of obstetric fistula, may be worth saving. Others are Potemkin facades erected to con critics and, as in the Matlab bait-and-switch experiments in Bangladesh, deceive women.[6]

Other governments, as well as human rights groups, have belatedly begun to pay attention to the suffering population control programs have caused women. The Human Rights Commission of the Mexican government in 2003 condemned the Ministry of Health's practice of sterilizing or contraception women immediately after childbirth (although these practices continue.) Both Amnesty International and Human Rights Watch have criticized forced abortion, especially in the Chinese context. One hopes that other human rights agencies and organizations will join them. Human rights are nonnegotiable, or they are not rights at all, merely privileges to be withdrawn at the whim of governments, international organizations, or both.

The Real Population Crisis

Once these steps have been taken, we can begin to address the real population crisis: Cascading birth rates around the world.

A bust, like a boom, moves in geometric progression, its effects magnifying over time. In many countries, as we saw in Chapter 1, the elderly population is exploding, while the number of babies being born is plummeting. The consequences of this demographic shift are mind-boggling. Economies will stagnate for lack of workers and consumers, while pension plans will hemorrhage red ink. Europe and Japan's anemic growth rates may be harbingers of far worse things to come.

"The specter haunting Europe today is the prospect of inexorable demographic decline," write Nicholas Eberstadt and Hans Groth in *Foreign Affairs*. Nevertheless, they argue, the continent can stave off relative economic decline for another generation if the elderly can be induced to give up *la dolce vita* and remain in the workforce.[7] While this is undoubtedly the baby-less continent's best option, it seems much more likely that the socialist-minded parliaments of Europe will respond to the economic demands made by the elderly by simply raising taxes, not by suggesting, however diffidently, that Wolfgang and Pierre go back to work. Even if Eberstadt and Roth's suggestion was adopted, this merely buys time, and not very much time at that. Let us imagine that by some robust combination of laws and incentives the average age of retirement is pushed back five, or even ten years. After this relatively brief up tick, the number of people in their productive years would still continue to decline. The worker to dependent ratio, after briefly righting itself, would continue its downward tumble. The elderly may be induced to put off retirement into the future, but they can hardly be induced to travel back 30 years into the past and reproduce themselves.

It is the reproductive behavior of those who are still able to reproduce that is important for the long-term health of the economy. How are young couples in Europe likely to respond to the ever-weightier tax burdens imposed by a growing population of elderly? Barring major improvements in productivity, they will have to work longer hours for less take-home pay. Many may postpone having children, perhaps indefinitely. In the worst case, government pension programs that transfer wealth from the young to the elderly will create what might be called a "low fertility trap," pulling fertility down into a maelstrom from which it will have trouble escaping.

The topsy-turvy demography found in present-day Europe will soon enough spread to many less-developed countries in South America and Asia. To the extent that Western-funded population control programs have succeeded in "artificially" driving down the birthrate, we will be responsible for visiting the "white pestilence" upon poor peoples who have far fewer resources than wealthy Europeans with which to cope.

How low can the birthrate go before all hope of recovery is lost? There is probably no way to say for certain. A productive remnant can reproduce very rapidly, and repopulate a country. But if the tax structure of a country penalizes those who have many children, as most of them do, then this kind of demographic renaissance is unlikely at best.

What is clear is that the time to begin preparing for the problems that depopulation will bring is now. The engineer of a fast-moving freight train does not slam on his brakes fifty feet from the end of the line; he begins slowing down miles from his destination. Depopulation trends have forward momentum, too, and are likewise best braked decades in advance. It is already too late to simply call off the dogs of population control where birthrates have fallen to below replacement; pro-natal programs must be enacted. But how do you go about convince people to have offspring again after you have spent decades of time, and billions of dollars, telling them that children are inconvenient, expensive and a threat to the environment?

Reversing the Plunge

Is it possible to escape the low fertility trap? This is not a rhetorical question. No government of a country whose birthrate has fallen significantly below replacement has ever succeeded in once again achieving replacement rate fertility. Once the birthrate falls to what the UN Population Division calls "low low fertility," no combination of policies and subsidies to which governments have had recourse has been sufficient to boost the birthrate back to 2.1 or above.

Viewing this problem, most observers simply conclude that the policies are simply not robust enough, nor the subsidies large enough, to alter fertility behavior. I believe that their position, however reasonable it sounds, is fundamentally wrongheaded. For a close examination of these policies and subsidies reveals that they are, in their effect on fertility, self-limiting and even self-defeating. That is to say, they create unintended anti-natal incentives that for the most part offset their ostensible pro-natal purposes. Moreover, the welfare state itself, with its extremely high tax rates and its usurpation of family functions, relentlessly drives down fertility. In this sense it is *paternalistic government itself that is the problem.*

Costs and Benefits

Conservatives are accustomed to thinking of reproduction from a moral perspective, while liberals view it from a "rights" perspective. But the act

of conception—or the frustrating of that act by contraception, sterilization and abortion—can be viewed from a financial perspective as well,
for it is freighted with economic consequences. Each baby represents a
valuable, if gradual, addition of human capital to society. Each abortion,
on the other hand, constitutes nothing less than the wanton destruction of
human capital. The abortion industry, it may be said, is the only sector of the
economy that does not create wealth, but destroys it, leaving us all (except
the abortionists themselves) materially poorer. The 1.1 million abortions
committed annually in the United States are the economic equivalent of a
massive anthrax attack on a mid-sized American city. Government-funded
contraception and sterilization programs, which deliberately suppress the
birth rate, may be said to prevent the formation of human capital.

The parents' see the matter quite differently, of course. However much
love they feel for their newborns, and however much pride they feel in
raising a useful member of society, they *experience* babies as a drain on
the family economy. They make tremendous investments of time and
money in each of their children over the years, only to watch them open
separate bank and checking accounts as soon as they become gainfully
employed. The Department of Agriculture estimates the cost of raising
a child born in 2005 at around $200,000 over twenty years.[8] Yet adult
children contribute precious little to the financial well being of their parents, either directly or through government-run pension programs. The
U.S. Social Security system, like its counterparts overseas, completely
ignores the vital contribution of human capital that parents make to the
system. In so doing it undermines their willingness to create that capital,
that is, to conceive, bear and raise children.

Yet the family's loss is society's gain, for these same children constitute the human capital that the larger society draws upon for its very
life. The economy continues to flourish—and government medical and
pension programs continue to operate—only because millions of parents
generously sacrifice their own well being by providing for the future in
the most fundamental way, by providing for the next generation. How
much human capital do parents create when they conceive, bear, and raise
a child? One way to assess their contribution is to calculate the economic
value of a baby at conception. Assuming that wages continue to rise at
their current rate, the future earnings of a child conceived today will be
probably in the neighborhood of $4 and $5 million. Discounting the future
costs and benefits to the present produces a figure of around $600,000.
How many people realize that every conception is the creation of a small
fortune? Most parents certainly don't, and with good reason.

As long as the costs borne by the family are disconnected from the benefits reaped by the larger society, the birthrate will continue to fall in many countries, with calamitous consequences.

Wrong-Headed Policies

Many European countries have long had policies and programs in place that are intended to raise the birth rate.[9] The policies, which offset some of the costs and consequences of childbearing, take the following forms:

(1) A one-time bonus: the government provides parents with a fixed sum of money, as in Russia, where each family receives a bonus of $9,600 following the birth of a second child and any subsequent children.

(2) A parental leave program, allowing parents to stop work after a child is born, as in Norway where Norwegian mothers can take 12 months off work with 80 percent pay, or 10 months off with full pay. Husbands are also *required* to take at least four weeks off from work after the birth of a child.

(3) A government subsidy for a set period of time, often pegged to the parental leave program, as in Sweden, where the mother can receive 80% of her salary during the period of leave.

(4) Government-run daycare centers that take babies to preschool-aged children, as in France and Sweden.

(5) Small monthly subsidies for dependent children, called, in German-speaking countries, "Kindergeld."

(6) Propaganda campaigns, as in France, where a government-sponsored national ad campaign trumpets *La France a besoin les enfants!* (France needs babies!). The Czech Republic, also, has erected billboards extolling the virtues of larger families.

Among the most ambitious of such efforts is the new "Elterngeld"—or "parent money"—program of Germany, which was adopted in 2007. This program allows an adult who stops work after a child is born to continue to claim two-thirds of their net wage, up to a maximum of $2,375 per month, for 12 months. Low earners can claim 100% compensation for lost wages. In an obvious bow to feminist sensibilities, if both parents take a turn, they can claim the benefit for two months longer, for a total of 14 months. These benefits mark a substantial increase over Germany's previous scheme: a flat $400 a month for low-income families for up to two years. But the early signs are that it is unlikely to have any more impact than its predecessor on the anemic German birth rate.

Sweden has the most generous parental leave laws, allowing either the mother (or the father) can take 480 days of parental leave with guaranteed reemployment. Despite these benefits, Sweden's fertility rate of 1.7 children per woman, though high for Europe, still falls short of replacement.[10] Not one of the schemes adopted by the European countries has succeeded in recovering the birth rate to replacement. Why?

One defect of these policies is that they ignore the dynamics of the natural family—that is, a family consisting of a father, a mother, and their natural and adopted children—in favor of gender—and marriage-neutral policies. The German program, by tempting fathers to leave the work force for long periods of time, will undoubtedly damage their career prospects, and thus impose long-term financial costs on the family. It is well-known that fathers work harder the more children they have, and this propensity should be encouraged, not discouraged by attempting to turn them into stay-at-home dads.

Another thing that must be said about these government subsidies is that they are an inefficient use of tax dollars. The administrative costs of these programs are generally quite high. Governments in general are very inefficient consumers, only able to recover 30 cents of value from every dollar they spend. This is why, in many states and municipalities, waste disposal services, and prisons, among other services, have been privatized. Young couples in Europe, who see half their income absorbed by the state and only get a fraction back in exchange for their fertility, know a bad bargain when they see one.

The countries of the European Union spend an average of 28 percent of GNP on the social sector. Nearly all of this goes into pension benefits and government-run health care programs, however, not to the family. According to a 2006 report from the Madrid-based Institute for Family Policies (IFP), only 2.2 percent of GNP is spent on the family, mostly on small subsidies to families with children.[11] With the exception of tiny Luxembourg, which offers a subsidy of 611 euros to a family with two children, these amounts are only a pittance compared with the cost of raising children. Germany offers only 308 euros, the United Kingdom only 270 euros. The rates are much lower in Spain, Italy, Portugal and Greece. Spain grants only 49 euros to a family with two children. The new, and far poorer, EU states do even less well. A couple with two children would receive only 38 euros in the Czech Republic, and a meager 22 euros in Poland.

Another failing of these policies is that they are overly egalitarian. That is to say, they seek to encourage *all* couples to have one more child. But given that couples vary widely in their fertility desires, the policy focus should rather be on empowering couples to achieve their own desired number of children. Those couples who, for reasons of religious conviction or personal fulfillment, desire to have larger than average families, should be particularly encouraged, since even a small percentage of large families can have a substantial demographic impact. Consider the ultra-Orthodox Jews of the United States. Although they constitute only about 6 percent of the Jewish population at present, households of four, six, or even eight children are not uncommon. This is many times the Jewish average. Within a few decades, their descendants will constitute the majority of the Jewish population. Put another way, without the generous fertility of the ultra-Orthodox, the Jewish population of the United States would be rapidly dying out.

But the most serious shortcoming of these policies is that they fail to address the *principal financial stress on the family*, namely, that which results from high tax rates. The cradle to grave welfare systems of the modern European state are enormously expensive and, in conjunction with other government programs, consume half of GNP. This means that, while America taxes away roughly one-third of the earnings of its citizens, European governments devour one-half. This massive redirection of economic resources away from the family leaves it bereft of the resources it needs to grow and thrive.

The IFP recommends increasing social welfare benefits aimed at families, but the problem cannot be resolved by marginally increasing child payments, or by tacking another month or two onto the parental leave policy. Such statist solutions will not solve the problem of the empty cradle, for it is the modern welfare state itself that relentlessly suppresses fertility. By its very existence, it discourages the formation of the very kind of strong, independent families that are necessary for robust fertility by fracturing the intergenerational dependency of the family, by adopting "gender-neutral" policies that undermine the complementarity that is at the heart of successful marriage, by providing abortion on demand, by mandating sex education for children, by pushing state-funded contraception schemes on teenagers and young adults and, above all, by high tax rates.

If young European couples could be sheltered from the exactions of the state, it is likely that the continent's birth dearth would largely disappear. This, in fact, has been the experience of the United States over the past quarter century.

Sheltering Young Couples

Fertility rates in America never dropped as far or as fast as they did in Europe or Japan. Still, by the late 1970s, the United States was averaging a TFR of 1.79.[12] Instead of offering government subsidies to families with children, the Congress sought in typical American fashion to address this and other problems through the tax code. The idea was to reduce the tax burden on families, in part so that they would be more open to new life.

The Tax Reform Act of 1986 almost doubled the "income tax deduction for dependents," from $1,080 to $2,000 and, more important over the long run, indexed it to inflation. The TFR rose in response to 1.92.[13] The next step forward came in 1997, when the tax reform act of that year created a new Child Tax Credit. Originally set at $400, this has since been gradually increased to $1,000 per child. This means that a family with three children can claim a credit against taxes of $3,000. If their total tax is less than this amount, as is often the case with families of modest income, they receive a rebate from the government. This measure, too, had a modest pro-natal effect, boosting the TFR up to just about replacement.[14] If countries of Europe—and others with anemic birth rates—want to seriously address their demographic deficit, then they should adopt the same approach.[15]

There is no reason why these tax proposals should not be acceptable even to those who speak of reproductive rights. Young women in America express a desire for 2.5 children or so, significantly above the current TFR of 2.1. Surveys also show that many mothers would choose to stay home with their children, rather than work outside the home, if they were financially able to do so. Allowing mothers the financial freedom to act on their fertility and mothering preferences, rather than being forced into the work force and away from their children by high taxes, expands their freedom of choice. Population control programs, on the other hand, act to constrict the choices made by young women.

Still, any policy that seeks to strengthen the family and raise the birth rate will obviously not receive universal applause. Strenuous objections will come from the same radical groups who continue to propagate the tired old myth of overpopulation. We will apparently always have the population controllers at the UNFPA and elsewhere with us, at least as long as long as they continue to receive billions of dollars in government funding. So-called equity feminists will continue to advocate shifting the tax burden onto "homemakers" and one-income families, forcing their reluctant "sisters" out of childbearing and into the workforce.[16] And eco-militants like Paul Watson will continue to compare humanity to the AIDS virus and advocate a human die-back to one billion.[17]

There is nothing to stop such individuals from acting on their dystopian impulses, if they chose to do so, but we should discourage their efforts to take vast numbers of their fellow human beings with them.

As my late friend Julian Simon was fond of remarking, human beings are the ultimate resource.

Notes

1. See, for instance, the proposed National Population Policy of the group Negative Population Growth.
2. Slogans of the 1960s continue to reverberate in the writings of younger activists, such as "All causes are lost causes unless we stop population growth." Such anachronistic slogans continue to appear in the mainstream press. See, for example, Yeh Ling-Ling, "Stop Population Growth-Here and Abroad," *San Francisco Chronicle*, 4 January 2005, B8.
3. This idea should be credited to Eileen Cosby of the Filipino Family Fund.
4. See the *Country Reports on Human Rights.*
5. After five years of holding its family planning funding request level, the Bush administration finally requested reduced funding in 2006, only to have the funding increased by the Congress.
6. The World Bank, USAID and other donor agencies set up what critic Betsy Hartmann calls a "human laboratory" at the International Center for Diarrheal Disease Research in Matlab, Bangladesh. Selected health services—such as prenatal care, training of traditional midwives, oral rehydration for diarrhea, tetanus immunization of pregnant women—were added, in Hartmann's words, "to its family planning program in different 'packages' in order to see which ones had the greatest effect on enhancing [family planning] field worker credibility and thus increasing contraceptive use. … Through a series of regression equations, the researchers concluded that only a minimal Mother and Child Health (MCH) package achieved the desired result and that further expansion of MCH services to include, for example, prenatal care and midwife training was not essential to increased contraceptive use." Betsy Hartmann, *Reproductive Rights and Wrongs: The Global Politics of Population Control and Contraceptive Choice*, (New York: Harper Collins, 1987), 235.
7. See "Healthy Old Europe," *Foreign Affairs* 86 (3) (May/June 2007), 55-68. Eberstadt and Groth are at pains to suggest that Europe's elderly are "exceptionally healthy," and constitute a great untapped resource for the continent.
8. I believe that this sum, which ignores the economies of scale achievable by families with more than one child, is somewhat exaggerated.
9. See Maurice Kirk, Massimo Vivi, and Egon Szabady, eds., *Law and Fertility in Europe: A Study of Legislation Directly or Indirectly Affecting Fertility in Europe* (International Union for the Scientific Study of Population, 1975). Although now dated, this provides an excellent summary of the early, and nonavailing, efforts of European states to raise their birth rates following World War Two.
10. U.S. Census Bureau figure, accessed 21 June 2007, at http://www.census.gov/cgi-bin/ipc/idbsum.pl?cty=SW See also, "Europe's Endangered Families: With Few Children, What are Countries to do?" Zenit.org, 5 May 2006.
11. "Report on the Evolution of the Family in Europe 2006," Institute for Family Policies (Madrid, Spain, 2006). www.ipfe.org/lineasestrategicas.htm.
12. U.N. Population Division, *World Population Prospects: the 2006 Revision, Highlights*, esp. Table A.15, "Total fertility by country for selected periods (medium variant)."
13. For an excellent summary of the relationship between tax policy and fertility see Allan C. Carlson, "Taxing the Family: An American Version of Paradise Lost?" *Family Policy Review* 1(1) (Spring 2003): 1-20.

Appendix
USAID Contraceptive Shipments Worldwide

Condoms
USAID Shipments Worldwide

Year	Units	Cost ($US)
2006	462,813,000	$19,926,631
2005	429,039,000	$20,876,893
2004	442,458,000	$24,659,867
2003	458,217,000	$24,093,940
2002	233,262,000	$14,688,946
2001	348,876,000	$24,365,932
2000	308,706,000	$20,171,844
1999	238,404,000	$14,298,928
1998	435,336,000	$23,856,398
1997	308,466,000	$17,713,222
1996	352,156,900	$19,892,211
1995	603,822,000	$31,836,438
1994	483,300,000	$25,300,000
1993	498,100,000	$29,100,000
1992	267,000,000	$15,500,000
1991	765,100,000	$38,100,000
1990	794,500,000	$37,700,000

Condom totals include condoms intended primarily to prevent HIV infection, as well as those for population control.

The number of condoms shipped declined sharply in 1996 because of decreases in contraceptives sent to Kenya and Nigeria. Kenya received condom shipments from other sources, and Nigeria was decertified, curtailing all shipments of contraceptives.

The 1999 decline in condom shipments is due to "manufacturing difficulties and an increased demand for quality assurance testing." Interestingly, "shipments to Africa were least affected by the decrease."

In FY2000, Bangladesh received almost as many condoms as the entire region of Africa, making it the largest condom recipient.

Source: 1990-2000 Statistics are from the Population, Health and Nutrition Projects Database; 2001-2006 Statistics are from the Global Summary of Shipment Reports, Reproductive Health Supplies Coalition.

Depo Provera (injective) USAID Shipments Worldwide		
Year	Units	Cost ($US)
2006	18,526,400	$19,766,999
2005	18,960,800	$20,649,354
2004	18,256,800	$20,617,769
2003	17,319,200	$17,374,790
2002	9,933,600	$9,258,382
2001	16,584,000	$17,564,371
2000	9,068,400	$9,504,017
1999	8,958,800	$9,364,690
1998	9,947,200	$9,697,501
1997	6,702,400	$6,517,141
1996	4,183,200	$4,224,774
1995	2,869,600	$3,107,144
1994	810,000	$900,000

Source: 1990-2000 Statistics are from the Population, Health and Nutrition Projects Database; 2001-2006 Statistics are from the Global Summary of Shipment Reports, Reproductive Health Supplies Coalition.

Female Condoms USAID Shipments Worldwide		
Year	Units	Cost ($US)
2006	4,855,000	$3,241,233
2005	1,284,000	$882,933
2004	1,941,000	$1,312,220
2003	1,009,000	$755,331
2002	119,000	$87,629
2001	20,000	$16,204
2000	168,000	$147,383
1999	69,000	$55,637
1998	22,000	$19,818

Female condoms were first shipped by USAID in 1998. They were sent exclusively to Kenya and Bolivia that year.

Source: 1990-2000 Statistics are from the Population, Health and Nutrition Projects Database; 2001-2006 Statistics are from the Global Summary of Shipment Reports, Reproductive Health Supplies Coalition.

Norplant (implant) USAID Shipments Worldwide		
Year	Units	Cost ($US)
2006	124,200	$3,145,789
2005	78,300	$2,001,908
2004	78,400	$1,992,638
2003	88,900	$2,261,697
2002	124,500	$3,118,544
2001	102,500	$2,586,368
2000	63,750	$1,612,012
1999	300,400	$7,390,179
1998	76,750	$1,859,792
1997	61,700	$1,497,406
1996	38,700	$935,721
1995	84,600	$2,016,152
1994	92,050	$2,170,000
1993	48,350	$1,120,000
1992	49,600	$1,180,000

Norplant first became available in 1992 following U.S. Food and Drug Administration (FDA) approval.

Shipments of Norplant increased 60 percent from 1996 to 1997, with most of the increase in shipments to Africa.

Source: 1990-2000 Statistics are from the Population, Health and Nutrition Projects Database; 2001-2006 Statistics are from the Global Summary of Shipment Reports, Reproductive Health Supplies Coalition.

Intrauterine Devices (IUDs) USAID Shipments Worldwide		
Year	Units	Cost ($US)
2006	458,600	$818,939
2005	1,365,600	$2,295,753
2004	1,986,600	$3,405,809
2003	1,808,200	$3,062,106
2002	2,168,400	$3,528,568
2001	1,830,800	$3,079,645
2000	1,243,200	$1,628,320
1999	2,736,000	$3,931,996
1998	3,311,400	$4,578,832
1997	1,863,000	$2,386,792
1996	3,772,200	$4,726,858
1995	2,993,000	$3,569,173
1994	3,500,000	$4,000,000
1993	2,690,000	$3,000,000
1992	5,560,000	$5,400,000
1991	3,590,000	$3,900,000
1990	5,770,000	$5,900,000

IUD shipments increased 78 percent in 1998, mainly because of an increase in the quantity shipped to Indonesia.

Source: 1990-2000 Statistics are from the Population, Health and Nutrition Projects Database; 2001-2006 Statistics are from the Global Summary of Shipment Reports, Reproductive Health Supplies Coalition.

Vaginal Foaming Tablets (VFTs) USAID Shipments Worldwide		
Year	Units	Cost ($US)
2004	182,400	$25,546
2003	1,108,800	$158,200
2002	5,923,200	$818,770
2001	3,691,200	$521,269
2000	8,961,600	$1,187,378
1999	10,089,600	$1,395,819
1998	13,934,400	$1,695,566
1997	10,857,600	$1,253,067
1996	15,528,000	$1,696,703
1995	15,067,200	$1,726,645
1994	15,200,000	$1,600,000
1993	19,100,000	$1,900,000
1992	16,400,000	$1,700,000
1991	19,900,000	$2,000,000
1990	19,400,000	$1,900,000

Source: 1990-2000 Statistics are from the Population, Health and Nutrition Projects Database; 2001-2006 Statistics are from the Global Summary of Shipment Reports, Reproductive Health Supplies Coalition.

Oral contraceptives (cycles) USAID Shipments Worldwide		
Year	Units	Cost ($US)
2006	73,162,800	$18,468,570
2005	87,008,400	$22,134,795
2004	77,432,400	$19,302,278
2003	85,176,000	$21,302,736
2002	73,448,400	$18,128,039
2001	77,350,800	$19,763,918
2000	74,640,000	$18,163,713
1999	57,944,400	$14,154,517
1998	60,930,000	$13,436,189
1997	42,610,800	$9,122,237
1996	69,816,000	$14,416,916
1995	52,507,200	$10,992,319
1994	65,000,000	$13,400,000
1993	90,000,000	$17,300,000
1992	76,800,000	$15,100,000
1991	68,500,000	$13,200,000
1990	60,700,000	$12,100,000

Source: 1990-2000 Statistics are from the Population, Health and Nutrition Projects Database; 2001-2006 Statistics are from the Summary of Shipment Reports, Reproductive Health Supplies Coalition.

Bibliography

Books

Abernathy, Virginia D. *Population Politics*. New Brunswick, NJ: Transaction, 2000.

Aird, John. *Slaughter of the Innocents*. Washington: AEI Press, 1990.

Alexandratos, Nikos. *World Agriculture: Towards 2010*. Chichester, England: Food and Agriculture Organization of the United Nations and Hon Wiley & Sons, 1995.

Avery, Dennis T. *Global Food Progress 1991: A Report from Hudson Institute's Center for Global Food Issues*. Indianapolis: The Hudson Institute, 1991.

———. "Saving the Planet with Pesticides." In *The True State of the Planet*, edited by Ronald Bailey. New York: Free Press, 1995.

Banister, Judith. "Vietnam's evolving population policies." In *International Conference on Population, New Delhi, September 1989*. Liege: International Union for the Scientific Study of Population, 1989.

Bauer, Peter T. and Basil S. Yamey. "The Third World and the West: An Economic Perspective." in *The Third World: Premises of U.S. Policy*, edited by W. Scott Thompson. San Francisco: Institute for Contemporary Studies, 1978.

Becker, Jasper. *Hungry Ghosts: Mao's Secret Famine*. New York: The Free Press, 1996.

Bork, Robert. *Slouching Towards Gomorrah*. New York: HarperCollins, 1997.

Borlaug, Norman. "Feeding a World of Ten Billion People: The Miracle Ahead." In *Global Warming and Other Eco-Myths*, edited by Ronald Bailey. New York: Random House, 2002.

Brown, Lester. "Population growth, food needs, and production problems." *World Population and Food Supplies 1989*, ASA special publication 6:17-20. Madison, WI: American Society of Agronomy, 1989.

Brown, Lester, et al, eds. *State of the World 1997*. New York: Norton, 1997.

———. *State of the World 1998*. New York: Norton, 1998.

———. *State of the World 2000*. New York: Norton, 2000.

Camp, Sharon. "Politics of U.S. Population Assistance." In *Beyond the Numbers*, edited by Laurie Ann Mazur. Washington, D.C.: Island Press, 1994.

Cassen, Robert *et al*. *Population and Development: Old Debates, New Conclusions*. New Brunswick, NJ: Transaction Publishers, 1994.

271

Cassen, Robert with Lisa M. Bates. *Population Policy: A New Consensus.* Washington, DC: Overseas Development Council, 1994.

Chase, Allan. *The Legacy of Malthus: The Social Costs of the New Scientific Racism.* New York: Knopf, 1977.

Choucri, Nazli. *Population Dynamics and International Violence.* Lexington, MA: Lexington Books, 1974.

Coale, Ansley J. and Edgar M. Hoover. *Population Growth and Economic Development in Low-Income Countries.* Princeton: Princeton University Press, 1958.

Cole, H.S.D., Christopher Freeman, Marie Jahoda, and K.L.R. Pavitt, eds. *Models of Doom: A Critique of The Limits to Growth.* New York: Universe, 1973.

Courbage, Youssef. *Nouveaux horizons démographiques in Méditerrané.* National Institute of Demographic Studies: Paris, February 27, 1995.

Critchlow, Donald T. *Intended Consequences: Birth Control, Abortion, and the Federal Government in Modern America.* Oxford: Oxford University Press, 1999.

Daly, Herman and John Cobb. *For the Common Good: Redirecting the Economy Towards Community, the Environment and a Sustainable Future.* London: Green Print, 1990.

Decter, Midge. "The Nine Lives of Population Control." In *The Nine Lives of Population Control*, edited by Michael Cromartie. Washington, D.C.: Ethics and Public Policy Center, 1995.

Desowitz, Robert S. *The Malaria Capers.* New York: W. W. Norton and Co., 1993.

Donaldson, Peter and Amy Ong Tsui. "The International Family Planning Movement." In *Beyond the Numbers*, edited by Laurie Ann Mazur. Washington, D.C.: Island Press, 1994.

Donaldson, Peter J. *Nature Against Us: The United States and the World Population Crisis 1965-1980.* Chapel Hill, NC: University of North Carolina, 1990.

D'Souza, Dinesh. *The Enemy at Home: The Cultural Left and Its Responsibility for 9/11.* New York: Doubleday, 2007.

Eberstadt, Nicholas. "The Premises of Population Policy: A Reexamination." In *The Nine Lives of Population Control,* edited by Michael Cromartie. Grand Rapids, MI: Eerdmans, 1995.

——. *Prosperous Paupers and Other Population Problems.* New Brunswick, NJ: Transaction, 2000.

Edwards, P.N. and S.H. Schneider. "Self-Governance and Peer Review in Science-for-Policy: The Case of the IPCC Second Assessment Report." In *Changing the Atmosphere; Expert Knowledge and Environmental Governance*, edited by C. Miller and P.N. Edwards. Cambridge, MA: MIT Press, 2001.

Ehrlich, Paul and Anne Ehrlich. *Betrayal of Science and Reason.* Washington: Island Press, 1996.

Ehrlich, Paul. *The Population Bomb.* San Francisco: Sierra Club, 1969.

Ehrlich, Paul and Anne Ehrlich. *The Population Explosion.* New York: Simon and Shuster, 1990.

Ethelston, Sally *et al. Progress and Promises: Trends in International Assistance for Reproductive Health and Population.* Washington, DC: Population Action International, 2004.

Engelmann, Robert. "A Response." In *The Nine Lives of Population Control,* edited by Michael Cromartie. Grand Rapids: Erdmann's, 1995.

Fingleton, Eamonn. *In Praise of Hard Industries.* Boston: Houghton Mifflin, 1999.

Flavin, Christopher et al, eds. *State of the World 2002.* New York: Norton, 2002.

Franks, Angela. *Margaret Sanger's Eugenic Legacy: The Control of Female Fertility.* Jefferson, N.C.: McFarland, 2005.

Freedman, Ronald. *The Sociology of Human Fertility: An Annotated Bibliography.* New York: Irvington Publishers, 1975.

Friedman, George and Meredith Lebard. *The Coming War with Japan.* New York: St. Martin's Press, 1991.

Fu, Zhengyuan. *China's Legalists: The Earliest Totalitarians and Their Art of Ruling.* Armonk, New York: M.E. Sharpe, 1996.

Grant, Nichole. *The Selling of Contraception: The Dalkon Shield Case.* Columbus: Ohio State University Press, 1992.

Gore, Al. *Earth in the Balance: Ecology and the Human Spirit.* Boston: Houghton Mifflin, 1992.

Guttmacher, Alan E. "The Planned Parenthood Federation of America, Inc., General Program." In *Manual of Family Planning and Contraceptive Practice,* edited by Mary Steichen Calderone. 2nd edition. Baltimore: Williams and Wilkins, 1970.

Hardin, Garret. *Population, Evolution, and Birth Control* Second Edition. San Francisco: W. H. Freeman, 1964.

Harr, John Ensor and Peter J. Johnson. *The Rockefeller Conscience.* New York: Scribner, 1991.

Hartmann, Betsy. *Reproductive Rights and Wrongs.* Boston: South End Press, 1995.

———. *Reproductive Rights and Wrongs: The Global Politics of Population Control and Contraceptive Choice.* New York: Harper Collins, 1987.

Hayward, Steven. *Index of Leading Environmental Indicators 2006.* Washington, D.C.: American Enterprise Institute and the Pacific Research Institute, 2006.

Hollander, Jack M. *The Real Environmental Crisis: Why Poverty, Not Affluence, is the Environment's Number One Enemy.* Berkeley: University of California Press, 2003.

Huntington, Samuel P. *The Clash of the Civilizations and the Remaking of World Order.* New York: Simon & Shuster, 1996.

Isaacs, Harold R. *Scratches on Our Minds: American Images of China and India.* New York: John Day, 1958.

Jacobs, Jane. *The Death and Life of Great American Cities.* New York: Vintage Books, 1961.

Jaquette, Jane S. and Kathleen A. Staudt. "Women as 'At Risk' Reproducers: Biology, Science, and Population in U.S. Foreign Policy." In *Women, Biology, and Public Policy*, edited by Virginia S. Shapiro. *Sage Yearbooks in Women's Policy Studies*. Beverly Hills: Sage Publications, 1985.

Johnson, Paul. *A History of the English People*. New York: Harper and Row, 1985.

Kasun, Jacqueline. *The War Against Population: The Ideology and Economics of World Population Control*. Rev. ed. San Francisco: Ignatius, 1988.

Kirk, Maurice, Massimo Vivi, and Egon Szabady, eds. *Law and Fertility in Europe: A Study of Legislation Directly or Indirectly Affecting Fertility in Europe*. Paris: International Union for the Scientific Study of Population, 1975.

Lader, Lawrence. *Breeding Ourselves to Death*. Foreword by Dr. Paul R. Ehrlich. New York: Ballantine Books, 1971.

Liagin, Elizabeth. *Excessive Force: Power, Politics and Population Control*. Washington, D.C: Information Project for Africa, 1995.

Livingstone, Tess. *George Pell: Defender of the Faith Down Under*. San Francisco: Ignatius Press, 2002.

Lomborg, Bjorn. *The Skeptical Environmentalist*. Cambridge: Cambridge University Press, 2001.

Longman, Phillip. *The Empty Cradle: How Falling Birthrates Threaten World Prosperity [And What To Do About It]*. New York: Basic Books, 2004.

Lyons, Daniel. *Is there a Population Explosion?* New York: Catholic Polls, 1970.

McNamara, Robert. *One Hundred Countries, Two Billion People*. London: Pall Mall Press, 1973.

Meadows, D.H., *et al. The Limits to Growth: A Report for the Club of Rome's Project on the Predicament of Mankind*. New York: Universe Books, 1972.

————. "The Only Feasible Solution." In *Mankind at the Turning Point: The Second Report to the Club of Rome* edited by Mesarovic, Mihajlo, and Eduard Pestel. New York: E.P. Dutton, 1974.

Meek, Ronald L., ed. *Marx and Engels on the Population Bomb*. Second Ed. Berkeley, CA: Ramparts Press, 1971.

Miller, C.A. and P.N. Edwards. "Introduction" to *Changing the Atmosphere; Expert Knowledge and Environmental Governance*. Cambridge, MA: MIT Press, 2001.

Mintz, Morton. *At Any Cost: Corporate Greed, Women, and the Dalkon Shield*. New York: Pantheon, 1985.

Moore, Hugh. *The Population Bomb*. New York: The Hugh Moore Fund, 1954.

Moore, Thomas Gale. *Environmental Fundamentalism*. Stanford, CA: Hoover Institution, 1992.

Mosher, Steven W. *Broken Earth: The Rural Chinese*. New York: Free Press, 1983.

————. *China Misperceived: American Illusions and Chinese Reality*. New York: Basic Books, 1990.

————. *A Mother's Ordeal: One Woman's Fight Against China's One-Child Policy*. New York: Harcourt Brace, 1993.

Mullan, Phil. *The Imaginary Time Bomb*. New York: I. B. Tauris, 2002.

Myrdal, Gunnar. *An American Dilemma: The Negro Problem and Modern Democracy*. New York: Harper and Row, 1944.

Organski, Katherine and A.F.K. Organski, *Population and World Power*. New York: Knopf, 1961.

Ortega y Gasset, Jose. *The Revolt of the Masses*. New York: W. W. Norton, 1957.

Paddock, William and Paul Paddock, *Famine-1975!*. London: Weidenfeld and Nicolson, 1968.

Petty, William. *The Economic Writings of Sir William Petty*, Edited by Charles Henry Hull. Cambridge: Cambridge University Press, 1899.

Piotrow, Phyllis. *Draper World Population Fund Report: Voluntary Sterilization*. Washington, D.C.: Draper World Population Fund, 1976.

————. *World Population Crisis*. Westport, CT: Praeger, 1973.

Ramirez de Arellano, Annette B. and Conrad Seipp. *Colonialism, Catholicism, and Contraception: A History of Birth Control in Puerto Rico*. Chapel Hill, N.C.: University of North Carolina Press, 1983.

Riggs, David. "Avoiding Water Wars." In *Global Warming and Other Eco-Myths*, edited by Ronald Bailey. New York: Random House, 2002.

Robbins, John. *Too Many Asians*. New York: Doubleday, 1959.

Sai, Fred T. and Lauren A. Chester. "The Role of the World Bank in Shaping Third World Population Policy." In *Population Policy: Contemporary Issues*, edited by Godfrey Roberts. New York: Praeger, 1990.

Sanger, Margaret. "The Children's Era." In *The Sixth International Neo-Malthusian and Birth Control Conference, vol. IV, Religious and Ethical Aspects of Birth Control*, edited by Margaret Sanger. New York: American Birth Control League, Inc., 1926.

————. *Pivot of Civilization*. New York: Brentano's, 1922.

Sassone, Robert. *Handbook on Population*. 5th Ed. Stafford: Virginia, American Life League, 1994.

Shilts, Randy. *And the Band Played On: Politics, People, and the AIDS Epidemic*. New York: St. Martin's Press, 2000.

Simon, Julian. *The Ultimate Resource*. Princeton: Princeton University Press, 1981.

Song Jian, Chi-Hsien Tuan, and Jing-Yuan Yu. *Population Control in China: Theory and Applications*. New York: Praeger, 1985.

Tien, H. Yuan. *China's Strategic Demographic Initiative*. New York: Praeger, 1991.

Tietze, Christopher. *A Speaker's and Debater's Guidebook*. Washington, D.C.: National Abortion Rights Action League, June 1978.

Vogel, Ezra. *Japan as Number One*. New York: Harper Torchbooks, 1979.

Vogt, William. *People! Challenge to Survival*. New York: William Sloane Associates, 1960.

————. *The Road to Survival*. With an introduction by Barnard Baruch. New York: William Sloane Associates, 1948.

Warwick, Donald P. *Bitter Pills: Population Policies and Their Implementation in Eight Developing Countries.* Cambridge: Cambridge University Press, 1982.

Wells, Robert V. *Revolutions in American Lives: A Demographic Perspective on the History of Americans, Their Families, and Their Societies.* Westport, CT: Greenwood Press, 1982.

Wells, Robert. *Uncle Sam's Family: Issues in and Perspectives on American Demographic History.* Albany: State University of New York Press, 1985.

Whelan, Robert. *Choices in Childbearing: When Does Family Planning Become Population Control?* London: Committee on Population & the Economy, 1992.

Official Documents

Bush, George W. "State of the Union Address." The United States Capitol, Washington, D.C., 28 January 2003.

Central Intelligence Agency. "Political Perspectives on Key Global Issues," March 1977 (declassified, in part, January 1995).

———. *The World FactBook.* https://www.cia.gov/cia/publications/factbook/geos/fr.html.

Chavez Chuchon, Hector. "A Doctor Speaks Out: What Happened to Medicine when the Sterilization Campaign Began?" Statement to the Subcommittee on Africa, Global Human Rights, and International Operations of the Committee on International Relations of the U.S. House of Representatives, 25 February 1998.

Fatkulin, Yemlibike. "The Plight of the Uyghur People." Statement to the Committee on International Relations of the U.S. House of Representatives, 17 October 2001.

Gao Xiaoduan. "Forced Abortion and Sterilization in China: The View from the Inside.", Statement to the Subcommittee on Africa, Global Human Rights and International Operations of the Committee on International Relations of the House Representatives. Hearing on "Human Rights in China: Improving or Deteriorating Conditions," 10 June 1998.

Guy, Josephine. "Women and Child Abuse in China." Statement to the Committee on International Relations of the U.S. House of Representatives, 17 October 2001.

Interagency Task Force on Population Policy. *U.S. International Population Policy: First Annual Report.* Washington, D.C., U.S. National Archives, May 1976.

International Development and Food Assistance Act of 1978. 22 U.S. Code, sec. 2151-1; 22 U.S. Code, sec. 2151(b). House Select Committee on Population, Report, Population and Development Assistance, 95th Congress, 2nd Session. Washington, D.C.: U.S. Government Printing Office, 1978.

International Monetary Fund. *International Monetary Fund Annual Report 1991.* Washington, D.C.: International Monetary Fund, 1991.

Joint United Nations Programme on HIV/AIDS. "AIDS Epidemic Update," Geneva: UNAIDS/World Health Organization, December 2002.

Ministry of Health of the Government of Kenya. "Procurement of Progestagen-only Injectable Contraceptives," Undated.

National Advisory Council on International Monetary and Financial Policies. *Annual Report to the President and to the Congress for the Fiscal year 1988.* Washington, D.C.: Department of the Treasury, 1989.

National Institute of Allergy and Infectious Diseases. "Scientific Evidence on Condom Effectiveness for Sexually Transmitted Disease (STD) Prevention." Washington, D.C.: National Institutes of Health, Department of Health and Human Services, 20 July 2001.

National Security Council. "Report of the Interagency Task Force on Population Policy for the Under Secretaries Committee of the NSC." Washington, D.C.: National Security Council, 1976.

Obaid, Thoraya Ahmed. "Reproductive Health and Reproductive Rights With Special Reference to HIV/AIDS." Statement to the U.N. Commission on Population and Development, 1 April 2002.

Office of Population. "Overview of AID Population Assistance, FY 1989." Washington, D.C.: Office of Population, April 1990.

Office of the White House Press Secretary. "Fact Sheet: The President's Emergency Plan for AIDS Relief." 29 January 2003.

Peruvian Congressional Subcommittee for Investigation of Persons and Institutions Involved in Voluntary Surgical Contraception. *Final Report Concerning Voluntary Surgical Contraception During the Years 1990-2000.* Lima, Peru: the Congress of Peru, June 2002.

The Population Institute et al v. M Peter McPherson et al. 85-3131, U.S. District Court for the District of Columbia, affidavit of Werner H. Fornos.

Powell, Colin. Letter from Secretary Colin Powell to Patrick J. Leahy, Chairman Subcommittee on Foreign Operations, Committee on Appropriations, U.S. Senate. 21 July 2002.

———. "Analysis of Determination that Kemp-Kasten Amendment Precludes further Funding to UNFPA under Pub. Law 107-115." Attachment to letter from Secretary Colin Powell to Patrick J. Leahy, Chairman Subcommittee on Foreign Operations, Committee on Appropriations, U.S. Senate, 21 July 2002.

"Regulation of Medical Devices (Intrauterine Contraceptive Devices)." Hearings of the Committee on Government Operations of the U.S. House of Representatives (93rd Congress, 1st session), 30, 31 May 1972, 1, 12, 13 June 1973.

Schneider, Mark. USAID Assistant Administrator for Latin America and the Caribbean, Statement to the Subcommittee on Africa, Global Human Rights and International Operations of the Committee on International Relations of the House Representatives. Hearing on 25 February 1998.

Tiahrt, Todd. HR 4569, amendment no.38. *Congressional Record*, 105th Cong., 2d session, 1998, 144, no.123:H7922.

UNAIDS (Joint United Nations Programme on HIV/AIDS). "AIDS Epidemic Update." Geneva: UNAIDS, December 2002.

United Nations. *"Programme of Action" of the 1994 International Conference on Population and Development*, Cairo, Egypt, 18 October. New York: United Nations, 1994.

United Nations Division for Sustainable Development. *Comprehensive Assessment of the Freshwater Resources of the World*. New York, United Nations, 1999.

United Nations Population Division. *World Population Policies 2005*. New York: UN Department of Economic and Social Affairs, 2006.

———. *World Population Prospects: The 1996 Revision*. New York: UN Department of Economic and Social Affairs, 1996.

———. *World Population Prospects: The 2000 Revision, Highlights*. New York: UN Department of Economic and Social Affairs, 2001.

———. *World Population Prospects: The 2004 Revision*. New York: UN Department of Economic and Social Affairs, 2005.

———. *World Population Prospects: the 2006 Revision, Highlights*. New York: UN Department of Economic and Social Affairs, 2006.

———. *World Population to 2300*. New York: UN Department of Economic and Social Affairs, 2004.

United Nations Population Fund. *Inventory of Population Projects in Developing Countries Around the World*. New York: UNFPA, 1996.

———. *The State of World Population 1997: The Right to Choose: Reproductive Rights and Reproductive Health*. New York: UNFPA, 1997.

———. *The State of the World Population 2000: Lives Together, Worlds Apart: Men and Women in a Time of Change*. New York: UNFPA, 2000.

———. *The State of World Population 2001: Footprints and Milestones: Population and Environmental Change*. New York: UNFPA, 2001.

———. *The State of World Population 2004: The Cairo Consensus at Ten: Population, Reproductive Health and the Global Effort to End Poverty*. New York: UNFPA, 2004.

———. *The State of World Population 2005: The Promise of Equality: Gender Equity, Reproductive Health and the Millennium Development Goals*. New York: UNFPA, 2005.

———. "UNFPA Country Programme Action Plan [for the Philippines], 2005-2009, Executive Summary." New York: UNFPA. http://www.unfpa.org.ph/6thcp/default.asp. Accessed on 3 November 2007.

U.S. Agency for International Development. "The ABC's of HIV Prevention." http://www.usaid.gov/pop_health/aids/News/abcfactsheet.html.

———. *Contracts and Grants and Cooperative Agreements with Universities, Firms and Non-Profit Institutions Active During the Period October 1, 1994 - September 30, 1995 (The Yellow Book, 1995)*. Washington, D.C.: USAID, 1995.

———. *Contracts and Grants and Cooperative Agreements with Universities, Firms and Non-Profit Institutions Active During the period October 1, 1995-September 30, 1996 (The Yellow Book, 1996)*. Washington, D.C.: USAID Office of Procurement, 1996.

———. *FY1998 Budget Presentation for Guinea*. http://www.info.usaid.gov/pubs/cp98/afr/countries/gn.htm.

———. *FY1998 Budget Presentation for Kenya*. http://www.info.usaid.gov/pubs/cp98/afr/countries/ke.htm.

————. *FY1999 Budget Presentation for Uganda.* http://www.usaid.gov/pubs/cp99/afr/ug.htm.

————. "HIV/AIDS: Frequently Asked Questions." http://www.usaid.gov/pop_health/aids/News/aidsfaq.html#deaths.

————. *USAID Highlights* 6:4 (1989).

————. "USAID: Leading the Fight Against HIV/AIDS." http://www.usaid.gov/pop_health/aids.

————. *User's Guide to the Office of Population.* Washington, D.C.: USAID, 1991.

U.S. Agency for International Development Center for Population, Health and Nutrition. *Population, Health and Nutrition Projects Database (PPD).* http://ppd.phnip.com.

U.S. Census Bureau. *1999 U.S. Census Bureau Statistical Abstract: Compendium for the Millennium* (December 1999).

————. *Global Population Profile 2002.* U.S. Government Printing Office. http://www.census.gov/prod/2004pubs/wp-02.pdf.

————. International Data Base. http://www.census.gov/ipc/www/idbnew.html.

————. *Statistical Abstract of the United States 1997 [117th Edition].* Washington, DC: United States Government Printing Office, 1997.

U.S. Congress Committee on Foreign Affairs, Committee on Foreign Relations. *Legislation on Foreign Relations Through 2005*, "Current Legislation and Related Executive Orders," Vol. 1. Washington, D.C.: Government Printing Office, January 2006.

U.S. Embassy, Lima, Peru. "Improved Health, including Family planning, of High-Risk Populations," 10 January 2000. http://ekeko.rep.net.pe/usa/aidsale.htm. Accessed on 5 May 2005.

U.S. House of Representatives Select Committee on Population. *Population and Development Assistance*", 95th Congress, 2nd session. Washington, D.C.: U.S. Government Printing Office, 1978.

U.S. National Security Council. *Implications of Worldwide Population Growth for U.S. Security and Overseas Interests*, National Security Study Memorandum 200. Washington, D.C.: National Security Council, 1974.

Vigo Espinoza, Victoria. "Sterilized after giving birth." Statement to the Subcommittee on International Operations and Human Rights of the Committee on International Relations of the U.S. House of Representatives, 25 February 1998.

World Bank. *1993 International Development Conference.* Washington, D.C.: World Bank, 11 January 1993.

————. *Dying Too Young: Addressing Premature Mortality and Ill Health Due to Non-Communicable Diseases and Injuries in the Russian Federation.* Washington, D.C.: World Bank, 2005.

————. *World Bank Annual Report 1991.* Washington, D.C.: World Bank, 1991.

————. *World Bank Annual Report 1995.* Washington, D.C.: World Bank, 1995.

————. *World Development Report 1984.* Washington, D.C.: World Bank, 1984.

————. *World Development Report 1993.* Washington, D.C.: World Bank, 1993.

————. *World Development Report 1998/99.* Washington, D.C.: World Bank, 1999.

World Health Organization. "AIDS diagnosis and control: current situation: report of a WHO meeting," WHO Regional Office for Europe, Munich, 16-18 March 1987.

————. "Children and Malaria," Roll Back Malaria Campaign. http://www.rbm.who.int/cmc_upload/0/000/015/367/RBMInfosheet_6.htm. Accessed 14 March 2007.

————. "Malaria in Africa," Roll Back Malaria Campaign. http://www.rbm.who.int/cmc_upload/0/000/015/370/RBMInfosheet_3.htm. Accessed 14 March 2007.

————. *Breastfeeding and Replacement Feeding Practices in the Context of Mother-to-child Transmission of HIV: An Assessment Tool for Research.* Geneva: World Health Organization, Department of Reproductive Health and Research, 2001.

————. *Coverage of Maternity Care: A Listing of Available Information.* Fourth Edition. Geneva: World Health Organization, 1997.

————. "Global Programme on AIDS, Progress Report 1992-1993." Geneva: World Health Organization, 1995.

————. "Human Rights, Women and HIV/AIDS," Fact Sheet No. 247. Geneva: World Health Organization, June 2000.

————. "Pregnancy and HIV/AIDS," Fact Sheet No. 25. Geneva: World Health Organization, June 2000.

————. *Reduction of Maternal Mortality: A joint WHO/UNFPA/UNICEF/ World Bank Statement.* Geneva: World Health Organization, 1999.

————. "Safety of Injections: Facts & Figures," Fact Sheet No. 232. Geneva: World Health Organization, October 1999.

————. "Safety of Injections: Misuse and Overuse of Injection Worldwide," Fact Sheet No. 231. Geneva: World Health Organization, April 2002.

————. *Unsafe abortion: Global and regional estimates of incidence of mortality due to unsafe abortion with a listing of available country data.* Third Edition. Geneva: World Health Organization, 1997.

————. "Wastes from Health-Care Activities," Fact Sheet No. 253. Geneva: World Health Organization, October 2000.

————. "The World Health Report 2002: Reducing Risks, Promoting Healthy Life." Geneva: World Health Organization. 2002.

Articles

"Abortion of 14-week Fetus Banned." *People's Daily* (Beijing), 16 December 2004.

Adekoya, Lawrence. "Nigeria objects." *PRI Review* 2(2) (March/April 1992).

Ahktar, Farida. "Norplant the Five Year Needle." *Issues in Reproductive Engineering* 3(3).

"Aiding a Holocaust: New UNFPA Program Designed to Tidy Up One-child Horror." *PRI Review* 7(2) (March/April 1998).

AIDS Weekly, 10 March 2003.

Aird, John. "The China Model." *PRI Review* 4(4) (July/August 1994).

Akapo, Barbara. "When family planning meets population control." *Gender Review*, June 1994.

Alan Guttmacher Institute. "Estimate of the Number of Additional Abortions, Maternal Deaths and Infant Deaths Resulting from a 35% Cut in USAID Funding for Family Planning for All Countries Excluding China." New York: Alan Guttmacher Institute, 6 March 1996.

"Al-Azhar Fatwa Committee's point of view on birth planning." *Population Sciences* (Cairo, Egypt), 1988.

Alstott, Anne L. "Tax Policy and Feminism: Competing goals and institutional Choices." *Columbia Law Review* 96 (December 1996).

"Asian Sex Selection a Problem." *PRI Review* 11(6) (November/December 2001).

Audubon Society. "Population Habitat: Making the Connection." http://www.audobonpopulation.org.

———. "Why Population? Why Audubon? Why Now?" http://www.audobon.org/campaign/population_habitat/why.html.

Auvert, B., R. Ballard, T. Mertens, *et al*. "HIV Infection Among Youth in a South African Mining Town is Associated with Herpes Simplex Virus-2, Seropositivity and Sexual Behavior." *AIDS,* 2001.

Bailey, Ronald. "Billions Served." *Reason* (April 2000).

Bairagi, R. and M. Rahman. "Contraceptive Failure in Matlab, Bangladesh." *International Family Planning Perspectives* 22(1) (March 1996).

"Bangladesh Sterilization Incentives." *PRI Review* 1(5) (September/October 1991).

Barinaga, Marcia. "Making plants aluminum tolerant." *Science* 276(5318) (6 June 1997).

Bedard, Paul. "Third World birth control tops Gore's list of 'greenhouse' cures." *Washington Times*, 1 October 1997.

Bennett-Jones, Owen. "Vietnam's Two-Child Policy." BBC, 8 November 2000.

Berelson, Bernard. "Beyond Family Planning." *Studies in Family Planning* 38 (February 1968).

Berelson, Bernard and Jonathan Lieberson. "Government Efforts to Influence Fertility: The Ethical Issues." *Population and Development Review*, December 1979.

Bermudez, Alexandro. "Sterilization without consent." *Catholic World Report*, March 1998.

Boaz, David. "Pro-Life." *Cato Policy Report* (July/August 2002).

Bongaarts, John. "Does Family Planning Reduce Infant Mortality Rates?" *Population and Development Review* 13(2) (1987).

Bonner, Raymond. "A Reporter at Large." *The New Yorker*, 13 March 1989.

Brewer, *et al*, "Mounting Anomalies in the Epidemiology of HIV in Africa: Cry the Beloved Paradigm." *International Journal of STD & AIDS,* 2003, 14.

Brinkman, U. and A. Brinkman. "Malaria and health in Africa: the present situation and epidemiological trends." *Tropical Medicine and Parasitology,* November 1991.

Bush, George H.W. "George Bush on Population: An Early Statement." *Population and Development Review* 14(4) (December 1988).

Buve, A., K. Bishikwabo-Nsarhaza, G. Mutangadura. "The Spread and Effect of HIV-1 in Sub-Saharan Africa." *The Lancet,* 2002, 359.

Camp, Sharon. *The Diane Rehm Show*, WAMU, 13 December 1991.

"Capacity Building for Eradicating Poverty, an Impact Evaluation of U.N. System Activities in Vietnam 1985-1997."

Carlson, Allan C. "Sexuality: A Litmus Test for Culture." *The Family In America*, May 2003.

———. "Taxing the Family: An American Version of Paradise Lost?" *Family Policy Review* 1(1) (Spring 2003).

Catholic Family and Human Rights Institute. "US-Sponsored Panel Calls for Focus on Main Causes of Maternal Mortality." *Friday FAX*, 22 October 2004.

Chesterton, G.K. "Introduction to 'The Christmas Carol'," *Illustrated London News*. 14 February 1925.

Chin, J., P.A. Sato, J.M. Mann. "Projections of HIV infections and AIDS cases to the year 2000." WHO *Bulletin*, 68(1) (1990).

"China Daily wins global media award." *China Daily* (Beijing), 16 March 1982.

"Chinese Province Passes Regulation to Stop Sex-Selective Abortion." *People's Daily* (Beijing), 6 December 2000.

Chivers, C.J. "Putin urges plan to reverse slide in the birth rate." *The New York Times*, 11 May 2006.

Chowdbury, Nina. *Bangladesh Daily Star*, 17 April 1995.

"Christopher defends U.S. population programs." *Reuters*, December 19, 1994.

Chun Muhua. "In order to Realize the Four Modernizations, We Must Control Population Growth in a Planned Way." *People's Daily* (Beijing), 11 August 1979.

Clowes, Brian. "Coercive Birth Control: Examining Antinatalist Thought and Action." *Yale Journal of Ethics* (Fall 1995).

Clumeck N., P.H. Van de Perre, D. Rouvroy, D. Nzaramba. "Heterosexual promiscuity among African patients with AIDS." *New England Journal of Medicine,* 1985, 310.

Cohen, Joel. "Human Population: The Next Half Century." *Science*, 2003, 302.

Cohen, Margot. "Success brings new problems." *Far Eastern Economic Review,* 18 April 1991.

Cohen, Susan A. "Beyond Slogans: Lessons from Uganda's Experience with ABC and HIV/AIDS." *The Guttmacher Report*, December 2003.

Colbert, Ronald. "Haiti: A quest for legislation for protecting public health and the rights of people living with HIV/AIDS." *The Panos Institute, Medianet Bulletin*, News from the Caribbean, October 1999.

"Condoms limited vs. HIV." *PRI Review* 7(3) (May/June 1997).

"Congress to USAID: Stop the Abuse." *PRI Review* 8(4) (July/October 1998).

"Contraception is Treason, Turkish Islamist Leader Says." *Agence France Presse*, 16 February 2002.

"Conventional wisdom challenged." *PRI Review* 3(5)(September/October 1993).

Coyle, David Cushman. "Japan's Population." *Population Bulletin* 15(7).

Crosson, Pierre. "Will Erosion Threaten Agricultural Productivity?" *Environment*, 39(8) (October 1997).

———. "Soil Erosion Estimates and Costs." *Science* 269.

D'Agostino, Joseph. "France's End." *PRI Review* 15(5) (November/December 2005).

Davis, K.R. and S.C. Weller. "The Effectiveness of Condoms in Reducing Heterosexual Transmission of HIV." *Family Planning Perspectives* 31(6) (1999).

de Marcellus, Robert. "A Foundering Civilization." *Human Life Review* 28(1-2).

Diamond, Jared. "Why We Must Feed the Hands that Could Bite Us." *The Washington Post,* 13 January 2002.

Diczfalusy, Egon. "Population Growth: Too Much, Too Little, or Both?" *IPPF Medical Bulletin* 36(1) (1 February 2002).

Dowie and Johnston. "A Case of Corporate Malpractice." *Mother Jones*, November 1976, 36-50.

Drucker, E.M. P.G. Alcabes, and P.A. Marx. "The Injection Century: Consequences of Massive Unsterile Injecting for the Emergence of Human Pathogens." *The Lancet,* 2001, 358.

Drucker, Peter. "The Future that Has Already Happened." *Harvard Business Review*, September/October 1997.

Dyck, Arthur. "Alternative Views of Moral Priorities in Population Policy." *Bioscience*, 27(4) (April 1977).

Eberstadt, Nicholas. "Birds, Bees, and Budget Cuts." *PRI Review* 6(3) (May/June 1996).

———. "Growing Old the Hard Way: China, Russia, India." *Policy Review*, April/May 2006.

———. "Population Change and National Security." *Foreign Affairs*, Summer 1991.

———. "UNFPA: A Runaway Agency." *PRI Review* 12(3) (May/June 2002).

———. "World Population Implosion." *The Public Interest*, 1996.

Eberstadt, Nicholas and Hans Groth. "Healthy Old Europe." *Foreign Affairs*, May/June 2007.

Egunjobi, J.K. "Science academies call for global goal of zero population growth." *Nature* 386, 4 November 1993.

Ehrenreich, Barbara, Mark Dowie, and Stephen Minkin. "The Charge: Gynocide; The Accused: The U.S. Government." *Mother Jones*, November 1979.

Ertelt, Steven. "China Offers Families Money to Have Girls Babies Instead of Abortions." LifeNews.com, 12 August 2004.

Ettling and Himonga. "Impact of malaria on Zambian children." *Zambian Health Information Digest,* April-June 1995.

"Europe's Endangered Families: With Few Children, What are Countries to do?" Zenit.org, 5 May 2006.

"Falling Population Alarms Europe." *The Washington Times*, 2 December 1987.

"Family planning by force." *San Francisco Chronicle*, 3 September 1995.

Family Planning Management Development Project. "About FPMD," http://www.msh.org/fpmd/main/about.htm.

"Family planning measures hopeful." *China Daily* (Beijing), 4 May 1983.

Fatkulin, Yemlibike. "The Plight of the Uyghur People." *PRI Review* 11(4) (September/October 2001).

Feuer, Lewis S. "Generations and the Theory of Revolution." *Survey*, 18 (Summer 1972).

"Fewer Means Better." *The Economist,* 5 August 1995.

"Flexible but Comprehensive: Developing Country HIV Prevention Efforts Show Promise." *The Guttmacher Report*, October 2002.

Foreign Broadcast Information Service (FBIS). *Daily Report: China,* no. 91-071, 12 April 1991.

———. *Daily Report: China*, no 88-82, 28 April 1988.

Foster, Gregory D. *et al.* "Global Demographic Trends to the Year 2010: Implications for U.S. Security." *Washington Quarterly*, Spring 1989.

Gardner, Gary. "Windows on the World." *World Watch*, July/August 2005.

Germain, Adrienne. "Addressing the demographic imperative through health, empowerment, and rights: ICPD implementation in Bangladesh." *Health Transition Review*, Supplement 4 to Volume 7.

Gillespie, Duff G. "Reimert T. Ravenholt, USAID's Population Program Stalwart." *Population Today* 28:7.

Gisselquist, David, John J. and Potterat. "Heterosexual Transmission of HIV in Africa: An Empiric Estimate." *International Journal of STD & AIDS,* 2003, 14.

Gisselquist, David, R. Rothenberg, J. Potterat, *et al.* "HIV Infections in Sub-Saharan Africa not Explained by Sexual or Vertical Transmission." *International Journal of STD & AIDS,* 2002, 13.

Gisselquist, David, John J. Potterat, Stuart Brody and Francois Vachon. "Let it be Sexual: how Health Care Transmission of AIDS in Africa was Ignored." *International Journal of STD & AIDS,* 2003, 14.

Goodkind, Daniel. "Vietnam's New Fertility Policy." *Population and Development Review* 15(1) (March 1989).

Goshko, John M. "Planned Parenthood gets AID grant ..." *Washington Post,* 23 November 1993.

"Government may legalize abortion." *Nigerian News Digest*, 20 September 1991.

"Government to Do Away With Birth Control Policy." *Korea* Time, 5 June 1996.

"Gratis to Nigeria from UNFPA." *PRI Review* 2(2) (March/April 1992).

Greenhalgh, Susan. "Science, Modernity, and the Making of China's One-Child Policy." *Population and Development Review* 29(2) (June 2003).

"Guangxi Province Residents Protest China's One-Child Policy, Call for Refunds of Fines." Kaisernet, 1 June 2007.

Guilfoyle, Jean M. "Abortion in Nigeria: U.S. Connection?" *PRI Review* 2(2) (March/April 1992).

———. "Islam and Family Planning." *PRI Review* 2(4) (July/August 1992).

———. "The United Nations' Civil Society." *PRI Review* 5(5) (July/August 1995).

———. "USAID: Enabling 'The Piper's Tune.'" *PRI Review* 2(6) (January/February 1993).

———. "World Bank Population Policy: Remote Control." *PRI Review* 1(4) (July/August 1991).

"Guojia jihua shengyu lianhehui Wu Kunhuang he Aluweihaier zhuren shuo: renmin xuanze Zhongguo de jihua shengyu shi renmin zijide xuanze." ("President Ng Khoon-Fong and Director Aluvihare of the International Planned Parenthood Federation say that China's family planning program is the people's own choice.") *Jiankang bao (Health Gazette)*, Beijing, 18 April 1983.

Guy, Josephine. "Story of a Beautiful Baby Boy." *PRI Review* 11(4) (September/October 2001).

———. "Women and Child Abuse in China." *PRI Review* 11(4) (September/October 2001).

Hafidz, Wardah, Adrina Taslim, and Sita Aripurnami. "Family planning in Indonesia: the case for policy reorientation." *Inside Indonesia*, March 1992.

Harrison, Kelsey A. "Maternal Mortality in Nigeria: The Real Issues." *African Journal of Reproductive Health* 1(1) (1997).

Hartmann, Betsy. "Population Control as Foreign Policy." *Covert Action* 39 (Winter 1991-92).

Henshaw, Stanley K. and Jennifer Van Vort. "Abortion Patients in 1994-1995: Characteristics and Contraceptive Use." *Family Planning Perspectives*, July/August 1996.

Hu Zuliu and Mohsin S. Khan, *Why is China Growing so Fast? IMF Economic Issues* 8 (1997).

Huntington, Samuel P. "Why International Primacy Matters." *International Security* (Spring 1993).

Instance, Gail. "Family Planners Attack the Philippines." *GFL News* 4(3) (June/July 2005).

"International News." *Ms. Magazine*, Nov/Dec. 1992.

"Iran Promoting Birth Control in Policy Switch." *The Washington Post*. 8 May 1992.

Kamali, Anatoli. "Interventions for HIV prevention in Africa." *The Lancet*, 2003, 361(9358).

Kang Shin-Who. "New Babies Rise Again in Seoul." *Korea Times*. 19 January 2007.

Kaplan, Robert D. "The African Killing Fields." *The Washington Monthly*, September 1988.

Kapo, Barbara. "When family planning meets population control." *Gender Review.* June 1994.

Karanja, Stephen. "Health System Collapsed." *PRI Review*, 7(2) (March/April 1997).

———. "Kenya, A Country of Graves." *PRI Review* 12(3) (May/June 2002).

———. "The Sword of Damocles: Population Control and AIDS Destroy African Families." *PRI Review* 10(5) (October/December 2000).

Kasun, Jacqueline. "The High Price of Population Control: Environmentalism and the economics of 'sustainable development.'" *PRI Review* 9(2) (February/March 1999).

Khan, K.S. *et al.* WHO Analysis of Causes of Maternal Death: A Systematic Review.» *The Lancet* 367 (2006).

Kingsley Davis. "Population Policy and the Theory of Reproductive Motivation." *Economic Development and Cultural Change* 25, Supplement, 1977.

Kristof, Nicholas. "A U.N. agency may leave China over coercive birth control." *The New York Times*, 15 May 1993.

Lardy, Nicholas R. "Food consumption in the People's Republic of China." In *The Chinese Agricultural Economy*, edited by Randolph Barker and Radha Sinha with Beth Road. Boulder, Co: Westview Press, 1983.

Larkin, G.L. and P.E. Thuma. "Congenital malaria in hyperendemic area." *American Journal of Tropical Medicine and Hygiene,* November 1991.

The Leader (Owerri, Nigeria), 15 September 1991.

Liagin, Elizabeth. "America vs. Everyone Else." *PRI Review* 6:6 (November/December 1996).

———. "Money for Lies." *PRI Review* 8(4) (July/October 1998).

———. "Profit or Loss: Cooking the Books at USAID." *PRI Review* 6(3) (November/December 1996).

Lim, Louisa. "China fears bachelor future," BBC News, 7 April 2004.

Liu, Jianguo, Gretchen C. Dally, Paul R. Ehrlich, and Gary W. Luck. "Effects of Household Dynamics on Resource Consumption and Biodiversity." *Nature* 421 (30 January 2003).

The London Observer, 1 April 1984.

Maine, Deborah, Lynn Freedman, Farida Shaheed, and Schuyler Frautschi. "Risk, Reproduction and Rights: The Uses of Reproductive Health Data." In *Population and Development: Old Debates, New Conclusions,* edited by Robert Cassen. New Brunswick, NJ: Transaction Publishers, 1994.

"Malaria: avoidable catastrophe?" *Nature*, 10 April 1997.

Mallet, Victor. "Procreation does not result in wealth creation." *Financial Times*. 4 January 2007.

"Matter of Scales Spending Priorities." *World Watch Magazine* January/February 1999.

McConnell, Scott. "Delayed Motherhood: Is it Good for Society?" *New York Post* 24 May 1995.

McElroy, Damien. "China's One-Child Policy Fine Rises." *The London Telegraph*, 30 July 2002.

McEwen, Pat. "Stupid American." *PRI Review* 10(4) (July/August 2001).

McGurn, William. "Population and the Wealth of Nations." *First Things*, December 1996.

Meaney, Joseph. "Refugees' Rights vs. 'Reproductive Rights': UNFPA Population Control Campaign Threatens Kosovars." *PRI Review* 9(3) (April/May 1999).

"Media Reports: Depo-Provera is hazardous to your Health." PRI Weekly Briefing 6(29) (7 September 2004).

Meng Fang and Chen Fenglan. "Heilongjiang sheng kaizhan cang wu jihua wai shengyu cun houdong qude chengxiao" (Heilongjiang Province carries out activities to create villages with no unplanned births and obtains results"). *Zhongguo renkou bao (China Population News)(ZGRKB)*, Beijing, 7 October 1988.

"Mexican 'Family Planning' by Force." *PRI Review* 5(5) (Sept/Oct 1995).

Miller, James A. "The Case of the Dalkon Shield." *PRI Review* 6(5) (September/October 1996).

———. "The Disassembly Lines." *PRI Review* 7:4 (July/August 1997).

———. "Fornos whines for population grants." *PRI Review* 5(5) (September/October 1995).

———. "Lester Brown's 'Grain Reserves' Shell Game." *PRI Review* 1(4) (July/August 1991).

Moeller, Herbert. "Youth as a Force in the Modern World." *Comparative Studies in Society and History*, 10 (April 1968).

"More Health Care Undermined ..." *PRI Review* 8(4) (July/October 1998).

Morrison, David. "Burn, Baby, Burn." *PRI Review* 6(5) (September/October 1996).

———. "Cutting the Poor: Peruvian Sterilization Program Targets Society's Weakest." *PRI Review* 7(2) (March/April 1998).

———. "Family Planning by the Numbers." *PRI Review* 8(2) (March/April 1998).

———. "Interview with Eduardo Yong Motta." *PRI Review* 7(2) (March/April 1998).

———. "Pop Control While People Die." *PRI Review* 7(6) (November/December 1997).

———. "Tiahrt Violations! USAID Continues to Fund Family Planning Programs in Peru, Despite Verifiable Abuses." *PRI Review* 10(1) (January/February 2000).

———. "Weaving a Wider Net: U.N. Move to Consolidate its Anti-Natalist Gains." *PRI Review*. 7:1 (January/February 1997).

Mosher, Steven W. "How Not to Win the War on Terror." PRI Weekly Briefing 9(11) (15 March 2007).

———. "The long arm of 'one-child' China." *The Washington Post,* 10 April 1988.

———. "The Malthusian Delusion and the Origins of Population Control." *PRI Review* 13(1) (January/February 2003).

———. "UNFPA Supports Coercion: Vietnamese are Victims of UNFPA." *PRI Review* 12(1) (January/February 2002).

————. "When Family Planning is Ethnic Cleansing." *PRI Review* 9(5) (August/September 1999).

————. "Why are Baby Girls Being Killed in China?" *Wall Street Journal*, 30 November 1981.

"Mr. Bush's Population Policy." *Washington Post*, 3 June 1989.

Nations and Needs, (newsletter of the Center for International Development and Conflict Resolution), March 1985.

Nelson, Julie A. "Tax Reform and Feminist theory in the United States: Incorporating Human connection." *Journal of Economic Studies* 18: 5/6 (1991).

"New Era for Injectables." *Population Reports,* 23(2) (August 1995).

"New Proof of Serb Plans to Use Reproductive Health as a Genocidal Tool." Kosovapress, 20 July 1999.

"New $200 m[illion] USAID package for Health Sector Likely." *The Daily Star* (Dhaka), 18 July 1996.

"New-born boys outnumber girls." *Viet Nam News*, 20 July 2006.

N'Galy, B., and R. Ryder. "Epidemiology of HIV Infection in Africa" *Journal of Acquired Immune Deficiency Syndrome,* 1988, 1.

"Nigeria: Population Policies," International Development Association, 19 April 1991.

"Norplant alleged to cause blindness: Abuse of women in Bangladesh, Haiti documented." *Population Research Institute Review* 6(3) (May/June 1996).

"Norway, Sweden and the United States are rated highest in commitment to world population assistance in 1991." *International Family Planning Perspectives* 19(4) (December 1993).

Onstad, Eric. "West Misses Cash Target to Curb Population Growth." Reuters, 12 February 1999.

Packard, R.M. and P. Epstein. "Epidemiologists, Social Scientists, and the Structure of Medical Research on AIDS in Africa." *Social Science and Medicine,* 1991, 33.

"Pakistan may lose $250 million aid for not agreeing to sex education. *Pakistan Business Recorder*, 8 August 2000.

Paton, David. "The Economics of Family Planning and Underage Conceptions." *Journal of Health Economics* 21(2) (March 2002).

Peng Peiyun. "Guanyu 1989-nian de gongzuo." ("On the work in 1989"). *Zhongguo Renkou Bao* (China Population News), 24 February 1989.

"A Peoples' Project in China." *JOICFP News* (234) (December 1994).

Peruvian Ministry of Health. "Number of Tubal Ligations." *PRI Review* 12(4) (July/August 2002).

Peterson, Herbert B., *et al.* "The Risk of Ectopic Pregnancy after Tubal Sterilization." *The New England Journal of Medicine,* 13 March 1997.

Pfizer Inc. "Depo-Provera Physician Information." http://www.pfizer.com/pfizer/download/uspi_depo_provera_contraceptive.pdf.

————. "New Important Safety Information about Depo-Provera," www.depo-provera.com/index.asp. Accessed on 3 November 3, 2007

Phillips, James F., Ruth Simmons, J. Chakraborty, and A. I. Chowdhury. "Integrating Health Services into an Maternal Child Health-Family Planning Program: Lessons from Matlab, Bangladesh." *Studies in Family Planning* 15(4) (July/August 1984).

Pimental, David, Mario Giampietro, and Sandra G.F. Bukkens. "An Optimum Population for North and Latin America." *Population and Environment* 20(2).

Piot, P., F.A. Plummer, F.S. Mhalu, J.L. Lamboray, J. Chin, J.M. Mann. "AIDS: An International Perspective." *Science,* 1988, 239.

Piot, P., M. Laga, R. Ryder, *et al.* "The Global Epidemiology of HIV Infection: Continuity, Heterogeneity, and Change." *Journal of Acquired Immune Deficiency Syndrome,* 1990.

"Plan to Reduce Population Growth Rate: Yusuf." *The Bangladesh Observer* (Dhaka), 13 July 1996.

"Plea to Stop Use of Norplant, Depo Provera on Women." *The Independent* (Bangladesh), 11 April 1996.

Population Action International. Fact Sheet: "How Donor Countries Fall Short of Meeting Reproductive Health Needs." Washington, DC: Population Action International, October 2005.

———. Fact Sheet: "How Reproductive Health Services and Supplies Are Key to HIV/AIDS Prevention," http://www.populationaction.org/resources/fact-sheets/FactSheet18_AIDS.htm.

"Population Control Hurts Elderly: UN Ambassador Stuns Pop Controllers Forum." *PRI Review* 8(3) (May/June 1998).

"Population Control of Third World Planned: Sterilization Storm in U.S." *Evening Press* (Dublin), 12 May 1979.

"Population Crisis Committee OK's Coercion." *PRI Review* 2(2) (March/April 1992).

Population Research Institute. "Media Reports: Depo-Provera is hazardous to your Health." PRI Weekly Briefing, 7 September 2004.

———. "UNFPA Supports Coercion in Vietnam." PRI Weekly Briefing, 1 February 2002.

"Population." In *Social Problems*, 4th ed. Chapter 17. Boston: Addison Wesley Educational Publishers, 1990.

Population Services International. "Bringing Mass Media to Rural Populations through Mobile Video Vans." Washington, D.C.: Population Services International, November 1994.

———. "HIV/AIDS." www.psi.org_program/hiv_aids.html.

Potts, Malcolm. "Fertility Rights." *The Guardian*, 25 April 1979.

Potts, Malcolm and Julia Walsh. "Making Cairo Work." *The Lancet*, 23 January 1999.

"Propaganda department tightens control on press." *Ming bao*, Hong Kong, 15 January 1994, FBIS, no. 94-011 (18 January 1994).

"Prime Minister Abe to set up a strategic council to counter the falling birthrate." *Asahi Shimbun,* 28 January 2007.

"Prime Minister reprimands health minister for his inappropriate remarks referring to women as 'child-bearing machines.'" *Tokyo Shimbun,* 29 January 2007.

Quinn, T.C., J. M. Mann, J. W. Curran, P. Piot. "AIDS in Africa: an Epidemiologic Paradigm." *Science,* 1986, 234.

Richens, J., J. Imrie, A. Copas. "Condoms and seat belts: the parallels and the lessons." *The Lancet* 355(9201) (29 January 2000).

Roberts, Dick, Promboon Panitchpakdi, and Benjamin Loevinson, editors. "Using Information on Discontinuation to Improve Services." *The Family Planning Manager* 2(3) (May/June 1993).

Robinson, Jr., Leonard H. "Report to Africa Bureau, Office of Regional Affairs, Agency for International Development." Columbus, OH: Battelle Human Affairs Research Centers, 6 November 1981.

Royce, R.A., A. Sena, W. Cates, Jr., M.S. Cohen. "Sexual Transmission of HIV." *New England Journal of Medicine,* 1997, 336.

Ruse, Austin. "Kosovar Refugee Women 'Just Say No.'" *PRI Review* 9(4) (June/July 1999).

"Russian population declining as births, life expectancy drop." *The Washington Times.* 26 September 2006, A12.

Sanger, Margaret. "Birth Control and Racial Betterment." *Birth Control Review.* February 1919.

———. "The Function of Sterilization." *Birth Control Review.* October 1926.

Sassen, Saskia. "America's immigration 'problem.'" *World Policy Journal* 4 (4) (Fall 1989).

Sauvy, Alfred. "Le 'Faux Problème' de la Population Mondiale." *Population* 4(3) (July/September 1949).

Seltzer, Judy and Stee Solter, editors. "Tracking the Progress of Reproductive Health Services in the Highland District." *The Family Planning Manager* 6(2) (Summer 1997).

———. "Using National and Local Data to Guide Reproductive Health Programs." *The Family Planning Manager* 6(2) (Summer 1997).

Sen, Amartya. "Population: Delusion and Reality." *New York Review of Books*, 22 September 1994.

"Several regulations of Jilin province for the administration and management of family planning." *Jilin Ribao* (Changchun, China), 29 October 1993.

"Shades of National Security Study Memo 200!" *PRI Review* 5(1) (January/February 1995).

Shell, Ellen. "Resurgence of a deadly disease." *The Atlantic Monthly*, August 1997.

Simon, Julian L. and Roy Gobin. "The Relationship between Population and Economic Growth in LDC's." In *Research in Population Economics*, Vol. 2, edited by Julian L. Simon and Julie deVanzo. Greenwich, Conn.: JAI Press, 1979.

Sierra Club. "Global Population and Environment: The United Nations Population Fund." http://www.sierraclub,org/population/UNFPA/.

Simon, Julian. "Population Growth is Not Bad for Humanity." *PRI Review* 3(6) (November/December 1993).

Sims, Calvin. "Using Gifts as Bait, Peru Sterilizes Poor Women." *New York Times,* 15 February 1998.

Smith, Christopher. "Judging a Civilization." *PRI Review* 11(4) (September/October 2001).

———. "Who is Al Gore to blame babies for pollution?" 3 October 1997.

"Snags in Population Management." *The Financial Times* (Islamabad), 18 March 1996.

Song Jian. "Cong xiandai kexue kan renkou wenti" (Population problems from the perspective of modern science). In Song Jian, *Song Jian kexue lunwen xuanji* (Selected scientific papers of Song Jian). Beijing: Kexue Chuban She, 1999.

Song Jian. "Population Development—Goals and Plans." In *China's Population: Problems and Prospects*, edited by Liu Zhen, Song Jian *et al.* Beijing: New World Press, 1981.

———. "Systems Science and China's Economic Reforms." In *Control Science and Technology for Development,* edited by Yang Jiachi. Oxford: Pergamon, 1986.

Song Jian, Tian Xueyuan, Li Guangyuan, and Yu Jingyuan. "Concerning the Issue of Our Country's Objective in Population Development." *Renmin Ribao* (People's Daily), 7 March 1980.

"Sri Lankan Population Atrocities." *PRI Review* 7(2) (March/April 1997).

"Starvation in a Fruitful Land." *Time*, 5 December 1988.

"Stoppage of Nor-plant Use Demanded." *The Morning Sun* (Dhaka), 1 January 1996.

Sylva, Douglas. "UNICEF Devolves." *National Review Online*, 31 October 2003.

"Thailand's Grim Harvest." *Population Research Institute Review.* 7(1) (January/February 1997).

Tien, H. Yuan. "Demography in China: From Zero to Now," *Population Index* 47(4).

Tietze, Christopher. "Abortion and Contraception." In *Abortion: Readings and Research.* Toronto: Butterworth & Co., 1981.

Tietze, Christopher and J. Bongaarts. "Fertility Rates and Abortion Rates, Simulation Family Limitations." *Studies in Family Planning*, 6 (1975).

Trussell, J. "Contraceptive Efficacy," In *Contraceptive Technology*, edited by R. A. Hatcher, *et al.* 17th Revised Ed. New York: Ardent Media, 1998.

Tyrer, Louise. "Letter to the editor." *Wall Street Journal,* 26 April 1991.

UBINIG. "The price of Norplant is TK.2000! You cannot remove it." *Issues in Reproductive and Genetic Engineering* 4:1 (1991).

"UN Attempts to 'Buy' Pakistan and Impose Population Control." Zenit, 16 August 2000.

"UN Offers $250 Million to Pakistan if it Teaches Population Control." CWNews, 9 August 2000.

UNFPA. "Stepping up Efforts to Save Mothers' Lives." http://www.unfpa.org/mothers/index.htm.

United Nations Children's Fund. "Pregnancy and childbirth: Major causes of death and disability for women in developing world, according to UNICEF." New York: UNICEF, 11 June 1996.

———. "Report focuses on 'conspiracy of silence.'" New York: UNICEF, http://www.unicef.org/ponannou.htm.

"USAID Targets Honduras Population." *PRI Review* 5(6) (September/October 1995).

Van de Perre, P., D. Rouvroy, P. Lapage, *et al.* "Acquired Immune Deficiency Syndrome in Rwanda." *The Lancet,* 1984, ii.

Veatch, Robert M. "Governmental Population Incentives: Ethical Issues at Stake." *Studies in Family Planning* 8:4 (April 1977).

"Vietnam Plans Law to Ban Tests on Sex of Fetus." *Reuters*, 16 November 2001.

"Vietnam's Two-Child Policy." *PRI Review* 5(5) (September/October 1995).

Vink, Michele. "Abortion and Birth Control in Canton, China," *Wall Street Journal*, 30 November 1981.

Waggoner, Paul. "How Much Land can Ten Billion People Spare for Nature?" *Daedalu*s 125(3) (Summer 1996).

Warwick, Donald P. "The Ethics of Population Control." In *Population Policy: Contemporary Issues,* edited by Godfrey Roberts. New York: Praeger, 1990.

Warwick, Donald P. "The Indonesian Family Planning Program: Government Influence and Client Choice." *Population and Development Review* 12:3 (September 1986).

Watson, Paul. "The Beginning of the End for Life as We Know it on Planet Earth? There is a Biocentric Solution." Friday Harbor, WA: Sea Shepherd Conservation Society, May 4, 2007.

Wattenberg, Ben. "The Bomb that Fizzled." *New York Times Magazine.* 23 April 1997.

Watts, Jonathan. "China offers parents cash incentives to produce more girls." *The Guardian*, 16 July 2004.

"Weapons of Mass Destruction." *WorldWatch* (July/August 2003).

Weiskopf, Michael. "One Couple, One Child." *Washington Post,* 7-10 January 1985.

Wilmoth, John R. and Patrick Ball. "The population debate in American popular magazines, 1946-90." *Population and Development Review* 18(4) (1992).

"Who Care if a Third World Woman Dies?" *The Daily Star* (Dhaka), 6 February 1996.

Wonnacott, Tom. "Census shows youth will be missing from next generation." *PRI Review.* 13(3) (May/June 2003).

"WB [World Bank] Conditions Aid to Population Control." *The New Nation.* 7 September 1994.

World Vision. "Uganda's 'ABC' Approach to AIDS Proven Effective." http://www.worldvision.org/worldvision/pr.nsf/stable/update_uganda_52902.

Wren. Christopher. "Chinese Region Showing Resistance to National Goals for Birth Control." *The New York Times,* 16 May 1982.

Wu, Harry. "China's population policy." *PRI Review* 11(4) (September/October 2001).

Yeh Ling-Ling. "Stop Population Growth-Here and Abroad." *San Francisco Chronicle*, 4 January 2005.

Yin Su and Li Zheng. "Liaoning Kaizhan cangjian 'Jihua shengyu hege cun' quanmian quanche jihua shengyu xianxing zhengce" ("Liaoning carries out activities for establishing 'qualified family planning villages' and Implements the current family planning policy fully." *Zhongguo Renkou Bao* (China Population News), 30 September 1988.

"Zimbabwe MP Says Condom Use Plot." Reuters, 16 December 1994.

Zinsmeister, Karl. "Supply-Side Demography." *PRI Review* 3(4) (July/August 1993).

Zuk, Gary. "National Growth and International Conflict: A Reevaluation of Choucri and North's Thesis." *Journal of Politics* 47 (1985).

Lectures

Borlaug, Norman E. "Feeding a World of 10 Billion People: The Miracle Ahead." Lecture given at de Montfort University, Leicester, UK, 31 May 1997.

Clinton, Hillary. "Address to the Hague Forum." United Nations Population Fund Press Release, 9 February 1999.

Foulkes, George. "Presentation at the Hague Forum." 11 February 1999.

Natsios, Andrew S. *"First Principles of Development."* Lecture give at the Heritage Foundation, 28 April 2002.

Reports and White Papers

Alan Guttmacher Institute. "Estimate of the Number of Additional Abortions, Maternal Deaths and Infant Deaths Resulting from a 35% Cut in USAID Funding for Family Planning for All Countries Excluding China." New York: Alan Guttmacher Institute, 6 March 1996.

Berelson, Bernard. "Where Do We Stand." Paper prepared for Conference on Technological change and Population Growth, California Institute of Technology, May 1970.

Casterline, John B. and Steven W. Sinding. *Unmet Need for Family Planning in Developing Countries and Implications for Population Policy.* Policy Division Working Paper No. 135. New York: The Population Council, 2000.

Engender Health. *Contraceptive Sterilization: Global Issues and Trends.* Engender Health: New York, 2002.

Family Health International. Avert. Global statistical information and tables, 2002. www.avert.org/globalstats.htm.

———. "Policy and Advocacy in HIV Prevention." http://www.fhi.org/en/aids/aidscap/aidspubs/handbooks/bccpol.pdf.

———. "PPFA clinics drop pre-test." *Network*, Winter 1997.

———. "Provider checklists for reproductive health services," 2002. http://www.fhi.org/en/fp/checklistse/chklstfpe/englishchecklists.pdf.

———. "Reproductive Health Service Integration." www.fhi.org/en/aids/wwdo/wwd23.html.

———. "Technical Services: HIV prevention for drug-using populations." http://www.fhi.org/en/aids/wwdo/wwd13.html.

Institute for Family Policies. "Report on the Evolution of the Family in Europe 2006." Madrid, Spain: Institute for Family Policies, 2006.

Intergovernmental Panel on Climate Change. "Summary for Policymakers: A Report of Working Group I of the Intergovernmental Panel on Climate Change." In *Climate Change 2001: Synthesis Report.* Geneva: Intergovernmental Panel on Climate Change, 2001.

International Planned Parenthood Federation of America. *Advancing Sexual and Reproductive Health in the America, AIDS Summary.* No. 5, *Strengthening*

Integrated Services: Prevention of STD/AIDS in Primary Health Care in Bahia and Ceará: Strategies for Impact, Institutionalization and Sustainability. London: IPPF, February 2002.

———. *IPPF in Action.* London: Typographic Press, 1982.

———. *Meeting Challenges: Promoting Choices A Report on the 40th Anniversary, IPPF Family Planning Congress, New Delhi, India.* New York: Parthenon Publishing Group, 1993.

Johnson, Bryan T. "The World Bank and Economic Growth: 50 Years of Failure." Washington, D.C: The Heritage Foundation, 16 May 1996.

Korea Institute for Health and Social Affairs and U.N. Population Fund. *Sex Preference for Children and Gender Discrimination in Asia.* Seoul: KIHASA, 1996.

International Planned Parenthood Federation, Western Hemisphere Region. "Integration of HIV/STI Prevention into SRH Services." New York: *IPPF/WHR Spotlight on HIV/STI*, No. 1 (1 January 2002).

Ipas. "Manual Vacuum Aspiration (MVA)." http://www.ipas.org/english/products/mva/cannulae.html.

Mahbub Ul Haq Human Development Center. *Human Development in South Asia 2000 Report.* Islamabad, Pakistan: Mahbub Ul Haq Human Development Center, 2000.

Mann, Donald. "A No-Growth Steady-State Economy Must Be Our Goal." Negative Population Growth Position Paper, June 2002.

Maternal Mortality in 2000: Estimates developed by WHO, UNICEF and UNFPA. Geneva: World Health Organization, 2004.

The Montagnard Foundation. "Vietnam Ambassador Admits Sterilization of Montagnard Hill Tribes: Crime of Genocide: Imposing measures to prevent births." Press release. Spartanburg, S.C.: The Montagnard Foundation, August 2001.

Moore, Emily C.. "The Major Issues and the Argumentation in the Abortion Debate." In a loose-leaf booklet entitled *Organizing for Action,* prepared by Vicki Z. Kaplan. New York: National Abortion Rights Action League, undated.

Population Action International. "Expanding Access to Safe Abortion: Key Policy Issues." Population Policy Information Kit 8 (September 1993).

———. "The "ABCs" of HIV/AIDS Prevention." In *Condoms Count.* Washington, D.C.: Population Action International, 1 June 2002.

Population Research Institute. *Know Your Rights: Women, Family Planning and U.S. Law.* Front Royal, VA: Population Research Institute, 1998.

———. *The Demographic, Social and Human rights consequences of U.S. Cuts in Population control funding: A Reassessment.* Front Royal, VA: Population Research Institute, 1996.

———. *Innocents Betrayed: A Side of Family Planning the White House Does Not Discuss.* Front Royal, VA: Population Research Institute, 1997.

Population Services International. "Bringing Mass Media to Rural Populations through Mobile Video Vans." Washington, D.C.: Population Services International, November 1994.

Sai, Fred T. and Lauren A. Chester. "The World Bank's Role in Shaping Third World Population Policy." Internal Working Paper of the World Bank, Washington, D.C., November 1990.

Sinding, Steven W. *Strengthening the Bank's Population Work in the Nineties.* Washington, D.C., World Bank Population and Human Resources Department, Working Paper WPS 802. November 1991.

Solter, Cathy, Suellen Miller, and Miguel Gutierrez. *Comprehensive Reproductive Health and Family Planning Training Curriculum, Module 11: Manual Vacuum Aspiration (MVA) for Treatment of Incomplete Abortion.* Watertown, MA: Pathfinder International, September 2000.

Sylva, Douglas A. "The United Nations Population Fund: Assault on the World's People." New York: Catholic Family and Human Rights Institute, 2002.

United Nations Population Fund. "Vietnam: Key Issues in Population and Development." Hanoi: UNFPA, 1999.

———. *Guide to Sources of International Population Assistance 1991.* New York: United Nations Population Fund, 1991.

Walley, R.L. *Preferential Option for Mothers.* St. John's, NF: Matercare International, undated.

Unpublished Papers

Berelson to files. Berelson Files, Population Council Papers (unprocessed), 31 October 1973.

Heaps, David. "Report on the Population Council Prepared for the Ford Foundation." Population Council Files (unprocessed). December 1973.

Hsia, Tao-tsi and Constance A. Johnson. "Recent legal developments in China's planned births campaign." Unpublished memorandum, 9 July 1991.

Karanja, Steven. "Population Control—The Kenyan Perspective." Unpublished paper, 2 August 1997.

Hugh Moore to Malcolm W. Davis, Carnegie Endowment for International Peace. 10 November 1949. Moore Papers, Box 2, Princeton University.

Marshall, Alexander. Letter from Alexander Marshall, UNFPA Chief of Media Services, July 2002.

Mosher, Steven W. Interview with Elena Zuñega. National Population Council headquarters, Mexico City, 31 March 2004.

———. Letter to Anne Peterson, Director of the Global Health Bureau, USAID, 7 January 2003.

———. Letter to Anne Peterson, Director of the Global Health Bureau, USAID, 10 February 2004.

Mosher, Steven W., James Mosimann, Raphael Wanjohi. "Reproductive Behavior of Kenyan Women and their Attitudes towards Health Aid." Unpublished study, 19 May 2004.

Mulloy, Clement. *Margaret Sanger vs. The Catholic Church.* Ph.D. Dissertation, University of Arkansas, 2000.

Notestein, Frank to Bernard Berelson. Notestein Papers, Box 8, Princeton University, 27 April 1971.

Peterson, Anne. Unpublished Letter to Steven Mosher from Anne Peterson, Director of USAID Global Health Bureau, 7 January 2004.

Population Research Institute. "Kenya Report." Unpublished Interviews by PRI investigators at the Kenyatta National Hospital, Nairobi, Kenya, March 2003.

Ravenholt, Reimert Thorolf. "Africa's Population-Driven Catastrophe Worsens." Unpublished paper, June 2000. Available at www.ravenholt.com.

———. "China's Birthrate: A Function of Collective Will." Paper presented to the Annual Meeting of the Population Association of America, 27 April 1979.

Sanger, Margaret. "Lasker Foundation Award Speech," 25 October 1950. Washington, D.C.: Margaret Sanger papers, Library of Congress.

Watchenheim, George. Remarks given at reproductive health conference. Lima, Peru, 1966.

Index

Abacha, Mohammed Sani, 113-115
Abe, Shinzo, 17
abortions,
  as birth control, 40-41, 55
  as population control, 56, 191-192
  forced, 59, 71, 73-74, 79-81
  legalization, 48, 51
  sex-selective, 18-19, 23, 79-80
  World Bank, 47-49
Abrams, Elliott, 80
Adekoya, Lawrence, 111
Africa,
  foreign intervention with population
    control, 42-43, 103-106
  life expectancies, 171
  malaria, 161-166
  primary health care, 161, 166-172,
    185-186
aging population, 6-8
AIDS,
  and health care, 177-178
  in Africa, 170-172
  demographics, 172-176, 179-180
  population control, 55
  prevention, 181-184
  spreading the disease, 186-191
Aird, John, 84, 87, 89
American Birth Control League, see
  Planned Parenthood
anti-natalism programs, 42, 49-51, 54,
  105-106, 110-111, 131, 241
artificial insemination, 21
Atwood, J. Brian, 223
Australia,
  population worries, 11

Babangida, Ibrahim, 112, 113
baby bonuses, 9

Bangladesh,
  healthcare, 170
  population control, 101-102
  sterilization, 135
Beauvoir, Simone de, 55
Berelson, Bernard, 49-50, 81
birth control,
  and religion, 13-14, 41-42, 103
  as population control, 42-44
  by the numbers, 145-148
  promoting the message, 44-45
  sterilization, 34
birthrates,
  and cost of living, 21-22
  Asia, 14-19
  Europe, 5, 9, 10
  on a global scale, 5-6
  Russian, 9
  South America, 24
Bolivia,
  population, 24
Bork, Robert, 225-226
Bowers, Richard, 54
Brandt, Karl, 53
Burkina Faso, 47-48
Bush, George H.W., 40

Camp, Sharon, 56, 58, 81, 197-198
Canada,
  population worries, 11
Cantella, Raul, 169
Cash, Richard, 82
Cassen, Robert, 245-246
Chaunu, Pierre, 8
Chesnais, Jean-Claude, 225
Chimano, Ruth, 241
China,
  bribes, 84-86